Water for All

Water for All

Global Solutions for a Changing Climate

DAVID SEDLAK

Yale UNIVERSITY PRESS/NEW HAVEN & LONDON

Published with assistance from the foundation established in memory of
Amasa Stone Mather of the Class of 1907, Yale College.

Title page image: iStock.com/Zffoto

Yale University Press books may be purchased in quantity for
educational, business, or promotional use. For information, please e-mail
sales.press@yale.edu (US office) or sales@yaleup.co.uk (UK office).

Designed by Sonia L. Shannon.
Set in Minion and Future Book types by Integrated Publishing Solutions.
Printed in the United States of America.

Library of Congress Control Number: 2023931532
ISBN 978-0-300-25693-2 (hardcover : alk. paper)

A catalogue record for this book is available from the British Library.

This paper meets the requirements of ANSI/NISO Z39.48-1992
(Permanence of Paper).

10 9 8 7 6 5 4 3 2 1

For Meg,
My companion on
The foggy mornings,
The sunny days,
The rainy nights, and
Back again.
My water cycle would be unimaginable without you.

CONTENTS

PREFACE

WHEN IT COMES TO water, it would be easy to be a pessimist, because wherever we look, catastrophe looms. Droughts have emptied reservoirs, damaged crops, and caused wells to run dry. Hundreds of millions of women and children in rural villages spend several hours every day hauling water. Even in places where tap water freely flows, millions fear that drinking it will make them sick. Elsewhere, ecosystems deprived of water or overcome by pollution from farms, industry, and cities teeter on the edge of collapse.

None of this is new. Water crises have been a nearly constant feature of human history. Civilization has been shaped by the need to secure water to grow food, power industry, and meet the demands of growing cities. As population density increases and communities accrue wealth, water supplies gradually expand through incremental investments. But the approach used to manage water eventually runs up against physical limitations. When this happens, a period of crisis often ensues as the institutions responsible for water management encounter reluctance from community members about the need to allocate more resources to solve the problem. For growing cities, this hesitancy might result in an unwillingness to raise money to transition from local groundwater wells to imported water supplies or to make investments in water and wastewater treatment plants needed to protect human health and the environment. Similarly, agrarian communities might resist the need to invest in reservoirs or precision irrigation systems as long-term droughts cut into crop yields.

Local economic conditions, geography, and politics make every water crisis different. As a result, there is no single solution. After an initial period of hesitation, the wealthy often respond to water crises with massive infrastructure projects, while communities at the other end of the income spectrum are usually forced to adjust their expectations about growth. Communities adjacent to mountains tend to build dams and use gravity to deliver water, while those living on land underlain by permeable rock formations drill groundwater wells. Strong central governments create top-down national water plans, while nations committed to the free market often leave it to individuals and local communities to solve their water crises independently.

Under normal circumstances, the process of water system expansion that has arisen over the centuries would continue much as it has for centuries. But these are not ordinary times. Humanity is entering a period when rapid growth is colliding with the earth's capacity to accommodate societal needs. A changing climate coupled with close to eight billion people striving for ever-increasing living standards means that many of the institutions and approaches being used to manage water are no longer viable. It is not your imagination; water crises are arriving at a greater frequency, and the twentieth-century approach cannot keep up.

This book provides an overview of the clever ways that people solve water crises. Some of the solutions involve big infrastructure, such as dams, canals, groundwater wells, and desalination plants. Others rely upon large numbers of smaller devices, such as drip irrigation tubing that delivers water directly to the roots of a plant or washing machines that need a fraction of the water used by their predecessors. And some solutions require no new equipment; many water crises can be solved through better policies and laws. Understanding the limitations of each of these approaches and the ways that they can be used in concert will be critical to making the right decisions about how to respond to water crises in the coming decades.

There is no simple formula for solving water crises, but seeing the connections among seemingly disparate problems is a powerful means of bringing about change. Because our minds crave organization, I have divided the world's water challenges into six distinct crises. This shorthand notation provides a convenient means of sorting out responses that are likely to make sense in communities with different economic conditions, geography, and politics. It also lines up with the institutions that are normally responsible for planning, financing, and operating water systems. The decision to depict water problems as crises is also a simplification. By emphasizing the critical period when change comes about as existing approaches fail to meet pressing needs, it is possible to gain insight into the attributes of successful solutions. But for every place that faces a water crisis, it is possible to find communities that managed to bring about change without reaching a point that can be characterized as a crisis. These cases are worthy of examination, but they tend to lack the drama needed to maintain the reader's attention (after all, this is not a textbook).

To provide insights into the underlying causes and possible solutions to the six water crises, I have chosen representative examples from around the world. In some cases, I have focused on problems taking place in my backyard or in places where I have been lucky enough to gain firsthand knowledge. Because my personal experience is limited, I have turned to primary sources and the reporting of others for examples from places where I do not have direct experience. I recognize that telling the stories about unfamiliar places is fraught with peril. With enough patience, an author might be able to gather the salient facts and figures, but it is too easy to filter information through preconceived notions of the way that the world works. I have done my best to present all my examples of water crises through the perspectives of those who are experiencing them, with an emphasis on the people who end up making the decisions about how they should be resolved. Thus, I have attempted to depict that world as it is and not how I wish it would be. I do not intend to preclude the possibility that perseverant people who are currently shut out of the decision-making process can bring about change. But anyone who aspires to be a changemaker needs to understand the status quo that they hope to disrupt.

Vignettes about water crises are a form of storytelling—a way of communicating that tends to oversimplify complex events by creating a linear narrative populated by heroes and villains. This approach may hold a reader's attention, but it is often inconsistent with reality; people who pursue careers in water usually do so because they have a sincere desire to solve problems. I have yet to meet someone who set out to be a polluter or to create an impenetrable bureaucracy that prevents their fellow citizens from accessing water. Rather, each actor has a different set of priorities that often results in unintended consequences that exacerbate water crises and create barriers to their solution.

For the sake of narrative, stories often give the reader a false impression that to those who were involved, the solutions were always evident and that there was no other way to succeed. In practice, water crises are harder to understand as they transpire because they tend to play out over multiple decades. In addition, many of the key facts are uncertain when the decisions are made. Successful solutions may have required years of experimentation in which the benefits that a revolutionary idea delivered were too small or the risks that accompanied them were too great to justify their adoption. In many cases, ideas that seem attractive today might turn out to be dead ends, while others that have lost their popularity will succeed in a different form in another decade or two.

Despite these limitations, I believe that the successes, failures, and speculative ideas that fill the pages of this book might temper the pessimism that you feel about the world's water crises. I hope that they will encourage you to become part of the change that must come about in the coming years. Optimism is a powerful tool, but the magnitude of the water challenges the world faces should not be underestimated. It is going to take hard work to avoid crises that are more severe than those we are already experiencing. Just as we should not underestimate our current challenges, so we should not misjudge the capacity of people to rise to the occasion. I wrote this book because I believe that with sufficient imagination, we have the capacity to solve any water crisis; working together, I am certain that we can realize water for all.

Water for All

THE SIX WATER CRISES

Through water our humanity is revealed.

AS WILL BECOME EVIDENT, it is easier to develop new solutions to water crises if they are thought of as fitting into six distinct categories: (1) water for the wealthy; (2) for the many; (3) for the unconnected; (4) for good health; (5) for food; and (6) for ecosystems. As opposed to the habit of journalists, pundits, and politicians to lump a diverse set of problems under the banner of "The Global Water Crisis," a more careful differentiation among the water problems faced by society provides greater insight into the reasons why current ways of solving crises are only partially effective and avoids the erroneous assumption

1

that one-size-fits-all solutions exist. To solve the world's water problems, we must recognize that no two water crises are alike. They differ
with respect to their underlying causes, how they manifest themselves,
and the resources available for fighting them.

The six water crises are defined by the economic status of the people who need the water, how the water is used, and the nature of the
problems caused by an inability to manage it properly. Although such
a classification scheme may prove helpful, it is worth recognizing that
the situation is more complicated because multiple types of water crises
often occur simultaneously. Within each category of water crisis, factors such as climate, geology, geography, and cultural attitudes affect the
magnitude of the problem and the likelihood that a specific response
will succeed. In fact, the distinctly local nature of humankind's relationship with water is one of the greatest challenges associated with efforts
to apply solutions that have worked for one crisis to a new situation.

1

~~~~~~~~

Water for Household Use

EVERYONE NEEDS WATER. But the amount of water that we use in our homes, the ways that we obtain it, and the institutions responsible for managing it vary considerably. When water scarcity arises, these differences determine how communities respond. As a result of the overriding effect of wealth on the available solutions, it is helpful to distinguish among three separate crises of household water use that face communities in different economic situations.

The first crisis is often the easiest to solve: water shortages affecting wealthy people who live in cities. This is not to imply that the threats faced by the world's affluent city dwellers are trivial. Rather, people who live in cities on the upper end of the income spectrum already have the means of overcoming almost any water crisis they are likely to encounter. In addition to being tractable, the consequences of rich people's water crises are often modest relative to those experienced by people with lower incomes: what passes for a water crisis in a wealthy city might be considered only a minor inconvenience for many of the world's less affluent water users. Nonetheless, people who live in well-off cities have no need ever to experience even a mild water shortage if they recognize that the best time to respond to a drought is about a decade before it occurs. Wealthy city dwellers also merit our attention because they play a crucial role in advancing new solutions to water crises; their investments in technologies that have not yet been perfected drive down costs and increase accessibility for the rest of the world's water users.

The water supply challenges recently faced by Santa Barbara, California, exemplify the first category of water crises.

You could be forgiven if you have never heard of this picturesque coastal city wedged between steep mountains and the Pacific Ocean, just north of Los Angeles. The movie stars who call Santa Barbara home probably prefer a little anonymity. With a median household income of over sixty-five thousand dollars per year, the hundred thousand or so people who call Santa Barbara home would seem like the last people who would face any kind of crisis. However, the steep hills that separate the city from the valley to the east initially prevented Santa Barbara from accessing the aqueduct that has protected over twenty-two million residents of Southern California from drought since the 1960s. For Santa Barbara, a water supply system consisting of a few reservoirs in the coastal hills supplemented by groundwater wells near the city allowed it to develop from a Spanish mission into a thriving city.

Santa Barbara's reliance on a local supply finally led to a water crisis in the late 1980s, after a six-year period when about half of the normal amount of rain fell. Because the city had few other options to compensate for its water shortage, it built a seawater desalination plant. Given the state of the art for desalination at that time, the water that the plant produced was almost eight times more expensive than the city's existing supply.[1] Paying for a desalination plant was not necessarily popular with the local citizens, but it was the best available option at the height of the drought.

As often seems to be the case when a city invests in an expensive, new water supply project, the drought ended a few months after the desalination plant was completed in 1991. Two years later, Santa Barbara's other response to its water shortage, which the city had initiated in parallel with the decision to pursue desalination, succeeded when a new branch of the state's imported water system was extended to a reservoir that served the city.[2] After a few years, the desalination plant was decommissioned.

The return of wet conditions and the connection of the city to California's imported water system may have ended the water crisis of 1991, but it did not resolve the underlying problem. Santa Barbara's latecomer status to the state's complicated water rights system meant that its imported water allocation was not guaranteed during future dry periods when the city would most need it. Of course, the operators of the state-run water supply canal would not let the city run out of water in a future drought, but they would expect the people of Santa Barbara to engage in water rationing, let their lawns and gardens wither, and adopt real estate development restrictions if a severe drought occurred. For a wealthy city, this would constitute a water crisis.

A little over twenty-five years later, when that severe drought finally materialized, the city looked to its decommissioned desalination plant for a solution. The passage of time worked in Santa Barbara's favor: during the intervening years, advances in seawater desalination, driven by investments from other wealthy, water-stressed cities, reduced the energy needed to produce drinking water from the sea by about 40 percent.[3] The desalinated seawater was still more expensive than the city's other water sources, but its reliability justified the cost. In 2017, the local utility invested over seventy million dollars to revive and upgrade its mothballed seawater desalination plant. When it is operating, the new plant provides about a third of the city's water. During wet periods, Santa Barbara can save money by putting its desalination plant into standby mode. If an even more severe drought someday were to overwhelm the capacity of the plant to augment the city's water supply, its capacity could be expanded.

Santa Barbara was able to solve its water crisis because its residents could afford desalinated seawater. They are not alone. About three hundred million people worldwide, in such wealthy cities as Riyadh, Tel Aviv, and Perth, have turned to seawater desalination plants for water security.[4]

Increasingly, cities that lack access to the ocean or where citizens are concerned about the energy consumption and environmental impacts of seawater desalination are adopting other technologies that allow them to recycle their wastewater or to obtain their drinking water from aquifers that only a few decades ago were considered to be too salty to serve as water supplies. Because water security is not the top priority of cities until a drought occurs, wealthy cities still undergo crises before adopting these high-tech solutions, but the existence of these easily deployable approaches has reduced the damage that a city experiences. As is the case with so many other situations, wealth goes a long way toward crisis mitigation.

The ability of wealthy communities to buy their way out of scarcity stands in stark contrast to the situation faced by people who can afford the infrastructure needed to store, treat, and deliver drinking water but for whom the extra cost of technologies such as desalination is out of reach. Almost half of the world's population currently fits into this category. Because a drought typically consists of an extended period of below-normal precipitation and not a complete absence of rain, during a drought, a city faces a merciless race against time in which it must develop new water resources and decrease the rate of water consumption before the water remaining in its reservoirs or groundwater aquifers is exhausted. If the public concludes that the city is losing the race, the result is a water crisis.

Water managers have a variety of tools at their disposal for increasing water supplies during a drought. They can purchase water rights from nearby farmers or cities that have excess capacity. When that is impractical, they can dig deeper wells or build new reservoirs. Alternatively, they can sacrifice water quality for quantity by blending groundwater or river water that would otherwise be too salty to drink into their remaining water supply.

Water managers also possess the means of reducing the rate at which their city consumes water. As a drought intensifies, they can ramp up the pressure on their customers to reduce water consumption, first through voluntary cutbacks, publicized by media campaigns on billboards, radio, and internet sites, and then by creating penalties for profligate water users and rewards for those who meet conservation goals. If all else fails, they can ration water by shutting off parts of the water distribution system during different times of the day.

The situation confronted by São Paulo when a drought hit the city in 2014 is representative of this second water crisis.

Despite its subtropical climate, Brazil's largest city has struggled with water provision.[5] The main cause has been explosive population growth: the metropolitan area grew from approximately eight million people in 1970 to more than twenty million by 2010. As a nation, Brazil tends to invest a much smaller fraction of its wealth in water infrastructure than other emerging economies. During the period when the city was rapidly expanding, its water utility extended its main water supply canal to a second watershed and built a few new reservoirs. But the extra water was not enough.

São Paulo needed to be more aggressive in expanding its capacity to deliver water because as its population was surging, parts of its previously built water supply were becoming unusable. As more people moved into the city, its informal settlements, or favelas, began to encroach on the watersheds where its urban reservoirs were located. Because the favelas were not connected to the city's sewers, some of the reservoirs became too polluted to use as drinking water sources. Failure of the local water utility to maintain the city's underground pipe network during this period also contributed to the problem. By the early 2000s about a quarter of the treated water put into the city's pipes was being lost through leaks.[6]

Despite the growing mismatch between supply and demand, the city did not invest aggressively in water conservation, which is the normal practice of utilities confronting water stress. According to its critics, the water utility believed that it was in the business of selling water and had little motivation to spend money on a program that could shrink its revenues by discouraging water use.[7]

Despite the growing stress on the system, São Paulo's water utility continued to serve the needs of the city for many years, thanks in part to the fact that over a meter of rain fell annually in the watersheds where the city's reservoirs are located. But regional changes in precipitation patterns have diminished the reservoirs' ability to capture water. The average amount of rain that fell west and north of São Paulo, where the reservoirs are located, actually increased slightly in the decades leading up to the drought, but more of the precipitation was arriving in short, intense summertime storms.[8] This meant that the capacity of the city's reservoirs would have needed to be expanded if they were to capture the summer rains for use during the dry season while simultaneously leaving enough excess capacity in the reservoirs to protect the city from flooding. Because the utility did not expand the city's reservoirs quickly enough, the system became more vulnerable to the drought of 2014.

São Paulo's changing rainfall patterns appear to be related to two main factors.[9] First, climate change has altered regional weather patterns, as higher ocean temperatures have increased the humidity of the offshore air and altered atmospheric circulation patterns. Second, conversion of the region's forests and farms into buildings and roads has changed the microclimate around the city through a phenomenon referred to as the urban heat island effect. In essence, the heat released by cars and air conditioners coupled with the tendency of concrete and asphalt to adsorb more of the sun's energy than the trees and crops that used to be there has made the air above the city slightly warmer. This subtle change has led to more intense storms in the watersheds where the reservoirs are located when the moisture-laden air from the city encounters cooler conditions after passing over São Paulo.

The discovery that cities can alter precipitation patterns at first came as a surprise to meteorologists. After all, this is the branch of science that debunked the false notion that rain would fall on the grasslands of North America's Great Plains when they were converted into farms, an idea that was popularized by the saying "Rain follows the plow" in the 1870s.[10]

Although Great Plains farmers did not make the Great Plains suitable for rainfed agriculture, paving over cities does have subtle effects on rainfall patterns. In São Paulo, as well as a host of other rapidly expanding cities, such as Atlanta and Dallas, it turns out that rain follows the bulldozer.[11]

Like many middle-income cities struggling with drought, water supply was not the only issue concerning São Paulo's politicians and members of the public. When the drought hit, Brazil was facing a severe recession, a political scandal, and an outbreak of an insect-borne disease (Zika virus) just as it was preparing to host the Summer Olympics in facilities that might not be ready when the crowds arrived.[12] The simultaneous occurrence of multiple political and social challenges may have prevented a stronger response from the distracted federal government.

When the level of water in the city's main reservoir fell below the system's intake pipe and the press showed up to take dramatic photographs and write about the upcoming water apocalypse, the government's response was muted. The severity of the water crisis in the eyes of the public was intensified when the utility announced that it would be installing pumps to access the part of the reservoir that engineers commonly call the "dead storage."

Despite the alarming tone of the media coverage, utility leaders knew that the situation was not as dire as it seemed.[13] In fact, the extra attention worked to their advantage because recognition by the public that their water supply was in danger meant that the utility could start spending money on its response without fear of a public relations backlash when consumers received higher water bills. Over a period of about twelve months, São Paulo built more than ten kilometers of pipelines connecting parts of the city to reservoirs that still had adequate capacity. This internal water transfer allowed the utility to reduce the daily demand on the city's stressed main reservoir by about 20 percent. With the public's attention focused on water shortage, the city turned its attention to water conservation. By offering consumers bonuses for saving water and penalties for exceeding their allocation, the utility drove down water demand by about 10 percent. Finally, the utility lowered the water pressure in the pipe network to reduce the amount of water that escaped through cracks in the underground pipes and repaired some of the system's worst leaks, which cut water use by an additional 20 percent.

Within a year, São Paulo's water demand was more closely balanced with its decreased supply. During the drought, the utility also gained approval for more than a billion dollars in new water projects to expand its water supply to reduce future risks of shortage. If the drought had continued for another year or two, the city might have faced some difficult decisions about who would have to go without water. The federal politicians might have even stepped up to help. The water crisis had moved onto the front page of the newspapers, but the city was not going to run out of water.

Although predictions that São Paulo was about to descend into chaos may have been exaggerated, the drought greatly inconvenienced the public. It also had economic consequences that will be felt for many years. During the drought, reduced water pressure was a major problem for people living in the hills surrounding the city, because water did not reach the higher elevations during the daytime periods when consumption elsewhere in the system was high. Poor and middle-income people were disproportionally affected by the reduced water pressure because only wealthy homeowners could afford water storage tanks that collected water when the pressure increased after the city went to sleep.[14]

Less water flowing out of the reservoirs stressed the power supply, causing rolling blackouts and increasing electricity costs because other, more expensive sources of energy had to be used when the turbines in the hydroelectric plants were idled.[15] From a long-term fiscal standpoint, the drought also was painful; the city will be paying back the loans that were taken out for the emergency construction projects and the new reservoirs for years to come. Almost as importantly, São Paulo's failure to prepare for the drought reduced the confidence of its citizens and potential investors in the city.

Many other cities in low- and middle-income countries also are confronting the second water crisis.[16] For example, in southern India in 2019, Chennai's reservoirs emptied and water rationing took place when the annual monsoon was delayed. Istanbul, Mexico City, and Manila also have struggled to adapt their water systems as their populations grow and their local climates change. The list of cities facing water shortages will likely grow in coming decades: projecting trends in population growth, water consumption patterns, and climate change, researchers predict that about a quarter of the world's cities that rely upon rivers and lakes will face severe shortages for at least one month per year by 2050. For those cities that rely upon groundwater, about half will be well on the way to running out of water by midcentury.

Residents of cities in the world's low- and middle-income countries are predicted to continue to face water shortages, but they ultimately have the means of mounting a robust response to water crises. If a drought reaches the crisis stage in one of these cities, money that might have otherwise gone into roads, power lines, and public transit can be redirected to water infrastructure. In addition, organizations such as the World Bank, the European Investment Bank, and the Asian Development Bank, which issue hundreds of billions of dollars in loans, are only a phone call away during a water crisis. For most of the world's city dwellers, water shortages are costly, inconvenient events that diminish the quality of life and impact the local economy, but they get addressed after the severity of the problem is recognized by the public.

This is not the case for the rural poor and for people who live in parts of cities that are not served by water utilities. These people often wake up to a water crisis every day. According to the United Nations, about eight hundred million people worldwide lack access to basic water services, which is a technocratic way of saying that they obtain their daily twenty liters (or less) of water from an old-fashioned, hand-dug well or by spending more than half an hour per day hauling water from a piped water source located far from their homes.[17] Hundreds of millions more people technically have access to basic water services, but purchasing water soaks up a large fraction of their income. Over half of the people who struggle to obtain drinking water live in sub-Saharan Africa. Of the remainder, most live in East and Southeast Asia.

Poverty also restricts water access in wealthy countries such as the United States, where the system of funding water systems raises water bills to levels that a substantial fraction of the community cannot afford.

To understand the implications of this third type of water crisis, we need to put the cost of a lack of water access into context.[18] Drinking untreated river water or water from a hand-dug well increases exposure to waterborne diseases. Obtaining water from other sources may be safer, but paying for them creates a different set of hardships. About two-thirds of the people who lack basic water services subsist on less than two dollars per day. Buying water from vendors can consume about 10 percent of the household income of indigent city dwellers. The terrible irony of this situation is that it typically costs a poor person about ten times more to buy a liter of water on the street than it does for a wealthy person to have it piped into their home in the same city. The crisis is even worse for the rural poor due to the extra cost of transporting water by road. If people who lack basic water services happen to live within a reasonable distance of a decent water source, they can save money by sending family members on a daily trip to collect water, but this often means pulling children out of school and using precious time that could be spent earning income.

Access to safe, affordable drinking water is not the only water-related problem facing the world's poor. More than twice as many people lack basic sanitation (that is, a toilet that is not shared with other households) as those who lack basic water services.[19] The larger number of people lacking access to sanitation reflects the added expense and difficulty of moving from shared sanitation services, such as a communal latrine, to basic sanitation. This is important because many diseases are transmitted more readily in shared facilities than when sanitation stays within the family.

Communal latrines are not an ideal sanitation solution, but they are a step up from the way in which millions of people still answer the call of nature: lacking reasonable alternatives, many people simply defecate in fields or the nearest available open space. In addition to the inconvenience and odors associated with open defecation, the disease-causing microbes in the human feces eventually get mixed into the street dust, spreading germs that lead to diarrhea and other illnesses to people who often cannot afford the soap and water required to maintain good hygiene.[20] Festering human waste also serves as breeding grounds for flies that transmit diseases such as trachoma, a bacterial eye infection that can cause blindness. Finally, pathogenic microbes from improperly managed feces eventually find their way into the rivers and the shallow, hand-dug wells that people who lack access to basic water services often rely upon for their drinking water.

This third water crisis jeopardizes health and holds back the economic progress of about a quarter of all people on earth. In recognition of the magnitude of the problem, the United Nations, nongovernmental organizations, and governments have been trying to decrease the number of people lacking adequate water, sanitation, and hygiene (sometimes abbreviated as WaSH) for decades. These efforts intensified after 2000, when the United Nations included access to safe water, sanitation, and hygiene in the Millennium Development Goals that served as the mechanism for prioritizing investments from aid organizations and their partner governments.[21]

After fifteen years of gradual progress, the United Nations elevated the importance of water and sanitation in 2015 through the creation of the Sustainable Development Goals (SDGs). A goal exclusively targeted at water, SDG 6, recognized that investments in water and sanitation were central to efforts alleviate poverty and to create a more equitable society.[22] Through concerted efforts to realize these goals, gradual progress has been made, with hundreds of millions of people gaining access to basic water services, basic sanitation, and hygiene through investments in community groups and construction of infrastructure serving the world's most vulnerable populations.

Ethiopia provides an example of how the focus on providing water services to the poor has begun to make a difference. Starting in the early 1990s, when the country's political situation stabilized after decades of civil war, the new government changed how funding was allocated to infrastructure projects. After the Tigray People's Liberation

Front took control, they created a system referred to as ethnic federalism in which the decision-making process for allocation of infrastructure funding was given to local and regional governments.[23]

Although it was criticized as a means of solidifying the ruling party's political control, Ethiopia's ethnic federalism system provided local accountability to aid organizations that ultimately led to more resources for water projects. As a result, between 1994 and 2015, thirty-five million poor people living in rural areas gained access to improved water supplies (water sources that are less likely to be contaminated with microbes than traditional hand-dug wells or unfiltered surface water).[24] Another ten million city dwellers obtained household water connections. This progress is remarkable considering that there were only sixty-three million people in the country in 2000 and more than half of them lived on less than $1.25 per day.

The approaches for bringing water to the people of Ethiopia employed a variety of well-established technologies.[25] In some rural communities, nongovernmental organizations focused on building capacity, assisting villagers with the construction of small dams, community wells, and rainwater cisterns. In larger towns and cities, the funding allowed local water agencies to drill water supply wells, construct reservoirs, and expand pipe networks. In Ethiopia and many other countries with large rural populations, the expansion of access to improved water services was catalyzed by the availability of money, technical assistance from international aid groups, a supportive government, and an engaged populace.

Foreign aid and local support for water projects was only part of the story in Ethiopia. The return of political stability, a better-educated, youthful workforce, and foreign investment dramatically expanded Ethiopia's economy. During the period between 2004 and 2011, Ethiopia's gross domestic product increased by an average of 11 percent per year, making it one of the five fastest growing economies in the world.[26] Although much of the wealth accrued to city dwellers, the expanded economy meant that more government resources were available to support water infrastructure projects. Richer people also spent more money buying food from the country's farmers.

As a result of Ethiopia's economic expansion, the percentage of people living below the poverty line decreased from 56 percent to 30 percent between 2000 and 2010.[27] As they transitioned out of poverty, more people gained access to water.

Efforts to expand sanitation and hygiene in Ethiopia have lagged that of drinking water provision. Between 2000 and 2015, access to basic sanitation increased only from 3 percent to 7 percent.[28] However, that does not mean that the situation did not improve. As the country's economy grew, Ethiopia invested in the construction of communal pit latrines and other forms of shared sanitation that do not count under the definition of basic sanitation applied by international aid organizations. Between 2000 and 2015, the percentage of the population that defecated in open spaces decreased from 80 percent to 27 percent. The situation has been similar in much of the rest of the world: progress toward expanding access to basic sanitation and hygiene worldwide tends to trail progress in water supply access, but the most problematic practice (open defecation) has become less prevalent.

The renewed conflict that broke out in November 2020 threatens the progress that has been made in Ethiopia in recent years.[29] That the war broke out as the region was entering a severe drought puts additional pressure on the country. Hopefully, progress that had been made during the prior peaceful period will resume after the conflict ends.

Despite recent progress, the third water crisis will not disappear anytime soon. Even the most optimistic projections indicate that more than three hundred million people will still lack access to basic water services in 2030.[30] A larger number of people also are predicted to lack basic sanitation and hygiene at that time. Furthermore, if the global economy falters, if conflicts break out, or if climate change reduces water supplies more than currently anticipated, progress toward solving the third water crisis could slow down.

2

Safe Drinking Water

VULNERABILITY TO drought and a lack of access to drinking water are problems currently faced by about a quarter of humanity. But being wealthy or having enough water does not guarantee that a community will never face a water crisis. An adequate quantity of water is only part of water security. Water also must be safe to drink.

Throughout history, safe drinking water has meant the absence of disease-causing microbes. Over two thousand years ago, people had already figured out that waterborne disease could be prevented by boiling water before drinking it. This helps explain why in much of the world hot tea or water that has recently been boiled are the preferred ways of consuming water, even during the heat of summer.[1]

By the end of the nineteenth century, engineers learned that they also could make water potable by passing it through sand filters and adding chemical disinfectants such as chlorine.[2] The advent of drinking water treatment in the early decades of the twentieth century improved public health and obviated the need to boil water before consumption throughout much of the world. But drinking water treatment plants did not alleviate all water quality concerns. Just because water treatment plants remove or inactivate waterborne pathogens, tap water is not always safe to drink.

In much of the world, treated water is recontaminated with microbes as it makes its way through water distribution pipes that deliver it to homes.[3] The inability of utilities in many low- and middle-income countries to maintain sufficient pressure in their water distribution systems cancels out much of the benefit of drinking water treatment and forces people to treat their tap water by boiling, purchase bottled water, or subject themselves to the risk of waterborne disease. Because most of the world has come to accept the idea that their tap water cannot be consumed without additional treatment, this shortcoming is not really a crisis but more of a missed opportunity.

The fourth water crisis—a water supply that is not safe to drink—occurs because conventional drinking water treatment methods do not remove chemicals that jeopardize human health. Rich and poor, urbanites and residents of rural villages, people who obtain their water from modern water treatment plants and those who rely upon hand-dug wells—all are at risk if their water supply contains unsafe levels of toxins. Rather than focusing on the thousands of chemicals that could make water unsafe to drink, it is easier to understand the fourth water crisis by considering the potential sources of contamination. A key to this approach is recognition that most of the dangerous chemicals in drinking water can be traced to either naturally occurring substances or industrial pollution.

When it comes to drinking water, natural does not always mean healthy. As water percolates into the soil or flows down a stream, the minerals that it encounters start to dissolve. Quite often, this process adds beneficial ions, such as calcium and magnesium—nutrients essential to good health that also make drinking water more palatable—but some minerals release toxic ions as they dissolve.[4] Among the toxins that can be released during mineral dissolution, arsenic is the worst offender, and Bangladesh is probably the place where it has caused the greatest suffering.

Much of the problem associated with arsenic-contaminated drinking water in Bangladesh can be traced back to a well-intentioned effort by UNICEF and other international aid groups in the 1970s. During that period, public health experts were trying to reduce the rates of waterborne disease caused by fecal contamination of the rivers and ponds that served as the country's main drinking water sources. Because most of Bangladesh's population lived in rural villages where the installation and operation of drinking water treatment plants would be challenging, the experts attempted to get people to switch their water supplies from unfiltered river water to shallow groundwater.[5] The approach was chosen because percolation of water through the soil usually filters out the microbes that cause waterborne diseases. In addition, the shallow wells used in Bangladesh, referred to as tube wells, were inexpensive and easy to install, maintain, and operate.

The effort to change the ways that Bangladeshis obtained their drinking water quickly succeeded. By the early 1990s, most people living outside of cities served by piped water systems were obtaining their drinking water from one of the ten million tube wells that had been installed with aid from the international donors or, for wealthier people, by their own investments in what they believed to be safer drinking water.[6] The incidence of waterborne disease decreased as people stopped consuming pathogen-contaminated surface water, but the change in water source set the stage for a different crisis.

Unfortunately, the experts who came up with the solution to the country's waterborne disease problem did not fully appreciate Bangladesh's geology. Over the millennia, the sediments carried down from the Himalayas by the rivers that bisect the country's river delta had deposited arsenic-containing minerals over the land surface.[7] When a well is installed in such sediments, dissolution of the naturally occurring minerals results in unsafe levels of arsenic in the water.

Although the concentrations of arsenic in the well water were too low to cause immediate illness, months or years of exposure to arsenic-contaminated water affected people's health. As early as 1983, doctors began reporting arsenic-induced skin lesions among people who had been drinking water from tube wells.[8]

Unsightly and painful skin lesions were the most visible sign that arsenic was compromising the health of Bangladeshis. Long-term exposure to low levels of arsenic also causes other disorders, including cancer, bronchiectasis (a respiratory disease), and hypertension.[9] To protect the public from these diseases, the World Health Organization recommends that drinking water not contain more than ten parts per billion of arsenic.

After the problem was recognized and the wells began to be tested, researchers estimated that between about 30 percent and 60 percent of the 125 million people living in Bangladesh were at risk of exposure to unsafe levels of arsenic in their drinking water.[10] Among the exposed population, around 5 percent were consuming water with arsenic concentrations that were at least twenty times higher than the World Health Organization recommendation.

Initial progress in addressing the arsenic crisis was slow because the options for protecting people simultaneously from arsenic and from waterborne pathogens were limited. More than two decades after the first cases of arsenic poisoning were reported, when consensus had finally been reached about the magnitude and cause of the problem, the government attempted to convince people to abandon their tube wells and drink pond water that had been treated to remove microbes.[11] However, this approach failed to catch on. After all, the population had expanded in the decades since tube wells had first become popular, meaning that disease-carrying microbes were now even more prevalent in the former water sources. In some places, ponds had been repurposed for aquaculture or had been polluted by industrial waste. In addition, people were accustomed to the ease and convenience of drawing water from wells located near their homes.

The government was able to convince a few communities to switch over to river water or groundwater that had passed through modern drinking water treatment plants capable of removing microbes and arsenic because they also provided better water delivery systems. However, the logistics and costs of operating drinking water treatment plants along with the associated pumps and pipe networks needed to distribute the water meant that this solution was infeasible in the countryside where much of the population resided.[12]

If people were unwilling to abandon their tube wells and conventional drinking water treatment was impractical, perhaps there was a way for well users to remove the arsenic on their own. To make the contaminated wells safe, aid groups donated or subsidized inexpensive arsenic-removing filters.[13] The filters employed a simple principle: before consuming the water, users would pass it through a container packed with a material with a high affinity for arsenic. After treatment, the clean water would be stored in a large container. Although these systems produced safe water, Bangladeshis tended to give up on them after a few months because they were tough to maintain. Furthermore, the cost of replacing the filters was often beyond the means of rural families, especially after the subsidies stopped.

Ultimately, the most effective strategy for reducing arsenic exposure in Bangladesh was related to the heterogeneous distribution of the buried arsenic-containing minerals. In much of the country, concentrations of arsenic-containing minerals in the shallow sediments varied widely over distances of tens of meters. Thus, a shallow well that produced safe water was often located within a short walk of a well with arsenic levels well above the World Health Organization guidelines. To take advantage of this quirk of nature, almost half of the country's shallow wells were tested for arsenic. Community members were made aware of the test results by a simple code: wells that were painted green were safe to use and those that were painted red contained unsafe levels of arsenic.[14]

Once people with contaminated water knew the locations of the nearest safe well, about a third of them switched their water supply.[15] The remainder stuck to their contaminated wells, despite efforts to educate them about the dangers of drinking arsenic-contaminated water. Although it did not remove the problem, this modest, one-time investment in testing—an approach that was far less costly than other options—protected millions of people from arsenic poisoning. In the few places where no safe wells could be found within about one hundred meters of a contaminated source, new wells were drilled into a deeper part of the aquifer where the amount of arsenic-containing minerals was usually much lower. By limiting the construction of expensive, deep wells to only those places where tube wells that produced safe water were unavailable, the overall cost of protecting Bangladesh's rural population from arsenic poisoning greatly decreased.

As a result of the trial-and-error approach of the past three decades, the proportion of Bangladesh's population that is being exposed to unsafe levels of arsenic in their drinking water has dropped to around a quarter.[16] Perhaps the continued efforts to test tube wells, educate community members, and provide alternative water supplies will eventually solve the country's arsenic crisis. However, the absence of inexpensive small-scale treatment systems that community members could readily adopt, coupled with the fact that most of the population is poor and lives in the countryside, means that around forty million Bangladeshis are still being exposed to unsafe levels of arsenic in their drinking water.

The attention that was directed at Bangladesh's arsenic crisis increased awareness in other places where people live atop arsenic-rich minerals. Another one hundred million people, mostly in Southeast Asia and South Asia, are exposed to unsafe concentrations of arsenic in their drinking water.[17] That statistic can mislead you into thinking that arsenic is a regional problem: it is not. Asia is home to the majority of the world's population, so it should not surprise anyone that the greatest number of people struggling with arsenic-contaminated drinking water live there.

In terms of its distribution, arsenic-contaminated groundwater is a worldwide problem. For example, in the United States, around two million people, mainly homeowners who rely upon domestic wells in the Midwest, New England, and the Southwest, are exposed to arsenic concentrations above the World Health Organization recommendations.[18] Millions more people in South America drink arsenic-contaminated water. Despite their affluence, the absence of practical treatment methods for household wells has meant that wealthy Americans with contaminated groundwater have not fared much better than low- and middle-income Asians when it comes to avoiding the health effects of arsenic.

Arsenic is not the only naturally occurring substance that contaminates drinking water.[19] More than two hundred million people in India, China, Argentina, and the Middle East are exposed to elevated concentrations of fluoride, which causes skeletal fluorosis—a disease related to the uptake of this element into the mineral matrix of bones. Many millions more are drinking groundwater containing unhealthy concentrations of uranium, chromium, or radon. Although there is less recognition of the drinking water crises associated with these other naturally occurring contaminants, the public health consequences are still severe. As was the case for arsenic, communities without easy access to alternative water supplies have few workable options after they learn that Mother Nature has rendered their drinking water unsafe.

Not all drinking water contamination by naturally occurring substances can be blamed on unfavorable geology. Since humans began scouring the earth in search of metals, we have been polluting our environment.[20] Ice cores in Europe and lake sediments in Asia contain elevated concentrations of metals such as lead and antimony from mineral exploitation that took place more than three thousand years ago. Because mines and smelters are usually located far from cities, remote forests, lakes, and rivers have usually borne the brunt of the damage from mineral extraction and processing. When it comes to drinking water, contamination typically occurs when the metals are improperly used in the places where people live.

One of the best-known cases of metal contamination of drinking water in modern times came to light in the 1980s in the desert east of Los Angeles. Just outside of the small town of Hinkley, California, a chromium-containing solution had been used to prevent metal corrosion in compressors at a natural gas pipeline. Due to the unsophisticated method of disposing of the waste (it was simply dumped into unlined pits near the facility), much of the town's groundwater became contaminated with chromate, a particularly toxic form of the metal. After a trial in which doctors described chromate-linked health effects in the community and lawyers showed evidence of a cover-up of unsafe disposal practices used by the pipeline's operators, a jury awarded 650 plaintiffs more than three hundred million dollars.[21] The trial also launched the career of Erin Brockovich, a tireless advocate for consumers exposed to pollution, and brought further stardom to Julia Roberts, who won an Academy Award for her depiction of the public health protector.

Naturally occurring substances are not the only chemicals that can contaminate drinking water. During the twentieth century, the synthetic organic chemicals that revolutionized our lives have sometimes contaminated our drinking water. As a result of innovations by the chemical industry, our grocery stores are filled with inexpensive food grown on farms that use synthetic pesticides to increase crop yields. In the morning, we put on clothing made from synthetic chemicals, including nylon, spandex, and Gore-Tex. The vehicles that we drive and the houses that we live in are loaded with plastics, flame retardants, and synthetic fragrances. Although it is hard to imagine modern life without these products, we have learned the hard way that synthetic organic chemicals can compromise our health. Among the numerous dangers associated with chemical exposure, contamination of drinking water is one of the most pernicious.

The first high-profile crisis related to contamination of water with synthetic organic chemicals occurred in 1977, near Niagara Falls, New York, where a housing development and school had been built on top of an abandoned waste disposal site.[22] The residents of the Love Canal neighborhood became ill because they breathed in air contaminated by toxic chemicals in the groundwater that routinely seeped into their basements. Although the community's health problems were not attributable to their drinking water, the coverage that the case received brought to national attention the idea that organic chemical-contaminated groundwater could make people sick.

A vague awareness that the lax approach that had been applied to chemical storage and disposal might pose a risk to the nation's water supplies had been a chief concern of the US Environmental Protection Agency (EPA) since its founding in 1970.[23] By 1976, the agency's analysis of the problem had led to modest regulations on chemical management through passage of the Resource Conservation and Recovery Act.

After the contamination at Love Canal came to light, the pace of the EPA's efforts accelerated: Congress passed the formidable Comprehensive Environmental Response, Compensation, and Liability Act (CERCLA) in 1980. Within a year, the EPA created an inventory of contaminated waste sites. Among the 282 contaminated sites reported by state regulators, the agency deemed 33 to be more dangerous than Love Canal.

By the early 1980s, it had become evident that one family of chemicals—the halogenated solvents—posed the greatest threat to drinking water. Industrial chemicals like trichloroethylene (TCE)—a liquid used to remove oil and grease from everything from metal machine parts to clothing (it is the chemical that made water-free "dry cleaning" possible)—were among the most common groundwater contaminants. They also proved to be among the most difficult to clean up.[24] In addition to the fact that most microbes living in the soil had a hard time breaking them down, these chemicals accumulated in a separate phase, referred to as a non-aqueous phase liquid, or NAPL, when they were released into groundwater (they act like the droplets of oil that float around when you mix oil and vinegar). Because the droplets of TCE were denser than water, the NAPL sunk through the groundwater until it hit a layer of clay or impermeable rock. The accumulated layer of pure chemical resisted attempts to remove the contamination by simply pumping out the dirty groundwater, because some of the droplets of NAPL that stayed behind would dissolve when the contaminated water was replaced by clean water.

The process for characterizing and cleaning up contaminated soil and groundwater was slow, expensive, and labor intensive. If the first impenetrable layer above the aquifer was only a meter or two below the ground surface, the soil could be excavated and incinerated. But if the organic contaminants had worked their way deep into the aquifer, the most common remedy was to install a network of wells and pump the groundwater to the surface. For volatile solvents such as TCE, the chemicals in the extracted water could simply be vented to the atmosphere. Irrespective of what happened to the organic chemicals after they were brought to the surface, this process had to be repeated for decades until all those droplets of NAPL had finally dissolved into the water.

By the 1980s, thousands of sites in the United States where groundwater, soil, and sediments were contaminated with halogenated solvents and metals were being cleaned up with this brute-force approach. Eventually, less expensive and more sophisticated technologies were developed. In some cases, soil microbes could be coaxed into consuming the organic chemicals after nutrients or oxygen were added to the groundwater. At other sites, the solvents could be transferred into the air pockets in the soil by injecting steam into the ground. Once the chemicals were transferred to the soil air, they could be sucked out of the soil with giant vacuums. None of this was cheap. The US Department of Defense alone spent more than thirty billion dollars cleaning up contaminated sites, while chemical companies, oil refineries, and manufacturing facilities spent hundreds of millions of dollars to undo the damage that they had done to drinking water supplies.[25] For contaminated sites where no responsible party could be found, the cleanup process was paid for with a federal government tax that was levied on chemical manufacturers. The orphan-site taxes created a "Superfund," the term that became synonymous with the entire CERCLA program.

More than forty years and many tens of billions of dollars spent cleaning up contamination succeeded in removing the hazardous waste disposal crisis from the American public's consciousness, but the problem has not been solved: in many places, industrial contamination still threatens drinking water supplies. For example, despite hundreds of millions of dollars in cleanup efforts, a plume of groundwater contaminated with TCE and chromium shut down the drinking water supply wells in a wide swath of Los Angeles's San Fernando Valley in 2018. In an effort to turn the contaminated sections of the aquifer back into a drinking water supply, the water-stressed city budgeted over $570 million to build a treatment plant to remove the contaminants from the water after it is pumped out of the ground.[26]

Outside of North America, the issue of contamination of groundwater by industrial waste has received far less attention. However, that does not mean that there are not undiscovered water crises lurking under the feet of the citizens of the rest of the world's cities. Maybe the greater sensitivity to groundwater contamination in North America is somehow related to the American media's penchant for serving up stories about citizens being betrayed by powerful institutions, such as chemical companies and pipeline operators. Or maybe concern for groundwater contamination never reached the same level elsewhere because the public was paying attention to crises involving surface water contamination.

Throughout history, rivers have served an important role in commerce, allowing merchants to move their goods easily over long distances. As a result, many of the world's great cities are located on rivers. When the chemical revolution of the second half of the twentieth century occurred, the refineries and chemical manufacturing facilities ended up on the waterfront. Rivers have also provided cities with easy access to drinking water. These two activities were able to coexist because most cities put their drinking water intake pipes upstream of the industrialized part of the city. The modest amounts of chemicals that routinely found their way into rivers were assumed to be diluted to safe levels before they reached drinking water intake pipes of the next city downriver. When dilution of chemical wastes, farm runoff, and other sources of chemical contamination proved to be insufficient, cities removed them by filtering their water through the sandy aquifers adjacent to the river or by passing it through activated carbon during the drinking water treatment process. However, these treatment processes can be overwhelmed by chemical spills.

In Europe, public awareness of the dangers posed by synthetic organic chemicals was raised in 1986, when a chemical factory in Basel, Switzerland, caught on fire. The ten million liters of water from the firefighting efforts at the Schweizerhalle industrial complex introduced massive amounts of pesticides and other toxic chemicals into the Rhine River—the source of drinking water for over twenty million people in Germany, France, and the Netherlands.[27] In the immediate aftermath of the fire, the pumping stations on the Rhine were shut off, leaving some cities without drinking water for several days.

The fire was instrumental to the growth of the European environmental movement. Unfortunately, Europe's lesson has not prevented spills in other parts of the world.[28] For example, an accident at a chemical factory in Harbin, China, in 2005 left more than four million people without water for almost a week, while a hole in a chemical storage tank in Parkersburg, West Virginia, in 2014 left the state's capital city without drinking water for ten days.

After forty years of experience and hundreds of billions of dollars spent responding to water contamination crises, we have many tools for detecting and cleaning up polluted drinking water. Nonetheless, the fourth water crisis has not been solved. In addition to the hundreds of millions of people who continue to consume water contaminated by naturally occurring contaminants such as arsenic and fluoride and the threats posed by the legacy of hazardous waste sites and improperly managed chemical facilities, drinking water constantly faces new dangers.

The most recent drinking water contamination crisis involves a family of chemicals referred to as PFAS (poly- and perfluoroalkyl substances). These chemicals, which are the key ingredients in nonstick coatings that keep grease from soaking through fast-food packages and that allow firefighters to put out fires at airports and chemical refineries, are effective because they contain multiple carbon-fluorine bonds.[29] These unusual chemical bonds impart superpowers to the PFAS when it comes to the products that chemists produce, but these same properties mean that they can wreak havoc in our bodies.

As a result of their widespread use, high toxicity, and resistance to treatment, PFAS are present at unsafe levels in the drinking water supplies of hundreds of millions of people worldwide, with tens of millions of people in the United States alone drinking water that contains PFAS at levels near or well above those that are considered safe.[30] It is likely that many more billions of dollars will be spent in the coming decades to fix this next drinking water crisis.

3

~~~~~~~~

Water to Grow Food

UP TO THIS POINT, our discussion has been limited to factors affecting the availability, cost, and quality of drinking water. But drinking
water is not the only source of water crises. It takes ten to a hundred
times more water to grow the food that a person living in a middle- or
upper-income country eats than it does to provide all the water they
use in their home.[1] The fifth water crisis—a shortage of water needed
to grow food—is probably the most complicated and potentially con-
fusing of the six water crises because food is often consumed far from
where it is grown. Furthermore, a complex labyrinth of subsidies, historic water rights, and long-standing habits determines what our food
costs, who grows it, and how water is used or overused in the process.

Before we delve into the complex world of water use in agriculture,
we should consider the ways that a lack of water for growing food can
affect farmers and the people who rely upon the food that they grow.

The most obvious victims of agricultural water shortfalls are those
who derive their livelihoods from food production. To understand how
the people who work in agriculture respond to a water crisis, we first
must recognize that farmers are in a business in which adapting to
adverse conditions is often the key to success. In addition to surviving
droughts, farming requires an ability to persist in the face of floods,
cold snaps, heat waves, diseases, and insect invasions. In agriculture, a
year of lower than expected crop yields caused by a normal, periodic

natural phenomenon is compensated for with money saved up during years in which favorable conditions produced profitable harvests. Thus, a resourceful farmer who had not already been facing other stresses will bounce back from the kind of drought that happens once every few decades, but water scarcity that is more severe than anything experienced over the past few centuries might push even the most resourceful farmer over the edge.

Insight into the effects of agricultural water shortages can be gained by looking at the historic record. Drawing upon evidence from pollen grains, geologic deposits, and archaeological artifacts, scientists are now reassessing their explanations for the declines of ancient civilizations. This new knowledge indicates that long periods of drought, caused by volcanic eruptions, meteor strikes, or changes in the intensity of the sun, were critical to the downfall of the Akkadians of ancient Mesopotamia, the Mayans of Mexico's Yucatán Peninsula, and the Mochica and Tiwanaku of Peru.[2] The fortunes of each of these great societies took a turn for the worse after severe droughts lasting for a decade or more took hold. In every case, collapse followed a similar pattern. First, a lack of water lowered crop yields. Then, birth rates dropped, large numbers of people emigrated, and the economy faltered. Eventually, invasions or political instability—symptoms of a prolonged drought rather than the cause of the problem—led to the downfall of the civilization.

Today, drought-induced drops in agricultural productivity do not normally result in the disappearance of cities and towns because we are essentially all part of one big civilization linked together by global commerce. Nonetheless, water shortages can affect entire regions and not just the people whose livelihoods are directly supported by agriculture. How a water shortfall moves beyond the farm is determined by the extent to which the neighboring economy depends upon water as well as the supply chains that bring food grown elsewhere into the region when local food production declines. As is normally the case, rich people are better insulated from this water crisis than those who struggle to make ends meet under normal circumstances.

In the wealthiest parts of the world, droughts are only crises for those whose livelihoods are directly connected to agriculture. For everyone else, they are more of a distant inconvenience. This dynamic is exemplified by the different ways that Australia's Millennium Drought of the 2000s—the country's most severe since European settlement—affected rural communities and city dwellers.[3] While many of Australia's farm communities struggled with increased rates of suicide and bankruptcy due to a lack of water, people living in the country's cities and suburbs thrived. For Australian consumers, the drought raised the cost of fresh fruits and vegetables and locally produced food, such as honey, but the prices of grains, meat, and dairy products barely budged because these commodities were imported from overseas. During the two-year period when the drought was at its peak, a typical family's grocery bill increased by 12 percent, about twice the rate of inflation. Outside of the agriculture sector, a robust economy fueled by industries that were not affected by drought, such as tourism and mining, led to brisk economic growth. The thriving economy also provided tax revenue that the government distributed to farmers in the most severely affected regions of the country.

The situation is often quite different when water shortages hit the world's poorest countries, because a higher proportion of the population typically derives their income from agriculture and industries that are intimately linked to water. The drought in Zimbabwe of 1991–92 illustrates the way that the effects of even a brief drought can extend beyond agricultural communities in countries where the economy has not yet reached the level of diversification characteristic of high-income countries.[4] When the drought hit, Zimbabwe was still adjusting to the effects of a controversial land redistribution policy. Lacking sufficient water for crops, agricultural productivity fell and food prices spiked. The damage did not stop there. Manufacturing output in important water-dependent industries such as textiles, clothing, and footwear fell by over 9 percent as the effects of a decline in domestic cotton production and interruptions in hydroelectric power rippled through the economy. Because so many of the country's wage earners were employed in agriculture and in water-dependent industries, unemployment grew and consumer spending shrank. As a result, the government had less tax revenue to support health care, salaries for government employees, and aid for farmers. Although catastrophe was averted with food and loans provided by international aid organizations, the drought was a major setback. For Zimbabwe and other countries with economies that are intimately tied to water availability, a drought can cause a national crisis that slows economic development for many years after the rains return.

For countries whose wealth falls between the extremes of Australia and Zimbabwe, increases in food prices can affect society in a more complex manner.[5] In low- and middle-income countries, food typically accounts for 15–40 percent of expenditures by families of average income. If prices for locally grown foods spike during a drought, middle-income consumers will usually change their diets, substituting foods grown elsewhere, such as grains, for fresh produce and other commodities that are not easily purchased on the global market. The situation is more problematic for the very poorest urban dwellers in these countries, who spend 60–70 percent of their income on food, because they tend to obtain most of their calories from one or two locally grown staples that typically become more expensive during a drought. Farmers also suffer more in countries that are not wealthy enough to offer government aid to those whose livelihoods are directly affected by droughts.

When economic stress on the urban poor is combined with hardship in rural communities during a drought, political instability may take place. According to several recent accounts, the civil war in Syria is a prime example of how droughts can destabilize countries.[6] Proponents of this theory note that when the most severe drought in modern times hit the country between 2006 and 2009, farms failed as wheat and barley production decreased and the country's livestock was lost. Unemployed farmworkers and their families moved to the edges of the country's six largest cities, where they struggled to find work. The drought-crisis theorists argue that the presence of large numbers of underemployed farmworkers and hungry urban poor led to protests and violence that sparked a civil war.

Although this might make intuitive sense and is supported by contemporaneous statements made by politicians and aid workers, several prominent experts on Middle Eastern affairs have argued that the drought was only a minor factor in the Syrian crisis. According to their interpretation, factors unrelated to drought, such as a reduction of government subsidies for agriculture, discontent with the regime of Bashar al-Assad, and the influence of revolutions that had recently occurred in other Middle Eastern and North African countries, dwarfed the impact of the drought when it came to ranking the many possible factors responsible for the civil war.[7]

Experts who study global conflict might not see eye to eye on the causes of the Syrian civil war, but they do agree that droughts are likely to play a more important role in destabilization of nations as climate change intensifies. Their shared expectation is that in much of the world, climate change–induced droughts will eventually be just as important to civil unrest as the other drivers of instability, such as frustration with inept or oppressive governments, tribal grudges, and memories of previous conflicts.[8] In the already volatile Middle East, hotter, drier conditions will quite likely lead to further destabilization. Water resource management challenges facing India, Pakistan, and sub-Saharan Africa also are likely to lead to problems as populations expand, weather patterns shift, and water to grow food becomes scarce.

Irrespective of how much the drought contributed to the Syrian civil war, that there is now serious discussion about the role of climate change–induced droughts in political instability has important implications for how the world will respond to the fifth water crisis. The experience in Syria has popularized the idea that droughts are threat multipliers, meaning that climate change is now linked to wars and refugee crises in the minds of the people who make policies and control large amounts of money that can be used to prevent or respond to water shortages.[9]

With a better understanding of who is most affected by a shortage of water for growing food and how those impacts are manifest, we can turn our attention to the tools that societies employ to avoid the fifth water crisis.

Since the earliest days of civilization, humans have tried to protect themselves from the damaging effects of droughts by storing and diverting surface water. Around four thousand years ago, the ancient Mesopotamians built a dam on the Tigris River to feed canals that moved water more than three hundred kilometers to a spot north of Baghdad where the water was used to irrigate farms.[10] The surface water irrigation system that the Mesopotamian engineers created not only alleviated farmers' worries about whether a dry spell at a critical time would lower crop yields, they allowed farmers to grow food in places where agriculture would otherwise have been impractical.

Today, surface water irrigation enables California's farmers to produce most of the United States' wintertime supply of fresh vegetables in a former desert east of Los Angeles.[11]

On the other side of the world, the Indus Basin Irrigation System—the largest irrigation system in the world—diverts snowmelt and rainfall runoff from the Himalayas to farmers in an arid region on the India-Pakistan border. On the Pakistani side of the border, the project provides about 90 percent of the water that the country uses to grow its food.[12]

Although surface water irrigation has greatly increased food production, it has not made farmers immune from water shortages. After all, the volume of water that can be stored behind a dam is finite. When too many farmers rely upon the same water source or when an extended drought hits, agricultural production will suffer. A prime example of the limitations of surface water irrigation can be found on the Colorado River, which serves as the main water source for 2.3 million hectares of farmland that grows alfalfa to feed livestock as well as much of the fruit, vegetables, wheat, and cotton produced in the western United States.[13]

The Colorado River's dams and canals have moved snowmelt and rainwater from the Rocky Mountains to farms and cities in the Southwest for more than a century, but the system is under stress.[14] As the climate warms, less snowmelt and rainwater is making its way into the rivers that feed the system's reservoirs because more of the water soaks into the dry soil or evaporates before it has a chance to drain to the river. Lower water yields upstream, growing demand from rapidly expanding cities downstream, and a need to apply more water to crops growing under hotter and drier conditions add up to an uncertain future. Unless Colorado River water users change their long-standing habits, the system's main reservoirs will become an increasingly unreliable water source for the region's farms and cities in the next two to three decades.

The second strategy that farmers have employed to liberate themselves from droughts involves groundwater. Unlike surface water irrigation, which relies upon the construction of shared infrastructure to move water over great distances, groundwater is a source of irrigation water that is accessible directly under the place where it is used. For much of human history, the main barrier to tapping into groundwater to grow food was figuring out how to bring large amounts of water to the surface.

In ancient times, the challenge was met with mechanical ingenuity. To obtain water from shallow wells, almost every ancient civilization came up with some version of a lifting device that the Egyptians called a shaduf. This simple invention consists of a long wooden pole with a counterweight at one side of a rope and water container on the other. After well water fills the container, the user gradually releases the rope to allow the counterweight to pull the water out of the well. Although this innovation was an improvement over the laborious approach of hauling a heavy bucket of water out of the well with brute force, its capacity was limited. An ambitious farmer equipped with a shaduf could haul around two thousand liters of water out of a well in an hour, which might have been enough to satisfy thirsty livestock but could not irrigate an entire farm.[15] Eventually, more sophisticated animal-powered mechanical water-lifting systems were developed, but these methods were still not a very practical way to deliver water to fields.

Around 1000 BCE, Persian engineers developed the qanat, a gently sloping tunnel dug into the side of a hill that collected large volumes of groundwater that then flowed out into a canal by gravity.[16] This ingenious technology spread to cities and farms throughout the region, but its overall impact on food production was limited to places where a sufficient quantity of groundwater was located near the surface and the local topography was favorable (for a qanat to be useful, the tunnel's outlet had to be located above the land where the water was to be applied).

The use of groundwater for irrigation of crops finally took off with the development of efficient mechanical pumps. Piston pumps—devices that sequentially apply pressure to columns of water that are expelled through a central chamber—had been used to move water since the time of the Roman Empire, but they were too expensive for irrigation.[17] It was not until the eighteenth century, when improvements in metallurgy and engineering led to the widespread availability of the familiar, lever-action cylinder hand pump, that large-scale irrigation with groundwater became a possibility. When the suction pump was coupled to a steam engine, a large quantity of water could be brought to the surface quickly. However, the expense of this cutting-edge technology meant that its use was initially limited to applications in which expense was not an issue, such as dewatering mine shafts and providing drinking water for wealthy city dwellers. Eventually, the price declined to a point at which farmers began to use suction pumps, too. By the end of the nineteenth century, better manufacturing methods meant that a suction pump coupled to a windmill or an internal combustion engine could pump around four hundred thousand liters of water to the surface in an hour at a price that a farmer could afford. The era of exploiting groundwater to grow food was underway.

In the early twentieth century, another type of pump made it possible to access water from depths of up to 150 meters below the ground surface. To overcome the struggles that suction pumps and related technologies have in accessing deep groundwater, rotodynamic pumps employ a different approach. Using an engine connected to a shaft inserted down the well, a small paddle, known as an impeller, is rapidly rotated inside of a chamber. The centrifugal force applied to water entering through one side of the chamber causes it to flow up and out of the well. As these groundwater pumps became more popular, windmills and inefficient internal combustion engines were replaced by reliable electric motors and more efficient diesel engines on many farms. By the time that the Great Depression hit in 1929, more than fifty thousand groundwater wells were being used for irrigation by farmers in the American West.[18] As part of the government's efforts to hasten economic recovery, rural electrification programs spread groundwater pumping over much of the western United States during the next two decades.

After World War II, yet another new type of pump—the submersible electric pump—further reduced the cost of using groundwater on farms. These devices, which were lowered into the bottom of the well after someone convinced the installer that they would not be electrocuted when the device hit the water, were less expensive to purchase and required less maintenance than their shaft-drive predecessors.[19]

During the second half of the twentieth century, the submersible electric pump coupled with an innovation in irrigation technology—the center pivot irrigation system—led to another rapid expansion in groundwater use in the American West. The genius of the center pivot was its simplicity. It reduced the cost of irrigation systems by eliminating the need to install permanent irrigation pipes. It also made it possible to apply fertilizer with the irrigation water. As a result of these technological advancements, the use of groundwater to irrigate fields on the arid plains of western Nebraska expanded tenfold in the period between 1972 and 1986.[20] If you want evidence of the importance of center pivot irrigation and submersible pumps, all you need to do is zoom in on a satellite image from an arid region of the world where food is

Satellite image of western Kansas where center pivot irrigation
and submersible pumps have remade the landscape.

grown or look out the window of an airplane as you fly over irrigated farmland. Those green circles that you see are being irrigated with groundwater from a center pivot system.

Irrigation with groundwater played an important role in the Green Revolution that made it possible to feed many of the 3.6 billion people who joined the world's population during the second half of the twentieth century. Among the many places where access to groundwater has been instrumental to agricultural productivity, India is exceptional.[21] Starting in the second half of the 1960s, the Indian government funded rural electrification projects and provided loans for farmers to purchase groundwater pumps. The government also provided subsidized electricity. As a result of the availability of cheap groundwater, the area of irrigated farmland increased sixfold over the next four decades, to over sixty million hectares. By 2000, over 40 percent of India's farmers were relying upon groundwater to produce food that accounted for about 10 percent of the country's gross domestic product.

Because the rate at which groundwater was being pumped out of India's aquifers far exceeded the rate at which it was being recharged by rainfall, groundwater levels soon began to decline. Between 1980 and 2000, groundwater levels in the state of Gujarat fell by more than eighty meters, which resulted in the need to dig deeper wells and to use more power to acquire irrigation water.[22]

Today, groundwater pumping consumes about 15 percent of India's electricity.[23] In the southern part of the country, where deep-groundwater use is concentrated, pumping consumes about 45 percent of the electricity. Pumps are also responsible for the consumption of large quantities of diesel fuel in the eastern parts of India, where internal combustion engines are used to access shallow groundwater. Although the Indian government is aware of the need to reduce groundwater use before the water recedes to a point where it cannot be accessed by farmers, efforts to regulate the resource have been challenging. India's rural communities rely upon the subsidized or free electricity that politicians have used over the years to win their votes. The nation's leaders fear their anger as well as the economic damage that would likely follow groundwater cutbacks in India's rural villages.

Overexploitation of groundwater extends beyond South Asia. Aquifers in China, North Africa, and North America also have been falling in recent decades.[24] Two of the most productive farming regions in the United States—located in the Great Plains and California's Central Valley—experienced substantial declines in groundwater levels during the second half of the twentieth century. Although California's farmers have begun to reverse the trend by bringing their groundwater use into balance with recharge rates, water levels in much of the Ogallala Aquifer continue to decline because the local geology is not conducive to recharge. On the Texas Panhandle, near the border with Oklahoma, if current trends continue, the day when the center pivot irrigation systems turn off for good will probably occur in the next three decades.

In addition to unsustainable use of irrigation water, the world's farmers face a serious challenge. Water use in agriculture needs to be adjusted to the conditions of a hotter, often drier planet just as the world's population is growing and acquiring a taste for meat and dairy products, which require more water to produce. By 2050, the world's farmers will need to produce 70 percent more food than what is grown today.[25]

The good news is that farmers and agricultural experts in water-stressed parts of the world have already developed tools for growing more food with less water. But even if we could overcome the economic, social, and political challenges that often slow the spread of these best practices, efficiency alone would get us less than halfway to meeting the world's irrigation water needs.[26] Some of the remaining shortfall could come from new dams, reservoirs, and groundwater wells, but much of the world's most productive farmland is already in use, and most of the easily accessed water sources are already being exploited or, as we have seen, overexploited.

4

~~~~~~~~~~

Water for Nature

TODAY, ABOUT 10 PERCENT of the precipitation that falls on the continents is intercepted by humanity and used to grow food, power cities, or provide drinking water.[1] But this number does not express the full extent to which humans have changed the flow of the world's water because a lot of rain falls in sparsely populated places, such as the rain forests of the Amazon and the jungles of Southeast Asia. In drier, more densely populated places, such as the Indo-Gangetic Plain, the North China Plain, and the Mediterranean, more than half of the water that falls on the land is used by people. In wetter, less crowded parts of the world, the amount of precipitation captured by humanity may be smaller, but the impacts of humanity's water use on the surrounding environment are far from negligible.

Much of the water that humanity exploits is returned to the world's rivers, lakes, and aquifers after it is used. These return flows are critical to the survival of ecosystems in arid parts of the world, but waterways that receive wastes from farms, power stations, and sewage treatment plants can become inhospitable to native plants and animals. Humanity has changed the way that water is released to the environment by eliminating the natural fluctuations between floods and dry periods that are characteristic of undisturbed ecosystems. The water flowing back to the environment also differs in composition from the water that was captured. During its use, water is warmed by passing through power plants and its composition is altered by the addition of fertilizers, pesticides, metals, and chemical wastes.

The effect of human water use extends well beyond water pollution and water diversion projects.[2] To protect cities from flooding, rivers have been straightened and reinforced with levees. When it has suited our needs, we also have reversed the flow of rivers and connected water bodies that had been separated for millions of years. In short, humans have taken control of the water cycle.

Our inability to act as good stewards to the world's water has led to the disappearance of sensitive species and has pushed entire ecosystems to the brink of collapse. Increasingly, our actions are also threatening our own health and standard of living. The sixth and final water crisis is related to the impact of humanity's use of water on the plants and animals with which we share the planet.

Some of the easiest places for observing the scale of humanity's impact on the world's waterways are terminal (endorheic) lakes. Because these water bodies do not have outlets, their size depends upon the balance between the flow of water into the basin and the rate at which it evaporates from the surface. Central Asia's Aral Sea serves as a prime example of how diminished river flows have altered terminal lakes.[3] Before the 1960s, when the Soviet Union expanded the irrigation system that diverted water from the Anu Darya and the Syr Darya Rivers to the region's cotton and rice farms, the Aral Sea was the fourth largest lake in the world. After the water project was built, the Aral Sea shrunk by over 90 percent. The lake now consists of three small lakes set amid a few formerly thriving towns where the air is polluted by salty, metal-rich dust blown up from the dried lakebed. In two of the remaining lakes, the water has become too salty and polluted for fish to survive. Local officials have managed to save the fish in the northernmost of the residual lakes by building a thirteen-kilometer-long dike to concentrate the diminished flow into a smaller area, but this stopgap measure will not bring back the lake's thriving ecosystem. Without a major change in upstream water use, the Aral Sea will remain a shadow of its former self.

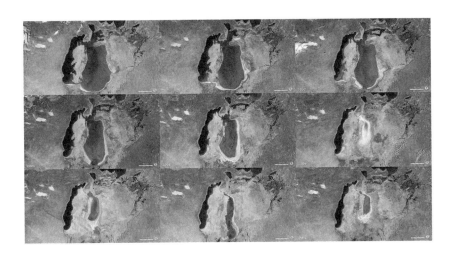

A set of satellite images depicting the near disappearance
of the Aral Sea between 2000 and 2013.

Although the damage that water diversion projects have caused
has not always been as obvious as what has happened to the Aral Sea,
Central Africa's Lake Chad, California's Salton Sea, and the rest of the
world's shrinking terminal lakes, such projects also have had profound
effects on rivers and lakes that are connected to the ocean.[4]

The recent fight over water rights on North America's Klamath
River system is representative of the ways that the sixth water crisis
feeds conflicts between ecosystems and nearby communities. Along the
border between Oregon and California, a set of dams built in the early
decades of the twentieth century turned a flat section of the river into
Upper Klamath Lake, a twenty-five-thousand-hectare shallow reservoir
that supplies farmers with irrigation water for growing alfalfa, potatoes,
and onions and hydroelectric power. After this initial modification of
the watershed, the salmon migration continued in the lower section
of the river because ample amounts of water continued to flow into the
river from tributaries entering the Klamath farther downstream. Conditions took a turn for the worse in the 1960s, when one of the biggest
rivers flowing into the lower reaches of the Klamath was redirected to

California's Central Valley.[5] Over the next three decades, the diminished flow combined with the effects of nutrients and pesticides in the irrigation water returning from farms greatly reduced the number of coho and chinook salmon in the lower section of the river.

In response to the decline in the salmon population, members of the native tribes that had been fishing the waters of the Klamath for thousands of years sued the US government. In 2001, a federal court ruled that use of water for irrigation had to decrease substantially. After the irrigation district complied with the decision, angry farmers pried open the locks that had been installed to prevent them from accessing the system's main irrigation canal.[6] The following year, tens of thousands of salmon died in the lower reaches of the river as a result of Vice President Dick Cheney's decision to intervene in support of the right of farmers to take irrigation water. After a few more tense, uncertain years, in which the value of agricultural land in the basin fell, farms failed, and members of the Hoopa Valley, Karuk, and Yurok tribes struggled to maintain their livelihood and pursue their cultural heritage on a river with fewer and fewer fish, a compromise was reached. To restore the Klamath River without destroying the region's agricultural economy, a series of hydroelectric dams downstream of Upper Klamath Lake would be removed and more water would be released to the lower section of the river during the period when the salmon were migrating.[7] Although the dam removal project, which has been making slow progress toward implementation, could stabilize the salmon population, the sixth water crisis is likely to continue along the Klamath for many decades.

In other parts of the world, controversies have been brewing in ecosystems where water diversion projects damaged ecosystems during the second half of the twentieth century. For example, Australia's Murray-Darling River, Southeast Asia's Mekong River, and South America's Amazon River have all experienced declines in native fish populations and ecosystem health due to the withdrawal of irrigation water and the construction of hydroelectric power projects.[8] When local community members have raised their voices in protest, more water has sometimes been released, but few places have seriously considered the possibility of removing the water infrastructure or making serious compromises in the ways in which projects are operated.

A retrospective analysis, conducted by the World Commission on Dams, indicates that, despite their popularity with engineers, bankers, and government officials, the net economic benefits of large dams and their associated flood control, power, and irrigation projects are often quite small. In most places, the regional economy receives an initial boost when these projects are built, but the costs associated with relocating communities displaced by the dams and the damage to ecosystems caused by alteration of water flow have often been of a similar magnitude as the benefits associated with the crops and electricity that the projects produced.[9]

The same data indicate that the livelihoods of over 450 million people already have been adversely impacted by large water diversion projects.[10] The unintended consequence of humanity's takeover of the water cycle has been the creation of water crises for scores of ecosystems and communities that had been relying upon the natural flow of water in river systems.

Water pollution has also led to crises in many of the world's rivers, lakes, and estuaries.

In terms of water quality, civilization's largest use of water—agriculture—is responsible for the most substantial impacts. Cropland and pastures take up approximately 12 percent and 26 percent, respectively, of the ice-free area of the world's continents.[11] Much of the water that falls on fields and grazing land or is piped in via irrigation projects eventually percolates into the groundwater or drains to a river or lake. As this water passes through the soil, it becomes contaminated with fertilizers, pesticides, and salt. It also can pick up pathogenic microbes from the feces of farm animals. Agricultural water pollution, often accompanied by changes in the amount of water flowing downstream and changes in the seasonal flow patterns, can eventually degrade ecosystems to a point of crisis.

Before the second half of the twentieth century, the effects of farm runoff were mostly confined to waters immediately adjacent to farms. The impacts did not extend further because the cost of fertilizer was high, synthetic pesticides were not widely used, and there were plenty of open spaces between farms to dilute the pollution. The intensification of agriculture after World War II increased the damage caused by farm runoff as the area of irrigated land under cultivation approximately doubled.[12] In wealthy countries, crop yields were increased by the application of large quantities of fertilizers and pesticides along with policies that favored the consolidation of farms that could take advantage of mechanical harvesting equipment and other economies of scale. Throughout the rest of the world, crop yields were driven up by new, disease-resistant, high-yielding grains; crop yields were increased further by access to pesticides and fertilizers.

As crop yields increased, the price of grain fell.[13] In parts of the world facing food shortages, hunger was reduced. In wealthy countries, where food shortages had been less of a problem, farmers began to sell their surplus grain as animal feed. As a result, the price of meat in North America, Western Europe, and Japan dropped just as people's incomes rose as part of the postwar economic boom. By the 1970s, a meal including a big slice of meat went from an occasional luxury to a daily ritual for wealthy people. Worldwide, meat consumption almost doubled between 1960 and 2013. As wealth spreads to Asia and Africa over the next three decades, it will likely double again.

The increasing popularity of an animal protein–rich diet has had serious consequences for the world's surface waters. The traditional way of producing meat and dairy products by putting animals out to pasture pollutes waterways because grazing animals are messy: as they wander across fields in search of fresh grass and drinking water, livestock erodes and compacts the soil, which reduces the amount of water that percolates into the ground and increases the amount of sediment flowing downstream.[14] In addition, animal waste, which contains nutrients, organic matter, and waterborne pathogens, easily finds its way into streams and rivers wherever animals graze. The modern way of raising animals by feeding them grain and housing them in a barn or on a feedlot reduces some of the pressure on pastureland. Unfortunately, the economic advantages of locating large numbers of feedlots, dairies, egg-laying barns, and food processing operations in the same place mean that local waterways are subject to concentrated pollution that can overwhelm their assimilative capacity.

The wastes generated by concentrated animal agriculture receive much less treatment than those produced by people in cities. For example, the state of North Carolina dealt with the doubling of its human population and the fourfold increase in its porcine population in recent decades in very different ways.[15] To serve North Carolina's expanding cities, the state's taxpayers invested billions of dollars in modern sewage treatment plants capable of processing human waste so that it can be discharged safely to the region's most sensitive waterways. In contrast, the waste produced on hog feedlots, which is similar in volume to the amount produced in the state's cities, is sent to one of three thousand animal waste lagoons—structures that are essentially uncovered ponds filled with two to six meters of pig excrement, urine, and hundreds of trillions of waste-eating bacteria. Within the lagoons, the bacteria convert some of the undigested food into carbon dioxide, dinitrogen, and water, but most of the nutrients, pathogens, antibiotics, and metabolites in the waste are simply sprayed back onto the land adjacent to the feedlot.

This low-tech approach to waste disposal does not violate water pollution regulations because it mimics the ways that farmers with smaller numbers of animals use animal waste as fertilizer. Nonetheless, the industrial-scale waste disposal practice employed in North Carolina has been controversial. Members of neighboring communities have protested and sued companies that operate the hog farms in an effort to control the odorous and toxic chemicals and bacteria-laden dust that drift into their homes and yards.[16] When the region gets hit by hurricanes, the entire contents of lagoons are often released to adjacent waterways all at once. Worldwide, continuation of the charade that wastes from industrial-scale animal agriculture are taken up by crops grown on inadequately sized plots adjacent to feedlots and barns means that life will become unpleasant and water quality will be diminished when intensive animal husbandry comes to town.

The impacts of modern agriculture on the world's waterways are not limited to animal agriculture. Intensive cultivation practices employed to grow grain, fruits, and vegetables also pollute waterways. Only about a third of the phosphorus and half of the nitrogen currently being applied to the land ends up in the food that we eat.[17] Much of the excess nutrient load eventually leaches into groundwater or gets carried away in runoff. A significant fraction of the 4.6 million tons of pesticides applied to fields and the 60,000 tons of antibiotics fed to livestock will also find their way into waterways.[18]

Because their impacts are easier to detect, the effects of nutrients are better documented and understood than those caused by other agricultural water pollutants. The tenfold increase in synthetic nitrogen fertilizer use that occurred between 1960 and 2000 was accompanied by a surge in the concentrations of nitrate—the most prevalent nutrient in farm runoff—by a factor of between two and ten in the world's rivers and lakes.[19] Concentrations of the other major plant nutrient, phosphorus, also increased, but to a lesser degree because it has a greater tendency to adsorb onto soil. Unsurprisingly, the presence of higher levels of nutrients in the world's waterways has given the Green Revolution a second, less positive meaning.

When modern agricultural practices are first adopted, most people barely notice the growth of a little more algae in rivers or lakes. Parents might recall a time during their childhood when they could easily see the bottom of the swimming hole and their drinking water did not have a musty taste from the algae growing on the surface of the town's drinking water reservoir, but the new conditions seem normal to their progeny. Fishermen, naturalists, and scientists often lament the loss of sensitive species that accompanies the decline in water quality from nutrient pollution. But measured against a backdrop of economic growth and cheap, plentiful food, few people consider this first stage of

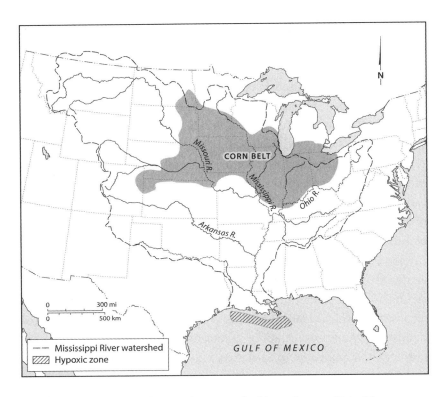

Nutrients applied to farms in the Corn Belt of the midwestern United States contribute the growth of algae that lead to the formation of an area that is often termed the Hypoxic (or Dead) Zone because the oxygen-free sediments and overlying water are often devoid of fish and aquatic organisms.

ecosystem decline a crisis. It is not until the cumulative effects of decades of nutrient pollution reach a point of serious ecosystem damage that a general diminution in water quality graduates to a crisis.

Conditions in and around the American Midwest over the past century vividly illustrate the decadal timescale over which modern agriculture has created regional water crises. If you were to take a trip from the rich agricultural land of western Ohio, through the productive farmland of Illinois, Iowa, and southern Minnesota, you would pass through the Corn Belt, which is one of the world's most productive grain-producing regions. Most of the seventy-six billion dollars' worth of corn and soybeans grown in this region are converted into high-fructose corn syrup or are fermented and distilled to make ethanol for biofuel.[20] In the north, some of the runoff from this rich farmland flows into the Great Lakes. But most of the runoff from the region's fields eventually finds its way into the Mississippi River, through which it enters the Gulf of Mexico near New Orleans.

Homesteaders arriving from the East had turned much of the region's forests, grasslands, and wetlands into farms by the middle of the 1800s. Over the next hundred years, towns and cities grew and locks were installed as the Mississippi was transformed into a major transportation artery. During the first part of the twentieth century, the river channel was deepened and more locks were built to facilitate shipping in the present-day Corn Belt.[21] In the Lower Mississippi, engineers installed flood control levees, deepened the channel, and straightened some of the river's characteristic meanders. Turning the Mississippi into a modern transportation network facilitated the movement of goods across the region, but it came at a steep cost. Sediments trapped by locks, dams, and wetlands in the northern section deprived wetlands and floodplains in the southern section of materials needed to maintain their ability to assimilate nutrients. As less sediment accumulated in the river's delta, New Orleans, Baton Rouge, and other cities along the Gulf Coast became more susceptible to the effects of rising seas and hurricane-driven storm surges.

Over a two-decade period starting in the 1960s, the amount of nitrogen that the Corn Belt delivered to the Gulf of Mexico tripled.[22] Algae growing in the nutrient-enriched Gulf waters fed the shrimp and fish, but the algae that did not end up as fish food as well as the feces produced by the well-fed shrimp and fish sank into the shallow sediments, where they were broken down by sediment-dwelling microbes. After years of accumulation of organic wastes, microbial activity in the sediments reached the point at which oxygen from the bottom waters was consumed faster than it could be replenished from the atmosphere.

The result was an area of oxygen-depleted waters devoid of shrimp, fish, and other aquatic organisms that is referred to as the Hypoxic or

Dead Zone.[23] Although a small area of oxygen-depleted water at the mouth of the Mississippi River may have been present much earlier, the size of the Hypoxic Zone has greatly expanded since the 1960s. Today, an area slightly smaller than the state of New Jersey (or, for those who are less familiar with the dimensions of Bruce Springsteen's home state, half the size of the Netherlands) forms in the Gulf every summer. In addition to clearing this gigantic area of marine life, nutrient pollution has reduced the clarity of the water, altered the composition of fish species, and created conditions favorable to swarms of jellyfish throughout the Gulf.

For decades, government officials ignored the expansion of the Hypoxic Zone because few people were complaining. The Gulf's maritime economy continued to prosper because the commercial fishing fleet and charter boats could set their nets or troll along the edge of the Hypoxic Zone where large schools of fish fed in the nutrient-enriched waters. Although local marine biologists published papers and gave lectures warning about an impending ecosystem collapse, people outside of the research community were too busy enjoying the Gulf to listen. The problem finally became too big to ignore in 1993, when an increase in nutrients associated with one of the wettest years on record in the Mississippi River watershed almost doubled the size of the Hypoxic Zone in one season.[24] In response to the increased attention being paid to the Hypoxic Zone, the federal government established the Mississippi River/Gulf of Mexico Watershed Hypoxia Task Force in 1997.

After two decades in which state and federal agencies spent tens of millions of dollars on research and retooled programs that had previously directed billions of dollars to projects designed to raise crop yields for the new goal of controlling nutrients in farm runoff, the amount of nitrogen being delivered to the Gulf decreased by almost 20 percent.[25] Despite the progress in reducing concentrations of one of the two nutrients responsible for algae growth, the Hypoxic Zone did not shrink. If healthy ecosystems are going to coexist with modern agriculture, something will need to be done to control the nutrient-laden runoff that has created hypoxic zones in the Gulf of Mexico, North America's Chesapeake Bay, Scandinavia's Kattegat (the bay at the outlet of the Baltic Sea), and Asia's East China Sea.[26]

Accounting for hypoxic zones, air pollution (mainly from the volatilization of ammonia in animal waste), and decreased quality of drinking water, the impacts of nitrogen pollution cost each citizen of the United States and Europe around fifty dollars per year.[27] Although this might seem to be a modest cost for access to cheap and abundant food, the brunt of these impacts are borne by the fraction of the population living close to where the food is produced. Rather than accepting this pollution as an inevitable part of modern life, it seems that the rest of us should be willing to spend more for our food to prevent this aspect of the sixth water crisis.

As described earlier, the world's farmers will have to grow 70 percent more food over the next three decades to keep up with population growth and a higher demand for meat.[28] The United Nations estimates that around 90 percent of the increase in food production will come from agricultural intensification. Although advanced plant breeding, market reform, and new practices that reduce food wastage are likely to play a major role in the next stage of agricultural intensification, it seems probable that the world's waterways will be subject to more pollution if nothing changes in the way that food is produced. The impacts on ecosystems of this next stage of agricultural intensification is likely to be exacerbated by climate change and the diversion of more water into irrigation projects.

Pollution of the world's waterways extends beyond nutrients in agricultural runoff. Pesticides contaminate rivers, lakes, and groundwater surrounding farms.[29] For example, much of the drinking water in the Corn Belt is contaminated with the herbicide atrazine at levels that have been tied to miscarriages and birth defects. The presence of atrazine in the region's waterways also may help explain the disappearance of native frogs that has occurred in recent decades.

Outside of regions polluted by farm runoff, cities and industry have also contributed to ecological crises.[30] The world's hunger for fossil fuels has been accompanied by oil spills that have crippled aquatic ecosystems in Alaska, Ecuador, and the Niger Delta. Looking beyond the rich parts of the world that are home to about 10 percent of humanity, only a small fraction of sewage produced in cities undergoes any form of treatment before it flows into the environment. The impacts of discharging untreated sewage often are compounded by the added insult of wastewater from textile dyeing, tanneries, and chemical refineries.

In our quest for a better life, we have forgotten that we cannot take water from the environment or pollute it when we return it to the environment without considering the impacts of our actions on the ecosystems and people that had grown accustomed to using that water. As we find excuses for shirking our duty as stewards of the world's waterways, the hardy aquatic survivors of the sixth water crisis silently suffer in the diminished environment that the civilized world has created.

ANTICIPATING AN
UNCERTAIN FUTURE

Change is inevitable, but sometimes it is also predictable.

DESPITE A GROWING recognition that a new approach is needed to address water crises that are becoming both more severe and more frequent, infrastructure and institutions that developed over four thousand years cannot be reinvented overnight. After figuring out better ways to obtain, treat, and use water, it still will be necessary to build political support to resolve issues that tend to slow the rate of change, such as the convoluted systems of water rights and financing that exist in many places. Even under the most optimistic of scenarios, water solutions developed today are unlikely to become widespread until the second half of the twenty-first century. By that time, the world is likely to be a very different place. To develop more robust and effective water systems, it will be necessary to design water systems that anticipate the future that awaits them. The best way to do this is by understanding the events that created modern civilization and some of the trends that are likely to shape it in the coming decades.

5

The Great Acceleration

IT IS IMPOSSIBLE TO say much about the future without considering the unprecedented changes that recently swept across the world.
Following a global economic depression and two world wars in the
first half of the twentieth century, each of the seven decades starting in
1950 ended with a bigger increase in population, amount of wealth created, and use of natural resources than the one that preceded it. This
trend of continuously increasing social and economic development,
which has been referred to as the Great Acceleration, has reshaped society and the natural world. But acceleration cannot continue forever.
At some point, the rate of change must slow as civilization either transitions to a more stable state or collapses. The decisions that our generation makes about how to navigate this period will likely affect the
state of the world for centuries to come.

There are many ways of interpreting the complex political, social,
and economic events of the first decades of the twentieth century. During that period national economies were becoming interlinked through
investments in new technologies such as the telegraph, railroad, and
steamship as regional powers came into conflict over political ideolo-
gies and issues related to the control of weaker countries.[1] For the purpose of trying to understand the impact of these changes on water, the
important point is that civilization entered the middle of the twentieth
century poised for big changes. Facing a world needing to be rebuilt, a

vacuum created by crumbled empires, and decades of pent-up techno-logical development from ideas that could not reach their full potential during the depression and wars, the Great Acceleration began.

The unprecedented social, economic, and environmental changes that took place during the second half of the twentieth century can best be understood by a set of iconic graphs popularized by researchers at Stockholm University.[2] For most of the trends depicted on the graphs, the rapid growth of civilization has not abated. But a closer look at the contributions from different regions provides evidence of a transition to a more stable state in some places. To project future water needs, it is important to consider these regional differences and the intercon-nected global trading that transfers food, energy, and goods between water-rich and water-scarce nations.

Irrespective of regional differences, the Great Acceleration has been accompanied by considerable population growth (see graphs on next page). Between 1950 and 2020, the world's population more than tripled, increasing from approximately 2.5 to 7.6 billion people. In group-ing countries according to their state of development at the start of the Great Acceleration, it becomes clear that growth has been distributed unevenly. The relatively wealthy people living in the OECD (Western Europe, North America, Japan, South Korea, Turkey, Israel, Australia, New Zealand, and Chile) contributed only about 10 percent of the pop-ulation increase. The BRICS countries (Brazil, Russia, India, China, and South Africa), which currently make up about half of the world's peo-ple, accounted for about 40 percent of the growth. The other half of the increase in population mostly occurred in less affluent countries in Africa, Southeast Asia, and the Middle East, with much of the growth taking place between 1990 and 2020. These rapidly growing parts of the world also are where most of the population increase will occur over the next thirty years, as populations in the OECD countries level off and growth rates slow in the BRICS countries. In particular, sub-Saharan Africa is poised to become a hotspot for population growth, account-ing for almost half of the global population increase as the region goes from about 1 to 2 billion people between 2020 and 2050.[3]

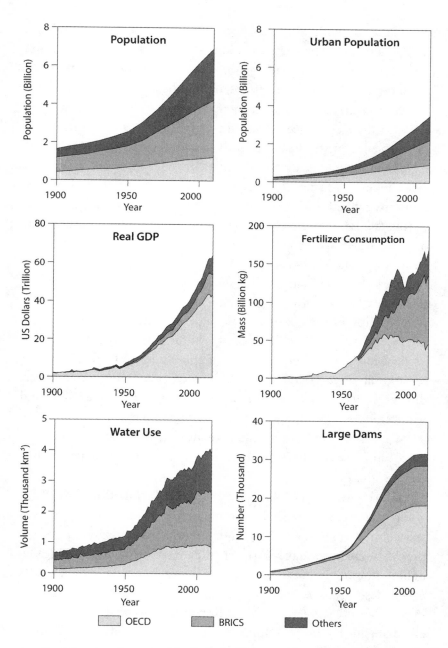

Six socioeconomic trends of the Great Acceleration. The shading depicts trends for the OECD countries, the BRICS (Brazil, Russia, India, China, and South Africa) countries, and the rest of the world (Others). Data on fertilizer use before 1960 were not available for separate regions.

Many factors help explain the explosive population growth that accompanied the Great Acceleration. Most of the population growth was tied to the fact that people lived longer, as opposed to increases in the number of children that they had. But the reasons for greater longevity are nearly impossible to untangle because so many things about the ways that people lived changed simultaneously after World War II. Looking back into the historic record in parts of the world where growth and development occurred before the Great Acceleration, we can find clues about the factors underlying more recent trends in decreased mortality rates: death rates in Western Europe and North America fell during the first four decades of the twentieth century as sanitation and drinking water treatment slowed the spread of communicable diseases such as typhoid fever and polio.[4] Mortality rates also decreased during that period as increasing wealth allowed people to adopt more nutritious diets. Starting around the middle of the twentieth century, the effects of vaccines and antibiotics drove the continued trend of decreasing mortality rates in wealthy nations. In the latter part of the century, modern medicine further increased lifespans through better treatments for chronic diseases afflicting older people, such as cancer and heart disease. When sanitation, water treatment, more nutritious food, and medical innovations spread to later entrants in the Great Acceleration in other parts of the world simultaneously, the net effect was an even more rapid increase in population than those that had happened during previous periods.

In Western Europe, North America, Japan, and other parts of the world that first experienced declining mortality rates, population has started to level off in a phenomenon known as a demographic transition.[5] The change usually starts when people move to cities in search of better-paying jobs: as a greater percentage of the population adopts urban lifestyles, birth rates drop because large families are less attractive in crowded cities. Decreases in birth rates among city dwellers eventually dampens the impact of longer lifespans on population. But these changes also affect the age structure of society, leading to fewer young people generating income to support their retired elders. Some countries compensate for the shortage of working-aged citizens by allowing or even encouraging immigration from less affluent parts of the world, while others put up barriers to outsiders and struggle with the economic drag associated with an aging population. Either way, as the demographic transition reaches its end, populations in Western Europe, Japan, North America, and China are predicted to level out or undergo modest declines during the twenty-first century. With respect to water supply, these trends imply that the expectations of continuous growth that drove the expansionist behavior of water planners during the twentieth century will end, as urban water demand levels off or decreases.

It would be tempting to assume that growth in the rest of the world will follow a similar trajectory, with development leading to wealth, an orderly process of urbanization, and a leveling off in water demand, but that is not necessarily the case.

One reason is that urban migration is now a lot faster.[6] For example, in the nineteenth century, the population of Greater London doubled approximately every forty years, as the metropolitan area grew from around one million to six million inhabitants. Today, the world's fifteen fastest growing cities—all in sub-Saharan Africa—are doubling in population every fifteen years. When urban population grows so quickly, water utilities struggle to build reservoirs, wells, and pipe networks as organizations responsible for other essential city services, such as public transit and hospitals, compete with them for a limited pool of government revenue.

The second reason that this round of growth is different is that, unlike the demographic transitions of the twentieth century, the next transitions may not be accompanied by the rapid decreases in poverty that accompanied previous periods of expansion.[7] If rapid population growth does not coincide with the creation of a large number of well-paying jobs, much of the future urban growth will happen in informal settlements—places that some people refer to as slums. Delivering water infrastructure to these areas is challenging because the normal rules for laying pipes and collecting revenue from new customers do not work when cities grow in an uncontrolled fashion.

Because much of the population growth in coming decades will occur in sub-Saharan Africa, the case of Nigeria—the African country with the biggest population and largest economy—may provide useful insights. Nigeria already has ten cities with populations above a million people, all of which will grow rapidly in the coming decades.[8] Many of Nigeria's small towns also are expected to turn into cities during this period. At first glance, Nigeria would seem to have many of the ingredients needed for a successful demographic transition: a rich culture, a young workforce, and, since 2000, a stable government, but the country faces challenges that render its future uncertain.

Despite its great potential, Nigeria has failed to bring much of its population out of poverty. It is not for a lack of trying.[9] Since the country obtained its independence from Britain in 1960, every government has had a plan for poverty alleviation. Nonetheless, approximately half of the country's rural population and a third of its urban population still lived below the poverty line in 2014. One of the main reasons that rural poverty persists is the low productivity of agriculture—the sector of the economy where the largest number of people work. The poor economic performance of Nigeria's farms is partially attributable to the inability of small landholders to finance investments in fertilizer and modern agricultural equipment. Inadequate transportation infrastructure also penalizes farmers when they try to move food to markets.

Escape to the city in search of better-paying jobs is no guarantee of success: urban poverty persists because many of the country's small businesses, operating outside of the formal economy, pay low wages, despite the relatively high cost of living in Nigerian cities.

Many of the most educated Nigerians seek stable, better-paying government jobs or emigrate to countries where their skills can be put to work rather than attempting to create private sector jobs that would lift less-skilled workers out of poverty.[10]

Although these explanations are valid descriptions of the symptoms that hold Nigeria back, focusing on their impact on the country's economic performance obscures the proximate cause of the problem: a historic reliance on the oil and gas industry to support the government has created conditions that make it hard to build up other parts of the economy.

In fact, Nigeria is often considered the epitome of a phenomenon that economists refer to as the Resource Curse.[11] The idea, which was popularized by Jeffrey Sachs and Andrew Warner in 1995, is that countries with abundant petroleum or mineral reserves easily get trapped in a cycle that prevents them from diversifying their economies beyond resource extraction. People who do not think like economists would likely presume that revenues from exporting abundant natural resources would accelerate development by providing income for building infrastructure and enabling spending on goods and services. However, income from resource extraction also leads to an appreciation of a nation's currency that makes domestically manufactured goods less attractive in global markets and depresses the local prices of competing imported goods. As a result, industries other than those that directly rely upon mineral or petroleum resources often are slow to develop in resource-rich nations. In addition, the concentration of wealth in the hands of a small number of companies and individuals tends to foster corruption, which both stifles democracy and leads to government investments in policies that do not always benefit the public.

Nigeria has struggled to overcome the Resource Curse since oil was discovered in the early 1960s.[12] Many of the country's problems— a civil war, government officials looting the nation's treasury, millions of dollars spent on a steel mill that never produced any steel—can be traced to the Resource Curse. Reliance on fossil fuel exploitation also has been detrimental to development because prices have risen and fallen in an unpredictable manner, causing recessions just as the economy seemed to be moving in the right direction. Although Nigeria's current government, which is well aware of the causes and symptoms of its past shortcomings, delivered impressive growth rates of approximately 6 percent per year between 2000 and 2018, the newfound wealth still is not leading to significant decreases in poverty.

Nigeria is not the region's only nation with abundant natural resources.[13] Countries with lucrative mines or rich petroleum reserves, which are home to about two-thirds of Africa's people, are struggling to escape the Resource Curse. But not all African nations are fated to a future of extreme income inequality and diminished economic prospects.[14] Botswana has managed to escape the Resource Curse by anticipating and planning for the boom-and-bust cycles of its diamond mines, while resource-poor Ethiopia recently had one of the fastest-growing economies in the world.

Irrespective of whether they will be held back by the Resource Curse, sub-Saharan African countries are unlikely to experience the same sort of rapid ascent to wealth that occurred in Japan, South Korea, and China during the Great Acceleration because the world is building fewer factories that employ large numbers of workers. The engine that will drive the development of sub-Saharan Africa in the twenty-first century is likely to be the demographic dividend—the economic advantage that is temporarily available to a country during the brief period when its labor force is growing faster than the rest of its population.[15] If sub-Saharan African nations can provide young workers with access to education, functioning infrastructure, and an environment free from rampant corruption, the demographic dividend might allow them to successfully navigate a path to prosperity and stability. For these countries, wealth will come from development of human capital that provides the goods and services needed to grow the economy and not from exploitation of natural resources or the construction of factories that manufacture products for the rest of the world.

According to the latest models, Africa's urban population will grow by close to a factor of four, to around 1.6 billion people, between 2020 and 2050. Although the sheer size of the megacities of Lagos and Kinshasa, which each are expected to be home to more than 35 million people by midcentury, is likely to continue to garner the media's attention, about 75 percent of the growth in African cities will probably occur in small- and medium-sized cities—many of which are still towns and villages today.[16] Planning water systems in settlements that are poised to undergo such rapid urbanization presents both challenges and opportunities.

First the challenges: much of the population increase in sub-Saharan Africa's cities likely will take place in informal settlements where city planners may have little control over population density or proximity to water resources. The water systems in these areas are often controlled by organizations that benefit from the sale of water by private vendors.[17] If growth is not accompanied by new jobs, rather than seeing informal settlements as places in need of infrastructure investment, the United Nations warns that governments may end up treating informal settlements as security problems due to the presence of underemployed young people and groups that resist government control.

The opportunities associated with the coming period of rapid growth stem from the fact that much of Africa's future urban development will take place in yet-to-be-built cities that are not already locked into the old ways of providing water, drainage, and waste management. Just as the continent's lack of centralized electrical infrastructure is making it easier to adopt renewable electricity production, the absence of a legacy of centralized water and sewer systems could provide an opportunity for African cities to avoid some of the mistakes that plague cities on other continents that struggle with infrastructure that is difficult to maintain and adapt.[18] Because sub-Saharan Africa's cities are likely to become more prosperous in the decades after they are built, they may be particularly well suited for smaller neighborhood- or building-scale systems that can be reconfigured as economic conditions improve. Such systems also may be better positioned for experimentation with new approaches for water recycling or the recovery of nutrients and energy from human waste. Although innovative new approaches may ultimately reduce costs and make water use more efficient, the construction of water infrastructure will still require a scale of investment and technological expertise that has not yet materialized on the continent.

Beyond sub-Saharan Africa, the other place where rapidly growing and urbanizing populations are likely to pose severe challenges to water management in coming decades is the Middle East and North Africa region (the MENA countries). The nations in this grouping, which stretches from Morocco to Iran and which, for reasons of cultural and economic similarities, is sometimes discussed in the same breath with Pakistan and Afghanistan (the MENAP countries), share some similar characteristics, including religion (Islam), petroleum resources (for most but not all members), and an arid climate. Egypt, Iran, Iraq, Algeria, Morocco, and Sudan collectively account for about 70 percent of the approximately half a billion people who live in the MENA countries.[19] Despite their cultural and climatic similarities, the MENA countries are at different stages of the demographic transition, with countries where development accelerated earlier, such as Iran, Morocco, and Lebanon, having already passed into the slow-growth stage, while nations where development was delayed, such as Iraq and Sudan, continuing to double in population every fifteen to twenty years.

Due to the region's low rainfall and soil degradation that took place over thousands of years of land cultivation, food security has been a major challenge for MENA countries. As a result, many governments have adopted policies that favor water-thirsty cereal crops as a means of reducing reliance on imports.[20] Today, close to 60 percent of the farmland in the region is used to grow staples such as wheat, sorghum, and barley. Government price supports for this practice have trapped many farmers into the production of crops with a low economic value. Yet in those MENA countries that lack petroleum wealth and price support for cereals, such as Lebanon and Tunisia, farmers have shifted to more profitable products, such as fruits, vegetables, and nuts. In rapidly growing countries where cereals are still the dominant crops, such as Iraq and Sudan, population growth has outstripped the ability of farmers to produce enough food to keep up with domestic demand.

As the MENA countries purchase a larger fraction of their cereals on the global market, the folly of chasing after the goal of food self-sufficiency is becoming more apparent. From an economic perspective, the logical solution is to take advantage of the region's warm temperatures and relatively low labor costs by growing high-value export crops and using the profits to pay for imported cereals. Looking beyond the agricultural sector, leaders of the more farsighted MENA countries are beginning to follow the advice of their economists by reforming water allocation policies and laws to assure that the limited water supply is dedicated to the most productive economic uses, such as supplying farms that grow food for export, as well as providing a secure water supply to factories and cities.[21]

This general idea, that water-stressed countries should rely upon domestic industry and high-value agriculture to generate income needed to pay for cereal imports from countries with ample water resources, has been referred to as trading in virtual water.[22] Embracing policies that de-emphasize cereal production also is logical because the cultivation of fruits and nuts provides more employment to rural communities than growing staple foods. However, cereal-producing farmers remain a powerful lobbying group, and attempts to alter the subsidy system that they have come to rely upon too quickly can be challenging.

Rather than attempting to restrict how their farmers use water, some leaders of MENA countries have chosen to gamble on expensive infrastructure projects that keep irrigation water flowing. One such risky investment has already paid off. Beginning in the early 1980s, Libya has spent about twenty billion dollars of its petroleum income to build one of the largest irrigation projects in the world.[23] Libya's Great Manmade River project currently provides about 70 percent of the country's water, with most of it being used to grow wheat, barley, fruits, and vegetables on farms located along the Mediterranean coast. This massive water project relies upon several hundred wells drilled to depths of five hundred meters or more in the parched center of the country. Giant pumps move the water to coastal cities and farms through a network of more than four thousand kilometers of pipes. The project was made possible by the existence of an extensive fossil aquifer where groundwater had been recharged more than ten thousand years ago when wetter conditions prevailed during the last ice age. Because the land above the Nubian Sandstone Aquifer receives less than two centimeters of rain per year, it is not being replenished. Depending on whether you believe the estimates made by the US Central Intelligence

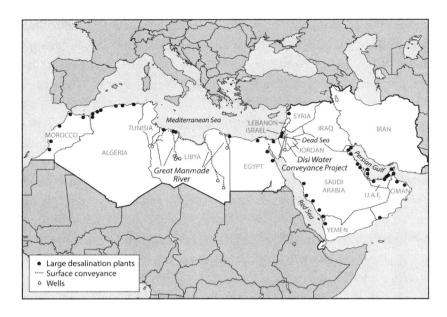

A few of the existing and proposed water megaprojects and large desalination plants of the Middle East and North Africa (MENA) region.

Agency, academic experts, or the Libyan government, the fossil aquifer will be depleted sometime between 50 and 4,625 years from now if Libya continues to use water at its current rate.[24]

Other MENA countries also have been attempting build their way out of water scarcity.[25] For example, in 2013, Jordan completed its own miniature version of the Great Manmade River project by building a pipeline to transport groundwater from the country's southern border with Saudi Arabia to farms and cities more than three hundred kilometers to the north. The $1.2 billion Disi Water Project is expected to provide about 40 percent of the country's water supply until it runs dry in about fifty years. In recognition of the temporary nature of its new groundwater supply, Jordan has set its sights on a bigger prize: the Red Sea. The country has been promoting the Red Sea–Dead Sea project, an ambitious $10 billion effort that would produce desalinated seawater with hydroelectric power generated as water flows downhill from the

Red Sea to the Dead Sea. Much of the freshwater produced by the desalination plants would be pumped into Jordan to satisfy its water needs. Israel and international donors would cover part of the cost of building the project because the brine produced during desalination would flow to the Dead Sea, which has been shrinking due to diversion of the river that serves as its source. Elsewhere in the region, Egypt has tapped into its own fossil aquifers and is investing in expensive projects to move water from the Nile River to farms in the desert. These and other infrastructure schemes may allow some of the MENA region's farmers to continue to grow subsidized cereal crops, but their high costs of construction, operation, and maintenance, paired with the unsustainable premise under which many of them were conceived, cast doubt on the future of efforts to grow the water supply to achieve food self-sufficiency in the region. Ultimately, the high-stakes gamble that some of the leaders of MENA countries are making is that they can continue to find enough water and money to keep up with the demands of their growing populations.

6

~~~~~~~~~~

Powering the Acceleration

RETURNING TO THE changes that took place during the Great Acceleration, energy use during the second half of the twentieth century also underwent exceptional growth. Considering how all that energy has been produced, another fact becomes clear: if population growth was the engine driving the Great Acceleration, coal, oil, and natural gas were the fuels that powered it. Between 1950 and 2019, these three fuels were responsible for 90 percent of the sixfold increase in the world's energy production.[1] As more dams were built, hydropower generation capacity expanded, and three additional sources of energy—nuclear, solar, and wind—became more prevalent during the last few decades. Nonetheless, on a global basis, these latter forms of energy still account for only about 5 percent of energy use.

The sheer scale of the energy sector assures that water use for energy will be important to the overall water budget of nearly every country on earth. In fact, cooling water used for power production is the top use of water in the United States and the European Union and the second largest use of water (after agricultural irrigation) in China.[2] Water use in the energy sector is also tied to a host of pollution problems. To understand the impact for water of the world's reliance on fossil fuels, it is necessary to consider both how these materials are obtained and how they are used.

Since the early days of the Industrial Revolution, the process of

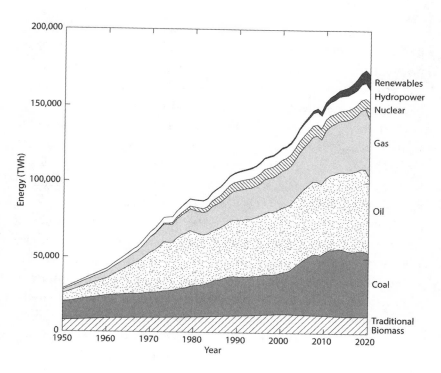

Energy use in the period between 1950 and 2020.

obtaining the first of three fossil fuels to be widely exploited—coal—has been intimately linked to the development of water-moving equipment because water removal from mine shafts requires powerful pumps.[3] If the coal contains the sulfur-containing mineral pyrite, oxygen-containing water that percolates into the mine allows microbes to catalyze the conversion of the mineral into sulfuric acid and iron oxides. The acid-contaminated water, which often contains elevated concentrations of toxic metals that were codeposited with iron, such as copper and nickel, has decimated many of the streams and rivers where the infiltrated water flowed after it was pumped out of the mine.

To minimize the formation of acidic water, operators quickly pump the incoming water to the surface and avoid the formation of pools within mines where water has opportunities to come into contact with pyrite-rich sediments.[4] But after all of the coal has been extracted, the pumps are shut off and mine shafts inevitably fill with water, which eventually leaks out of the mine, leaving severely degraded streams and rivers in areas where coal mines used to operate. For example, by 1967, approximately seventeen thousand kilometers of streams and rivers in the Appalachian coal mining region of the United States—the main source of the country's coal in prior decades—had been damaged by active and abandoned coal mines. Damage to surface waters is not unique to the United States; most countries where coal has been mined struggle to control the impacts of acid mine drainage.

Drilling for oil does not require the construction and dewatering of mine shafts, but it still poses water management challenges because the geologic formations where oil occurs almost always contain a lot of water. As a result, for every barrel of oil that is pumped to the surface, anywhere from three to ten barrels of water typically are brought to the surface as well.[5] In many respects, this form of energy production is as much a matter of water management as of oil extraction. A smaller volume of water is produced when natural gas is extracted, but it, too, requires extensive water management efforts. During the early decades of the Great Acceleration, nearly all the salty, oil-contaminated water produced in the oil and gas extraction process (aptly named produced water) was pumped back into the formation where it originated to maintain the pressure needed to get more petroleum products out of the ground.

After the easily obtained oil had been pumped out, the water story became messier. When oil production in Central and Southern California started to decline in the 1960s, engineers devised a way of injecting steam into the ground to liberate the residual oil trapped in the pores of the rock.[6] The early experience with enhanced oil recovery was followed by the development of more sophisticated ways of using water to get residual oil and natural gas out of the ground. First, petroleum engineers figured out how to access trapped hydrocarbons more efficiently by drilling horizontal wells. Then, they invented a technique for increasing the porosity of geologic deposits where oil and gas were stuck in the pores. When horizontal drilling was combined with the fracturing of bedrock with a pressurized mixture of water, sand, and chemicals, the result was a process known as hydraulic fracturing, which is commonly referred to as fracking.

Between 2010 and 2020, the rapid spread of fracking, mainly in Texas, Montana, and North Dakota, increased oil and gas production in the United States by 60–80 percent.[7] After the initial fracking process was completed, anywhere from about 10–70 percent of the injected water, along with the residual chemicals, dissolved petroleum hydrocarbons, salts, and toxic metals, was returned to the wells. The imaginatively named flowback water had to be removed before oil and gas could be brought to the surface.

The most expedient solution was to follow the playbook that had worked so well in the oil fields of California and Texas. Because the flowback water could not be injected back into the same tightly packed formation where the oil was being pumped, it was usually injected deeper underground. This worked well in some places, but in others the injected water set off earthquakes. The hotspot for this phenomenon was Oklahoma, which went from having a handful of earthquakes before the fracking boom to having around three thousand earthquakes per year at its height. Concerned about the damage the quakes were causing to homes, businesses, and highways, Oklahoma began shutting down the state's injection wells in 2016.[8]

The alternatives to injecting the flowback and produced water into a deep formation include cleaning it to a point where it can be released to surface waters or reusing it in the creation of a new fracking well. Given the challenge of making the contaminated water clean enough to safely discharge and the scarcity of water in many of the places where new wells were being drilled, it is hardly surprising that reuse became more popular. But this approach is not sustainable: because each new fracking well generates a larger volume of flowback and produced water than what is needed in the initial fracking process, reuse only makes sense when the number of fracking wells is growing.[9]

Looking beyond the United States, several other countries, including China, Argentina, and Russia, have large reserves of oil or gas that could be accessed by fracking.[10] In addition to coping with the greenhouse gas implications of burning more fossil fuels, future efforts to expand fracking would have to overcome several water challenges. For example, much of China's immense shale gas reserves occurs in arid parts of the country where obtaining fracking water would come at the expense of agriculture, municipal supply, and industrial uses.

On a local or regional scale, obtaining fossil fuels sometimes competes with other uses of water, but energy extraction accounts for a tiny fraction of water use when considered on a national scale.[11] For example, at the height of the recent boom in oil and gas production in the United States, fracking, which played a major role in much of the country's oil and gas production, was responsible for only about 0.04 percent of national water use. In contrast, cooling water used by power plants was responsible for about 40 percent of water taken out of the environment in the United States during the same period.

To anticipate future water crises and the role that new technologies could play in their solution, the ways that fossil fuels are converted into energy is much more important than the way they are obtained. To understand this issue, it is best to break energy into the two largest uses: electricity production and transportation. Moving people and goods— a process that mainly involves cars and trucks—accounts for about a quarter of global energy use.[12] Although internal combustion engines are important contributors to greenhouse gas emissions, their operation has little impact on water resources because vehicle engines are cooled by air. In contrast, the process of turning coal and natural gas into electricity currently requires vast quantities of water.

Thermoelectric power production—the process through which coal, natural gas, and nuclear power plants create electricity—involves a cycle in which water is heated to produce pressurized steam to power a turbine. (The way that a turbine is coupled with a generator to produce electricity is something that you either did or didn't already learn in your high school physics class.) After it passes through the turbine, the steam is condensed back into water to reinitiate the cycle. The most efficient way to cool steam rapidly involves a heat exchanger, and the best heat-transfer fluid for this purpose is water.

There are two ways that water is used for cooling in thermoelectric power plants. The first, known as once-through cooling, is exactly what it sounds like. If a large body of water is located near the power plant, or rather, if the power plant has been built next to a large body of water, as is often the case, water is passed through a heat exchanger before it is returned to the waterway. Under typical operating conditions, a power plant raises the temperature of about 150 cubic meters of water by about 10 degrees Celsius for each megawatt-hour of power that it produces.[13] Put into terms that are easier to visualize, if your electricity is produced at a thermoelectric plant that uses once-through cooling, every day about one hundred liters of water will be heated up by about 10 degrees Celsius (17 degrees Fahrenheit) just to run your refrigerator. Aside from making a river a little less conducive to a refreshing summertime swim, the power plant's discharge, if insufficiently diluted by cold water from other sources, will stress fish and other aquatic organisms and make them more vulnerable to the adverse effects of pollutants.

The other approach, recirculating cooling, which is also referred to as closed-loop cooling, uses a much smaller volume of water to soak up the heat by taking advantage of the fact that a lot of energy is needed to vaporize water. Thus, a plant that employs recirculating cooling needs only about 2 percent of the water of a once-through cooling plant of the same size. Closed-loop cooling systems do not heat up waterways, but over half of the water that goes into the plant is dissipated to the atmosphere, where it is sometimes seen as billowing clouds of steam coming out of cooling towers.[14]

Other approaches for managing the heat produced by thermoelectric power plants exist but are much less popular than the two approaches described above. Dry cooling—the use of air on the cold side of the heat exchanger—currently accounts for less than 3 percent of thermoelectric power cooling in the United States and is similarly unpopular in most of the rest of the world because it raises the cost of electricity by reducing the amount of power that can be produced in a thermoelectric plant by about 5 percent.[15]

Another approach involves using the heat for a beneficial purpose.[16] If you have ever been curious about the source of the steam billowing up from the manholes of New York City, it is coming from a combined heat and power system that employs steam from nearby power plants to heat around two thousand of the city's buildings. Because these systems are most efficient when power plants are located near densely populated cities, it is relatively unpopular beyond New York and Europe, where it is used for about 10 percent of the electricity produced.

Excess heat from thermoelectric plants also is used for desalination, especially in the Middle East, where power plants were often built next to desalination plants that employ some form of distillation. In fact, the co-location of power and desalination plants in Abu Dhabi produces more water than the city's buildings need during summer due to the high electricity demand for air conditioning. The extra water is used on golf courses, which in turn elevates water demand to keep the grass alive during winter, which in turn requires the power plants to use even more energy.[17] The co-location of power and thermal desalination plants is less attractive in other parts of the world, where energy costs are higher and power plants had already been built when water shortages started to occur.

Irrespective of the way in which steam is cooled, most power plants cannot function without access to large quantities of water. Power plants located near the ocean or large lakes are less vulnerable to water shortages than those that rely upon rivers, where power production sometimes has to be curtailed during a drought or when an extended period of hot weather would stress the ecosystem even in the absence of hot water discharged by power plants.[18] For example, during the summers of 2007, 2010, and 2011, the Brown's Ferry nuclear power plant— the second largest nuclear facility in the United States—had to greatly reduce its electricity production because its inlet pipes were close to being above the water line and local officials were concerned about the effect of its hot water discharges on the already warm river. In 2003,

France shut down a quarter of its nuclear power plants to protect its riverine ecosystems from high water temperatures during what was then the country's hottest summer on record. Power production was curtailed again in 2022 as the country faced another hot, dry summer.

Policies to minimize the environmental impacts of power plant discharges and the uncertain availability of cooling water combined with efforts to shift the ways that electricity is produced will change how water is used for electricity production in North America, Europe, and many other countries during the next three decades.[19] In the United States, despite a relatively stable demand for electricity, the volume of water used for power plant cooling is expected to decrease by about 80 percent between 2020 and 2050. As the country's mix of energy sources evolves in response to market forces and environmental concerns, thirsty coal and nuclear power plants will be replaced by more efficient natural gas-fired plants and renewable sources of electricity that do not employ water for cooling (such as wind and solar photovoltaics). The use of recirculating cooling in new power plants and retrofits of once-through cooling power plants will mean that the amount of water *consumed* in electricity production (water is consumed when it is transferred to the air rather than being returned to the water body from which it was taken) is expected to remain relatively constant until 2040 before decreasing by about 30 percent by 2050. In Europe, the same driving forces are projected to lead to a decrease in water withdrawals of around 40 percent by 2050, with similar reductions in water consumption over the same period. Once-through cooling is likely to continue to be important along some of Europe's major waterways because nuclear power plants will continue to operate in France and several other countries, but solar, wind, and gas-fired power plants are likely to displace nuclear and coal-fired plants over much of the continent.

Of course, these future projections depend upon the continuation of current trends: more rapid progress in transitioning away from coal, gas, and nuclear power plants, because of the perceived dangers associated with greenhouse gas emissions, national security efforts associated with reducing reliance on imports, and perceived dangers associated with nuclear power could accelerate the trend of decreasing water use for electricity production.

Looking beyond the OECD countries, predictions about water needed for electricity production are more uncertain, especially in China. The Great Acceleration, which created the world's second largest economy in China, was accompanied by a fourfold increase in electricity production in the first decade of the twenty-first century. China has powered its burgeoning cities and factories with coal—its cheapest and most readily available domestic source of energy. Between 2020 and 2050, China is expected to increase its electricity-generating capacity by another 50 percent.[20] Despite a recognition by the nation's leaders of the problems that coal causes with respect to urban air pollution and climate change, the amount of electricity generated by coal-fired power plants may continue to increase even as the country builds more wind farms, solar farms, and nuclear power plants. China also has been the world's most prolific dam-building country in recent years, doubling its hydroelectric capacity between 2005 and 2012, with an increase in installed capacity equivalent to that of all of France's electric generation capacity. These projects generate about 10 percent of the country's electricity and, almost as importantly, provide a means for managing flows along rivers where thermoelectric power plants are located. But political controversies over building more dams in watersheds that China shares with its neighbors could limit further expansion of hydropower in coming decades. Overall, thermoelectric power production, with coal and nuclear power creating most of the electricity, is likely to account for over half of the country's increase in power production between 2020 and 2050.

The availability of cooling water already is a major concern for China because thermoelectric power plants tend to be located near where electricity is needed, which, in this case, is the water-stressed part of the country that extends from the Beijing metropolitan area in the north to the province of Henan, about a thousand kilometers to the south.[21] Before the Fukushima-Daiichi nuclear disaster, the Chinese government had been planning to build nuclear power plants along inland rivers in this densely populated region, but safety concerns have led to a reconsideration of the strategy. To minimize risks to the public and reduce the chances that water shortages will curtail electricity production, China has been building new thermoelectric plants and expanding existing facilities along its coast. The nation's power companies also have started building dry-cooled power plants in inland locations.

To improve living standards, India is the next big country that needs to dramatically expand its electrical grid.[22] Current projections indicate that the country's electricity demand will increase by a factor of four between 2020 and 2050, with coal and, to a lesser degree, nuclear and natural gas accounting for about half of the increased power production and a combination of solar and wind making up the remainder. As one of the most water-stressed countries in the world, India banned construction of new inland once-through cooling systems back in 1999. Nonetheless, water use for electricity production is likely to become a larger problem for the country in coming decades. If India manages to upgrade its existing once-through power plants to recirculating cooling, water consumption for power is likely to triple between 2020 and 2050.

Water is likely to be especially problematic along India's inland rivers, where power plants will compete for water with farmers during the dry season when irrigation demand peaks.[23] As a result, the power grid may be unreliable in much of the country for several months per year. Following China's lead, India could start building more dry-cooling power plants, but utilities currently are hesitant to take on the cost of construction and operation of these more sophisticated power plants.

Elsewhere in the world, other countries undergoing rapid urbanization and industrialization, including Vietnam, Indonesia, and Pakistan, will grapple with the same kinds of water problems facing India and China. In contrast, sub-Saharan Africa, where the acceleration in electricity demand is still more than a decade away, is likely to have less of a problem because the region can access technological advances that are making renewable energy cheaper than thermoelectric power. Parts of the continent with ample water resources may even follow the lead of Brazil, where about three-quarters of the electricity currently comes from hydroelectric power.[24] Among the water crises awaiting Africa and other parts of the world where wealth and development have been slow to arrive, cooling water is one for which going through the Great Acceleration last may prove to be an advantage.

7

~~~~~~~~

Impacts of Climate Change
on Water Resources

THE GREAT ACCELERATION increased global population and raised
the standards of living for billions of people, but it also resulted in steep
increases in the atmospheric concentrations of carbon dioxide, meth-
ane, and nitrous oxide—the three main greenhouse gases responsible
for climate change. About three-quarters of the rise in greenhouse gas
concentrations was due to fossil fuel use while the remainder was related to changes in land use, as agriculture intensified and forests and
grasslands were cleared to make room for more farms and cities. About
half of the historic greenhouse gas emissions can be attributed to activities that have taken place in the OECD countries, but the contributions of the BRICS and other rapidly growing nations are rising as they
continue on their economic transformation.[1]

In the latter part of the twentieth century politicians could put a
low priority on addressing climate change because most of the damage was expected to take place after they left office. As heat waves,
droughts, floods, and wildfires have become more common and more
intense, that approach is becoming less viable. Voices calling for concrete action to stabilize the world's climate are getting louder, but
that is no guarantee that change will come fast enough to avoid severe
problems. In the mid-2010s in the United States, only about half of the

population agreed with the experts about the cause of climate change, while 40 percent expected that climate change would not affect their way of life over the next fifty years.[2] Elsewhere, attitudes varied considerably. People in Europe, India, sub-Saharan Africa, and Latin America were more worried about the issue than Americans, while climate change was less concerning to the public in China, Pakistan, and Russia.

Although public sentiment is important to decisions about emissions controls, many of the key decisions will be made by politicians and business leaders whose success depends upon near-term economic impacts of their actions. The shared view among mainstream economists who advise the people who make these decisions has been that climate change will not have major impacts on growth until the second half of the twenty-first century. According to models that take into account the incremental ways that governments and companies are likely to adjust their behaviors in response to the risks of climate change, the world's economy in 2050 will be only about 3 percent smaller than it would have been if the climate had not been altered.[3] Although that adds up to trillions of dollars of damage, the world economy is still expected to be about four times larger in 2050 than it was in 2020. Thus, from the perspective of the people who run much of the world's economy, the small decrease in growth due to climate change in the first half of the century will be possible to ignore when considered at a global scale, especially if taking action to protect the climate slows short-term economic growth.

The belief among many of the world's most influential people that the overall output of the global economy will not be severely hampered by climate change in the short term is of little comfort to communities suffering from climate change–driven crises as well as those who believe that people alive today have an obligation to future generations. Despite the near-term suffering from climate-related disasters in low- and middle-income countries, unaccounted for damage to ecosystems, and the long-term consequences of climate change, market forces can be expected to resist attempts to aggressively reduce greenhouse gas emissions because growth that happens today is compounded over time, rendering losses that might occur three or four decades from now of little importance to economic decision-making. The tools that most economists employ to discount future impacts of climate change reduce the urgency for corporate and government leaders to act in ways that do not generate profits and growth over the span of a quarterly report or an election cycle. It does not help matters that people who have little incentive to act can point to reports from like-minded groups that continue to emphasize uncertainty in climate change predictions.

The work of Yale economist William Nordhaus is helpful to anyone trying to understand the inability of the market to address the climate crisis more aggressively. In his Nobel Prize address in 2018, he described the ways that the global economy is likely to respond as the damage associated with climate change starts to take a larger toll on the economy.[4] Under the existing system, in which the economic damage due to climate change is assumed to be balanced by the benefits of continued growth and development, his coupled economic-climate models predict that the average temperature on earth will increase by around 3 degrees Celsius between 2020 and 2100, an amount that is twice as high as the target set by the international community. This means that if the world is serious about avoiding severe disruption to the climate, a bigger shift in public attitudes will be needed to bring about fundamental changes in the way that future consequences are accounted for by decision makers.

There are numerous reasons that the scenario laid out by Nordhaus may not come to pass. Activists and concerned leaders could prevail over the interests of those who stand to profit from continued reliance on fossil fuels. Technologies that enable a transition away from fossil fuels may decrease in cost at rates that are faster than those predicted in current models. It is also possible that growing awareness of the climate crisis will spur political action. The path that the world will take on climate will be determined by the events of the next few decades; it is impossible to predict how the world will respond to the droughts, floods, pandemics, wars, scientific discoveries, and social conflicts that will influence political discussions about policies affecting greenhouse gas emissions.

Irrespective of where the world ends up in its response to these challenges, it is nearly certain that climate change will substantially alter the water cycle in the coming decades. To anticipate the future water needs of cities, farms, and factories, it is important to understand the ways that a changing climate is likely to affect the movement of water between the ocean, atmosphere, and land. It may be impossible to predict future greenhouse gas emissions precisely, but insights can be gained about the changes in the water cycle by considering the ways that the movement of water through the atmosphere will be altered in a warming world.

The best place to start understanding the effects of increasing concentrations of greenhouse gases on water resources is to consider the region where water evaporation rates are the highest—an approximately thousand-kilometer-wide band centered at the equator known as the intertropical convergence zone. Because about 80 percent of this equatorial region consists of warm ocean waters where the sunlight intensity is strong throughout the year, massive quantities of moisture are introduced into the atmosphere in this part of the world. The moist air released from the equatorial ocean cools as it rises and moves north and south, where it condenses to produce rain that falls on the world's tropical rain forests. At about 30 degrees latitude, the now dry equatorial air returns to earth, where it creates arid subtropical areas exemplified by the Sahara and Kalahari Deserts. The features created by this atmospheric circulation pattern—a phenomenon that is also responsible for the trade winds and jet streams—are known as Hadley cells.

At 60 degrees latitude, water evaporating from the ocean rises and heads toward the polar regions, creating the polar cells. Wedged between the Hadley and polar cells, a weaker system of rising and falling air produces midlatitude cells in the section of the globe that is home to most of humanity. Over the course of the year, the circulating band of moist air at the equator meanders north and south, where it plays a major role in precipitation in the midlatitude region as it encounters

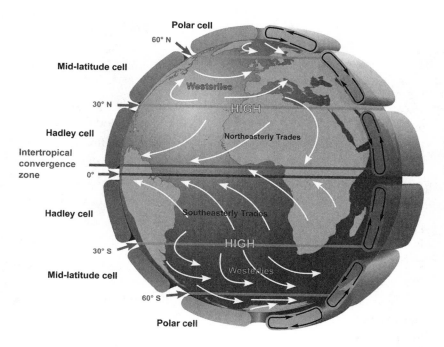

Moisture patterns in different regions of the earth are strongly affected by global circulation patterns related to the interplay between evaporation of water from the ocean and the movement of air in the atmosphere. As the earth warms, the size and intensity of the cells responsible for these patterns are likely to change.

the region's continents and ocean currents.[5] These interactions play an important role in seasonal weather patterns affecting the midlatitudes, such as the extratropical cyclones that bring hurricanes to North America's Gulf and East Coasts and the monsoons that are responsible for much of the annual precipitation on the Indian subcontinent and in East Asia.

As the planet warms, more moisture will enter the atmosphere in the equatorial region. As a result, rainfall is expected to increase over much of the tropics. In the midlatitudes, changes in precipitation patterns are tougher to predict accurately, but most models suggest that more precipitation will fall annually in the region, with a larger fraction occurring in a few intense storms. As a result, flooding likely will become more frequent as runoff overwhelms drainage systems that cannot accommodate a larger volume of water arriving over a shorter period.[6] For example, researchers studying flooding in Europe concluded that the 25–50 percent increase in large floods in Northwestern Europe observed between 1970 and 2020 is an early sign of how climate change will affect the region. Relative to the period from 1950 to 1989, worldwide economic losses associated with large floods have increased by about a factor of ten, to around ten billion dollars per year. Although most of the overall increase in damage was due to population growth and development in low-lying flood-prone locations, some portion was attributable to climate change–induced increases in storm intensity. In the future, the combination of more people and property in vulnerable areas and a growing frequency of large storms is expected to amplify flood damage.

It might seem that an increase in annual rainfall in the world's most populated regions would solve problems related to water scarcity, but that is not necessarily the case, especially when more rain arrives over a shorter period. Large storms may not alleviate water shortages under our current system of water management because floodwaters quickly flow to the sea. A larger fraction of precipitation is retained by the land when water has time to percolate through the soil. When water arrives in large storms, much of it flows over the land. This leads to increased river flows that pose challenges to the operators of dams who must balance the need to capture water against the risk of overfilling their reservoirs. Thus, an increased likelihood of large storms will force water managers to adopt more conservative practices, meaning that they will keep reservoir levels lower during the wet season just in case a big storm hits. Because warmer temperatures also tend to increase the demand for water during summer, regions that rely upon dams may struggle to capture enough water to supply farms and cities during the summertime period of peak demand.[7]

In terms of average annual rainfall in the midlatitude region, the general expectation is that wet places will get wetter and dry places will get drier as the planet warms.[8] The underlying explanation is an intensification of the Hadley cell circulation as more water evaporates along the equator. When this happens, subtropical regions where the downward flow of dry, equatorial air already contributes to arid conditions, such as the Mediterranean, the American Southwest, and Southern Africa, are expected to receive 10–20 percent less rainfall in typical years by the middle of the twenty-first century. Temperate zones in Central and Northern Europe, Asia, and North America, where precipitation patterns are affected by other phenomena, are expected to receive 10–20 percent more precipitation by midcentury.

As more water evaporates along the equator, the Hadley cells also are expected to widen, moving subtropical deserts farther from the equator.[9] This shift already appears to be impacting Australia. In the southeastern part of the continent, the Millennium Drought has been linked to expansion of the Southern Hemisphere's Hadley cell. During the twelve years of drought that ended in 2009, the dry air that descended onto southern Australia pushed winter storms that delivered much of the continent's rainfall offshore.

The situation has been particularly acute in the southwestern tip of Australia, where the amount of water flowing into Perth's reservoirs has already decreased by about 50 percent relative to conditions experienced in the twentieth century.[10] Although the average annual precipitation in the city's main watershed has decreased by only around 15 percent, the decline in the city's water supply has been more severe because less of the region's rain arrives in winter storms. Wintertime storms produce more flow in the streams and rivers that feed into the city's reservoirs because less of it evaporates or is taken up by trees and grasses in the catchment. Predictions based upon the latest climate models suggest that the amount of water flowing into Perth's reservoirs will decrease by another 50 percent between 2020 and 2050 as climate change further alters regional precipitation patterns. Rather than building more water storage capacity, the city is attempting to wean itself from reliance on rainfall. Through an aggressive campaign to reduce per capita water use coupled with the construction of seawater desalination plants that provide about half of the city's drinking water, Perth avoided water rationing during the Millennium Drought. With plans to recycle about half of its wastewater by 2030 and the possibility of building additional desalination plants, the city's water suppliers appear to be on track to adapt to its new climate.

In addition to altering precipitation patterns, warmer conditions cause the rate that water evaporates from the land to increase, leaving less moisture in the soil. When soils dry out, vegetation is stressed, resulting in crop losses and greater risks of forest fires.[11] Soil moisture also plays an important role in moderating heat waves because evaporation of water from the soil cools the land surface when hot weather arrives. The net effect of reduced soil moisture and less springtime rainfall is intensification of summer heat waves, such as those that Europe experienced in 2003 and 2022. During the two-month extreme heat event in 2003, more than thirty thousand people died of heat-related causes, crop yields dropped by 10–30 percent, and wildfires burned about a million hectares of land (an area approximately equal to the size of Lebanon).[12] According to climate models that account for the feedback between soil moisture and warmer temperatures, such heat waves will become more frequent, last longer, and affect larger land areas in Europe during the twenty-first century. Under a more extreme scenario in which average global temperatures increase by 3 degrees Celsius, southern Spain, Italy, and Greece will become deserts.

The loss of soil water due to warmer temperatures will likely be counterbalanced by increases in precipitation in many temperate regions. But in arid places, such as the Mediterranean and the American Southwest, the combination of less precipitation and warmer temperatures will lower soil moisture considerably. Drier conditions make farmers practicing rainfed agriculture more vulnerable to crop failure during heat waves. For farmers with irrigation systems, more water will be needed to produce the same amount of food. Beyond agricultural lands, heat waves may hasten shifts in vegetation patterns, favoring plant species that are better adapted to dry conditions.[13]

Higher temperatures also will affect watersheds where melting snow and ice feed rivers.[14] Currently, about 15 percent of the world's population relies upon snowmelt to provide water needed for irrigation, power plant cooling, and municipal water supply during the summer. As the mountains and high-latitude plains warm, a switch in precipitation patterns from snow to rain during the winter and early spring will decrease the size of the snowpack and cause peak flows to arrive earlier in the year. A shift in the timing of peak flows in snowmelt-fed rivers is likely to be particularly pronounced in the western United States, where the fraction of river flows derived from melting snow in the three main mountain ranges (the Rocky Mountains, Sierra Nevada, and Cascades), will decrease from around 70 percent today to about 40 percent by the end of the twenty-first century. Aside from putting a damper on the winter sports industry, the smaller snowpack will affect the ability of the region's reservoirs to provide water during the summer and fall.

Climate change is also changing water flows in glacier-fed rivers. Before the Great Acceleration, the size of most glaciers did not change much from year to year. As a result, glaciers had little effect on the annual flow of water in nearby rivers: during winter, a blanket of snow covered them, which fed rivers as it melted during summer. Today, due to increasing temperatures, nearly all the glaciers on earth are shrinking. As ice that accumulated over thousands of years disappears, the flows of the rivers that they feed have increased during the warm season in a phenomenon known as the meltwater dividend. For example, in Peru, along the arid coastal shelf north of Lima, a major economic boom has occurred as increased flows in glacier-fed rivers have been harnessed by the Chavimochic Irrigation Project. Starting in the 1990s, this more than two-billion-dollar set of canals and reservoirs has provided water to farms that grow valuable export crops such as asparagus, avocados, and blueberries on land that used to be sandy desert.[15] According to the latest projections, the flow of water from the region's melting glaciers has already started to decrease. By 2050, most of the glaciers feeding the Chavimochic Irrigation Project will have disappeared, leaving the viability of the farms and towns that have developed around the meltwater dividend in doubt.

The melting of glaciers in the Andes Mountains of Peru temporarily increases river flows through a phenomenon referred to as the meltwater dividend. After the glaciers disappear, the flow of water in rivers that people have come to rely on are likely to decrease quickly.

This phenomenon also is affecting Europe and Asia. Glaciers in the Alps and the Tibetan Plateau are shrinking, with the peak of the meltwater dividend projected to occur between 2020 and 2050 in most watersheds.[16] After the ice disappears, the operators of dams and reservoirs will have to adjust to the same shifts in timing of peak runoff that are being encountered in river systems where flow is dictated by annual precipitation patterns.

The final major water issue associated with a warming climate is sea-level rise. The popular view of this phenomenon is that melting ice returning to the oceans is expanding the volume of the world's oceans. Although melting ice is important, it contributes only about half of the increase in sea levels. The remainder of the sea-level rise is due to changes in the molecular structure of water that take place as it warms. Essentially, the addition of heat energy prevents the water molecules from packing together as tightly as they do when under colder conditions. The combination of more water in the oceans and water's thermal expansion translates to sea levels that are expected to be at least a half-meter higher by the end of the twenty-first century.[17] Moreover, it takes a long time for water returned to the surface by deep ocean currents to reequilibrate with a warmer atmosphere. As a result, thermal expansion of the oceans will continue for several centuries after the temperature stabilizes, even under the most optimistic of greenhouse gas emission scenarios.

The increase in sea level will cause the most damage to coastal communities during storm surges that accompany severe weather because higher ocean levels allow more water to flow into cities during storms. To protect themselves from flooding, wealthy cities will likely follow the lead of low-lying European countries that have pioneered the modern practice of coastal adaptation. By investing hundreds of billions of dollars in infrastructure such as tidal gates that can close over river mouths during storms and drainage systems that divert flood-waters to places where few people live, it is possible for the wealthy to coexist with an expanded ocean.[18]

Unfortunately, cities in low- and middle-income countries and rural areas within poor and wealthy countries often lack the means to pay for elaborate coastal infrastructure.[19] As a result, millions of people are likely to suffer through decades of increasing flood damage before relocating to higher ground. However, such moves are expensive, complicated, and politically unpopular.

In the United States, the first experiment in abandoning a coastal settlement began in 2016, when the federal government provided a forty-eight-million-dollar grant to help about sixty people living on Isle de Jean Charles, Louisiana, move to a newly built community located on higher ground about eighty kilometers inland.[20] This kind of spending may have been feasible for a small community, but spending almost a million dollars per person to relocate at-risk communities quickly adds up to more than a state or nation can afford when hundreds of thousands of people face rising sea levels.

Although the planned investment of fifty billion dollars in levees and water diversion projects may temporarily protect New Orleans and people living on low-lying land south of the city for the next few decades, some existing communities are outside of the planned area of protection. For example, the settlement of Jean Lafitte, located just outside of the planned protection zone, may not succeed in its effort to convince the government to provide the $1.2 billion levee that engineers estimate would be necessary to extend the seawall far enough to include the town's two thousand people.[21] If the people of Jean Lafitte and other towns outside of the planned coastal protection cannot obtain protection, a day will come when the banks stop making loans, insurance companies stop writing homeowner policies, and people will be forced to move to higher ground.

Communities in low-lying regions in low- and middle-income countries face even larger threats from sea-level rise because their nations lack the wealth needed to pay for protective infrastructure.[22] The problem is particularly acute in the river deltas that are home to more than 340 million people worldwide because many of these regions are sinking as the seas are rising: deltas subside when upstream dams and erosion-control projects starve the land of sediment needed to replenish local storm-related losses. The problem is made worse if excessive groundwater pumping on the delta also causes the land to subside.

In addition to the human suffering associated with relocation, flooding of river deltas could deprive the world of some of its most productive farmland. For example, over the past few decades, farmers on the Mekong Delta—the source of nearly half of Vietnam's rice—have struggled to maintain their high levels of productivity as salty water has begun flowing farther up the region's rivers during the dry season.[23] Because river water is used for irrigation of rice paddies when rainfall is insufficient, some farmers have not been able to plant the second or third annual crop that has been integral to the region's high agricultural productivity. New elevation measurements indicate that the average height of the Mekong Delta is only about 0.8 meters above sea level, meaning that much of the region could be below sea level by the end of the twenty-first century.

Any prediction about civilization's future is fraught with uncertainty, but a useful picture of the state of the world's water resources around the middle of the twenty-first century emerges when the trajectory of the Great Acceleration and the latest predictions of climate models are considered.

For the approximately one billion people living in wealthy countries, populations are forecasted to stabilize and maybe even shrink slightly by midcentury. Assuming that economic conditions do not substantially deteriorate, these parts of the world should be able to afford technological solutions to any water crises that cannot be addressed by changes in policies that make existing systems more efficient. People living in the BRICS will likely continue to invest in water infrastructure and adopt land-use practices to provide water to expanding populations living at a higher standard. For people living in parts of Africa, Southeast Asia, and Central and South America, where economic growth is forecast to start catching up to the rest of the world in the coming decades, rapidly expanding cities are likely to confront water stress with water demand outpacing local resources just as people are making the transition out of poverty. Water resources are likely to shape and, in some cases, constrain growth in these parts of the world.

Predictions of water availability and the capacity of nations to respond are harder to make beyond 2050, but some trends are clear. During the second half of the twenty-first century, it is likely that climate change will replace growth as the dominant factor affecting water resources. Even under the optimistic scenario in which greenhouse gas emissions are reduced enough to keep the average global temperature increase below 1.5 degrees Celsius, the American Southwest, the Mediterranean, Southern Africa, and Australia will likely become substantially warmer and drier than they are today. Other parts of the world are expected to experience periodic shortages as seasonal rainfall patterns associated with monsoons and the El Niño–Southern Oscillation change and the meltwater dividend comes to an end. Without major changes in current practices, the aquifers, dams, and reservoirs that many of the world's farms, factories, and cities rely upon will no longer be able to provide enough water. The second half of the twenty-first century may seem far away, but when one considers the effort needed to change long-standing water practices and the decades of work needed to finance and build new infrastructure, the time for action has already arrived.

USING WATER
MORE EFFICIENTLY

*Conservation is the cheapest, least damaging
form of water infrastructure.*

IF A RESOURCE IS plentiful and inexpensive, there is little incentive
to conserve it. But if widespread use decreases reliability and drives
up cost, people find creative ways to use the resource more efficiently.
Conservation also can be driven by a desire to reduce the environmental impacts of resource use. This dynamic drove the development
of fuel-efficient vehicles, energy-efficient appliances, and renewable en-

ergy technologies that have gained momentum as the challenges posed by climate change became clear. Although it lags the energy sector, a similar transformation in the water sector has the potential to reduce the impacts of each of the six water crises.

Water efficiency takes numerous forms. Gains can be made by reducing water losses that occur during storage and transport. Water savings also can be realized by adoption of new ways of watering plants or by using water more sparingly in factories and homes. Water demand can be further reduced through policies that encourage changes in the crops that are grown or the density of housing. Stark reductions in water use are evident on farms that had been employing inefficient flood irrigation methods to water crops. Government regulations, financial incentives, and a desire to grow more food with less water has resulted in widespread conversion of flood irrigation to efficient sprinklers and drip irrigation methods throughout much of the world, allowing more food to be grown in places with limited water resources.

Despite its great promise, water efficiency often loses out to investments in new water infrastructure during times of crisis. Sometimes the decision not to pursue conservation is tied to the lower cost of alternative supplies or the slow rate at which benefits are realized. But more often the failure of water efficiency to prevail over infrastructure expansion is related to the political power of groups that benefit from the status quo and the inability of institutions responsible for water management to embrace their role in advancing conservation. By considering recent successes and failures in making water systems more efficient, it is possible to gain insight into the role that this powerful approach can play in solving future crises.

8

~~~~~~~~

Reducing Water Use
in Wealthy Communities

OVER THE PAST THIRTY years, an approach that puts conservation before construction has quietly made inroads in many cities facing water scarcity. Seattle exemplifies the power of this approach. In the early 1980s, when projections indicated that the city's growing population would soon outstrip its water supply, Seattle adopted a comprehensive conservation program.[1] Four decades later, per capita water use has been cut in half and the city has not invested in any new supply projects despite an increase in population of around 50 percent. Seattle was able to avoid the need to expand its water supply by creating public awareness of the need for conservation and by redirecting funds that might otherwise have been spent on new supply projects to rebates for customers who retrofitted their homes with water-efficient appliances. The city also used money that it saved from avoided construction projects to provide free technical assistance to homeowners who wanted to install more efficient irrigation systems in their yards. For those residents who were immune to conservation messaging and financial incentives, Seattle's utility adopted a water pricing structure that greatly increased water costs when customers exceeded a specified monthly allotment.

Seattle is not the only city that minimized spending on new infrastructure by reducing water use.[2] When the Millennium Drought hit Australia, both Sydney and Melbourne reduced their per capita water use by about a third over a five-year period, without experiencing a bounce back after the rains returned. In Spain—a country where residential water use was already low—campaigns to increase public awareness about the need for water conservation helped cut per capita urban water use by about 20 percent between 2000 and 2015.

When a drought is not motivating change, conservation can be more challenging, especially in densely populated, modern cities where the easiest water efficiency measures have already been implemented. Nonetheless, if a city continues to focus on water conservation between crises, savings can continue to be realized for decades. For example, in 2017, Singapore, a city that was already on the lower end of per capita water use worldwide, provided incentives for residents to replace the city's remaining nine-liter-per-flush toilets even though they were considered to be state of the art in terms of water use when they were installed in the early 1990s. Through this program, along with the expansion of efforts to integrate knowledge about water security into school curricula and other efficiency measures, Singapore's utility anticipates an additional 9 percent reduction in per capita water use between 2020 and 2030.[3]

The answer to the question of exactly how much water a city can save through conservation depends upon its existing water use patterns. On one end of the spectrum, the potential for further residential water savings is probably limited in such European cities as Berlin, Brussels, and Prague, where per capita water use is among the lowest in the wealthy world at about one hundred liters per person per day.[4] Considering modern habits related to bathing, clothes washing, and cooking, policies that further reduce residential water use in these cities might be perceived as unacceptable outside of times of dire shortage.

In addition to possibly alienating the public, driving water use to extremely low levels can create a new set of management challenges because most water and sewer pipes were designed under assumptions about per capita water use at the time when they were built. If the population density of a city has not been increasing, extreme reductions in water use could necessitate expensive system modifications because lower-than-planned-for water flows increase the time that water spends moving through the pipe network, making pipes more susceptible to corrosion and diminishing drinking water quality between the treatment plant and the home.[5]

Although a handful of places may be approaching the lower limits of per capita water use, most of the world's cities still have the potential to realize substantial savings if they can bring the public along in their water conservation efforts. To avoid the backlash that is often associated with higher water bills, most utility managers would gladly employ conservation as a means of avoiding the need for expensive new water projects. But following through on conservation efforts can be hard work. In their effort to reduce water demand, utility managers frequently find themselves constrained by their local climate, land use patterns, and politics.

Cities seeking to avoid new water supply projects often turn to outdoor landscape irrigation for water savings, especially in arid regions where population increased substantially during the second half of the twentieth century, when automobiles made longer commuting distances and single-family homes on large lots attractive. For example, on average, about half of the four hundred liters per person per day of residential water use in Phoenix, Arizona, occurs outside of the home.[6]

Turfgrass plays a disproportionate role in outdoor water consumption: in an arid climate, each year, approximately 1,600 liters of water is needed to maintain each square meter of healthy lawn.[7] That is equivalent to flooding the entire grass-covered part of the yard to a depth of 1.6 meters once per year.

Recognizing the thirsty nature of lawns, Phoenix started to cut back on the amount of turf that could be planted on residential properties in the 1980s. As a result, fewer than 5 percent of the homes built in the city in recent decades have had extensive lawn coverage (defined as turfgrass on more than about a third of the lot). Despite the city's long-standing efforts, it is hard to correct past mistakes: as of 2019, about 7 percent of Phoenix's single-family dwellings still had extensive lawn coverage, and about 60 percent of homes had some turfgrass.[8] Replacing an arid city's remaining lawns offers only a partial solution; substantial quantities of water (about half as much as it takes to grow grass) are needed to maintain even the best-adapted types of green (but turfgrass-free) yards in a desert climate.

Because lot sizes in Phoenix's older neighborhoods are unlikely to shrink and there is a limited appetite for stones, painted concrete, and cactus landscaping in the city, the lowest outdoor per capita water use that is likely to be achieved in the next few decades would be about one hundred liters per person per day (a 50 percent reduction from the amount used in 2020). Such a change would require a substantial increase in spending on incentive programs for removing the city's remaining lawns, installing more efficient watering systems, and educational programs that increase public awareness about outdoor water waste. If similar reductions in outdoor water use also could be realized at office parks, shopping malls, and public spaces, the city's overall average per capita water use might decrease by about 25 percent.

This would be welcome news, because the population of the Phoenix metropolitan area is projected to increase by about 70 percent between 2020 and 2050.[9] Considering the way that climate change is likely to stress the city's existing water supply and the projected need for more water to maintain yards, playing fields, and parks as the local climate becomes hotter, replacing the city's remaining lawns and making landscape irrigation more efficient will likely be an important part of Phoenix's strategy to address its coming water challenges.

In the rainier, eastern half of the United States, turfgrass covers a larger fraction of the space that is not covered by houses or roads, but the potential to save water by replacing lawns or by installing more efficient irrigation systems is lower than in the arid West because the region's cooler temperatures and more abundant precipitation reduce the need for irrigation.[10] Thus, landscape irrigation typically accounts for about 30 percent of overall residential water use in the wet part of Texas. Farther north, in New Jersey, where the temperatures are lower and the growing season is shorter, only about 15 percent of municipal water use takes place outdoors. Attempts to reduce outdoor water use still could be worthwhile in less arid eastern cities and suburbs, but until recently, this form of conservation was pursued with less gusto than infrastructure expansion. This is particularly true in the Southeast part of the United States, where development-friendly policies, abundant job opportunities, and mild winters created some of the fastest-growing cities in the country. When a city and its tax base are rapidly expanding and water scarcity has not yet taken hold, it is a lot easier to justify spending on new infrastructure projects.

Atlanta, Dallas, and Tampa—three of the largest and most prosperous cities in the wetter part of the American South—exemplify the ways that urban water supplies have been managed in the region. All three cities have been transformed by growth: new suburbs proliferated as the populations of Dallas and Tampa tripled, while Atlanta has expanded by sixfold since the 1970s. Although the three cities each receive about four times as much rain in a typical year as Phoenix, their flat topographies and the absence of conveniently accessible water sources have made it challenging to increase water supplies fast enough to keep up with increasing populations. During the first few decades of rapid growth, reservoirs and groundwater wells were installed in all the obvious places. To keep the water flowing after the easy sources of water had been tapped, the cities turned to innovative supply projects.[11] Since the early 2000s, Atlanta and Dallas have spent hundreds of millions of dollars on projects to reuse treated wastewater. In 2003, Tampa, which was already recycling over half of its wastewater, invested $158 million on what at the time was the largest seawater desalination plant in the Western Hemisphere. Two years later, the city spent another $200 million on a new reservoir.

Facing the prospect of decades of continued population growth and few easy options for further expanding their water supplies, the cities started getting more serious about conservation around the turn of the century. Like their compatriots in the arid West, leaders of the southeastern cities first looked to landscape irrigation for water savings.

In 2001, Dallas passed an ordinance prohibiting lawn watering during the middle of the day. By 2012, the city had tightened up its policy by limiting lawn watering to twice per week, and in 2020, they unveiled a program encouraging homeowners and businesses to replace their lawns with drought-tolerant landscaping.[12]

Starting in the early 2000s, Tampa and other cities in the surrounding metropolitan area began requiring new homes to be built with more efficient automated irrigation systems. The city also has limited the fraction of property that can be irrigated when new homes are built.[13]

At around forty liters per person, Atlanta's daily per capita residential outdoor water use is already much lower than that of its neighbors, so the city took a different approach to reducing outdoor water use by tying its conservation strategy to smart growth. Increasing the density of housing through land use regulations and financial incentives can reduce per capita outdoor water use by lowering the area of land needing irrigation. Building up the region's population density instead of continuing expansion to the outer suburbs may also make the city more livable by reducing its notorious traffic problems.[14]

Although considerable progress is being made in reducing outdoor water use in these and other cities in the southeastern United States, there is a practical limit to the amount of outdoor water savings that can be realized. As was the case in Phoenix, the prevalence of single-family homes on ample lots coupled with the desire of homeowners to keep their lawns, trees, and gardens makes it likely that some outdoor water use (somewhere between twenty and fifty liters per person per day) will continue after the easy outdoor conservation policies have been implemented. The same holds true in the cooler northeastern and midwestern regions, where the demand for water might ultimately be a bit lower than that of the South after all the locally acceptable outdoor water conservation policies have been enacted.

Recognizing that reductions in outdoor water use will not solve their water supply challenges, some American cities turned their attention indoors. Luckily, progress was already being made on that front, thanks to the work of an unlikely water conservation champion. The movement to save water within homes began in earnest in the United States in the 1990s when a group of water-stressed states followed the example set by Connecticut—a state that was better known for its leadership in water pollution control than water conservation. After sixteen states plus the District of Columbia had joined Connecticut in setting efficiency standards for toilets and bathroom sinks, the manufacturers of plumbing fixtures threw their support behind the Energy Policy Act of 1992, which set national standards for water efficiency. Indoor water conservation was extended to the entire country because plumbing manufacturers wanted to avoid a situation in which they had to sell multiple versions of the same product in different parts of the country.[15]

To encourage even more substantial indoor water savings, in 2006 the EPA created a voluntary program known as WaterSmart. By adding a label articulating a water efficiency standing to washing machines and dishwashers (two items that were not covered by the act) as well as fixtures that used at least 20 percent less water than stipulated by the federal guidelines, the voluntary program gave further momentum to the indoor water conservation movement. Due to the combined effects of the Energy Policy Act, the WaterSmart program, and improvements in the efficiency of appliances, per capita indoor residential water use declined by about 15 percent in the United States between 1999 and 2016.[16]

Utilities seeking even greater water savings were able to accelerate the rate that inefficient fixtures were replaced by offering incentives for household retrofits.[17] For example, between 1994 and 2001, California provided over two hundred million dollars in rebates to homeowners to replace more than 1.5 million older toilets with more efficient models.

Despite these efforts, the rate of change was slow at a national scale.[18] As of 2016, fewer than 40 percent of the older, inefficient toilets had been replaced, in part because toilets tend not to be replaced until a bathroom is remodeled. In contrast, washing machines would be expected to be easier to change because they wear out much more frequently. By 2009, water-efficient, front-loading washing machines had grown to about 45 percent of total sales, but that number slipped down to around 30 percent over the next five years, as some consumers became disillusioned with the higher costs of the machines, longer run times, and tendency to accumulate mold on their rubber seals. More recently, the lost progress has been made up as newer, WaterSmart-certified top-loading machines closed the gap in water efficiency with front-loading machines. Whichever way people choose to wash their clothes, American cities can expect an additional decrease in per capita indoor water use of up to around a third as the remaining older plumbing fixtures and appliances are replaced by more efficient models.

Although the country has made progress in both outdoor and indoor conservation, per capita residential water use in the United States is still about two to three times higher than that of Europe. With continued effort, this gap may narrow in the future, but most American households will likely use more water than their European counterparts for the foreseeable future. Some of these differences can be ascribed to differences in the ways that people live on the two continents: European cities are more compact than North American cities, with a greater fraction of the population living in multifamily dwellings and single-family dwellings on smaller lots.[19] For example, the population densities of sprawling cities such as Atlanta and Houston are only about a third of those of Berlin and London. Due to their extensive suburbs, even crowded metropolitan areas, such as Washington, DC, and Los Angeles, are less than half as densely populated as their European counterparts. As a result of these density differences, outdoor water use accounts for less than 3 percent of residential water use in Europe, whereas, as we have seen, between about 15 percent and 50 percent of water use in the United States takes place outside of the home. But the differences in how people in these two places use water do not end there.

Households in the United States also differ from those in Europe in terms of demographics, socioeconomic characteristics, and individual attitudes in ways that affect indoor water use.[20] With respect to

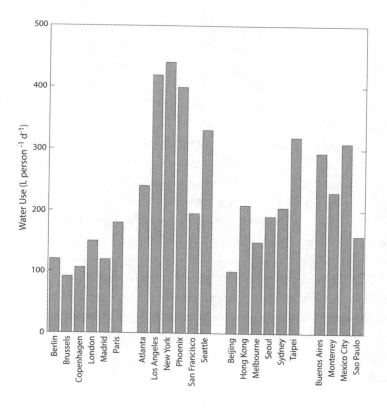

Per capita residential water use by city for Europe,
North America, Asia, and Central and South America.

demographics, the median age in the United States (38.5) is ten years lower than that of Germany and three years lower than that of France. This translates into higher per capita water use because, as parents have long suspected, teenagers really do use more water than adults. Retirees also tend to shower less often and wash fewer clothes. Beyond age, there is evidence that income, education level, and employment status affect the number of showers or baths that people take as well as their duration. In addition, household water is considerably more expensive in Europe than it is in the United States. For example, in Germany, Belgium, and the Czech Republic—three countries that are home to cities with some of the lowest per capita water use in the wealthy world—the monthly water bill for a typical family is about three times as high as it is in the United States or Canada. Thus, some aspect of the lower water use in Europe may be related to the tendency of a family to pay attention to leaky faucets and teenagers taking long showers when they feel the sting of higher monthly bills.

Cities also have realized substantial water savings by reducing the volume of water that leaks out of water distribution networks.[21] Before the 1990s, cities in wealthy countries typically lost between 10 percent and 30 percent of their water between the drinking water treatment plant and the home through leaky valves and pipes. But as water and energy conservation became priorities, many utilities were required to report data on water losses and implement leak control programs. Utilities also began to employ more sophisticated ways of operating their water distribution systems, lowering the pressure during late-night hours when fewer people were using water. Pressure modulation reduces the amount of water that escapes from water distribution pipes in much the same way that turning down the pressure will reduce the amount of water that leaks from an old garden hose that has a pinhole leak.

As a result of these efforts, water-stressed Phoenix, Dallas, Tampa, and other American cities reduced water losses due to leaks to between 5 percent and 10 percent of their total flow.[22] Cities like Atlanta, which still loses around 20 percent of its water through distribution system leaks, now face criticism from conservation watchdogs when they fail to get their leaks under control.

The last place where additional water savings may be realized is in the industrial sector. In terms of the volume of water used at a national scale, steel mills, paper manufacturing plants, and oil refineries are often the largest industrial water users.[23] However, many of these water-intensive operations have their own supplies or are located in regions where water is abundant. Thus, most water-stressed cities need to look elsewhere for savings. Although they use less water, other, less water-reliant types of manufacturing facilities, which rely upon municipal water, are still among the biggest customers of utilities, often accounting for 5–10 percent of a city's overall water use. Such industrial water users are logical places to seek greater water efficiency, but utilities tend to approach the issue of water use in factories with considerable caution. After all, if conservation measures increase the cost of doing business to a point that threatens employment and tax revenues, there will likely be pushback from politicians, local chambers of commerce, and other friends of the business community. But quite often this is less of an impediment than it might seem; industrial water users are often willing partners in conservation efforts because saving water can reduce manufacturing costs and burnish their reputations as environmental stewards.

In the United States, the potential impact of further efforts to increase water efficiency in the industrial sector must be understood within the context of the changing nature of the economy.[24] Between 1960 and 2010, the share of economic activity related to manufacturing decreased by over half nationally as the financial services, health care, and technical services sectors flourished. Within the manufacturing sector, steel mills and automobile factories gave way to less water-intensive industries, such as electronics, pharmaceuticals, and biotechnology. Between 1985 and 2015, industrial water use decreased by around 40 percent among the self-supplied water users, which as a group accounted for about three-quarters of industrial water use. Among users of municipal water, demand shifted from factories to the commercial sector, with a larger fraction of water being used in the office parks, convention centers, and hotels that supported the new economy. In terms of the amount of water needed to generate economic activity, jobs in health care, finance, and education require much less water than the heavy industries they replaced.

Although the water footprint of American industry has been shrinking as part of this long-term economic trend, water consumption in one unlikely place has received more scrutiny in recent years: the internet. As commerce, business, and entertainment have migrated online, a vast network of data centers has been created. In the United States, electricity used by data centers more than doubled in the first decade of the new millennium. By 2014, data centers accounted for almost 2 percent of nationwide electricity use.[25] Considering only the cooling water used to generate electricity, data centers have an average daily water footprint of about four liters for every person in the United States. Although this is a lot of water, it is lost in the noise of the massive volume of cooling water used to meet remaining electricity needs. As we have seen, the use of cooling water in electricity production will continue to decline in the coming decades as once-through cooling systems are replaced by evaporative cooling and as more wind and solar power plants come online.

But the thirst of the internet does not end there. In addition to increasing cooling water use at power plants, data centers need water to dissipate the heat produced by their hard-working computers. The most efficient way to cool data centers involves evaporative cooling—a practice that consumes an average of about three hundred million liters of water per day in the United States.[26] Because the performance of the internet improves when server farms are located close to their users, these facilities are often built in or near metropolitan areas.

When a new data center is proposed in a region that has been attempting to cut its water use, concerns are frequently raised about the impact of the new operation on the local water supply. For example, in 2020, Google announced plans to build new data centers near Dallas and Phoenix that each could consume up to around fifteen million liters of water per day—an amount corresponding to about 1 percent of the total water use in both water-stressed metropolitan regions.[27] Google is not the only company that has been on a server-farm building spree: Amazon, Meta, Microsoft, and a variety of other tech companies need water to operate data centers that they plan to build in water-stressed urban areas. Although it may be possible to cut the water demand of data centers by improving the efficiency of computers or by employing cooling methods that do not directly consume water, it is becoming evident that some of the need for water that was eliminated in recent decades might be replaced by the need to cool the internet.

Looking beyond cities in North America and Europe, similar opportunities and limitations for increasing efficiency are evident in other wealthy parts of the world. For example, due to changes made in response to the Millennium Drought and the country's growing recognition of its water challenges, Australian cities have made great strides in reducing per capita water use. However, due to the prevalence of single-family homes, youthful demographics, and a host of socioeconomic and climatic factors, Australia's city dwellers still use almost twice as much water as their European counterparts. Further investments in rain barrels, leak detection programs, and plumbing retrofits may continue the trend of decreasing per capita water use in Australia, but they are unlikely to close the gap with Europe in the near term.

In Asia, residential water use varies considerably, with water-stressed Beijing and Singapore exhibiting per capita residential water use comparable to that of European cities, while residents of Hong Kong, Seoul, and Tokyo use about twice as much water as Europe's most efficient cities, despite their higher population densities. Among Asia's big cities, Taipei stands out when it comes to residential water use, consuming about three times as much water per capita as Europe's efficient cities.[28] The large demand for residential water has been vexing to the city's water resource planners because agricultural irrigation, underinvestment in water infrastructure, and climate change have led to occasional municipal water rationing in the Taipei metropolitan area and have raised concerns about the impacts of water shortages on the high-tech manufacturing sector. Although Taipei would be better off if its per capita water demand could be brought into line with that of European cities, or even of its Asian neighbors, a long history of some of the lowest residential water prices in the world coupled with a sense of complacency among members of a public who believe that abundant rainfall translates into an ample water supply has slowed progress toward implementing bold urban water conservation measures.

Due to their aging populations, rainy climates, and high population densities, it seems likely that many wealthy Asian cities could drop their per capita residential water use by 25–50 percent over the next two decades if they were to make water conservation a higher priority. Yet other than in water-stressed cities such as Beijing and Singapore, there has been little effort to achieve deep reductions in residential water use in this populous, but often wet, part of the world.

9

~~~~~

Reducing Water Use in Low- and Middle-Income Communities

ALTHOUGH THEY COULD benefit substantially from conservation, cities in low- and middle-income countries have a hard time reducing water use. Mexico City exemplifies the complexity of the challenge facing middle-income countries.[1] As Mexico's largest metropolitan area grew from fewer than nine million people in 1970 to more than twenty-one million in 2020, its thirst depleted the massive aquifer underneath the city. After decades of groundwater overuse, the central part of the city has sunk by about ten meters, causing apartments, municipal buildings, and the city's main cathedral to tilt and buckle as the land under them subsided. The damage to the city's roads, metro system, and water supply infrastructure from land subsidence has recently exceeded one billion dollars per year. In response to the recognition that the local water source could not meet its needs, Mexico City had already invested in a pair of imported water systems that provide about a third of its water. The larger and more recently constructed of the two, the Cutzamala System, which was completed in 1993, brings water to the city from over 120 kilometers away. Due to the altitude difference between the city and the adjacent valley, this imported water must be pumped up by a net height of 1,200 meters—an endeavor that consumes almost twice as much energy as it takes to desalinate seawater.

The challenge of obtaining, transporting, treating, and distributing water coupled with the need to get wastewater out of the city and repair the damage caused by land subsidence gives Mexico City the distinction of having one of the most expensive water systems in the world. Despite the city's high production cost, the typical citizen of Mexico City pays only about 10 percent of the price of supplying their household water through water bills.[2] To make up for the revenue shortfall, the government provides more than a billion dollars per year in subsidies to the local water utility. Nonetheless, the utility still struggles to keep the water flowing, with intermittent delivery common in most parts of the city and leaks consuming about 40 percent of the water that is put into the system. Given the high cost of importing water, the damage that aquifer depletion has caused, and the prospects for future shortages, Mexico City would seem to be the ideal location to implement the types of water efficiency measures that have become common in wealthier parts of the world. Yet that has not been the case: efforts to raise water prices as a means of incentivizing conservation, repair the city's leaky pipes, and provide rebates for the replacement of water-consuming plumbing fixtures have consistently lagged perennial plans to expand the imported water system. Mexico City is not alone in its struggle to save water in the face of surging population growth and a dwindling water supply. For numerous other cities in low- and middle-income countries, water efficiency has been the road less traveled.

Part of the reason that it has been hard for cities in low- and middle-income countries to reduce water use is the inability of consumers of municipal water to pay anywhere near the full cost of its provision.[3] Despite their perpetual struggles with scarcity, chronically underfunded utilities are ill equipped to implement water-saving measures. In sub-Saharan Africa, the MENA region, and the Asia-Pacific region, the amount of money that utilities collect from their customers for each cubic meter of water delivered is usually about half of the amount collected by utilities in the United States and a third of the amount collected in Europe. Although some of this difference can be explained by the higher costs of building and maintaining water systems in wealthy countries, much of the gap is related to the inability of the utilities in low- and middle-income countries to collect money from their customers. About 20 percent of the water utilities in middle-income countries recoup less than 75 percent of their operating costs from bill-paying customers. In low-income countries, where it is even harder to collect revenue from cash-strapped users, most utilities need sources other than bill-paying customers to keep the water flowing.

The answer to the question of how much money a water utility can obtain from bill-paying customers depends upon the city's wealth and how that wealth is distributed. Aid agencies, government regulators, and nongovernmental organizations typically recommend that a family's water and sewer bill not exceed 4–5 percent of its income.[4] If only a fraction of the water users cannot afford their water bills, a utility can subsidize service to the poor by charging their richer customers a little bit more. If too many people need discounts, the price of water for those who are providing the cross-subsidy can escalate to a point where they push back.

Experience has shown that once water bills become unaffordable to the poor in low- and middle-income countries, they stop paying or seek other ways of obtaining water, which usually involves accessing unsafe sources such as shallow wells that are vulnerable to contamination. Because disconnecting a customer's water can have serious health and safety implications, utilities often let unpaid bills accumulate.[5] For example, in the 1990s, about half of the residential customers of Uganda's water utilities were not paying their bills. In Yerevan, the capital and largest city in Armenia, customers owed the water utility more than three times its annual operating budget in 2002.

Frustrated by the uncollected revenue in parts of their cities where people appear to have enough money for cell phones and cars, some utilities have taken out contracts with private bill collection agencies, while others have installed water meters that require payments to be made before they will let water flow.[6] Although such measures do increase revenues, squeezing money out of poor people is rarely a viable means of closing a revenue shortfall.

Faced with a customer base unable to fund their operations, many water utilities turn to their local governments and international aid agencies. Politicians in low- and middle-income countries often have been willing to support municipal water funding because it is a relatively inexpensive way to garner public support. Aid agencies are motivated to provide grants or loans for water projects because they stimulate economic growth and improve public health. However, these outside sources of money tend to lead utilities toward new infrastructure construction. After all, most politicians would rather be photographed cutting ribbons on new, government-funded water supply projects as opposed to getting the credit for a water conservation program that results in the installation of water meters and pamphlets educating people about the evils of leaky faucets. Managers of water utilities also tend to be happy to oblige the desires of the politicians to engage in ribbon-cutting; if the government is going to provide funding, most engineers would rather spend their time supervising a complex water supply project as opposed to badgering their staff to work harder repairing leaks and chasing down plumbers responsible for illicit water connections.[7] Aid agencies and banks also tend to favor new infrastructure because their organizations were set up to finance capital projects. As a result, their employees are rewarded for producing reports that tally up the number of new reservoirs and wells that they have funded rather than gaining recognition for funding water conservation programs that might or might not curb per capita water use.

When utilities are unable to raise enough money from their customers, local governments, and international aid agencies, the only option is to cut back on service. To save money, about a third of the water systems in low- and middle-income countries save electricity by operating intermittently. The nearly one billion people who are served by such utilities have come to accept the fact that their tap water, which is likely to be more contaminated with pathogenic microbes than it would be if it flowed continuously, might not be available when they need it.[8]

As budgets tighten, water utilities also fall behind in their efforts to repair leaky pipes with predictable results: on average, about 20 percent of the water put into water distribution networks in low- and middle-income countries is lost to leaks, with losses of 40 percent or more typical among the most underfunded and poorly managed utilities.[9]

Faced with water utilities trapped in a spiral of declining service quality, many governments in low- and middle-income countries were receptive in the 1990s when multinational corporations approached them with proposals to operate their municipal water systems. According to the contract-seeking companies, underperforming public water systems could be improved by leveraging the technical proficiency, management expertise, and access to financing available to globalized organizations that specialized in running water systems.[10] The World Bank and its counterpart regional development banks were receptive to arguments for privatization of water systems, often forcing cities to set up contracts with consortia consisting of multinational corporations partnered with local businesses as a precondition for loans and grants.

Between 1995 and 2014, the International Finance Corporation—the private-banking arm of the World Bank—led the privatization charge as it lent cities more than seventy-five billion dollars for water and sanitation projects.[11] In many cases, the private water companies improved the financial performance of water systems by trimming excess staff, optimizing treatment plants, and cutting down on water losses, but gains in efficiency can take a struggling utility only so far.

If a privately controlled water utility is going to improve service and extend access without government subsidies, it needs to collect more money from its customers. But this is no easy task. When the higher water bills show up, privatized utilities become lightning rods for public resentment. For example, in 2000, the government of Bolivia declared martial law in Cochabamba, the third largest city in the country, when street protests broke out in response to price hikes by a private consortium led by the American company Bechtel.[12] The conflict, which came to be known as the Cochabamba Water War, ended the consortium's involvement in the city's water system and became a potent symbol of the antiglobalization movement, but the push toward privatization continued elsewhere. Proponents claimed that, done correctly, privatization could solve many of the problems faced by utilities in low- and middle-income countries, while opponents contended that access to affordable water is a human right that should not be handed over to for-profit companies.

The potential benefits and pitfalls of water privatization are evident in the experience of Manila, where the world's largest water system privatization effort provided contrasting examples of this approach to water system management. The task of privatizing water services for more than ten million Filipinos was so large that the government granted two separate contracts when it began its privatization effort in the late 1990s. The contract for the east side of the city was awarded to a consortium owned by a group of influential local families that teamed up with the American company Bechtel, while the western side of the city became the responsibility of a consortium led by another set of well-connected locals who partnered with the French water giant Suez. In exchange for twenty-five-year contracts, both consortia promised to expand water service from 67 percent to 96 percent of the city's population while simultaneously paying off more than one billion dollars in debt incurred by the public utility that they were replacing.[13] As a result of the competitive bidding process, the utility's consumers initially found relief: the price of water for a typical household dropped by more than 50 percent in both parts of the city at the start of the privatization process. But within five years, it had spiked back up to levels comparable to those that existed when the public agency had run the system. Some of the price increases could be blamed on the effects of the Asian Financial Crisis of 1997, which raised the cost of paying back debts incurred from the foreign currency-denominated loans that were used to modernize the water system. A drought that arrived just after the consortia took control of the water system also strained the privatization effort.

The effects of the economic crisis coupled with the drought and poor management practices proved to be too much for the Suez-led team. In their attempts to deliver better and expanded water service they continued to raise water rates. But that was not enough to save them. By 2003, their consortium had gone bankrupt, turning control of the water system back to the city. In contrast, the managers of the Bechtel-led consortium improved service and avoided serious public backlash through a combination of management prowess and popular programs that engaged residents of informal settlements in the construction of water access stations. They also benefitted by starting out with less debt on their books than the consortium on the other side of the city. In 2005, the successfully privatized consortium went public, selling shares on the Philippine stock market for around twenty-five million dollars. For Bechtel and the other consortium partners, the privatization venture had achieved its goals. Arguably, it also was a win for the residents of the eastern side of the city, where service had been extended to 94 percent of households by 1996. By 2012, nearly everyone in their section of the city had access to water.[14]

Public opposition, coupled with the fact that the lucrative corporate profits often failed to materialize, dampened enthusiasm for water privatization in low- and middle-income countries.[15] Between 2000 and 2019, 75 percent of the contracts between cities and private water service providers were not renewed, and 11 percent were ended early. Privatization was trendy, but it was never dominant: even at the height of enthusiasm for the practice, about 90 percent of the world's water utilities remained under the control of public agencies.

Although privatized water companies continue to operate in low- and middle-income countries, banks and aid agencies no longer view them as a panacea. Nevertheless, the inefficiencies of traditional public utilities and expectations from lenders of better financial performance led to a change of attitude among many municipal water suppliers.[16] They are not beholden to shareholders, but a new generation of corporatized public water utilities operate more like their private counterparts than the bureaucratic organizations of the past, with fewer archaic rules and less oversight from elected officials. As they focus on balancing their budgets, these semiautonomous utilities tend to pay more attention to such issues as cost recovery and financial stability than the need to expand service to people who cannot pay their bills.

In 2010, the United Nations stepped into the debate about whether water utilities should be operated like businesses and essential services by passing a resolution that defined a human right to water. Five years later, it established the Sixth Sustainable Development Goal, which specified full access to safe *and* affordable water as an objective of global development.[17] But these two statements of principle were not always accompanied by the resources necessary to realize universal water access. Nonetheless, they offered a counterbalance to the trend of treating water as a commodity subject to market forces.

Eventually, communities need to pay most of the cost of operating and maintaining water systems through utility bills or through subsidies provided from their fellow citizens by way of taxes collected by the government. But until enough of the people living in the cities of low- and middle-income countries climb out of poverty, incremental policy reforms and corporatization or privatization of public utilities are unlikely to close the gap between the expense of extending water access to the poor and the inability of local governments and bill-paying customers and taxpayers to provide enough money to operate water infrastructure. The same holds true for efforts to provide safe sanitation. According to the World Bank, the amount of outside development funds being directed toward new water and sanitation projects will need to increase by a factor of three if the Sixth Sustainable Development Goal, associated with universal access to safe and affordable water, sanitation, and hygiene, is to be achieved by 2030.[18]

Tripling support for water system improvement would not be easy. The amount of money already being spent on water infrastructure is quite large: in recent years, approximately ten billion dollars per year in grants and low-interest loans have been directed to water and sanitation projects in low- and middle-income countries by such organizations as the World Bank, the Asian Development Bank, and the Inter-American Development Bank. These funds, when combined with billions more in annual spending by local governments, have built reservoirs, pipelines, treatment plants, and underground pipe networks that have extended access to water and sanitation to tens of millions of people per year in low- and middle-income countries.[19] After these new water and sewer systems are built, billions of dollars are needed just as outside support decreases and responsibility for operation and maintenance of the new systems shifts to bill-paying customers and local governments, which, as we have seen, often struggle to keep the water flowing.

Tripling the amount of funding to improve water access and affordability would require the allocation of about an additional twenty billion dollars per year to outside development agencies for grants and loans. It also would require local governments to provide billions more for their share of project funding. One option for obtaining these large sums of money would be to turn to the private sector in a process known as blended financing.[20] To access this support, resources from outside development agencies would have to be reallocated in ways that reduce the risk that private investors take when they make loans for infrastructure in countries where currency fluctuations, corruption, or political instability might prevent the full repayment of debt. By subsidizing loans and promising to step in when a project stalls, the outside development agencies could leverage private funding for new water projects. But for blended financing to be effective, the parties writing the contracts must strike the right balance between risks to the investor and the terms of debt repayment—a process that requires transparency, experience, and trust that has yet to mature to a point at which such transactions are routine and predictable. Although access to more money from the private sector could increase spending on water systems in low- and middle-income countries, blended finance is probably best suited for less risky water projects in wealthier middle-income countries where a smaller portion of the residents still lack access to running water. Furthermore, due to the mixed experience that many countries have had with privatization, there might not be a lot of public enthusiasm for borrowing large sums of money from multinational banks and private investors who are drawn in by the promise that water is another liquid commodity that will be just as profitable as oil.

If private investments cannot provide the additional funding for extending water systems to the urban poor, the international development agencies could turn to their government sponsors. Providing another twenty billion dollars per year to international development agencies is not unthinkable for the world's wealthiest nations. If the additional funding was spread out among the world's wealthy, it is unlikely that the billion or so people living in donor countries would notice the small increase in their taxes that would take place if their governments contributed about twenty dollars annually for every person that they represent to improve water, sanitation, and hygiene in low- and middle-income countries.

Of course, support for water and sanitation must compete with other critical societal needs within the portfolios of international aid agencies. If the budgets of outside development agencies suddenly were to receive an extra twenty billion dollars per year, water funding would likely receive only a fraction of the windfall after allocations were made for projects that support public health, energy access, government, and civil society—all of which currently receive over twice as much annual funding from development agencies as water and sanitation.[21] Absent a groundswell in public opinion, it seems unlikely that the governments of wealthy countries will raise taxes or redirect revenues on the scale needed to provide low- and middle-income countries with the hundreds of billions of dollars per year needed to more rapidly address the long list of problems that the urban poor currently face.

Irrespective of whether a tripling in outside development funding occurs, billions of dollars per year in grants and loans combined with billions more from local governments will continue to be directed at infrastructure projects in low- and middle-income countries in the coming decades. These projects will greatly increase the volume of water flowing into cities as utilities endeavor to keep up with the water demands of their expanding populations. With the right policy incentives coupled with a growing urban middle class that has a greater capacity to pay for water, hundreds of millions of people living in informal settlements in the world's cities will likely gain access to safe and affordable water and sanitation. But better urban water systems alone will not achieve the Sixth Sustainable Development Goal for water and sanitation because development aid and new wealth are not distributed evenly in low- and middle-income countries: only about a quarter of international development grants and loans reach people living in small towns and rural communities even though much of the population needing access to water and sanitation resides outside of cities.[22]

The water problems of city dwellers are easier to address than those of rural communities because the rapidly expanding cities of low- and middle-income countries tend to attract more investment than the countryside. Economic growth generates tax revenue and middle-class bill payers that provide a means of building, operating, and maintaining urban water systems. Cities also are easier for international development agencies to work with because each large urban water project provides water or sanitation access to tens of thousands of people. For aid agencies and governments, it can be a daunting task to manage and distribute large sums of money for the installation of the thousands of hand pumps, rainwater cisterns, small-scale water distribution systems, and latrines needed to provide a similar amount of access in rural communities. Historically, development agencies also have operated under the assumption that their funds will have a larger impact in cities because loans that are paid back by urban utilities can be reinvested elsewhere, whereas grants needed in rural areas do not provide any monetary return for reinvestment.

Rather than working directly with giant development banks or their central governments, communities that are not served by urban water utilities tend to partner with aid groups that specialize in rural access to water and sanitation. Government-funded aid organizations, such as the Japan International Cooperation Agency (JICA), the US Agency for International Development (USAID), and the German Federal Ministry of Economic Cooperation and Development (BMZ), each spend more than a hundred million dollars per year building capacity and providing grants for water and sanitation projects in rural communities in sub-Saharan Africa, South America, South Asia, and Southeast Asia.[23] As part of these efforts, technical experts are dispatched to rural villages to maintain and repair hand pumps on community wells, local government officials are given specialized training, wells that serve rural settlements are drilled, and grants are given to schools to install toilets and hand-washing stations.[24] Increasingly, more of the funding from these groups supports efforts to reform local policies and reduce inefficiencies in the ways that government aid is dispensed.

Nongovernmental organizations that acquire their money from private foundations, individual donors, and government grants also play an important role in increasing access to water and sanitation in rural communities. Just like their government-funded counterparts, these private groups partner with local communities to deliver rural water and sanitation services. For example, World Vision—one of the largest of these groups—spent over $140 million in 2019 to bring water to more than three million people and sanitation to more than two million people in rural communities in low- and middle-income countries.[25]

A more recent arrival to the nongovernmental organization scene, Water.org, has taken a different approach to the water and sanitation access problem by challenging the assumption that rural communities cannot pay back loans. By working with local banks and governments, the organization uses its modest budget (about twenty-five million dollars in 2019) to help local banks and government agencies make small loans to individuals and community groups for water projects that provide water and sanitation for about eight million people per year.[26] Unlike aid programs that rely upon grants, the group's focus on loans yields returns that further advance water and sanitation access: as the hundreds of millions of dollars in loans are paid back, local banks gain confidence in their ability to fund community water projects, and the pool of funding available for water and sanitation access grows.

Altogether, organizations that specialize in rural water and sanitation spend about two billion dollars per year supporting efforts to improve conditions for rural communities in low- and middle-income countries.[27] Based on the important role that these groups play in advancing the Sixth Sustainable Development Goal in places that often are outside of the reach of the big development banks, it would seem like a good idea to allocate more money to these efforts. Despite the evidence of success and the compelling nature of work done by these groups, finding more money to support their efforts is difficult. Government-funded organizations that provide rural water and sanitation support compete with the needs of other government development agencies when it is time for wealthy countries to set their annual aid budgets, while nongovernmental organizations already have teams of fundraisers doing their best to acquire more money from individual donors and charitable foundations.

In recognition of the challenge of creating additional support for water and sanitation access, nongovernmental organizations have proposed some creative funding mechanisms.[28] One approach that has started to gain traction involves directing one cent from every liter of bottled water sold to an investment fund dedicated to advancing the Sixth Sustainable Development Goal. The thinking behind this idea is that tiny payments from a product with global revenues of almost two hundred billion dollars per year will fill the funding gap without requiring a major realignment in government or private foundation spending priorities. Based on initial discussions with leaders from the beverage industry, there is evidence that tiny donations for each bottle of water sold, a practice that is sometimes referred to as a micro-levy, could be embraced by the industry to help them counteract the public criticism they receive for the litter, energy consumption, and plastic pollution associated with their product.

Thus, a voluntary program to redirect some of their advertising budgets to water and sanitation access could create goodwill that advances the industry's business interests. Because the public associates bottled water with safe water, the money raised by the micro-levy would also not have to compete with other development needs. In 2019, the idea began to move ahead through the efforts of Water Unite, a non-governmental organization based in the United Kingdom.[29] The amount of money being collected through bottled water micro-levies is still quite small, and media attention on issues related to plastic pollution means that some of the spending is likely going to go toward efforts to cut down on litter. Nonetheless, the micro-levy approach has the potential to raise hundreds of millions of dollars or perhaps even billions of dollars for water and sanitation.

Even without new funding sources, between 2000 and 2015, about 1.5 billion people gained access to basic water services and 1.4 billion people gained access to basic sanitation.[30] Some of this progress was due to the patchwork system of international development aid, local government spending, and the efforts of charitable organizations. Economic growth and development also played a role in increasing access by lifting people out of poverty and providing them with the ability to pay for their own water and sanitation services. As the world attempts to bring about universal water and sanitation access, disruptive events including pandemics, wars, and climate change could slow or reverse recent progress. Those people who still struggle for access are, by definition, living in the places that the current system of aid and economic growth are having the hardest time reaching. A large infusion of additional funding could help speed progress, but it seems unlikely that the goal of universal access by 2030 will be reached without new approaches.

Through the hard work of people employed by governments, non-governmental organizations, and private companies a lot of progress has been made in recent decades resolving the second and third water crises in low- and middle-income countries (water for the many and water for the unconnected) through the implementation of better policies. Using well-established technologies for providing and treating water, crises have been averted by increasing the efficiency in water use and finding more effective ways of funding the construction, operation, and maintenance of water and sanitation systems in low- and middle-income countries. The continued spread of these reforms along with economic growth will help counter some of the worst elements of these two water crises, but they will not necessarily create water systems that are well suited for the challenges of the second half of the twenty-first century.

While fighting the immediate water crises, municipal water suppliers have run into a paradox. At one end of the development spectrum, about a billion people lack basic water access or are being supplied with piped water from utilities that operate intermittently and resort to rationing during droughts. As these people move up the economic ladder and benefit from development aid, they will likely gain access to the kind of piped water infrastructure that serves many middle-income countries. The quantity of water that they consume will increase from subsistence levels (ten to fifty liters per person per day) to those typical of cities where cash-strapped utilities plagued by leaks struggle to implement conservation measures (per capita consumption over two hundred liters per day). Eventually, water-stressed cities that run out of inexpensive new supply options will adopt policies to reduce their per capita water use, but it is unlikely that it will ever drop much below around one hundred liters per day. By the time that the low- and middle-income countries reach the conditions that prevail in many of the world's wealthiest countries, billions of dollars will have been invested in imported water systems and underground pipe networks that lock communities into water supply and sanitation systems that are difficult to change.

As a result of the immediate need to address the second and third water crises, few of the hard-working people responsible for creating new policies and infrastructure have time to question the approach that they are reinforcing. This is unfortunate, because the world ultimately needs water systems that are better suited for the challenges associated with a changing climate and a less predictable future.

10

Reducing Agricultural Water Demand

TO UNDERSTAND THE potential for using demand management to avert water crises in agriculture, it is important to recognize the dual nature of the challenge. First, agricultural water use is driven by the need to increase global food production by about 70 percent between 2020 and 2050 to feed another two billion people plus the billions of newly middle-income people who will be able to afford to get a larger fraction of their calories from meat and other water-intensive foods. This already formidable task will be complicated by the simultaneous need to adapt the way food is grown to a changing climate. The second part of the problem is related to the effect of agriculture on the environment. In addition to reducing river flows, destroying wetlands, and drying up terminal lakes, modern agricultural practices have polluted many of the world's rivers, lakes, and estuaries with a cocktail of nutrients, pesticides, toxic metals, and salts to a point where ecosystems are showing signs of severe stress.

Considering the ways that water is presently used in agriculture, it would appear that there are plenty of opportunities for farmers to produce more food with less water while simultaneously cutting pollution.[1] Thirsty crops such as cotton are being grown in arid regions with surface irrigation methods that are nearly identical to those employed in ancient times. Farmers in water-stressed parts of India, the United States, China, and Iran are engaged in a race to the bottom, extracting groundwater at rates faster than it can be replenished. Modern farming practices are causing erosion, degrading soil fertility, and expanding hypoxic zones in coastal regions worldwide. For decades, these and other unsustainable practices have been highlighted by experts as places where better farming techniques could help save water and reduce environmental damage. Yet, despite an abundance of ideas on how agricultural practices can be made more efficient and less damaging, change has been slow to arrive.

To gain insight into why efforts to improve how water is used in agriculture have not always achieved their goals, it is important to consider both the means and the motivation for change. In many ways, identifying approaches for improving water use efficiency in food production is the easy part. Numerous proven methods exist for better managing water in agriculture; the hard work involves convincing people to use them to avert water crises.

Individual farmers are the ultimate deciders when it comes to water management. They choose the crops as well as how fields are plowed, fertilized, and harvested. But farmers are not completely independent; their decisions are strongly influenced by local economic conditions outside of their control, such as the cost of irrigation water, electricity, and fertilizer as well as the price that their crops command at harvest. As farmers endeavor to strike a balance between financial risks and economic rewards, a myriad of institutions alters their economic landscape. For example, to enhance the regional economy, government officials might fund a new reservoir or introduce subsidies to encourage production of a specific crop. To decrease pollution of downstream fisheries, water supplies, or tourist attractions, government policies might make it less attractive to grow crops that require certain pesticides and fertilization practices.[2] Beyond government rules, fluctuations in labor costs, agricultural commodity prices, and interest rates alter economics in ways that affect the decisions about what farmers grow and how they grow it.

Efforts to change the ways that water is used in agriculture will succeed only if they make sense to farmers in the larger context of their many other decisions. Water-saving or pollution-reducing practices that increase profits (for example, by raising crop yields) without requiring major alterations in established farming methods are likely to spread quickly after early adopters have demonstrated that they are effective in the local context. Government policies favoring more sustainable farming practices tend to alter the decisions of farmers in more subtle ways, by tilting their economic decisions in a desired direction. In practice, neither of these simplified characterizations fully captures the ways that change comes about in agriculture. Decisions are rarely straightforward because every farm differs in terms of such attributes as size, soil type, and topography and every farmer differs with respect to such factors as economic status, technical capacity, and willingness to take risks. Short of the extreme cases in which a policy change or a new way of growing food changes economic conditions to a degree that no other decision could possibly make sense, successful efforts to alter the ways that food is grown require an in-depth understanding of how a region's farms are operated as well as support and trust of the community. Due to the complicated nature of the decision-making process, making agricultural water use more efficient tends to be more challenging than reducing water use by municipal water systems, but the potential rewards of water savings and reductions in pollution are usually much greater.

Returning to the idea that water crises can be averted with preemptive action, it is important to recognize that the need to grow more food is the force driving water efficiency efforts and not the actual crisis. Most experts agree that the world's farmers will figure out how to meet the world's food needs by midcentury.[3] However, in the process, the two water crises that are most closely tied to agriculture—farmers experiencing economic calamity due to water shortages and ecosystems collapsing—are likely to occur more frequently. To avert crises related to idled farmers and collapsed ecosystems, agricultural efficiency must go beyond simply increasing the amount of food that can be grown on a particular plot of land with a specific amount of water; practices will have to change in a manner that allows farmers to bring their water use

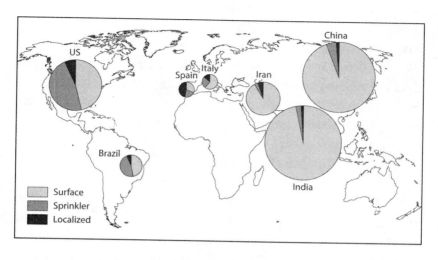

Annual volumes of water applied and methods of application for large users of irrigation water in the period 2004–2009. The size of the circle is proportional to the volume of irrigation water applied.

into balance with local availability and the needs of downstream ecosystems.

The first place to look for agricultural water efficiency improvements is on irrigated fields—the places that are most connected to water shortages. Although only about 20 percent of cropland is equipped for irrigation, fields receiving groundwater or water diverted from a river or reservoir produce about 40 percent of the world's food.[4] Irrigation is especially critical to food security in China, India, and Iran, which together account for almost half of the world's irrigated farmland. Among the different approaches for applying water, surface irrigation—the ancient practice of temporarily flooding farmland or routing water through unlined ditches or furrows running through fields—is by far the most common method used worldwide, accounting for about 86 percent of the applied water. These practices are labor-intensive to build and maintain, but they remain popular due to their low cost, simplicity, and familiarity to farmers whose families have used them for generations.

Surface irrigation is inherently inefficient because in most cases only about half of the water released onto a field is used by crops. The remaining water either evaporates from flooded fields or moist soil, is taken up by weeds, percolates to a depth that cannot be reached by plant roots, or drains off the land at the end of the application period. For comparison, between 65 percent and 95 percent of the water applied by the two other commonly practiced irrigation methods (sprinklers and microirrigation) typically makes it to crops.[5]

For an individual farmer, realizing water savings by shifting away from surface irrigation requires an investment of approximately $1,500 per hectare for conventional sprinklers to between $2,500 and $7,500 per hectare for drip irrigation or low-flow microsprinklers.[6] Even in the world's wealthiest countries, many farmers lack the means to make the transition on their own. Absent subsidies, investments in more efficient irrigation systems will tend to occur in water-scarce places where farmers grow specialty crops—fruits, vegetables, and nuts—that can be sold at high prices.

Among the world's water-stressed agricultural regions, few were better suited to adopt more efficient irrigation methods than California, a place that became the main source of specialty crops for most of the United States in the mid-twentieth century. Despite decades of effort by agricultural experts and vendors of microirrigation systems to convince farmers to abandon low-efficiency surface irrigation, change was slow in coming because the combination of imported water and ample groundwater made irrigation water abundant and inexpensive. Up until the late 1980s, surface irrigation was still used on over three-quarters of the state's cropland.[7] A shift to microirrigation methods, particularly drip irrigation, an Israeli technology that had already transformed that country's irrigation systems, did not gain momentum until the system was strained by a severe drought between 1987 and 1991. Over the next two decades, the acreage using surface irrigation was cut in half as more efficient irrigation methods proliferated.

A close look at the transition of California's irrigation practices reveals the circuitous path through which agricultural practices change.[8] Shortly after drip irrigation was commercialized in Israel in the mid-

1960s, extension agents—professionals employed by the state university system to support agricultural development—realized the potential of the new irrigation technology. During the twenty years that preceded the drought, extension agents and company representatives fanned out across the state seeking farmers willing to become early adopters of drip irrigation. They found their partners on groundwater-reliant farms, particularly those where well-drained soils were likely to lead to large savings in energy due to the need to pump less water. The knowledge gained by these early experiences led to reductions in equipment costs, increases in crop yields, and improvements in fertigation—a technique that delivered fertilizers dissolved in the irrigation water. This period of learning-by-doing expanded local expertise and created relationships that set the stage for rapid uptake of the technology that occurred when the drought hit.

The hard work of extension agents and their partners enabled farmers to weather the drought of 1987 to 1991 and to thrive in the subsequent decades. However, their efforts did not insulate California from water crises. The microirrigation transition mainly helped farmers achieve greater profits with the water available to them (that is, according to the mantra of the time, it supported "more crop per drop" and not a decline in overall agricultural water use). Despite the improvements in irrigation efficiency, the amount of water used by California's farmers barely budged between the mid-1960s and the 2010s. Instead, productivity gains from drip-irrigation coupled with increases in demand for high-value crops such as almonds, avocadoes, and wine grapes helped transform the state's agricultural economy.

Twenty years after the drought, surface irrigation was still being used to grow rice, hay, and cotton, but much of the state's water was now devoted to valuable permanent crops (that is, vineyards and fruit and nut trees) that, unlike those that used to be grown, could not take a year off when a severe drought hit the state in 2011. As the amount of water stored in reservoirs decreased, farmers flipped the switches on their pumps, turning to groundwater to make up for surface water deficits. In response, aquifer levels rapidly dropped, causing land in some parts of the agricultural Central Valley to subside by as much as 0.6 meter per year.[9] Not seeing an end in sight to the long-term trend of declining water levels, the state passed legislation requiring landowners to bring their groundwater use into balance with the availability of the resource.

The Sustainable Groundwater Management Act (SGMA) of 2015 broke California into approximately three hundred separate geographic zones managed by consortia of local water users that acted as groundwater sustainability agencies.[10] Under the threat that the state would step in with draconian solutions, each local organization was given five years to come up with a plan to bring local groundwater use into balance with water availability by 2040. By shifting the discussion from more crop per drop to stewardship of a shared resource, the state forced agricultural water users to put long-term sustainability ahead of short-term profits.

In the initial phase of the process, California's groundwater sustainability agencies are attempting to minimize the economic pain as groundwater use comes into balance with its availability. Despite the progress being made, the amount of irrigated farmland in the area with the greatest current groundwater deficit, the San Joaquin Valley, is predicted to decrease by about 10 percent in the coming decades.[11] Although some farmers will likely be hurt during the transition, the regional impacts of decreasing irrigation will be dampened by shifts in cropping patterns that favor more profitable water uses. If no further innovation occurs in plant breeding or farming practices, total farm revenues in the San Joaquin Valley are predicted to decline by about 5 percent. If researchers, extension agents, and private companies continue to find ways to increase the profitability of farming, the fear revenue declines might not happen.

Although full-blown crisis involving widespread farm failure may be averted, unresolved issues related to the hydraulic engineering projects of the twentieth century combined with the irrigation transition and the effects of a changing climate have the potential to exacerbate two additional water crises on irrigation-dependent California farms.

The first crisis is related to salt. Since the late nineteenth century, agronomists have warned that irrigation projects in arid regions have the potential to decrease soil fertility if the salt that remains behind when water evaporates is not removed from the basin.[12] Imported water aggravates the problem because bringing more water into a formerly dry area causes the water table to rise. If the water rises into the root zone, crops can be damaged through a process referred to as waterlogging. Groundwater pumping can lower the water table, but the practice of frequently flushing large volumes of water through the soil results in dissolution of naturally occurring minerals that release salts and toxic elements such as selenium into groundwater. In the wetter, northern part of California, winter rains carry away much of the accumulated salt. But in the southern half of the Central Valley, salt is accumulating.

The federal government had recognized the need to drain salts from the southern San Joaquin Valley when it built the region's irrigation project in the 1960s, but a lack of funding to complete the drainage system and years of finger-pointing about who has the responsibility for its construction means that salt continues to accumulate. According to current estimates, about 5 percent of irrigated farmland in the valley has already been lost to salinization, and about a quarter of the land is showing signs of salinity-caused losses in productivity.[13] In California and most other dry places where irrigation is practiced, on-farm water efficiency increases make it harder to wash salts out of the system.

The second challenge is an impending ecological crisis in California's inland and coastal waters. When water is used more efficiently by farmers, flows in downstream rivers and estuaries decline. As a result, water temperatures increase, and less clean water is available to dilute salts, nutrients, and pesticides released by farms and cities. Because these changes came on top of other stresses—an increased frequency of droughts, warmer temperatures, diminished habitat, and invasive species—threatened and endangered fish, such as the delta smelt and coho and chinook salmon, are teetering on the edge of extinction. Although state and federal laws are supposed to assure that enough water flows downstream to assure fish survival, reality is often quite different, especially during severe droughts. When farmers and cities started to run out of water during the drought that started in 2011, political wrangling led to delays in water releases, causing flows to fall below the minimum safe levels for ecosystem protection in several of California's largest waterways.[14]

Recognizing that groundwater management alone will not avert ecosystem crises, California has begun to set aside money for habitat restoration and the construction of additional water storage systems (expanded reservoirs and so-called off-channel reservoirs that collect high flows during the wettest times of the year) that will release cold, clean water to rivers during critical months when fish are migrating or experiencing stress from low flows. For example, in order to secure money from the state, about half of the water in the proposed five-billion-dollar Sites Reservoir will be dedicated to ecosystem protection.[15] Whether the interventions will be enough to avert an ecological crises is still uncertain.

A similar move toward more efficient irrigation methods has also occurred in the Mediterranean, with similar outcomes to those experienced in California. Among the region's agricultural leaders, Spain is most like California, with millions of hectares of irrigated fields growing much of Europe's fresh fruit and vegetables. In the aftermath of drought-induced shortages of the mid-1990s, the Spanish government incentivized more efficient agricultural water use. With subsidies from the government, farmers increased the percentage of land employing drip irrigation from about 20 percent to 50 percent between 2002 and 2012.[16] But just as in California, the declining popularity of surface irrigation did not free up any water: the area of irrigated farmland expanded by close to 10 percent as efficiency gains and higher profits from exports led to the redirection of water savings into greater food production.

Spain's decades-long trend of agricultural intensification threatens the long-term sustainability of groundwater and has put pressure on groundwater-fed streams.[17] As the country adapts to a hotter, drier future, its farmers may ultimately end up with less irrigation water, but their transition to efficient irrigation practices means that farmers are well insulated from the severe economic damage, at least for the next few decades.

Although irrigation efficiency improvements will likely prevent water shortages on Spain's farms, additional action will be needed to save the country's already stressed ecosystems. Many of the wetlands and rivers in arid parts of the country had already been severely impacted by decades of surface water diversions, groundwater pumping, and habitat destruction when the country's integration into the European Union made ecosystem protection and restoration a priority in the early 2000s.[18] As the country attempts to come into compliance with the European Union's Water Framework Directive, it has begun to invest more money in pollution control, habitat restoration, and measures to increase environmental flows. Whether these efforts will avert crises in freshwater and coastal ecosystems remains to be seen.

Elsewhere in the Mediterranean, farmers are following a similar path of adopting more efficient irrigation methods to grow specialty crops. In Israel and Cyprus—two of the region's most water-limited countries—about 75 percent of farmland already employs microirrigation, a means of delivering drops of water to plants.[19] Microirrigation also is becoming increasingly popular for specialty crop production throughout the rest of the region, but its overall impact on water use at a national scale is not as obvious as in Spain, Cyprus, and Israel because drip and microirrigation are not widely used for grains and other commodity crops. A similar pattern is evident worldwide: farmers in water-limited parts of South Africa, Chile, and Australia are using microirrigation to grow high-value specialty crops, while many of their neighbors still rely upon surface irrigation and other techniques to grow less valuable commodities.

Microirrigation has had little impact at a global scale because farmers have a hard time justifying its high cost on less profitable crops.

When water savings are needed for commodity crops, farmers turn to less expensive approaches. Chief among them has been overhead sprinklers.

Water efficiency gradually took hold in the American West through the replacement of surface irrigation with center pivot irrigation and systems employing sprinklers mounted or fixed on moving platforms. After California, the sixteen remaining states in the arid American West are the next biggest users of irrigation, accounting for about three-quarters of the remainder of the agricultural water use. Excluding California's specialty crops and the orchards and vegetable farms of the Pacific Northwest, most of the West's irrigation water is applied to corn, alfalfa, wheat, soybeans, and cotton.[20]

In response to water stress, many farmers growing these commodity crops turned to water efficiency. Between 1984 and 2013, the volume of water applied by surface irrigation in the western United States declined from about 70 percent to 40 percent as center pivot irrigation systems became the dominant means of applying water.[21] However, as was the case elsewhere, the irrigation transition did not reduce overall water use. For example, with the help of government subsidies, farmers in water-stressed western Kansas upgraded to center pivot irrigation by the mid-1990s. When those investments did not reverse declining aquifer levels, they replaced most of the high-pressure sprinklers on their irrigation equipment with dropped nozzles. These low-pressure sprinklers, which deliver water just above the plant canopy, decreased evaporative water losses by another 10 percent. Instead of reducing water use, farmers shifted from less water intensive crops such as wheat and sorghum to thirstier, higher value crops such as corn, soybeans, and alfalfa. Once again, the more-crop-per-drop mentality increased profits without reducing vulnerability to water crises.

Aside from changing the way that water is delivered to crops, there are plenty of other, less obvious ways to make irrigation more efficient.[22] For example, 15–45 percent of the water used by large-scale irrigation projects is typically lost in transit, by seepage through the bottoms of unlined canals. By lining canals with concrete, clay, or some other low-permeability material, substantial water savings can be realized. Likewise, soil moisture sensors save water by allowing farmers to irrigate when plants need water. Often, these approaches are more cost-effective than new irrigation systems, but if they are made in the name of more crop per drop, they are just as unlikely to avert agricultural crises as investments in drip irrigation or low-pressure sprinklers.

Irrigation has an obvious connection to water shortages and ecosystem stress, but in many places rainfed agriculture—the cultivation method that produces most of the world's food—has a greater effect on water availability and pollution.[23] To gain insight into the role that rainfed agriculture can play in water crises, it is useful to focus on wheat, maize, and rice—the staple foods that account for much of the world's cereal production. About 75 percent of wheat is grown in China, India, North America, the European Union, and the western part of the Eurasian Steppe (Russia, Ukraine, and Kazakhstan). The United States, China, and Brazil produce over 70 percent of the world's corn (maize), with much of it going to animal feed, while about 90 percent of the last of the world's rice is grown in Asia.

During the Great Acceleration, these three staples helped feed growing populations. Although land clearing and irrigation projects played roles in meeting food needs, especially in China and India, the surge in food production known as the Green Revolution was driven by innovations in plant breeding, fertilizers, and pesticides. During this period, staple production tripled, while the area of cultivated land only increased by about 30 percent. The discovery of wheat and rice cultivars that were resistant to rust—a common plant disease that reduces crop yields—as well as the breeding of plants that matured quickly enough to allow for a second annual planting made it possible to grow a lot more food on existing fields.[24] Although some of the techniques used in rainfed agriculture may have reduced the fraction of the precipitation falling on the land that made it to rivers, the water scarcity caused by rainfed agriculture was less severe than what would have transpired if farmers had relied exclusively on irrigation to meet food needs. The Green Revolution may have had only modest impacts on water scarcity, but it played a major role in the sixth water crisis through application of nutrients and pesticides that eventually ended up in downstream waterways.

As the world faces the need to grow more food, agricultural technology is once again being seen as a means of expanding food production, in what some people term the Second Green Revolution. Increasingly, the cultivation of high-value crops such as grapes, strawberries, and nuts has taken on the look and feel of a modern factory, with data from soil moisture sensors, satellite imagery, and drones being integrated to provide more precise control over decisions that farmers used to make by experience and instinct. Seeing the potential for profits if sensors and software can lower the cost of producing food, Silicon Valley entrepreneurs have rushed into agriculture, creating tech start-ups to capitalize on the potential for increasing agricultural productivity through real-time data analysis.[25]

While it is too soon to tell if any of these efforts will succeed, precision agriculture has already arrived on large farms in wealthy countries. For example, by 2010, approximately half of the corn and soybean in the United States was grown on farms that used GPS-enabled tractors that employed data on the previous year's yields at specific locations to determine where and when to apply fertilizers.[26] From the perspective of their impact on water efficiency and downstream pollution, the potential for these new techniques is high.

As the world pursues a Second Green Revolution, it would be wise to consider the social consequences of altering the traditional ways in which food is grown, especially in low- and middle-income countries. Cheaper food and rural wealth stimulated growth throughout Asia, Central America, and South America during the first Green Revolution, facilitating investments in manufacturing and infrastructure that drove migration to cities.[27] But not everyone benefitted. In some countries, many farmers slipped deeper into poverty because they were unable to compete with cheap imported food. In addition, the gains in productivity tended to strengthen large landholders, chemical companies, and food processors at the expense of small farmers. The winners and losers of a Second Green Revolution are not preordained. Lessons learned during the Great Acceleration can help assure that the social and economic benefits of new technologies and the impacts of farming on the environment are distributed equitably.

11

Navigating the Jevons Paradox

THE INABILITY OF irrigation efficiency improvements to solve the problems associated with unsustainable water use is an example of the Jevons paradox—a phenomenon identified in the 1860s by the English economist William Stanley Jevons to describe the unanticipated increase in coal consumption that accompanied introduction of the Watt steam engine. Increased resource consumption often follows inventions that improve efficiency because decreased costs encourage practices that would have otherwise been impractical.

The existence of the Jevons paradox in agricultural water management is not unique to the United States and Spain.[1] The failure of irrigation efficiency measures to yield substantial reductions in water use has also been observed in most places where people have bothered to collect data. Governments around the world continue to subsidize overhead sprinklers and microirrigation systems as well as a host of other water-saving measures because it is easier to support the goal of growing more crop per drop than it is to suggest that agricultural water use might need to be curtailed.

When a depleted aquifer or an ecological crisis finally forces policy makers to confront the Jevons paradox, the hard work of reducing agricultural water use at the basin scale can finally begin. The Australian government's response to the effects of the Millennium Drought in the country's agricultural heartland is an instructive example of the challenge of transitioning a heavily irrigated region to more sustainable water practices. After years of ecosystem decline across the Murray-Darling River Basin, the Water Act of 2007 changed the ways that water was allocated for around half of the arid country's irrigated agricultural production.[2] Had it not been for the unprecedented length of the drought, it is unlikely that the sustainability advocates could have succeeded in getting water users to renegotiate the ways that water was allocated in a watershed that covers almost 15 percent of the Australian continent.

The agreement that emerged after five years of consultation contained provisions for increasing environmental flows while simultaneously providing government support to minimize economic damage caused by reduced agricultural water use.[3] The key innovation in the plan was the way that the way that the government's thirteen billion dollars in financial incentives were deployed. Unlike programs that had been adopted in other countries, the Murray-Darling Basin Plan required that farmers return half of the water saved by irrigation efficiency improvements to environmental purposes.

Because those savings phased in slowly and provided only a portion of the necessary environmental flows, the government purchased additional water from an existing trading market—an action that drove up the profits that farmers could realize by selling their water rights. After the drought ended, the government investments began to have their intended effect: environmental flows increased and ecosystems in certain parts of the basin improved without detrimental impacts on the economic prospects of irrigation-reliant agricultural communities.[4]

When it was launched, water resource managers worldwide hailed the Murray-Darling Basin Plan as a model for sustainable water management. But having a good plan is no guarantee of success. During the postdrought period, when the public's attention turned elsewhere, agricultural interest groups gradually increased their share of the basin's water. Within a few years, experts who had helped establish the program began to question whether the promised environmental flows were actually being realized, citing poor monitoring of irrigation water use and return flows as weaknesses that prevented the plan from providing its promised ecosystem improvements.[5]

When another severe drought began in 2018, political warfare erupted, as water-stressed farmers threatened to pull out of the agreement if environmental flows were not returned to them. In response, environmentalists cited a massive fish kill in a lake that had been deprived of flows by upstream water diversions and the increased risk that tides would carry saltwater into the city of Adelaide's drinking water intakes if flows were further reduced as reasons to maintain the program's environmental water allocations.[6] Although tensions dissipated when the drought ended in 2020, it is evident that the hard work of preparing the basin for a drier future is far from over. Irrespective of the ultimate outcome, the Murray-Darling Basin Plan demonstrates that elevating the water needs of the environment to the same status as those of farms and cities is an important step in averting ecosystem crises.

Countries that rely upon surface irrigation for food production and rural economic security—particularly China, India, and Pakistan—are grappling with similar challenges as they face water scarcity. Although water managers in these countries are trying to learn from their counterparts in places where the Jevons paradox has frustrated efforts to achieve sustainability, the transition to new ways of supplying, allocating, and using water resources thus far has proven to be just as difficult. If anything, the challenge is even greater because the motivation to single-mindedly pursue more crop per drop is driven by such hard-to-ignore goals as the alleviation of rural poverty, hunger, and malnutrition.

China's efforts to achieve sustainable water use are shaping up to be a lot like those of the western United States, especially in the dry north, where much of the country's grain is grown. Although advancements in plant breeding, fertilizers, and pesticides have been important, China's agricultural productivity would not have increased so much without the water infrastructure projects that broke the country's reliance on rainfed agriculture.[7] Between 1950 and 1980, the area of irrigated land in China tripled as the country built tens of thousands of reservoirs and installed or modernized more than two million groundwater wells. Only after those water supply projects were completed did China turn its attention to water efficiency, funding canal-lining programs, and subsidies for sprinklers and micro-drip irrigation.

Like most other parts of the world, water savings were channeled back into food production. Between 1990 and 2015, China's agricultural water use barely budged as crop yields grew and the area of cultivated land expanded by about 15 percent. Presently, about three-quarters of the country's food is grown on irrigated land. Gains in irrigation efficiency have been highest in the water-limited north, where thirsty crops have slowly become more popular.[8] In fact, corn—a water-intensive crop that is used mainly for animal feed—replaced rice as the nation's top crop in 2012. As the country's wealth continues to increase, feeding livestock to satisfy growing consumer demand for meat will further stress China's agricultural water supply.

The demands of China's demographic and economic transformation have stressed its water resources. Across much of North China, groundwater levels fell between 2003 and 2010, mainly as the result of increasing water demands from farms and booming metropolitan areas, such as Beijing and Tianjin.[9] By 2017, the South-to-North Water Diversion Project—a water transfer project that cost more than eighty billion dollars—had reversed the trend of groundwater depletion in and around Beijing (fig. 11). It also freed up water for farmers. However, in the long run, only a modest share of North China's agricultural water deficit will be met by new sources because the extra profits that can be made by irrigating farmland cannot justify the high costs of water megaprojects. Whether the Jevons paradox will prevent China from achieving a sustainable water balance is still an open question.

As is the case in other water-stressed places, China's challenge in achieving water sustainability is neither a lack of knowledge nor the absence of cost-effective irrigation technologies. Rather, after four decades of employing the more-crop-per-drop attitude to end hunger and rural poverty, local water management institutions are optimized

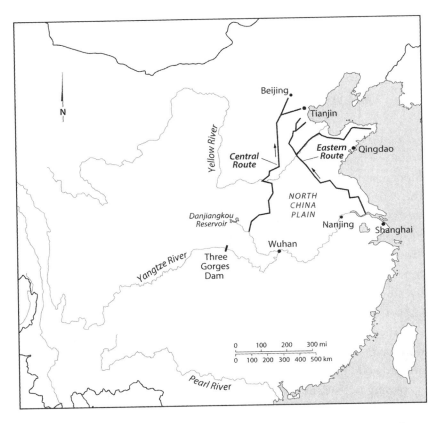

China's water megaprojects: the South-to-North Water Diversion Project, which was started in 2003, can move up to 25 billion cubic meters of water per year to the dry northern part of the country, while the Three Gorges Dam regulates the flow of the longest river in Asia (the Yangtze River).

to help farmers produce more food. To achieve water sustainability, incentives will need to induce them to balance agricultural productivity, ecosystem protection, and long-term water security.

On the Indian subcontinent, the ability to store and move water has been central to agriculture for millennia because much of the potential water supply arrives each year during about a week of intense monsoon rain.[10] In the dry northwest, those who controlled access to irrigation water historically held much of the wealth and political power. In the south, reservoirs built over the centuries played a critical role in both food production and economic development. When the British East India Company seized control in the 1800s, they expanded India's irrigation systems and centralized control of the subcontinent's water resources, in many cases displacing local water management practices that had been in place for hundreds of years. Between the mid-1800s and the 1940s, the colonial government built or rehabilitated more than 120,000 kilometers of irrigation canals while simultaneously fixing many poorly maintained or disused reservoirs. The new infrastructure, along with previously built reservoirs and individual farm-sized water storage tanks, irrigated almost half of the country's cropland at the time of independence.

The extensive irrigation system built in the Punjab province of British-controlled India represents the kind of big infrastructure thinking that forever changed the way that food is grown across much of the subcontinent. Before colonization, farmers relied on canals for irrigation during periods of high river flow. Outside of the flat areas adjacent to rivers that could be flooded easily, most of Punjab's drylands were used for grazing. When the British took control, they partnered with local elites to repair the canal system and build an irrigation project that triggered a mass migration to British-administered canal colonies. Through control of land ownership and irrigation water, a system was established in which sharecroppers living in the colonies worked the land for wealthy landlords.[11] By the 1950s, the peasant farmers were growing wheat, rice, and cotton on more than ten million hectares of irrigated farmland.

After independence, both India and Pakistan continued to expand the surface water irrigation network while maintaining the land ownership system set up by the British.[12] Presently, the Indus Basin Project—the largest contiguous irrigation system in the world—provides over 95 percent of Pakistan's irrigation water, serving nineteen million hectares of farmland. On the Indian side of the border, the modern descendent of the colonial canal project supplies almost seven million hectares of farmland with water supporting Punjab's role as India's most irrigated state.

Building upon the legacy of big water projects, the Indian government has continued to expand its water infrastructure.[13] Between 1950 to 2000, the area being irrigated with surface water more than doubled as the country invested billions of dollars in reservoirs and canals. Government-funded water infrastructure projects are still going strong, with ambitious new systems, such as the eleven-billion-dollar Kaleshwaram Lift Irrigation Project—the world's biggest water-lifting project—opening in the central part of the country in 2019 and construction of a long-discussed eighty-seven-billion-dollar project to connect northern rivers receiving Himalayan snowmelt to rivers that deliver irrigation water to canals in the south getting underway in 2017.

Access to irrigation water has always offered Indian farmers the promise of higher crop yields and protection from droughts, but during the first half of the twentieth century, the country's canals were inaccessible to millions of small landholders who lacked political influence or the good fortune of being located on land served by a government water project. An alternative water source had always been present beneath many of the fields of the excluded farmers, but not until a three-year drought that started in 1964 did they acquire the means to exploit it. In response to a drought-driven decline in domestic food production, the government began to subsidize well drilling and the provision of electricity for pumps that could access shallow groundwater.[14] The shallow wells allowed farmers to take advantage of the new seed varieties and inexpensive fertilizers that accompanied the Green Revolution while simultaneously helping to relieve some of the problems of waterlogged soils that had been brought about when the canal system had raised the region's water table.

This government subsidy program quickly spread from the Punjab region.[15] Between 1960 and 2000, the number of irrigation wells in India increased from fewer than two hundred thousand to around nineteen million. Within a decade, groundwater had surpassed surface water as the main source of irrigation water in India. Despite the government spending on new surface water storage projects, groundwater use continued to increase. Between 1991 and 2007, the area of fields irrigated by surface water decreased by almost four million hectares as farmers turned their backs on poorly maintained yet highly regulated canal systems. Today, India is the world's groundwater extraction leader, with its farmers pumping more than twice as much groundwater each year as their counterparts in the United States or China.

The growing popularity of groundwater required a vast expansion of electricity service across rural India. After power lines were extended to remote locations, the effort required to read meters and protect them from tampering accounted for about a third of the costs incurred by the electricity providers. To simplify matters and fight corruption, state-run utilities made a fateful decision to switch to flat-rate billing starting in the 1980s.[16] Under the new system, electricity charges were based on the horsepower rating of groundwater pumps. The change created an incentive for farmers to extract groundwater around the clock, selling any excess water to neighbors who could not afford their own wells. At about the same time, politicians began attracting rural voters to their parties with promises of cheap electricity. In some cases, the electricity to run groundwater pumps was provided for free.

Because the utilities could not keep up with growing electricity demands, rural service became less reliable.[17] In response, farmers in the eastern part of the country switched to diesel-powered pumps to access groundwater from the region's shallow alluvial aquifers. But electricity was essential in the western and peninsular regions, where a greater depth to groundwater rendered the use of diesel-powered pumps impractical. Facing growing demand and shrinking revenues, the cash-strapped utilities underinvested in maintenance and cut power provision to a few hours per day. Farmers responded by installing bigger pumps to maximize the amount of water that they could obtain during the hours when electricity was available. This chaotic situation resulted in frequent interruptions in service and higher bills for people living in villages who relied upon electricity to operate their businesses, light their schools, and run their medical clinics.

By 2007, groundwater pumps were consuming close to 15 percent of India's power, while electricity subsidies were soaking up around ten billion dollars of the government's annual budget. The expansion of groundwater irrigation was also depleting the country's aquifers. For example, in the Kukarwada subdistrict of Gujarat's Mehsana region, average groundwater levels fell by about eighty meters between 1980 and 2000.[18] As the water levels in Kukarwada's aquifer dropped, the amount of electricity needed to pump water to the surface tripled. By the early 2000s, the actual cost of the electricity needed for irrigation was approximately equal to the value of the food produced in the Indian states that were relying upon subsidies to run their groundwater pumps.[19]

A promising remedy to the situation was proposed by the International Water Management Institute in the early 2000s. By separating the electricity lines going to groundwater pumps from those that powered homes and businesses, the government could control the amount of groundwater being pumped while simultaneously assuring a continuous supply in towns and villages. Between 2003 and 2006, the state of Gujarat invested about $250 million to separate its electric lines as part of the Jyotirgram Yojana (literally "village lighting") scheme.[20] After the program got underway, power use by the agricultural sector dropped by about 20 percent. While villagers praised the uninterrupted electricity, farmers complained about government control of their water supply. But the change was not as disruptive as many had feared. Despite the inability of farmers to pump unlimited supplies of groundwater, agricultural productivity was maintained because irrigation water was available during the crucial thirty-to-forty-day window when demand peaked.

The main innovation of the Jyotirgram Yojana scheme—separating power supplies for pumps and villages—soon spread to other water-stressed states through government investments of around $3.5 billion.[21]

The decision to copy the program could be justified by the benefits that continuous power brought to rural villages, but evidence that the scheme would solve the groundwater depletion problem was hard to find because many other aspects of Gujarat's hydrology had changed simultaneously.[22] As it was untangling the agricultural and municipal power supplies, the state government had invested in local programs to install hundreds of thousands of small ponds and check dams to enhance groundwater recharge. Gujarat also began to receive water from the newly opened Sardar Sarovar project—a massive reservoir and canal system that is home to the second largest concrete dam in the world. Finally, the region entered a wetter period, with average rainfall increasing by about 30–50 percent. All these favorable factors meant that between 2003 and 2014 the trend of groundwater depletion was reversed throughout much of the state. Nevertheless, it is clear that the demand-side approach of the Jyotirgram Yojana scheme had not been able to steer clear of the Jevons paradox: after a brief period of decline between 2003 and 2006, which took place as the power lines were being separated, groundwater use by Gujarat's farmers gradually increased, reaching preintervention levels by 2012.[23] Because electricity subsidies had not been removed, farmers who could no longer buy groundwater from their neighbors had simply installed their own wells, proving once again that increases in water use efficiency or importation of water in the absence of effective programs to regulate its use will not bring about sustainable water management.

Despite declining aquifer levels in productive agricultural regions and a growing recognition that megaprojects are not keeping up with demand for irrigation water, demand reduction remains the road less traveled in India.[24] An effort to improve water use efficiency got underway in 2021, with the government providing around one billion dollars to help transition farmers away from inefficient flood irrigation practices by subsidizing the purchase of sprinklers and microirrigation systems. However, the program is probably out of reach of most small landholders, who lack the resources needed to buy and maintain irrigation equipment. Moreover, the Indian government's policies related to water efficiency rarely include provisions for reducing overall water use. As a result, if India stays on its current path, it is quite likely that gains made by investment in sprinklers and microirrigation systems will fall victim to the Jevons paradox.

If India's growing water demands continue to outpace its efforts to increase supply and adopt more efficient irrigation practices, groundwater levels in many regions will eventually recede to a point at which pumping will become impractical. When that happens, some farmers will either fallow their fields or return to the practices that their predecessors employed before cheap pumps and subsidized electricity. Rainfed agriculture had long been a way of life for small landholders in all but the most arid parts of the country, because irrigation offered only modest yield increases for such drought-tolerant crops as sorghum, pearl millet, and chickpeas.[25] The big attraction of irrigation water has always been profitable crops such as sugarcane and wheat as well as the ability to plant a second crop during wintertime, after residual moisture from the monsoon runs out. Groundwater also has offered security during drought years, when water scarcity would have caused severe economic hardship.

Although it is usually less profitable, rainfed agriculture exists side by side with irrigation in most of the world's major agricultural regions. Outside of desert climates where rainfed agriculture is impossible, the decisions that farmers make about which fields to irrigate is dictated by a complex set of calculations that consider market conditions, the cost of irrigation water, and its effect on yields. In India, about half of the food is currently grown without irrigation, often adjacent to fields where irrigation is taking place.[26] In places that have not made large investments in water infrastructure, irrigation is still the exception to the rule. When water is in short supply, irrigation tends to be reserved for crops that generate the greatest profit, such as fresh fruits and vegetables.

Rainfed agriculture is especially important to sub-Saharan Africa, where only about 5 percent of farmland is irrigated. As the region's population growth and economic expansion drives up food demand, large surface water storage projects once again are becoming attractive to development banks and government officials, despite shortcomings in design and a lack of maintenance, which caused the majority of the large irrigation projects built in the region during the twentieth century to be characterized as failures.[27]

Starting around 2010, donor banks, national governments, and private companies began pouring in hundreds of millions of dollars to rehabilitate failed projects and initiate new projects in Kenya, Tanzania, and Malawi.[28] Nonetheless, many African water resource experts remain skeptical about the prospects for big infrastructure projects to play a major role in sub-Saharan Africa's future food system. Despite a newfound enthusiasm for irrigation schemes among development banks and governments, cost overruns, a mismatch between projects and the needs of local communities, as well as the logistical challenges that farmers face in getting crops to markets, seems likely to slow or prevent the widespread growth of irrigation in the region.

Unless development banks and governments can change the way that the continent's irrigation projects are designed, built, and operated, sub-Saharan Africa's farmers will be relying upon rainfed agriculture as they respond to the region's growing food needs. Fortunately, there are many opportunities for them to increase crop yields without big irrigation projects. Agronomists have identified a substantial yield gap— a difference between the currently crop yields and the amount that can be grown if farmers were to use all the best available practices— throughout much of sub-Saharan Africa.[29] In the savannah and steppe biomes where the bulk of the region's food is grown, modest changes in farming practices have the potential to double yields of many popular crops.

Water scarcity in rainfed agriculture can be addressed without resorting to big infrastructure projects. By contouring the land, terracing hillsides, and building drainage ditches in the right places, farmers can better use the rainfall they receive. African farmers have also created small-scale surface water storage systems that provide irrigation water during critical dry periods when water stress would otherwise lower crop yields. Other practices that reduce water evaporation from the soil, such as cover crops and mulch, or minimizing the frequency and intensity of plowing, also conserve water. To spread these kinds of best practices throughout the region, proponents advocate for policies that channel some of the money that would have gone into irrigation infrastructure into farmer education programs and subsidies for more efficient water practices.

The potential for making rainfed agriculture more productive is not limited to sub-Saharan Africa. Farmers in water-stressed parts of Asia and Latin America can adapt the techniques being pioneered in sub-Saharan Africa. However, efforts to spread best practices for rainfed agriculture have been hampered by a lack of funding. Many of the world's donor agencies and national governments still view rainfed agriculture as a risky, inefficient endeavor that leaves farmers vulnerable to droughts. When they do succeed, big infrastructure projects rapidly increase agricultural productivity and make farming more predictable. They also attract outside investments in large farming operations that further enhance domestic food production. But in terms of poverty alleviation and fighting hunger, putting resources into programs that improve rainfed agriculture have the potential to yield greater benefits for rural communities.[30] The main challenge in closing the yield gap in rainfed agriculture will be to overcome the attitudes of institutions that are still enamored with big irrigation projects.

If water use in rainfed agriculture does become more efficient, rivers, lakes, and estuaries would likely receive less water. After all, any practice that retains more water on large swaths of land means that less runoff moves downstream. Eventually, more efficient use of rainfall could be just as deleterious to ecosystems as diversion for irrigation. Yet in watersheds where best practices for water retention in rainfed agriculture have been adopted, there is little evidence that downstream flows have substantially decreased. In part, this could be because even in places where adoption of water retention practices is common, there is still plenty of undeveloped land where water migration to streams is unchanged. Nonetheless, water resource managers will need to remain vigilant about possible unintended consequences of more efficient water use in places where water retention practices are widely implemented.

Despite the great promise of demand management solutions, making water use more efficient does not always prevent water crises. All too often, gains in water efficiency fall victim to the Jevons paradox. In many cities, decreases in per capita water consumption have simply enabled additional urban growth without returning flows to the environment. In agriculture, efficient irrigation technologies frequently have provided the means for farmers to shift to more water-intensive crops and to expand the amount of land they irrigate. As long as the institutions responsible for applying these practices do not prioritize policies that decrease the overall amount of water being taken from the environment, the world will be just as susceptible to ecological crises and water scarcity.

EXPANDING CONVENTIONAL
WATER SUPPLIES

Water infrastructure is the circulatory system of civilization.

DURING THE GREAT Acceleration, the world went on a water infrastructure spending spree, building tens of thousands of reservoirs and drilling wells wherever a decent yield of water could be obtained. As a result, in the most densely populated parts of the world, it is hard to find a river that is not dammed or an aquifer without wells.

Only after decades of investment did the true cost of water infrastructure projects become evident. Beyond the labor and materials needed for construction, society sacrificed other forms of wealth in the name of water security. Tens of millions of people were displaced to make way for reservoirs; millions more lost their livelihoods as fisheries were decimated by changing river flows. Dams also contributed to public health crises by creating conditions ideal for disease. The damage was not limited to people: dams blocked the paths of migrating fish and starved rivers of the sediments needed to maintain fertile floodplains.

Groundwater exploitation created its own set of problems. When aquifers were pumped faster than they could be replenished, wetlands and rivers dried up. Overuse of groundwater also led to land subsidence that placed river deltas and coastal communities at greater risk of flooding.

By the latter part of the twentieth century, an exclusive focus on meeting water needs by building big water projects had lost its luster in wealthy countries. In rapidly developing countries, international banks began to question investments in water infrastructure projects. Although the rate of construction has slowed and project designs have been modified to minimize their impacts, reservoirs, canals, and wells remain the dominant water sources throughout most of the world. Projects that fostered the development of farms and cities in the twentieth century may become obsolete in a more arid climate. Humanity now faces important questions about the best ways to manage, modify, and in some cases expand water infrastructure as the climate changes and projects built during the twentieth century reach the end of their design lives.

12

~~~~~~

A Dam Legacy

TO MOST PEOPLE, THE large dam is synonymous with water supply. According to the most widely used definition, large dams are over fifteen meters high. Dams between five and fifteen meters tall also are classified as large if they impound more than three million cubic meters of water. In 2020, the world had about 58,700 large dams capable of storing approximately eight trillion cubic meters (or, if you prefer, eight thousand cubic kilometers) of water—an amount that is roughly equivalent to 16 percent of annual global river flow.[1] Four countries—the United States, China, Brazil, and India—accounted for over two-thirds of the global storage capacity of large dams.

The ways that large dams are used varies with location. In Asia and Africa, most are used for irrigation, whereas in Europe and South America, hydropower was the most popular reason for building large dams. In North America, most large dams were built for flood control. However, simplistic classifications can be misleading because dams frequently serve multiple purposes. After all, if a dam is built to prevent flooding, it does not take much additional effort to include a turbine to generate electricity as it fulfills its obligations to deliver water to downstream users who divert it into irrigation canals and drinking water treatment plants. And if a huge lake sits behind the dam, its owners might as well set up a marina for boating and fishing. In many cases, the multiple functions of dams—flood control, power production, provision of irrigation water, municipal water supply, and the creation of recreational opportunities—have been used in different combinations to build support for new projects.

Beyond large dams, humanity has created almost too many small dams to count.[2] Using satellite imagery, researchers estimate that there are around 16.7 million surface water impoundments larger than one hundred square meters on Earth, most of which were built for the same purposes as large dams, but at a smaller scale. Although the world's large dams store over four times as much water, these less impressive structures play a critical role in water management. Ponds and small reservoirs provide water for livestock and supplemental irrigation for farmers. Small dams protect communities from floods and supply water and power to remote villages. They can also wreak havoc on ecosystems by creating barriers to the movement of fish, nutrients, and sediments.

Concerns about the adverse impacts of large dams were instrumental in the birth of the environmental movement.[3] Opposition to San Francisco's plan to build a dam across Yosemite National Park's Hetch Hetchy Valley brought John Muir and the Sierra Club to prominence in the United States in the early twentieth century as they questioned the assumption that nature is less important than the need for water and power. In the 1950s, opposition to a series of proposed dams along the Colorado River, first at Echo Park, Colorado, and then at Glen Canyon, on the southern border of Utah, brought the Sierra Club and its new leader, David Brower, back into the spotlight. Although the group eventually lost its battle to stop the Glen Canyon Dam, the Sierra Club's fights against water projects increased awareness of the nascent environmental movement that went on to lobby for the laws and policies to prevent further dam construction in the United States.

Elsewhere in the world, efforts to stop large dams and water diversion projects got started later than they did in the United States. Often, the rights of communities affected by big water projects were the main motivation for the groups leading these efforts. As a result of their focus on affected communities, their struggles had impacts that spread well beyond water resource management: opposition to big water projects nurtured a social movement that advocated for the rights of Indigenous people and gave voice to poor people who were being ignored by governments focused on satisfying the needs of wealthy urbanites and large corporations.

In Europe, an eight-billion-dollar government plan to divert much of the flow of northern Spain's Ebro River to farms and cities in the south served as a focal point for the country's successful antidam movement. Organized opposition to the project began in the early 1990s, after a team of academics from the University of Zaragoza, located in the heart of the Ebro River watershed, documented the damage that the Francisco Franco dictatorship's dams had caused to the region's rural communities during the 1960s.[4] To stop a newly proposed water transfer project that would have affected scores of villages and altered the ecology of the entire river basin, a consortium of researchers and community groups partnered with the environmental advocacy group Greenpeace to create the Association of People Affected by Large Reservoirs and Water Transfers (COAGRET) in 1995. Rallying behind the concept of a "new water culture" in which rivers have social and environmental values that supersede the state's interests in economic development, Spain's antidam movement held a series of well-attended protests in Barcelona, Madrid, and Brussels.

The attention that the group brought to the likely impacts of the water transfer turned public opinion against the project and influenced the European Union's decision to withdraw its financial support. In 2004, the government canceled the Ebro River project and announced that it would invest in agricultural water use efficiency and seawater desalination plants along the southern coast.[5] After its victory, Spain's antidam movement continued its efforts, slowing other domestic water projects and sharing its experiences with groups opposing water supply projects in Europe and Latin America.

In India, completion of Gujarat's Sardar Sarovar Dam was delayed by decades as a progression of groups protested and litigated against the project. The massive dam had been a key element of a larger plan conceived by the government of Prime Minister Jawaharlal Nehru to wean the newly independent country from its reliance on imported food. The delay commenced shortly after construction began in 1961 as the three provinces that relied upon the Narmada River fought over water rights.[6] After the dispute was resolved in 1978, middle-income and wealthy farmers in communities that were slated to be flooded rallied against the dam. To expand the opposition's appeal beyond the interests of affluent farmers, they linked their struggle with the growing sentiment in Indian society that economic development unleashed by the Green Revolution was inconsistent with the goal of alleviating poverty and income inequality.

By 1987, leadership of the struggle had shifted to Medha Patkar, a charismatic activist who turned the focus of the movement to the quarter-million poor people who would be displaced by the project.[7] In addition to criticizing the technical details, Patkar and her fellow dam opponents tied their struggle to the larger cause of resisting neoliberalism and globalization. To convince foreign donors to rescind funding promised for the dam, the activists placed more emphasis on the ecological impacts of the project while expanding their reach through a partnership with the Environmental Defense Fund—a US-based group that was engaged in a global campaign against problematic international development projects.

These efforts convinced the World Bank and the Overseas Economic Cooperation Fund of Japan (JICA) to pull out of the project in 1993. Afterward, Patkar and her allies used the courts to delay the project for another decade. The Sardar Sarovar Dam's proponents persevered, ultimately prevailing in their legal arguments and obtaining the money needed for completion of the project by issuing domestic bonds. In 2017, over half a century after Nehru laid the foundation stone of the structure, Prime Minister Narendra Modi celebrated his sixty-seventh birthday by opening the dam's gates to officially mark the end of construction.[8]

By the late 1990s, controversies over the Ebro River scheme, the Sardar Sarovar Dam, and other large dams and water transfer projects had contributed to a growing sense among many staff members at development banks and aid agencies that the adverse impacts of their loans and grants were not receiving enough consideration in the decision-making process. It would be difficult for financiers to walk away from big water entirely, because the projects were still seen as crucial to the fight against hunger and poverty. In an effort to make better decisions, the World Bank helped establish the World Commission on Dams—an independent body with a mission of evaluating the costs and benefits of large dams and identifying approaches for improving the ways that they were planned, built, and operated.[9]

The commission was chaired by Kader Asmal, a well-regarded leader of the antiapartheid movement who had gained experience in water management by running South Africa's Ministry of Water and Forestry. To ensure a diversity of perspectives, the other eleven members of the commission included scientists who had studied the impacts of dams, engineers who had built and operated them, and advocates who had opposed projects. Between 1998 and 2000, the group held regional consultations where they met with about 1,400 participants from fifty-nine countries. Commission members and their staff also analyzed case studies and pulled together data on the economic performance and impacts of hundreds of projects worldwide.

The team's final report endorsed much of what opponents to large dams had been saying—namely, that the damage caused by dams often outweighed their benefits.[10] Perhaps more importantly, the commission offered guidance on how large dam projects could benefit from participatory decision-making and explicit consideration of risks associated with projects.

Although the World Commission on Dams had no official power, it received a lot of attention. After the group's report was released, financing for dams declined as the World Bank and European development banks gave greater scrutiny to dams and water transfer projects. In places where such infrastructure could be built without support from donor countries, the report's concerns served as a focal point for antidam groups. The work of the commission also affected the dam industry, with many construction companies and consultants integrating

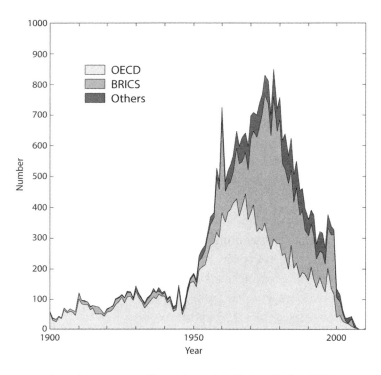

Annual construction of large dams globally from 1900 to 2010.

limited versions of the report's recommended participatory planning process to gain support from affected communities and local governments. Despite its prominence, the World Commission on Dams' report had less of an effect in the three countries that had the most active dam-building enterprises because the governments of China, India, and Brazil did not abide by the commission's findings.

Perhaps the steep decline in dam construction that occurred during the first decade of the twenty-first century would have taken place without the World Commission on Dams' report. After all, the most obvious projects had already been built and much of society had already soured on big water projects by the time the commission started its work. Nonetheless, the report is a milestone in the history of water resource development because it succinctly summarized the controversies surrounding dam construction and provided guidance on ways that the decision-making process could be made more inclusive. After the report was released, it was unlikely that a construction company, a bank, and government officials could design a successful dam project without soliciting input from the people who would be most affected.

Despite the recent decrease in the rate of construction of large dams, water supply infrastructure continues to be built.[11] In response to growing water demands, twenty-five big water transfer projects, representing a 75 percent increase in number relative to the number of existing projects, currently are under construction, mostly in Asia, the Middle East, and Southern Africa. A surge in the construction of small- and medium-sized hydroelectric dams has also begun recently as countries have initiated projects to help them meet their greenhouse gas emission reduction targets. By 2015, enough projects were being built or were in the planning stage in Asia, South America, Africa, and the Caucasus to nearly double the world's hydroelectric production capacity. Many of these efforts consist of run-of-the-river power plants where the construction of large dams is avoided by diverting a portion of a river's flow through turbines inside of pipes or tunnels running parallel to the river. The recent popularity of such projects is particularly concerning in the biodiversity hotspots of Southeastern Europe (Slovenia, Croatia, Bosnia and Herzegovina, Serbia, and Montenegro), where some of the last free-running rivers on the continent are being harnessed for electricity production.

Whether or not all the water transfer projects and hydroelectric plants currently under construction or in the planning stage come to fruition, it seems reasonable to assume that new projects, especially those where the primary purpose is water supply, will never again be built at the rates seen during the height of the Great Acceleration. However, a lack of new projects does not mean that the industry's bulldozers, concrete mixers, and backhoes will be silenced. The water infrastructure projects of the twentieth century are poised to receive billions of dollars in additional spending in the coming decades for three main reasons.

First, many of the world's dams are reaching the end of their design lives. When they were being built, engineers established schedules for maintaining or replacing mechanical and electronic control systems on dams as they aged. Although their contracts may have stipulated that the dams had to last only fifty years, project designers recognized that the structures that they were creating might remain in place for centuries. To decrease the risk of failure, they used the most durable materials that they could find for the difficult-to-repair load-bearing parts of the projects. Nonetheless, there are limitations to the lifetime of concrete and other durable materials that are integral to most large dams. The need to pay more attention to deterioration of these materials and to renovate other parts of aging structures is particularly pressing in North America and Asia, where about 2,300 large dams are already more than a century old.[12] The situation for small- and medium-sized dams is even worse; worldwide, tens of thousands of dams have already reached the end of their design lifetimes, often without owners who consider it their responsibility to keep up with the necessary maintenance.

If society skimps on dam upkeep or fails to detect weaknesses in aging structures, the consequences could be catastrophic. For example, a disaster nearly took place during the winter of 2017, when a storm dumped more than twenty centimeters of warm rain onto the foothills of California's Sierra Nevada.[13] As an exceptionally large volume of rainwater and melted snow flowed into Lake Oroville, the operators of the tallest dam in the United States attempted to release water to reduce the risk of overtopping the structure—a dangerous condition that can lead to dam collapse. Because parts of the spillway had worn away over the five decades since the structure had been built, a design flaw allowed water to get under the weakened concrete, causing a section of the channel to fail, which in turn necessitated the evacuation of more than 180,000 people and about a billion dollars in repairs.

According to the American Society of Civil Engineers, rehabilitation of dams in the United States will cost approximately ninety billion dollars in the next two to three decades. In places where construction took place later in the last century, the need for spending on dam maintenance is just starting to become apparent, with China and India allocating billions of dollars for rehabilitation projects recently. As the world's dams continue to age, simply maintaining the status quo will keep the construction industry busy.[14]

The second reason that more activity is likely is that many obsolete dams will need to be removed.[15] This is especially true in Europe and the northeastern United States, where tens of thousands of small dams were built to power factories and provide water to towns during the Industrial Revolution. A recent analysis conducted in the United Kingdom, France, Spain, and Poland identified about thirty thousand small dams that are no longer needed, with a similar number of obsolete structures present throughout New England. China also has tens of thousands of obsolete dams, many of which were built as the country pursued rapid development in the second half of the twentieth century. Although the ponds and engineered channels associated with old dams may seem like part of the landscape, they have had substantial impacts on ecosystems, altering the movement of biota, nutrients, and sediments. They also damaged downstream habitats by altering water temperatures, depleting oxygen from water that they retain, and creating conditions conducive to the growth of toxic algae. Now that many of these structures are no longer needed, their removal could help restore riverine habitats. However, the safe removal of dams requires more than demolishing an unwanted structure.

Before taking down a dam, project planners must figure out how to manage the many tons of sediments that have accumulated behind the structure. These materials may require careful handling because they could contain elevated concentrations of toxic manmade chemicals, as was the case when the obsolete Fort Edward Dam on New York's Hudson River was demolished by the Niagara Mohawk Power Company in 1973.[16] Unbeknown to the construction workers who removed the decaying dam, the sediments behind the nine-meter-high structure were contaminated with polychlorinated biphenyls (PCBs) from a pair of nearby General Electric factories. Although the dam removal project was not the cause of the contamination, its removal spread toxic PCBs hundreds of kilometers downstream. Cleaning up the PCB-contaminated sediment in the Hudson River ultimately cost around $1.6 billion and caused considerable damage to the ecosystem and fishery.

Even if the sediments trapped behind obsolete dams are not contaminated, their fate must be considered during the demolition process because the release of large amounts of material over a short period alters river features, burying aquatic habitat and frustrating landowners and recreational users for years as the riverbed adjusts to its new conditions.[17]

Despite the potential risks associated with the release of sediments, dam removal is often the best way to restore damaged river systems. As a result, obsolete dams have been coming down at a rapid pace in countries where there is a strong desire for river restoration.[18] In the United States, approximately 1,800 dams were removed between 1912 and 2021, with a nearly exponential growth in the number of projects taking place since the 1980s. In Europe, more than 5,000 small dams, weirs, and culverts have been taken down over the past two decades. The demolition of small dams and other obsolete structures usually requires only a modest amount of planning and permitting because the volume of sediments mobilized by projects tends to be relatively small, which allows the river and the communities that rely upon it to adjust rapidly to the new conditions.

The removal of large dams is another matter. Decades of hard work are often required to obtain funding, navigate local politics, and develop a credible plan to manage sediments. As a result, only about a hundred large dams have ever been removed in the United States.[19] Among these projects, the demolition of a pair of dams in Washington's Olympic National Park—the largest project yet completed—provides insight into the magnitude of the challenge.

Removal of the sixty-four-meter-high Glines Canyon Dam and the nearby thirty-two-meter-high Elwha Dam, cost over $320 million and required over three decades of sustained effort.[20] The struggle to take down the dams got underway in earnest in the mid-1980s, when the

Lower Elwha Klallam Tribe—the Indigenous people living at the mouth of the Elwha River—and local environmental groups began lobbying for dam removal to restore the river's salmon migration. In 1992, Congress authorized the purchase of the dams from the timber company that owned them. But that was just the start; bringing the project to fruition took two more decades. First, the dam removal proponents were thwarted by Washington's Republican senator Slade Gorton, who tied his support for the project to passage of unpopular legislation that would have prevented future removal of large dams on the Columbia and Snake Rivers. After Gorton lost his reelection bid in 2000, another decade passed as the government negotiated with the tribe on plans to manage the twenty million cubic meters of sediment that would be released by the project. The dams finally were removed in 2011, after two treatment plants were opened to provide downstream communities with access to sediment-free drinking water along with a salmon hatchery that was installed to speed up the restoration process. Within a few years, most of the sediment had been flushed out of the river, the salmon had returned, and the ecosystem was restored to a much healthier state.

The third reason that an increase in spending on dams is likely to take place in the near term involves the expansion of existing reservoirs. Raising the height of a dam is usually the easiest way to increase water storage capacity, especially in places where opposition to new dams and water transfer projects is well established. Furthermore, as a changing climate increases variability in weather patterns, proposals to raise the height of dams become more attractive: access to larger reservoirs gives water managers more flexibility to protect communities from more variable river flows as droughts and floods intensify. In terms of project cost and the amount of effort required to overcome public opposition, raising an existing dam tends to be faster and cheaper than acquiring land, flooding pristine land, and building the necessary access roads and related infrastructure.

As water managers in the western United States have sought out additional water storage, dam expansion has started to become more popular.[21] The trend picked up momentum in 2012, when the capacity of San Diego's largest reservoir was more than doubled through an $840 million dam-raising project. In 2020, Denver Water received a permit for a $460 million project to triple the storage capacity of its Gross Reservoir, thereby increasing the city's water storage capacity by around 10 percent. Proponents of supply-side solutions now are pursuing a $1.4 billion project to expand California's Shasta Reservoir (the largest in the state) and another $3 billion to expand two reservoirs that provide water to cities in the San Francisco Bay Area.

It is unclear whether the rest of the world will follow the lead of the western United States in investments in dam expansion projects. The trend has recently spread to Australia, with construction planning getting underway on a dam-raising project that could end up costing as much as $1.6 billion to provide more irrigation water to farmers in the Murray-Darling River system.[22]

13

A Second Chance for Dams

AS THE WORLD PREPARES to spend hundreds of billions of dollars to rehabilitate, remove, and raise dams, along with vast sums of money that might yet end up going toward additional water transfer projects and a few more large dams in Asia, Africa, and South America, it is worth reflecting on a few of the lessons of the Great Acceleration. Recent experience has provided considerable insight into the ways that surface water storage and water diversion projects can damage aquatic ecosystems and decrease the standard of living for people who rely upon the rivers where the projects have been built. In some cases, engineers have figured out how to retrofit dams or adapt their operations to reduce these impacts. If additional spending on dams and water transfer projects is going to take place, it seems prudent to use some of those funds to improve the situation. In other words, now that humanity has taken control of the world's rivers, some future funding could support a more deliberate approach for managing the sediments, biota, and water that this infrastructure is disrupting.

Starting with the sediments, the problem stems from a simple physical phenomenon: suspended particles carried by flowing water settle out when the velocity drops at the entrance to a reservoir.[1] Over time, the accumulation of sediments behind dams, a process referred to as siltation, substantially reduces water storage capacity. It also deprives downstream sections of rivers of the minerals and organic matter needed to renew habitat, replace eroded soil, build up deltas, and reduce flood risks. Worldwide, dams trap about a quarter of all sediments carried by rivers. Due to siltation, global surface water storage actually peaked around 2006, as reservoirs started filling with sediments faster than new storage capacity was being created.

Current projections that siltation will cut the world's surface water storage capacity in half by the end of the twenty-first century would not have surprised the people who designed the dams of the Great Acceleration: the gradual loss of water storage and eventual obsolescence of dams by siltation has always been part of the plan. During the twentieth century, the decision about building a dam was dictated by whether the economic benefits of water storage, power production, and flood control delivered over the project's design lifetime (typically fifty years) would be greater than the cost of building and maintaining it.[2] Because the economic models used to conduct these assessments employed discounting, the first few decades of operation—before siltation reduced the project's water storage capacity—were much more important than the later period when the storage capacity was expected to be shrunk by siltation. Discounting also meant that the impact of changing river flows as well as the eventual costs borne by future generations who would manage obsolete reservoirs had little bearing on the decision about whether the structures would be built.

Siltation was simply accepted as an inevitable process that would gradually shrink water storage capacity and in many cases lead to the retirement of dams. Nonetheless, some projects could not be justified from an economic standpoint if they did not include measures to slow siltation. When sediment management was deemed necessary, engineers offered a host of ways to attack the problem.[3]

The simplest and least disruptive approach followed the saying attributed to Laozi, "Muddy water, let stand, becomes clear." For example, at China's Three Gorges Dam—the largest producer of hydroelectric power in the world—the water level is lowered at the start of the flood season to allow the sediment-laden waters of the Yangtze River to pass through the reservoir. At the tail end of the flood season, when suspended particle concentrations drop, the height of the reservoir is raised, impounding water that drops less sediment as it slows down. This approach decreases the rate of siltation, but a substantial fraction of the river's sediment load still gets deposited behind the dam.[4] In about a century, sediments from the Yangtze are expected to have filled about 40 percent of the reservoir. After this point, the depth of the sediments will be such that flowing water moving through the long, narrow reservoir (water impounded behind the dam covers an area that is about seven hundred kilometers long and only around one kilometer wide) will assure that the deposition of new sediment will be balanced by the resuspension of previously deposited material. Losing close to half of the reservoir to siltation will cut its storage capacity, but the project will still be able to deliver plenty of electricity and flood protection. Until that equilibrium state is reached, retention of nutrient-rich sediments in the reservoir will continue to shrink the Yangtze Delta and reduce the productivity of the East China Sea.

Another strategy for managing siltation is to periodically remove accumulated sediments from reservoirs.[5] The intuitively obvious ways of taking out sediments, dredging the bottom or draining the reservoir and hauling sediments away in dump trucks, are prohibitively expensive. As a result, these techniques tend to be employed only in small reservoirs or are used in a targeted manner to remove sediments that threaten to bury dam intake structures. A more cost-effective approach for reversing the effects of siltation is to drop the water level to a point at which the inflow of water will create the turbulent conditions needed to resuspend accumulated sediment. The muddy water then is routed through an exit gate at the base of the dam. The limitation of this method is that it is only practical to empty reservoirs that hold a small fraction of a river's annual flow (draining a reservoir is usually impractical if it takes more than a few months to refill it). For some reservoirs, it is also possible to employ this idea without emptying the reservoir if turbidity currents (dense, sediment-laden flows along the bottom of the reservoir) can be routed through low-level exit gates. Either way, the water that scours the accumulated sediments tends to follow the original river channel, meaning that sediments accumulated on the edges of the reservoir often remain in place after the sediment removal process has been completed.

Considering these experiences, it seems reasonable to conclude that the lifetimes of some reservoirs can be extended, provided that dam operators can break free of the attitude that projects must be cheap to build and can retain water whenever it suits their needs. In places where they could be installed, tunnels or bypass channels could be used to route sediment-laden water around dams, provided that someone is willing to pay their relatively high installation costs. Alterations in reservoir operations for siltation control might not require large capital investments, but they would come at a cost; they usually reduce water storage, hydroelectric power production, and flood control—the very benefits that were used to justify construction of dams. Perhaps such sacrifices in the economic performance of dams, compromises that would not have been acceptable under the decision-making process that originally justified the projects, are worthwhile in light of the long-term costs of siltation.

The need to consider the benefits of sediment management is becoming increasingly important as the operators of dams attempt to strike a balance between controlling siltation and providing water storage and electricity production. The hundreds of billions of dollars of spending on dam rehabilitation and siltation control that is about to take place will determine the future of the world's rivers for the rest of the century and beyond. Unlike the benefits-focused decision-making process of the Great Acceleration, this time society will pay more attention to the ecological and social costs of dams. For some dams, it will still make sense to invest in renovations, bypass channels, and operational changes that slow siltation rates, especially if there is a possibility that they will enable the projects to operate for longer periods. For others, recognition that the Sisyphean effort needed to stop siltation cannot be justified will force managers to confront choices between dam removal and more modest investments needed to maintain recreational reservoirs with little water storage capacity. Such reservoirs still might produce electricity in a less profitable run-of-the-river mode, with energy production dictated by river flows rather than consumer demand.

Knowledge gained during the Great Acceleration can also guide investments in other changes that can reduce the ecological damage caused by dams and water transfer projects. Beyond their impacts on sediments, water projects alter the ecology of river systems by changing flow patterns in a manner that favors a different set of fish, algae, and sediment-dwelling creatures than those found in undisturbed rivers. Although some of these alterations are unavoidable, there are usually ways of modifying dams to reduce these impacts. As is the case for siltation control, these changes typically require either large capital investments or changes in operating procedures that decrease the economic performance of the projects.

The first way of decreasing the impact of dams is to make it easier for fish to move around them.[6] To accommodate the need of migratory fish, such as salmon, shad, and herring, to return to their upstream spawning grounds, some dams have been equipped with fish passage structures. Because not all fish navigate these structures successfully, many experts prefer to use the more neutral term "fishways." Fish also need to move downstream, but it is generally assumed that they get around dams by traveling over weirs, swimming through underwater outlet gates, or, with varying degrees of success, passing through power turbines.

One of the most common ways to help fish move upstream is to install a fish ladder—a series of inclined chutes with baffles that break up the flow. Using such ladders, fish can gradually climb over a large dam, much in the manner that they would have navigated short ledges and pools in a steep section of a river.[7] For species that are disinclined to use ladders, a dam can be equipped with a fish elevator—a device that is exactly what it sounds like. Because fish do not naturally congregate in a square box and engage in idle conversation while staring up at lit numbers near the ceiling, they must be lured into elevators. In most cases, this is done by directing the flow of water in a manner that signals a path around the obstruction. After enough fish have entered the elevator, the door closes, and the elevator whisks them up the side of the dam. Upon arrival, the door opens, and the fish continue their journey. In rivers that contain several dams in close proximity, the elevator might exit into the back of a truck, making it possible for dam operators to chauffeur fish around a series of barriers.

Finally, on the more comical end of the spectrum, trapped fish can be routed into a pneumatic tube that literally shoots them up and over the dam.[8] In case you are curious, the internet has plenty of videos showing fish passing through an invention that is sometimes referred to as a salmon cannon.

The main problem with fishways is that one size does not fit all. Each species and set of river conditions require a slightly different fish passage solution. Fishways have worked out reasonably well for the energetic salmon of America's Pacific Northwest, whereas efforts to ensure the passage of less adventurous migrants, such as shad and eels in the northeast United States and Europe, have been less successful. When it comes to fishways, every dam must be equipped with a system that is easy to navigate: if only half of the fish manage to make it through each fishway, the probability that they will reach their spawning grounds will be low, especially on rivers consisting of a gauntlet of ten to twenty dams.

Even on rivers where biologists and engineers have figured out how to make dams passable to fish, the cost of retrofits can be prohibitive. For example, in 2010, the prospect of spending $250 million on fish ladders along with another $200 million in structural upgrades as part of the relicensing of four hydroelectric dams on the Klamath River led a power company to cut a deal with the State of California that kicked off the largest dam removal project in US history.[9] But it is not just cost that prevents the building of fish passage structures.

Beyond the West Coast of the United States, where there is some confidence that fishways can accomplish their purpose, knowledge about how to design and effectively operate fishways is still incomplete.[10] Furthermore, fishways are rarely built for nonmigratory fish, in part because enabling movement of species that do not need to travel up- and downstream as part of their reproductive cycle is often perceived to be unworthy of investment.

The other way that the ecological impacts of dams can be reduced is by altering the daily and seasonal flow of water to more closely match conditions that existed before the project was built.[11] For most of the dams designed at the height of the Great Acceleration, the release of water was scheduled in a manner that maximized economic returns. Thus, the daily and seasonal needs of power production, downstream water deliveries, and flood control led to radical changes in downstream flow patterns. Before the late 1960s, the effects of the altered flows on ecosystems usually received little consideration. As the environmental movement brought greater scrutiny to the damage caused by dams in the United States, many operators became subject to rules that ensured that river flows never dropped below some mandated minimum— usually 30–50 percent of the pre-project amount. Over time, increasingly complicated formulas were developed to determine the minimum instream flow needed to protect threatened rivers. By the 1980s, it had become evident that simply focusing on the period of lowest flow and its effect on a single prized species was ineffective. As fishery biologists learned more about the impacts of altered flow patterns, they concluded that the annual cycles of high and low flows were essential to ecosystem health. If alteration of the hydrology of a river was too extreme, the entire ecosystem would change as fish and insects that were better adapted to the new conditions replaced the natives.

With their newfound knowledge about the effect of flow and water quality on river ecology, dam operators can make better decisions about how to release water.[12] Knowing how to release water from a dam is not enough; river restoration often means giving up some of the economic benefits that dams are supposed to deliver. By its very nature, if a dam or diversion project is going to provide water, electricity, or flood protection, downstream flow patterns will be altered. Sending a little bit more water downstream during critical times of the year and refraining from the most disruptive actions, like releasing water of the wrong temperature or abruptly turning on and off the flow in response to afternoon surges in power demand, will improve conditions, but they will never return a river to its pristine, premodification state.

Today, an increasing number of dams are being operated in a manner that recognizes the needs of the downstream environment. More sediments are being sent downstream. Fishways are allowing migratory species to access their spawning grounds. Biologists work side by side with dam operators to find compromises between the needs of water supply, flood control, power production, and ecosystem protection. Despite these efforts, many of the world's rivers remain in a diminished state, vulnerable to additional stress from a changing climate. Although obsolete small dams that have subdivided rivers are gradually disappearing, the widespread removal of large dams is unlikely to happen anytime soon. Nor are we likely to see radical changes in the ways that large dams are operated. Humanity's need for water is just too great for us to kick the dam habit.

14

Storing Water Underground

IN RESPONSE TO GROWING water scarcity and the slowdown in dam construction, managers are facing the seemingly impossible task of increasing the water supply without expanding the storage capacity of reservoirs. Some believe that they have found a solution in a source that thus far has eluded their best efforts to control it: capturing high flows during wet years or during parts of normal years when dams are too full to retain any more water and storing it below ground.

In the western United States, where much of the precipitation arrives in a few large storms, dam operators believe that they have figured out how to do this simply by paying better attention to the weather. To reduce the risk that a storm might overtop their dams, water managers historically have taken a cautious approach when setting reservoir levels, especially during the rainy season or periods when a thick layer of snow is present in the watershed. To safely capture more of this water, dam operators can take advantage of the increasing accuracy of long-range weather forecasts.[1]

Equipped with better predictions about the size of incoming storms and the amount of water that is likely to flow into their reservoirs, operators can continually adjust water levels to strike a better balance between flood risk and water storage. Several days before a major storm is expected to arrive, operators release just enough water to create the storage capacity needed to accommodate the predicted flows. The result is that, except for the period when a storm is approaching, the reservoir remains nearly full. This approach, known as forecast-informed reservoir operation, increases the water supply by cutting back on the portion of the reservoir set aside for incoming water. The impact of this seemingly minor change can be substantial. For example, the operators of a dam located one hundred kilometers north of San Francisco reckon that they will be able to increase the volume of water stored in their reservoir at the end of the rainy season by about a third.[2]

Forecast-enhanced reservoir operation may help managers capture more wet-weather flows without raising dam heights, but it is an efficiency measure rather than a comprehensive solution. During the wettest years, a lot of water will still not be captured. Before the Great Acceleration, dam-free rivers delivered water and sediments onto floodplains in a cycle that shaped the landscape. The impact of floods extended beyond the deposition of sediments that maintained soil fertility and the creation of temporary water bodies that served as habitats for waterfowl, insects, mammals, and amphibians. Floodwater that percolated into the ground gradually seeped back into rivers, nurturing wetlands and establishing a base flow of cold water that sustained ecosystems during dry periods. Today, in many places, the need to protect cities, transportation networks, and farms from floods has severed the connection between rivers and the adjacent land. During high-flow periods, swollen rivers bypass the floodplain, as water rushes to the sea through concrete channels protected by levees. By returning some of this water to the floodplain it may be possible to increase water supplies while simultaneously improving ecosystem health.

Insights about the management of high flows can be gained by considering the ways that farmers in arid and semiarid parts of the world capture water that is available for a few hours or days immediately after storms. Around five thousand years ago, farmers in Yemen built an eighteen-meter-high rock and soil dam across part of a river where water flowed only during the period immediately after a storm. This massive structure diverted a portion of the floodwater that occasionally came barreling downstream onto their unplanted fields.[3] By not

blocking the entire channel, they avoided the problem of rapid siltation that would have made operation of a conventional dam impractical. The moisture remaining in the soil after the floodwater had percolated into the ground provided the ancient Yemeni farmers with a
means of producing food in a region where an increasingly arid climate
was making it difficult to grow crops. The diversion of floodwaters
onto dormant farm fields, which is known as spate irrigation, is still
practiced in the Middle East, North Africa, Central Asia, and the Horn
of Africa. It is also used in a few watersheds in arid parts of Chile and
Bolivia. Despite its effectiveness, spate irrigation occurs on less than
1 percent of the world's irrigated land because it works only in places
that have the right combination of weather, topography, and geology.
It also requires considerable knowledge about local conditions and a
high level of cooperation among water users.

Spate irrigation changed during the Great Acceleration due to the
widespread availability of inexpensive submersible pumps that helped
farmers access groundwater. For example, in the 1970s, World Bank
funding made it possible for farmers on Wadi Zabid—an ephemeral
river in Yemen's agricultural heartland—to capture larger floods. The
increased water diversion capacity allowed them to apply more floodwater to their fields, where it quickly percolated through the sandy
soil.[4] In other words, the larger volume of floodwater reaching the land
was saved for a later time when it could be recovered as groundwater.
By pumping shallow wells that had been recharged by spate irrigation,
the farmers were able to grow profitable cash crops, such as bananas
and mangoes. The change was not without costs, as the increased diversion deprived downstream farmers of the flows needed to maintain
their date groves. Eventually, the change in practice also threatened the
drinking water supply of the downstream communities. Existing laws
that gave the upstream farmers the right to take much of the extra water
during the rainy season made no provisions for assuring an equitable
distribution of this limited resource.

In 2019, as the communities downstream of Wadi Zabid teetered
on the edge of collapse, the government brought farmers from differ-

ent parts of the watershed together to work out an agreement to share the floodwater.[5] Beyond serving as an example of the possibility of renegotiating historic water rights in the name of fairness, the episode demonstrated the ways that "wasted" water flowing past a farmer's fields might be essential to the livelihood of their downstream neighbors.

Although the climate is quite different from the places where spate irrigation is practiced, the application of floodwaters to dormant farmland is receiving considerable attention in other water-stressed parts of the world. In California, much of the current interest in flood irrigation can be traced to an experiment that began in an orchard near Fresno during the winter of 2011. Frustrated by his inability to use the floodwaters that flowed past his fields, Dan Cameron, the manager of Terranova Ranch, opened a valve and flooded a few hundred hectares of vineyards.[6] Cameron's action was considered risky by his neighbors because farmers normally do everything in their power to keep floods off their fields.

Inundation of the dormant fields went against conventional wisdom that standing water would cause plant disease and that the roots of submerged plants would suffocate after soil microbes consumed the oxygen contained in the soil. Yet Terranova's dormant vines were not damaged by the temporary ponding of water because the water rapidly percolated into the ground. Subsequent research indicated that proper timing of floodwater application could simultaneously raise groundwater levels and minimize downstream flooding, which had been responsible for losses exceeding $1.4 billion in the surrounding region during the previous three decades.[7]

Following the successful experiments on Terranova Ranch, interest in this Californian version of spate irrigation grew in other parts of the Central Valley. Because most storms hit the northern part of the state, the farms in the southern part of the valley, where groundwater depletion has been most severe, do not receive enough floodwater to refill their aquifers. Without infrastructure that can send high flows south, researchers predict that, at best, expansion of flood recharge might eventually make up for about 10–20 percent of the valley's long-term groundwater deficit.[8] If a way could be found to divert the water to where it is needed, most of the groundwater deficit might be reversed over the course of a few decades.

Rerouting the valley's drainage would be a challenge because the flood control system was designed to move water to the ocean. Because irrigation canals are managed at the local level, a coordinated regional effort would be needed to alter the path of the valley's drainage. Furthermore, not all the water can be taken; a portion of that "wasted" water that currently flows out to sea is crucial to the downstream ecosystem. Unless someone finds the funding and political will to bring about such changes, only those farms with permeable soils lucky enough to be located on canals or rivers that periodically swell with excess floodwater will be able to take advantage of what is likely the least expensive and environmentally damaging way of ensuring continued access to irrigation water. Those who cannot easily infiltrate water will need to find a more creative way to access underexploited floodwaters.

Fortunately for farmers who cannot take advantage of flood recharge, there are plenty of other options. Over the millennia, humanity has come up with ingenious ways to get water into the ground while still protecting farm fields and cities from flooding. For example, due to the episodic nature of its monsoon, residents of India have developed the world's most diverse set of tools for storing water underground. Throughout the subcontinent but especially in the peninsular region—a large area in the center of India where shallow bedrock slows groundwater recharge—hundreds of thousands of small reservoirs and ponds have been built.[9] After the monsoon fills the storage structures, they provide a shared water supply for communities. These structures have a secondary purpose that becomes critical during droughts: a portion of the rainwater flowing into the storage tanks and reservoirs percolates into the ground through recharge wells located in their bottoms or along their walls. In ancient times, these hand-dug wells recharged enough groundwater to help towns make it through dry periods. Due to the ability of this system to alleviate suffering, kings, local leaders, and wealthy benefactors came to consider the building of recharge structures as a civic duty and acted accordingly.

After modern drilling technology and submersible pumps lowered the cost of groundwater irrigation, recharge wells were converted from drought insurance to tools for replenishing depleted aquifers during normal years. Influenced by the region's long history of operating shared water storage structures, many communities quickly embraced small-scale recharge projects during the Green Revolution. Modern efforts to expand and adapt traditional recharge methods got underway in the 1960s, as the owners of depleted wells started routing rainwater into the wide openings of their hand-dug wells. Although a modest amount of water could be recharged by running the wells in reverse, the approach was far from optimal because the rate of recharge was slow, and wells could easily clog if suspended clay and silt was not settled out before the water was introduced to the well.

Recognizing the need to get more water into the ground during the brief period when it was available, the Indian government promoted alternative approaches.[10] By providing grants and technical support to build check dams—low barriers running perpendicular to the flow of rivers—and small recharge basins situated in the porous sediments adjacent to rivers, the government helped rural communities capture and store water that could be used later to irrigate crops. They also encouraged people living in cities to route the drains from their roofs into wells to recharge groundwater while simultaneously reducing the risk of flooding city streets.

Check dams, infiltration ponds, and other locally controlled infiltration structures can be a potent means of counteracting groundwater depletion. But in some cases, their effectiveness has led to problems downstream. For example, on the Gujarat peninsula, a religious guru and his followers initiated a program to build recharge wells and check dams in response to a drought that hit the region in the early 1980s. The network of locally controlled recharge structures decreased the drought vulnerability of rural communities, but the victory came at the expense of people living downstream in Rajkot—a rapidly growing city that relied upon the runoff that was now being captured upstream to fill its reservoir.[11] Once again, the illusion that "wasted" water could be captured and recharged without consequences for downstream users had transferred scarcity between groups of people who shared the same watershed.

Recognizing that locally controlled recharge projects were taking place in a haphazard manner, the Indian government initiated an effort in 1996 to coordinate the country's disparate programs. By 2002, they had developed the *Master Plan for Artificial Recharge into Groundwater in India*—a document describing the creation of a national network of check dams and recharge basins in the countryside and roof water infiltration systems in the cities that would serve as a blueprint for future efforts. Following the advice of the country's leading hydrologists and geologists, government officials sought to maximize recharge by focusing on places where excess water existed over depleted aquifers. As local projects were built, the federal government's Central Ground Water Board refined the master plan, releasing new versions in 2005, 2013, and 2020. Each time the document was revised, its estimate of both the amount of money that was required and the volume of water that could be recharged increased.[12] By 2020, the master plan identified the need for around eighteen billion dollars to projects capable of recharging about a third of the groundwater that was pumped out of the ground annually.

Although India's federal government has been promoting centralized management of groundwater recharge for over two decades, projects still proceed in a relatively uncoordinated manner.[13] Local government agencies and nongovernmental organizations often pursue their objectives opportunistically, building in places where it is easiest to obtain public cooperation and outside financing. As a result, the program tends to reinforce the status quo, serving wealthy farmers and communities where groundwater has not yet been severely depleted. There is hope that the situation will change; in 2018, the federal government received a loan from the World Bank that provided one billion dollars to coordinate more equitable groundwater recharge projects within the provinces where they will be most impactful.

Despite its often chaotic nature, locally controlled groundwater recharge remains popular in India because it fits into a long-standing tradition of community water management. In some parts of the country, such as the floodplains of the Ganges River, where large quantities of excess water are available most years, local recharge programs may eventually make irrigated agriculture more sustainable.[14]

In contrast, in Gujarat, Rajasthan, and other provinces where groundwater has been severely depleted, there is simply not enough excess water to recharge the depleted aquifers.[15] Recharge simply cannot provide water security if all the water is already spoken for. To solve scarcity problems in the world's most stressed regions, an additional source of water will be needed.

Under certain circumstances, dams might provide that supplemental source of water. By sending stored surface water downstream during dry periods, water can be transferred to an underground reservoir, freeing up space for dams to capture more floodwater. Over the past three decades, the coordinated operation of dams and groundwater recharge systems has proven to be an effective way of expanding storage in the water-stressed American Southwest.

This practice has been particularly impactful in Arizona, where it has been employed to manage the state's share of Colorado River water. In 1944, the sparsely populated state of around two hundred thousand people negotiated the right to almost 3.5 cubic kilometers per year of river water—an amount sufficient for the homes and lawns of over twenty million people—when the US government established a system for dividing up the resource. In the years following the signing of the Colorado River Compact, Arizona was able to use only a fraction of its water allocation because most of the state's people and farms were located far from the river, in the areas around Phoenix and Tucson.

The construction and operation of several hundred kilometers of canals along with the tunnels and pumps needed to move water uphill and then back into the valley where the demand originated initially was deemed impractical by the federal government.[16] As it became clear to the state's leaders that their plans for agriculture and urbanization could not be realized without additional water resources, Arizona redoubled its efforts to secure federal loans necessary to build a canal, finally succeeding in 1968. The $3.6 billion Central Arizona Project was designed to bring approximately half of the state's Colorado River allocation into the region, almost doubling the region's surface water supply.

When the canal was completed in 1993, the need for imported water had increased: Arizona's bountiful aquifers had already shrunk by around a hundred cubic kilometers through decades of pumping for irrigation and domestic water supply.[17] For anyone thinking about the long term, drawing down aquifers filled with eight-thousand-year-old groundwater to farm a desert would seem to be a misguided approach to water management. But the distant future was not on the agenda during the first decades of the twentieth century, when inexpensive modern pumps first allowed farmers to access the region's groundwater.

The timing was perfect for the early twentieth-century farmers seeking to fill the demand for cotton from the Goodyear Tire & Rubber factory in the imaginatively named company town of Goodyear, where tires were being made for cars and trucks.[18] When cotton prices fell after World War I ended, groundwater was redirected to forage crops such as alfalfa, which was fed to cattle, and citrus, which was shipped back east in refrigerated train cars. The shift solidified the last two of the "five C's" essential to the state's prosperity that every child in Arizona learns in their first local history class: cotton, cattle, citrus, climate, and copper (the last of which was the basis for the first major influx of European settlers).

Cotton production surged again during World War II and remained one of Arizona's main cash crops after US Department of Agriculture researchers developed Pima cotton, a superior form of the plant named in honor of the Indians who helped in its development.[19] Eventually, competition from other states and conversion of farmland into suburbs diminished the importance of cotton to the state's economy.

By the early 2010s, cotton production had declined by about 80 percent relative to its postwar peak as metropolitan Phoenix consumed more of the region's land and water.[20] Despite its decline, cotton remained the second largest crop in the state in the first decades of the twenty-first century, in large part because federal government subsidies guaranteed handsome profits to farmers who historically had been planting it.

The arrival of Colorado River water meant that there would be enough water to continue growing cotton, citrus, and cattle fodder even as the burgeoning cities of Phoenix and Tucson expanded to several million people. However, there was a problem: as junior water rights holders, Central Arizona Project water users would see their supplies curtailed first when a drought was declared in the Colorado River Basin. The effects of cutbacks, such as the one that took place in 2022, would be particularly challenging because Lake Pleasant, the project's reservoir, could only hold about half of a normal year's supply of water. Building more dams was not a viable option when the project was being designed because reservoir construction projects were already facing vigorous opposition from environmentalists who had successfully challenged a proposed dam at the nearby Grand Canyon. In addition, the new administration of President Jimmy Carter had expressed strong concerns about the environmental impacts of dams.[21]

To expand the storage capacity of the Central Arizona Project, water managers turned to the region's depleted aquifers. Luckily for them, local engineers had been conducting pioneering research on groundwater recharge since the late 1960s.[22] Faced with falling groundwater levels, Phoenix and Tucson had been seeking ways to recharge drinking water aquifers with treated wastewater and runoff from city streets. By the 1980s, engineers from the US Water Conservation Laboratory in Phoenix and the University of Arizona in Tucson had demonstrated that they could recharge aquifers using dry riverbeds and off-channel infiltration basins.

The key to getting water into the ground was overcoming the tendency of fine particles to plug the pores through which water percolated. The riverbeds unplugged themselves naturally when storm flows scoured the sandy stream bottoms, releasing trapped particles. At the off-channel recharge basins, suspended particles were removed by holding water in pretreatment ponds before sending it into the recharge basins. When the rate of infiltration eventually slowed due to the accumulation of particles that refused to settle out, the engineers turned off the flow. After the desert sun dried out the drained basin, cracks formed across the surface that served as conduits for water.[23] When that did not restore permeability, engineers sent in graders to scrape the surface and remove the accumulated gunk, much in the same way that water treatment plant operators unclog slow sand filters in water treatment plants, but on a much larger scale.

Although technical knowledge about how to operate recharge projects effectively provided confidence in aquifer storage systems, holding excess Colorado River water underground was still challenging because Arizona's legal system was incompatible with the practice. To provide operators of recharge systems with a means of assuring that other aquifer users would not simply pump out the stored water, the legislature revised state laws on groundwater rights in 1986 and 1994.[24] They also created the Arizona Water Banking Authority—a regional entity with a mandate to coordinate recharge and recovery of water from the region's aquifers. As groundwater regulations were being clarified, the state established a system for prioritizing water deliveries during times of shortage; cities and Indian tribes would have the highest priority for water deliveries while non-Indigenous farmers would bear the brunt of any future cutbacks.

When water from the Central Arizona Project arrived, recharge basins were waiting to infiltrate water left over after cities, tribes, and farmers had taken their shares. Today, the region has over forty-four square kilometers of recharge basins along with hundreds of kilometers of unlined canals and leaky riverbeds that are capable of recharging aquifers. In places where space was not available or where local geology precluded the construction of infiltration basins, recharge wells were installed to get water into the aquifer. After thirty years of operation, excess water from the Central Arizona Project has reversed the trend of groundwater depletion, making up for about 3 percent of the region's long-term water deficit.[25]

The massive aquifer that serves as the local underground reservoir contains about three times as much water as nearby Lake Mead, the largest surface water reservoir in the United States. Although it lacks the recreational opportunities afforded by the artificial lake, the aquifer loses far less water through evaporation (less than 1 percent of the water being recharged evaporates during the recharge process, whereas Lake Mead loses about 5 percent of the water that it receives).[26]

All the effort that went into turning central Arizona's depleted aquifers into a water bank will be put to the test in the coming decades as growing water demand and climate change increase water stress throughout the Southwest.[27] Pressure on the water bank ratcheted up in 2021, when the federal government reduced the amount of water that the Central Arizona Project could take from the river by about 20 percent. In anticipation of the cutbacks, some farmers already had fallowed their fields when the cuts were announced. If the shortage continues, cities and tribes will draw down their stored water as they redouble their efforts to implement conservation measures and seek out rights to other water resources. A few fortunate farmers also may take advantage of the water bank, but their low priority will make it a short-term solution. Most will continue to pump their wells, gradually drawing down the aquifers under their farms until their piece of the ancient aquifer recedes to a point when it will be too expensive to pump.

Farther to the west, California also has used aquifers to store excess surface water. Aquifer recharge projects currently provide about 15 percent of the drinking water used by Los Angeles, with a network of recharge basins located on the edge of the city infiltrating water throughout the lengthy dry season. About two-thirds of the excess water originates in flood control dams in the mountains above the city, while the other third comes from imported water sources, including the Colorado River.[28]

Groundwater banking also has been adopted as a means of storing excess water from dams in other parts of California. Between 1995 and 2020, infiltration basins and recharge wells, strategically placed adjacent to the aqueduct that moves water through the San Joaquin Valley, have infiltrated about 3.5 cubic kilometers of excess water in aquifers near Bakersfield.[29] The original concept behind the Kern Water Bank was that water recharged during wet years would be sold to cities in the south to make up for dry-year cutbacks. Although a lot of banked water has been delivered to Southern California's cities, demand for water to keep valuable orchards alive during droughts has meant that a substantial fraction of the banked water is being used by local farmers.

Coordination of dams and groundwater recharge facilities can expand water storage capacity without exacerbating the social and environmental consequences associated with new surface water reservoirs. However, the approaches employed in Arizona and California have not spread to many other places. One possible explanation is that there just are not a lot of water-stressed regions where the expansion of reservoirs has been blocked while, at the same time, partially emptied aquifers capable of storing excess water are available in a convenient location downstream. Layered on top of this is the absence in most jurisdictions of policies and regulations that prevent unauthorized withdrawals from water banks. But probably just as important is the issue of where the banked water originates: despite the great potential for aquifers to store water, they cannot create it. As was the case with flood irrigation and community-scale recharge operations, if a watershed cannot meet the combined demands of local cities, farms, and ecosystems, new sources of freshwater are the only way of expanding the supply.

TAPPING UNCONVENTIONAL
WATER SOURCES

Water awaits those who pursue the less traveled path.

HIDDEN IN PLAIN SIGHT, traveling through the atmosphere or waiting underground for tens of thousands of years, untapped water resources surround us. For those who are new to water technology, there is only one yet-to-be-exploited water resource—the ocean—a nearly inexhaustible supply that is already being used by desperate cities that can afford seawater desalination. Yet there are plenty of other unconventional water sources that for reasons of tradition and a lack of imagination humanity has failed to access. With few exceptions, rain that falls on roofs, sewage flowing out of cities, and aquifers from which water is too salty to drink are missed opportunities for averting water crises.

For cities facing water stress, rainwater and treated sewage are attractive because they are already being collected and managed. Historically, both were considered nuisances that had to be moved away from populated areas as quickly as possible to reduce the risks of disease and flooding. Because most downstream users were not interested in someone else's polluted water, cities have rarely needed to worry about securing the right to use these unconventional sources when they change their minds about getting rid of it.

The other main unconventional water source—brackish water—has periodically been exploited by water-stressed cities and industries for more than two hundred years. However, recent technological breakthroughs have lowered costs and extended applications to a point that makes desalination technology attractive well beyond wealthy coastal cities that obtain freshwater from the ocean.

The degree to which these underexploited water sources will solve the world's water crises depends upon the magnitude of the cost reduction that takes place as experience is acquired in their design and operation. The spread of these approaches will also be determined by how they fit into existing water management systems as well as concerns about the unintended consequences resulting from their adoption.

15

A New Source of Water
Falling from the Sky

THE FRACTION OF A city's water supply that could be satisfied by capturing local precipitation depends upon climate and population density. In North American cities, rainwater harvesting could be impactful because population densities are low. For example, Houston could satisfy its entire water demand if it were to capture about 20 percent of the water that falls within city limits in a typical year.[1] Even a more densely populated city in a drier location, such as Los Angeles, could meet close to 20 percent of its household water demand if it were to capture 20 percent of its rainfall.[2] In European and Asian cities, where population densities are typically five to ten times higher than that of Houston or Los Angeles, local precipitation capture still might be a useful tool for satisfying water demand, especially if it were employed in the less crowded outer edges of cities.[3]

If a city decides to tap this unconventional water resource, it must first figure out how to hold onto the water it captures. Keeping rainwater in or near buildings would seem to be a logical approach because it is easy to pipe roof water into storage tanks. This approach has another benefit; compared to the water flowing in storm sewers and streets, harvested roof water is often quite clean. Precipitation itself is among the purest forms of water, but as it flows across the roof, it can

Rainwater storage tanks can store much of the water needed for a single-family dwelling in many different climate zones.

be contaminated by chemicals from building materials. It also picks up dust and soot along with waterborne pathogens left behind by animals that use roofs as toilets. As a result, the use of roof water is often limited to nonpotable applications, such as landscape irrigation, laundry, and toilet flushing, in wealthy countries. In rural communities and in less affluent countries, where other sources of water are often dirtier than anything that might come off a roof, harvested rainwater is routinely used for drinking, cooking, and hygiene, often with little or no treatment.[4]

Cisterns and rain barrels have been employed as drinking water sources for at least five thousand years, but their use has fallen out of fashion in wealthy cities due to the storage space that would be needed to satisfy the water needs of a modern lifestyle.[5] For example, a rainwater storage tank capable of holding several cubic meters of water could meet about a quarter of the demand of a typical single-family home in much of the wealthy world. In Mediterranean climate zones where little rain falls during summer months, as in those of California, a tank of this size could only meet about 5 percent of annual household demand. For multifamily dwellings in any climate zone, the benefits of rainwater tanks would be much smaller because everyone shares the same roof. Thus, harvesting roof water from a six-story apartment building in a city that has abundant rainfall might, at best, meet about 5 percent of the water needs of its residents.

Despite the limited ability of roof water collection to provide enough water for a modern lifestyle, the installation of rainwater tanks has become increasingly popular in some wealthy countries. The most enthusiastic practitioners of roof water collection are probably the Australians. Driven by government subsidies and, in some places, policies mandating their installation in new construction, more than a million rainwater storage tanks were installed on the world's driest inhabited continent between 1994 and 2010.[6] Adoption of the practice has been highest in the most stressed parts of the country; in arid South Australia, about half of the homes are equipped with rainwater tanks.

Despite growing interest in roof water, the economic case for storage tanks is not overwhelming. Considering the costs of installation, maintenance, and electricity, water produced by household rainwater collection systems costs around nine dollars per cubic meter, which makes it more than twice as expensive as seawater desalination.[7] And this seemingly simple, low-tech solution also consumes a considerable amount of electricity; the inefficient pumps typically used to deliver stored rainwater to a home generally consume somewhere between 1.4 and 2.0 kilowatt hours per cubic meter—about half as much as what it takes to produce water in a modern seawater desalination plant—to move water from the storage tank to the home or garden.

From an economic and energy standpoint, rainwater harvesting would seem to be a bad investment in wealthy, water-stressed countries because, in addition to providing water of a lower quality than most of their existing supplies, rainwater tanks tend to run dry during droughts—exactly when a supplemental water source is most needed. For better or worse, this approach continues to attract investments because societal decisions about how to respond to water crises are often made for reasons unrelated to cost-benefit analysis. Roof water harvesting garners strong support among community members who feel a sense of agency as they help solve a local water challenge. Tanks also shift some of the economic burden from water agencies that are cautious about raising utility bills to city councils, real estate developers, and homeowners who consider rainwater collection tanks as desirable features of state-of-the-art green homes. Although the billions of dollars that have been invested in rainwater tanks might have had a larger impact on water security if they had been used to build desalination plants, expand existing reservoirs, and fix leaky pipes, water managers have little cause for complaint because the expenditures of others has relieved some of the needs that would otherwise have forced them to face customer ire when they raised water rates.

In wetter parts of Europe, Japan, and North America, the installation of rainwater tanks has often been driven by reasons unrelated to water security.[8] For example, more than 1.6 million storage tanks were installed recently in Germany to reduce the flow of rainwater into combined sewer systems—the underground urban drainage network that is shared by roof gutters, storm drains, and sewage collection systems. By cutting the amount of water flowing into sewers on rainy days, the tanks reduce how often treatment plants are forced to release a mixture of rainwater and untreated sewage to local waterways. That rainwater tanks also allow homeowners to save money by purchasing less water is an added attraction because this reduces the volume of water taken out of the environment. As in Australia, savings on water bills in Germany rarely justify the costs of purchasing, installing, and maintaining rainwater collection systems, even with generous government subsidies. Nonetheless, rainwater tanks remain popular, especially in new construction, because they increase the overall cost of buying and maintaining property by only a small increment. For the owners of many homes and commercial buildings in wealthy countries, the perceived value of protecting the environment is enough to warrant the cost of the storage system.

Beyond the world's wealthy, environmentally conscious cities, a rainwater tank can be an important household water source, especially in rural settings where other water resources are scarce. A good example of the potential benefits of rainwater collection is the One Million Cisterns program of Brazil's Sertão—the sparsely populated, semiarid region in the northeast part of the country.[9] Starting in the early 2000s, a coalition of church groups, rural trade unions, and a nongovernmental organization began to train local residents about how to build and maintain standardized sixteen-cubic-meter cement cisterns that could provide enough drinking water to get a family through the region's long dry season. The popularity of the program among community members who were not benefitting substantially from the government's investments in reservoirs and piped water systems eventually attracted subsidies that allowed the program to expand. Although the alliance has only gotten about halfway to its million-cistern goal, the locally made water systems have reduced reliance on tanker-truck water and have educated millions of people about how to live in a drought-prone climate.

The challenge associated with expansion of One Million Cisterns is its relatively high price. Although the construction materials are locally sourced and installation is performed by community members, each cistern still costs about a thousand dollars—a lot of money for families that might only earn about twice that in a year. Considering the limited quantity of water that can be collected from roofs and the availability of other local water supply options, aid agencies and governments that could provide loans or grants have not shown a lot of interest in dramatically expanding funding for roof water capture.

Rainwater tanks have a role to play in reducing water stress and protecting the environment in some parts of the world, but it is unlikely that planners in water-stressed cities are going to turn to them to solve their supply problems. If cities are going to tap the full potential of local precipitation, a less expensive approach for storing large quantities of water will be necessary. Due to the high cost of acquiring land combined with the practical limitations of maintaining small reservoirs or networks of storage tanks within cities, the best options may be underground. As discussed previously, India's *Master Plan for Artificial Recharge* to Groundwater encourages the infiltration of roof water recharge systems next to buildings.[10] To quickly transfer large volumes of water into the ground without flooding basements and damaging foundations, roof water infiltration often employs dry wells—wide-diameter boreholes that extend tens of meters below the surface, typically ending a few meters before they reach the aquifer (hence the "dry" nature of the well).

Although dry wells can offer an inexpensive means of storing large quantities of roof water, the challenge of retrofitting enough buildings to make a dent in water supply needs requires patience, community enthusiasm, and considerable organizational skill. Furthermore, an exclusive focus on roofs, even in places where not all the buildings are tightly clustered, misses the opportunity to collect a much larger volume of water. As a result, some cities have turned to water flowing in gutters, ditches, and storm sewers. Solving the logistical problem of roof water collection by collecting water at street level comes at a price: when rainwater interacts with streets, sidewalks, and parking lots, it picks up contaminants that are not usually present in roof water. Street-level rainwater often contains oil, metals, and synthetic chemicals released from vehicles along with pesticides and fertilizers used outside of the home.[11] This mixture of drainage water, which is sometimes referred to as stormwater runoff, also tends to contain waterborne pathogens from the feces of pets, wildlife, and livestock along with sewage-derived pathogens from leaky sanitary sewers and informal settlements that lack proper waste collection systems.

An instructive example of the potential benefits and risks of recharging drinking water aquifers with water that in other places would be sent downstream can be found just east of New York. As modern American suburbs were starting to cover the surface of Long Island—the 160-kilometer mass of sand and gravel left behind when the glaciers receded at the end of the last ice age—planners needed somewhere to put the water draining from the paved surfaces that accompanied the automobile-centric lifestyle of the suburbs. Due to the island's sandy soil and flat topography, the most cost-effective way of disposing of the excess water was to route storm runoff into shallow infiltration basins. The basins also served a second purpose: they recharged the island's aquifers—its sole water supply. Between 1950 and 1974, more than two thousand infiltration basins were built across the rapidly suburbanizing region.[12]

The stormwater basins were not the only engineered infiltration structures built with the new housing tracts. To avoid the expense of installing sanitary sewers and wastewater treatment plants, most of Long Island's developers equipped their homes with cesspools—structures that are essentially dry wells for disposing of sewage. The liquid part of the sewage quickly percolated into the ground, leaving behind solids that were slowly degraded by microbes. During the Great Acceleration, more than half a million cesspools were built across Long Island.[13] By the 1970s, it became clear that these primitive sewage disposal systems were contaminating aquifers in the more densely populated western half of the island (Nassau County) with nitrate concentrations that made the groundwater unsafe to drink. As a result, towns in the affected areas invested in sewers and wastewater treatment plants that discharged to Long Island Sound or the Atlantic Ocean. In a decision that later came to haunt them, officials on the eastern half of the island, Suffolk County, did not follow the lead of their neighbor because their population density was lower due to its longer commuting distance from New York.

Although treatment plants eventually were built to serve Suffolk's largest towns, about two-thirds of the county's 1.5 million people still infiltrate their sewage into the groundwater through cesspools or their updated relatives—septic systems—slightly more sophisticated versions of the cesspool.[14]

Since the 1970s, further increases in population and decades of sewage infiltration have polluted much of Suffolk's groundwater with nitrate. In the intervening decades the cost of retrofitting the communities with sewers has surged to more than fifty thousand dollars per home. Fearful of the public's response to the massive increases in taxes or water bills that would be required to transition to centralized sewage treatment, local politicians and regulatory agency officials are developing policies that require the gradual retrofitting of septic tanks with modules that convert the nitrate into dinitrogen (the inert gas that makes up 80 percent of the atmosphere).[15]

Despite the revulsion that some residents might feel when they realize that their parking lots, washing machines, and toilets are an integral part of their drinking water supply, Long Island is an example of a densely populated region that does not require dams or imported water. Each year, about 2.5 cubic kilometers of water percolates into the island's aquifers; almost 80 percent of the infiltrating water consists of rainwater and melting snow that make their way underground by passing through soil in areas that have not been covered by pavement or buildings.[16] The remaining 20 percent of the recharge water flows into aquifers from stormwater basins and, on the eastern part of the island, cesspools and septic systems. Although it is difficult to come up with an exact value, the local fraction of drinking water derived from the engineered infiltration structures in the larger towns is considerably higher than the average for the entire island.

Long Island's three million residents, along with its businesses and its few remaining farms, pump about a third of the infiltrated water back out of the aquifer each year. The water that does not return to groundwater through infiltration basins, septic tanks, and excess lawn irrigation flows into the ocean by way of sewage treatment plants or evaporates from lawns, gardens, and industrial cooling towers. The remaining two-thirds of the water that remains underground seeps out through springs that feed coastal streams and wetlands or flows away from the island in aquifers that extend under the seabed.

Without infiltration basins and septic systems, many of the island's coastal streams and wetlands might have dried up. Deprived of recharge water, the seaward flow of the offshore aquifers would have decreased or reversed, allowing salty ocean water to contaminate the island's drinking water wells.[17] With an overall population density that is approximately equal to Houston's, Long Island proves that it is possible to live a modern lifestyle on local water provided that you have enough precipitation, an ample aquifer under your feet, and the infrastructure in place to ensure that precipitation falling on your community finds its way into the ground. If local leaders can figure out how to keep nitrate and other contaminants from septic systems out of their drinking water, it could be a model for other communities with similar geologic conditions.

Relative to Long Island, where in an average year about 1.2 meters of precipitation falls, most water-stressed cities have far less water to infiltrate. For example, the Phoenix metropolitan area typically receives less than a fifth of Long Island's rainfall. Nonetheless, the city captures much of the stormwater that it does receive. To recharge groundwater while simultaneously reducing the risk of flooding, builders in the Phoenix metropolitan area are required to install structures capable of capturing the water produced during the first two hours of the largest storm that the area is expected to experience each century (the hundred-year storm). As specified by local ordinance, the captured water must be either infiltrated into the ground within thirty-six hours or drained to regional canals that have been designated as stormwater conduits. To comply, Phoenix has built more than ten thousand infiltration basins and forty thousand dry wells.[18]

Although reliable data on the contributions of dry wells to the water supply are scarce, a study from 2004 indicated that about 10 percent of the water falling on the Phoenix suburb of Chandler was infiltrated into the aquifer through dry wells and storage ponds.[19] (Much of the remainder of the rainwater was used by plants or evaporated from the soil.) Capturing and recharging a tenth of the rain that falls in a desert climate might not seem like a lot, but at the relatively low population density of the area (at the time of the study, Chandler was about as crowded as Houston or Long Island), recharged stormwater made up about 10 percent of the community's water supply.

Adelaide, a water-stressed Australian city of about 1.3 million with a population density approximately equal to that of Long Island, Houston, and suburban Phoenix, has made the infiltration of urban runoff a priority in its long-term quest for water security. However, the city has taken a different approach than its North American counterparts: rather than placing infiltration basins behind locked gates or relying upon unobtrusive dry wells, the city has made stormwater capture systems into community amenities.[20] Most of the stormwater projects in Adelaide include constructed wetlands that provide attractive greenspaces in places that otherwise might have consisted of concrete culverts and pipes. The wetlands also are functional, filtering out particles that might have otherwise clogged the infiltration ponds, dry wells, or injection wells—infiltration structures that extend deeper into the aquifer than most dry wells. Currently, the total volume of stormwater recharged by all these structures is equivalent to about 3 percent of the city's annual water use. Because stormwater recharge fits into the city's commitment to minimize its impact on the surrounding environment, expansion of Adelaide's stormwater infiltration systems is likely to continue, with plans in place for recharging a volume equivalent to about 10 percent of the city's overall water use.

Although urban runoff typically is much more contaminated than roof water, water extracted from aquifers that have been recharged with urban runoff tends to be quite clean.[21] Purification of water taking place during recharge exemplifies the power of natural systems to purify water. As water percolates through the subsurface, microbes living on the soil and sediments as well as the mineral surfaces adsorb waterborne pathogens, toxic metals, and synthetic chemicals. This process slows the migration of pathogens and chemicals to such a degree that most will not reach drinking water wells for hundreds or even thousands of years. In fact, many contaminants will never complete the trip because they are broken down by microbes within the biofilm.

Although soil-associated microbes can greatly improve the quality of stormwater runoff, they have their limitations.[22] Certain viruses and organic chemicals exhibit surface properties that allow them to move around the microbes or mineral surfaces that they encounter below ground. Despite the risk of contamination, people who consume water from aquifers recharged with stormwater do not appear to suffer from waterborne diseases at a higher frequency than those who get their drinking water from other sources. Some reduction in the spread of viral disease associated with stormwater infiltration may be attributable to the slow decrease in virus infectivity that takes place during the months or years that it takes viruses to travel through aquifers. Further protection is afforded the users of infiltrated stormwater because many utilities disinfect their groundwater after it is pumped out of the ground. Concentrations of the chemicals that were not removed during infiltration also drop as contaminated water mixes with water from cleaner sources within the aquifer.

Despite the purifying properties of the infiltration process, concern about the risks associated with stormwater recharge has increased recently due to discoveries about PFAS, a family of toxic, fluorine-containing chemicals used in firefighting foams and stain-resistant consumer products that have been detected in stormwater at concentrations exceeding stringent drinking water standards.[23]

PFAS-contaminated industrial sites can often explain the presence of these difficult-to-degrade compounds in stormwater runoff. For example, in the early 2000s, elevated levels of PFAS detected in the blood of residents of a suburb of Minneapolis were attributed to an industrial waste landfill located elsewhere in the city. The pathway through which the chemicals found their way to the suburb's water supply involved leachate from the landfill that drained into a stormwater channel. The channel provided a path for the water to flow a distance of about ten kilometers to a lake that recharged a nearby drinking water aquifer.[24] Although the stormwater channel and the lake had not been intended as a groundwater recharge system, the incident illustrates the ways in which difficult-to-remove industrial contaminants can migrate to far-flung aquifers by way of urban drainage systems.

PFAS are only the latest example of drinking water contamination risks from stormwater infiltration.[25] Before PFAS became the focus of so much attention, regulators expressed concerns about persistent, mobile compounds like fipronil and imidacloprid (insecticides used to kill ants, termites, and fleas) and MTBE (a gasoline additive that imparts a foul odor to drinking water). They also recommended vigilance and periodic water testing to guard against the possibility that someone might pour a container of unwanted pesticides or organic solvents into a storm sewer or that the fuel tank or radiator of a car might rupture, spewing its contents onto a parking lot connected to an infiltration basin.

If communities want to take advantage of the untapped potential of stormwater runoff without compromising public health, a more deliberate strategy will be needed to avoid groundwater contamination.

The first step in protecting urban aquifers is to do a better job managing toxic chemicals. In addition to tightening up on chemical handling at industrial facilities, residential chemical use could benefit from a new level of vigilance, particularly when it comes to pesticides.[26] In 2012, more money was spent on insecticides for homes and gardens than for farms in the United States, with expenditures of close to three billion dollars for purposes including termite control and the killing of bugs in lawns and gardens. Urban pesticides are also popular beyond the wooden homes and suburban yards of the United States: large quantities of insecticides are used in cities worldwide to control disease-carrying mosquitoes, which often breed in stormwater collection basins and drainage ditches. Herbicides also are liberally sprayed onto hard surfaces to keep weeds from growing out of cracks in the pavement. Likewise, that carpetlike appearance of the turfgrass in parks, playing fields, and golf courses would be impossible without the application of insecticides, weed killers, and fungicides. Pesticide use is not limited to the ground; increasingly, herbicides and fungicides are being incorporated into building materials and paints. By design, these more durable surfaces release pesticides to stormwater every time rain hits a roof or the side of a building. As a result of these and other uses, concentrations of pesticides in stormwater runoff typically are comparable to those measured in agricultural drainage.

Beyond a reliance on source control, the risk of groundwater contamination from stormwater infiltration might be lowered by adding additional treatment capabilities to infiltration systems.[27] Treatment wetlands, such as those employed in Adelaide, remove nitrate, pathogenic bacteria, and some of the more easily degradable pesticides and industrial chemicals from stormwater. More active treatment could be incorporated into the infiltration process by adding a small amount of hydrogen peroxide to the water and exposing it to ultraviolet light before recharge.

Alternatively, the top layer of sand and gravel within an infiltration basin or a dry well can be amended with inexpensive materials that adsorb contaminants more efficiently than native geologic materials.[28] For example, a modest amount of biochar—a charcoal-like substance produced by heating wood or organic waste in the absence of oxygen—can prevent mobile stormwater contaminants from reaching groundwater for decades or centuries. The ability of infiltration basins to improve water quality can also be increased by treating it with a solution of permanganate (a common form of manganese) and household bleach. The manganese-oxide-coated sand formed by this process retains toxic metals and degrades certain synthetic organic chemicals in stormwater.

Finally, groundwater contamination from a spill or malicious behavior can be detected with inexpensive electronic sensors that identify pulses of water containing high chemical concentrations or changes in easily measured properties, such as conductivity, temperature, and light absorption.[29] When a sensor encounters unusual conditions, it can close a valve or gate to keep potentially contaminated water out of the infiltration system. The sensor system can also notify water managers, who respond by visiting the site to ascertain the nature of the problem.

16

Replenishing Groundwater
with Treated Sewage

ALTHOUGH STORMWATER runoff can supplement local supplies, there usually is not enough of it to meet the needs of places facing scarcity. As an alternative, the clean water produced by sewage treatment, which is sometimes referred to as wastewater effluent, is often available in abundant quantities and is nearly clean enough to drink. Due to its availability and relatively high quality, wastewater effluent or surface waters where effluent makes up most of the flow (termed effluent-dominated rivers) have long been employed for aquifer recharge.

To understand the extent to which wastewater effluent can contribute to a city's water supply, consider Berlin, where concerns that the water supply could be cut off for political reasons led to the creation of an extensive water recycling system during the early years of the Cold War. To eliminate its reliance on a river originating in the Soviet-aligned German Democratic Republic, West Germany spent almost four billion dollars to turn West Berlin's sewage into drinking water. As part of this effort, wastewater effluent was piped into ponds and canals throughout the city.[1] Nearby wells sucked the treated wastewater into the aquifer as groundwater was pumped. As the infiltrated wastewater effluent traveled toward the water supply wells, it underwent the same natural treatment process that purifies stormwater.

In West Berlin's reconfigured water system, treated sewage made up about 70 percent of the drinking water, with the remainder coming from infiltration of rainwater in unpaved areas within the city and groundwater that had migrated into the city from the surrounding region. A portion of the wastewater effluent that was piped to the ponds and canals had originated in the city's stormwater collection system—a set of pipes that routed roof water and street runoff into the combined sewers. This urban drainage, along with the rainwater and snowmelt that had percolated through the soil, meant that Berlin's treated water was not stuck in a closed loop. The constant addition of water that had not already been recycled prevented the accumulation of salts and synthetic chemicals that were not removed during treatment.

The water recycling system built to address West Berlin's water security concerns was so effective that it remained in place after Germany was reunified. Despite the water's unpristine source, Berlin's utility touts the high quality of the city's drinking water, emphasizing its excellent taste and the fact that there is no need to add chlorine or other disinfectants before distributing groundwater to the city's 3.4 million inhabitants.[2]

Berlin's water recycling system is unique, but it is not unprecedented. The practice of obtaining drinking water from groundwater wells located next to polluted rivers—a process referred to as riverbank filtration—was pioneered in the 1870s as Düsseldorf, Hamburg, and other European cities responded to cholera and typhoid fever outbreaks caused by sewage contamination.[3]

The riverbank filtration process also was attractive because it eliminated many of the compounds that gave the river water its musty taste and yellow-brown color. After chemists learned how to measure trace concentrations of industrial chemicals, it became evident that the microbes living on the sand through which the water flowed broke down many of the industrial chemicals and pesticides during riverbank filtration.[4]

As a result of the efficacy and low cost of riverbank filtration, German water utilities rarely pump water directly from rivers. In places where the local geology is not conducive to riverbank filtration, water engineers access its benefits by routing water into shallow basins or permeable, flat areas next to rivers where extraction wells can be used to recapture the water after it has been infiltrated. Today, about 15 percent of Germany's drinking water is produced by riverbank filtration and related methods.[5] The processes are also quite common elsewhere in Europe, with Hungary obtaining nearly its entire drinking water supply from riverbank filtration systems located along the Danube River. The Netherlands and Switzerland have invested heavily in riverbank filtration too, using it to produce about a quarter of their drinking water.

Due to the clustering of European cities along rivers, treated sewage accounts for a significant fraction of the overall river flow in many places where riverbank filtration is practiced. For example, during dry periods, over half of the flow of the Rhine River—the drinking water source for about twenty million people—can be traced back to sewage treatment plants.[6] Thus, it is quite possible that a water molecule will have passed through several sets of kidneys before arriving at a faucet in Amsterdam. But it is just as likely that the same molecule will have already encountered just as many riverbank filtration systems during its downstream trip.

Building upon the positive experiences of the European cities that pioneered riverbank filtration, water-stressed cities in other parts of the world are starting to adopt the practice, with India, Egypt, Thailand, and Malaysia initiating projects in the 2010s.[7]

As is the case with stormwater infiltration, riverbank filtration has limitations. During the 1970s, when large quantities of waste from pulp and paper manufacturing operations and chemical factories were being dumped into European rivers, drinking water quality declined as the purifying capabilities of riverbank filtration systems were overwhelmed.[8] In response, many cities installed additional treatment processes, such as ozonation and activated carbon filtration, to remove the chemicals that passed through the subsurface. Now that European rivers are less polluted, post-riverbank-filtration treatment processes are providing an additional layer of protection. In countries that have not yet reined in the discharge to rivers of raw sewage and pollution from industries and farms, riverbank filtration alone will not be sufficient to produce safe drinking water.

European experiences with riverbank filtration also influenced early water recycling efforts in the United States. When Phoenix turned to treated sewage and stormwater runoff to recharge depleted aquifers in the late 1960s, its engineers were already aware of the purification that took place during infiltration. Some of that knowledge came from Herman Bouwer, an engineer who grew up in the Netherlands, where he had firsthand experience drinking Rhine River water that had been infiltrated into Amsterdam's aquifers in the sand dunes west of the city.[9] Bouwer and other early practitioners of groundwater recharge in the American West kept the lines of communication between American and European water experts open, organizing international conferences and personnel exchanges where they shared the latest knowledge about aquifer treatment.

By the time that Bouwer and his colleagues were experimenting with the effluent from Phoenix's wastewater treatment plants, Los Angeles was already infiltrating a portion of its treated sewage. Engineers from the county's water utility had been piping water from a newly constructed wastewater treatment plant into a dry riverbed on the eastern edge of the city since 1962.[10] When the Rio Hondo spreading grounds were first built, wastewater effluent accounted for only about a third of the infiltrating water. As imported water became more expensive and the city's engineers gained confidence in the ability of the treatment process to remove waterborne pathogens and chemicals, the wastewater effluent contribution crept upward.

By 2009, state regulators had granted Los Angeles permission to increase the wastewater effluent contribution to 50 percent during dry years.[11] Although the project made up only a few percent of the city's total water supply, the infiltrated mix of wastewater effluent, stormwater runoff, and imported water serves as the sole drinking water source for thousands of homes next to the spreading basin.

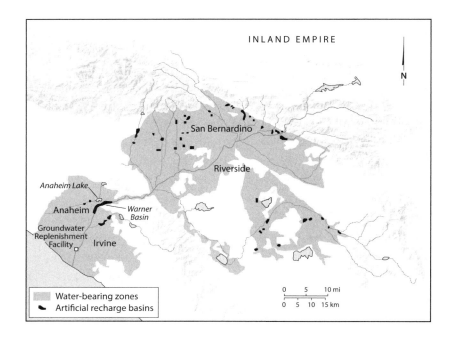

Southern California's Santa Ana River Watershed, which mainly consists of treated wastewater during the region's dry summer and fall period, has been engineered to maximize infiltration of water within the populated region along the coast.

During the same period, about fifty kilometers to the south, groundwater managers in Orange County built a series of infiltration projects that gradually morphed into a massive wastewater effluent recycling system. As Southern California's suburbs expanded, the Santa Ana River—the conduit to the sea for snowmelt and runoff from meadows and farmland in a sparsely populated inland valley—emerged as the solution to the supply needs of water-stressed communities in the rapidly growing coastal region.[12] Starting in the 1940s, Orange County's water managers updated a page from the book written by the Yemeni practitioners of spate irrigation. Using bulldozers and backhoes instead of hand tools, they sculpted the Santa Ana's sand into circuitous channels that spread the flow across the leaky riverbed. To increase the amount of water that percolated into the ground still further, they installed infiltration basins in the riverside sand quarries that had been dug out when the region's highways had been built.

When the infiltration systems were constructed in the 1950s, all attention was on the quantity of water that could be intercepted. Over time, the source and quality of the water also became important. As Southern California's population expanded, the farms of the upper watershed turned into the suburbs of the Inland Empire and the Santa Ana became an effluent-dominated river. By the early 2000s, Orange County's infiltration system was delivering the treated sewage of more than three million upstream residents into the drinking water aquifers of Anaheim (home of Disneyland) and other communities next to the river. The concentrations of salts and nitrate in the river crept upward throughout this period as mountain snowmelt was replaced by wastewater effluent from the upstream suburbs.[13]

After the Inland Empire suburbanized, about a third of Orange County's drinking water supply could be traced back to treated sewage that had been infiltrated along the Santa Ana River.[14] What had started out as a masterful exploitation of an underused resource had turned into a vulnerability because Orange County had come to rely upon water from a source that it did not control.

As the Inland Empire continued its expansion, that water supply was threatened because the upstream region began recycling wastewater to address its own water scarcity problems. Due to the arid conditions in the upper watershed, the flow of the Santa Ana River declined because a substantial fraction of the recycled water evaporated from lawns and gardens. In 2008, to compensate for the decreases in the Santa Ana River's flow, Orange County's groundwater managers built a twenty-kilometer-long pipeline to bring recycled water from the coast inland to the Anaheim infiltration basins.[15]

For over half a century, aquifers recharged with treated sewage and water from effluent-dominated rivers have met the drinking water needs of millions of people in the United States and Europe. But that approach did not prevail when several new projects were proposed in the 1990s in the western United States. Aside from the revulsion that many people felt upon recognizing that their drinking water had recently been sewage, some of the hesitation probably can be traced to a lack of trust in the judgment of experts and government officials that became more prevalent after the upheavals of the Vietnam War era. This attitude may have been reinforced by media accounts of trace amounts of pharmaceuticals and household chemicals showing up in the drinking water of Berlin and other cities that had pioneered water recycling.[16]

Resistance to the idea of adding treated wastewater to the water supply started killing off new projects in 1993, when an infiltration basin for treated wastewater was proposed at a location about ten kilometers east of the Rio Hondo spreading grounds—the site where Los Angeles had been operating a nearly identical system for more than thirty years. After a contentious public meeting in which a brewery led the opposition with accusations that treated wastewater would contaminate their beer, the local water agency abandoned its plans.[17] After several more projects in California met a similar fate, water engineers and regulators regrouped. To reduce the risks that wastewater-derived chemicals would enter the drinking water supply, from that point onward, proposed aquifer recharge projects would include additional treatment steps, such as ozonation and activated carbon filtration. Although scores of cities had been using riverbank filtration and effluent recharge for decades without incident, the extra layers of protection were needed to quell opposition to new projects.

Although additional treatment processes increased costs, wastewater recycling remained the most practical option for expanding water supplies in many water-scarce American cities.[18] For example, in 2004, a rapidly growing suburb of Denver built a riverbank filtration system adjacent to the effluent-dominated South Platte River. To assure the complete removal of contaminants, the system's designers included a second infiltration and groundwater recovery step, followed by a state-of-the-art drinking water treatment plant equipped with ultraviolet light and hydrogen peroxide to oxidize chemicals before activated carbon filtration and chlorine disinfection. A few years later, the designers of a massive groundwater recharge project in Virginia adopted a similar set of advanced treatment processes to remove chemicals and pathogens before injecting treated wastewater into a drinking water aquifer. The extra level of safety provided by oxidation, this time with ozone, followed by two activated carbon filtration steps and two disinfection processes (ultraviolet light irradiation and chlorination) assured that water from the Hampton Roads Sanitary District's advanced treatment facility would be exceptionally clean. Recharge of the depleted aquifer with treated wastewater was particularly attractive because it promised to reverse land subsidence that was increasing the vulnerability of communities at the mouth of the Chesapeake Bay to sea-level rise. When it is completed in the early 2030s, the Sustainable Water Initiative for Tomorrow (SWIFT) project will be one of the largest water recycling systems in the world.

Despite the continent's historic reliance on effluent-dominated rivers, the European Union implicitly discouraged the use of treated wastewater for aquifer recharge when it drew up its groundwater regulations in the late 1990s.[19] Infiltration of wastewater effluent was allowed when the groundwater was to be used for irrigation or industrial purposes, provided that strict testing guidelines were followed. Existing infiltration projects involving effluent-dominated rivers also were allowed to continue. But the application of similar practices to projects that would replenish drinking water aquifers with treated wastewater was discouraged by European regulators. The reluctance to embrace a practice that had been used elsewhere without incident was tied to larger concerns among regulators about harmonization of European Union regulations and the need to focus on pollution prevention and restoration of aquatic ecosystems. Adoption of the precautionary principle—the idea that unknown risks should be avoided until safety could be demonstrated—along with efforts to eliminate pollution sources took precedence over solving the supply challenges of water-stressed cities.

European ambivalence about using treated wastewater as a drinking water source led to strange situations where effluent could be used to supplement water supplies provided that no one admitted that it had been part of an intentional plan. For example, in Spain, treated wastewater had gradually become an essential part of Barcelona's water supply as Catalonia's population grew during the Great Acceleration. As a result, the contribution of upstream discharges from wastewater treatment plants to one of the city's two main drinking water sources—the Llobregat River—had grown to a point at which it accounted for about a quarter of the flow during the dry season.[20] Although the city spent large sums of money to install ozonation and activated carbon systems to purify Llobregat River water, the idea of using locally produced wastewater to meet the city's growing needs was considered to be too risky by local politicians and regulators. Nevertheless, that did not stop Barcelona's water utility from accessing the underexploited resource that flowed into the Mediterranean from its main wastewater treatment plant.

When a drought hit the region in the late 2000s, the city invested more than a hundred million dollars in a state-of-the-art water recycling plant.[21] A portion of the highly treated wastewater was pumped to a spot just below the intake to the furthest downstream of the city's Llobregat River drinking water treatment plants. The treated wastewater, which was often of better quality than the river water, allowed the drinking water treatment plant operators to take more low-quality water out of the river without causing its flow to drop below levels that could affect fish. Another portion of the highly treated wastewater was used for wetland restoration and irrigation. The remainder was treated by reverse osmosis, an advanced technique that further purified the water, before injection into the coastal aquifer. The stated purpose of the groundwater recharge project was the creation of a barrier to prevent seawater from getting pulled into coastal drinking water wells. Although they never said so in public, the project's scientists and engineers understood that a substantial fraction of the injected water would reach their supply wells. Rather than stating the obvious, it was more polite to follow the unwritten rule that Europe does not put treated wastewater into its drinking water aquifers.

The extra layers of protection provided by advanced treatment in the United States and the cautious attitude about using treated waste-water to recharge aquifers in Europe may have been the right decisions made for the wrong reasons.[22] By the early 2000s, elevated concentrations of PFAS were being detected in drinking water produced by riverbank filtration systems on Germany's effluent-dominated Ruhr River. About fifteen years later, the compounds started showing up in Southern California's drinking water wells near places where Santa Ana River water was infiltrated. Although the specific sources of the chemical could not be identified in all cases, it appeared that runoff from factories, airports, and waste disposal sites were the main culprits. The presence of PFAS and other riverbank filtration–resistant industrial chemicals in effluent-dominated surface waters means that drinking water suppliers will have to spend considerable sums upgrading their treatment systems.

When people living in wealthy countries became concerned about the impacts of pollution, billions of dollars were invested in modern wastewater treatment plants. To protect the microbes that were integral to the treatment process from toxic chemicals, regulations on industrial discharges were put into place. In the early 1970s, these pre-treatment regulations were extended to include DDT, PCBs, and other industrial chemicals that often contaminated the solid wastes produced by sewage treatment plants. Unfortunately, the regulations have not kept up with the times: as more cities turn to wastewater effluent for drinking water, factories that discharge their industrial wastes to public sewers will need to do more to prevent difficult-to-treat chemicals from entering the drinking water supply via water recycling projects.[23]

17

Refilling Reservoirs with Treated Sewage

THE USE OF TREATED sewage or water from effluent-dominated rivers to replenish depleted aquifers or, in the case of riverbank filtration, to purify contaminated water supplies helped wealthy, water-stressed cities address their supply needs. But not every city can take advantage of the power of subsurface water purification. For various reasons related to geography (for example, water from coastal wells is often too salty to drink) and geology (for example, many aquifers simply cannot produce enough water to meet urban water demands), groundwater accounts for only about 20 percent of the water consumed by the world's big cities.[1] Although recharge can purify treated wastewater to a point at which it becomes safe to drink, in most places aquifer treatment can process only a fraction of a city's treated sewage. Despite the water quality benefits of underground treatment, an increasing number of cities are foregoing infiltration as they bring treated wastewater into their drinking water supplies.

The community that convinced many engineers that they could skip the aquifer treatment step was a reluctant participant in an experiment necessitated by an inability to keep treated wastewater out of a drinking water reservoir. Before construction in the mid-1960s of Interstate 66—the highway connecting Northern Virginia to Washington, DC—most of the water flowing into the Occoquan Reservoir originated in bucolic countryside covered with forests, pastures, and farms. To protect its drinking water reservoir from the wastes produced by would-be commuters, government officials established strict zoning laws designed to keep population density low in the Occoquan watershed.[2] But the pull of the suburbs proved to be too strong. Despite the best efforts of planners to limit development, the volume of wastewater flowing into the reservoir from eleven decrepit sewage treatment plants located on upstream tributaries steadily increased.

By the early 1970s, nutrient pollution from the treated sewage of about fifty thousand people was causing severe algal blooms that clogged the filters at the reservoir's water treatment plant and imparted a musty taste and odor to the drinking water.[3] Within the reservoir, depletion of oxygen by decomposing algae killed fish and released foul-smelling hydrogen sulfide gas.

To reduce nutrient pollution, local politicians convinced the federal government to underwrite a single state-of-the-art treatment plant to replace the outdated facilities that were unable to keep up with the added wastewater flows. When the new system began operating in 1978, sewage passed through a treatment plant that was optimized for nutrient removal. Afterward, the water ran a gauntlet of additional treatment processes that removed the remaining nutrients along with anthropogenic chemicals and waterborne pathogens that had made it through the sewage treatment plant. Next, the unusually pure treated wastewater was released to a tributary located about ten kilometers above the reservoir.[4]

Despite the investment of around one hundred million dollars in a high-tech wastewater treatment plant, algal blooms persisted. The combination of stormwater runoff from new housing developments and the release of phosphorus from the reservoir's already contaminated sediments assured that, despite the near elimination of the sewage-associated nutrient sources, conditions remained conducive to algal growth.

To keep the algae in check, the water utility dumped almost four hundred metric tons of copper sulfate into the reservoir and its tributaries every year.[5] Copper is routinely used as an algicide in drinking water reservoirs and ornamental fountains (hence the blue color of the water in some of them) because the concentrations of the metal needed to kill off the tiny photosynthetic organisms are well below levels that can harm people. The seasonal poisoning of algae that had begun about a decade before construction of the advanced wastewater treatment plant had already caused collateral damage, eliminating copper-sensitive species of fish from several of the reservoir's tributaries. But a safe water supply took precedence over the ecology of the reservoir or, for that matter, of sections of the Potomac River and Chesapeake Bay where water that was not pumped into the drinking water plant eventually flowed.

Despite the presence of a deluxe wastewater treatment plant and its annual copper applications, there was nothing unusual about the Occoquan Reservoir. Plenty of other drinking water suppliers struggled with algal blooms as they pumped water from rivers or reservoirs situated downstream of sewage treatment plants. But conditions changed shortly after the strict zoning laws that had limited development in the watershed were overturned in court.[6] As housing construction took off, the volume of sewage flowing into the advanced treatment plant increased. To keep up, the capacity of the facility was doubled in 1985 and doubled again in the mid-1990s. By 2013, the highly purified wastewater of almost half a million people was flowing into the reservoir.

Averaged over a year, treated wastewater accounts for only about 10 percent of the water entering the Occoquan Reservoir. During dry periods, it makes up over 90 percent of the incoming flow. It has become such an important part of the water supply that without the contribution of the advanced treatment plant, the reservoir would be unable to deliver drinking water during an extended drought.[7]

To safeguard the community from waterborne pathogens and wastewater-derived chemicals, the operators of the water system remain vigilant, carefully monitoring water at the advanced treatment plant, the reservoir, and its tributaries. They also work closely with local industries to avoid the discharge of hazardous chemicals to the sewer system. As was the case in the early years of the project, nutrients from stormwater runoff remain the most immediate threat to water quality. Over the years, watershed managers have made considerable progress reducing nutrient concentrations in stormwater runoff through the installation of passive stormwater treatment systems and outreach programs to educate residents about the threat to water quality posed by overuse of lawn fertilizers. Due to the low nutrient content of treated wastewater and its critical role in providing water during droughts, attitudes about it have shifted; instead of being seen as a water quality problem, it is considered a critical tool in protecting the region's drinking water. In fact, the managers of the Occoquan Reservoir project periodically call for additional funding to enable them to pipe more sewage into their advanced treatment plant from surrounding communities.[8]

In the late 1990s, the successful experiment in Northern Virginia inspired a similar project near Atlanta. The F. Wayne Hill Water Resource Center—named after the county board supervisor and amateur pilot who routinely flew influential decision makers to the Occoquan Reservoir to experience the power of water recycling firsthand—is integral to the drinking water supply of millions of people living in and around Atlanta.[9] Two decades after the Occoquan project was built, the F. Wayne Hill advanced treatment plant became operational. It has been sending eighty million cubic meters per year of treated wastewater into the main drinking water reservoir for Atlanta's northern suburbs, Lake Lanier, since the pipeline connecting the treatment plant to the lake was completed in 2010. In addition to serving as the home for several drinking water treatment plants, the reservoir feeds the Chattahoochee River—Atlanta's main drinking water source.

Although the cost of advanced wastewater treatment had dropped as technologies improved in the years since the Occoquan project was built, the quality of the recycled water and the approach to monitoring were similar in both locations. Likewise, the same problem has threatened water quality: since 2020, algal blooms in Lake Lanier have been causing taste and odor problems in the drinking water and annoying recreational users of the lake.[10] As was the case in the Occoquan Reservoir, the advanced treatment system is not the culprit. Rather, runoff from residential and agricultural land within the watershed together with discharges from septic tanks and poorly performing sewage treatment plants on the lake's tributaries are the main sources of nutrient pollution.

Advanced treatment plants in Virginia and Atlanta along with a few smaller, less well-known projects in the southeastern United States demonstrated that treated wastewater could be converted into drinking water without an intermediate aquifer treatment step.[11] In the two most prominent examples, the greatest challenges to water quality have been related to the inability of water suppliers to keep runoff and polluted water from other sources out of the reservoirs where recycled water is stored. Because it is so difficult to prevent nutrients from getting into waterways in populated areas and it is usually too expensive to pump treated wastewater over great distances to reservoirs located far from cities, the most practical way to keep recycled water free from contamination is to store it in a reservoir that receives only highly treated wastewater.

This is exactly the approach employed by a water-stressed city in sub-Saharan Africa's driest country.[12] In the late 1950s, when an upstream reservoir and the local aquifer could not keep up with surging water demand, the utility responsible for supplying water to Namibia's growing capitol, Windhoek, built a second reservoir at the downstream end of the city. To keep sewage out of their new water supply, city managers also invested in a wastewater treatment plant that discharged below the reservoir. This arrangement met the city's needs until the mid-1960s, when growth again exceeded the city's water production capacity. This time, the utility turned to its wastewater treatment plant. Rather than rerouting the wastewater effluent into the reservoir, the utility sent it to a storage pond, where it was held for about two weeks before undergoing an extensive set of water treatment processes that included algae removal, sand filtration, chlorination, and activated carbon filtration. The recycled water was blended with copious quantities of disinfected water from the city's reservoirs along with groundwater before being put into the distribution network. When the treatment plant came online in 1968, recycled wastewater accounted for about 20 percent of Windhoek's drinking water supply.

Over the next twenty years, Windhoek's population underwent a fourfold increase. To keep up with the growth in water demand, another reservoir was built about fifty kilometers outside of the city. Eventually, this also proved to be inadequate. Luckily, recycled water could make up much of the shortfall; as Windhoek grew, the volume of sewage flowing into the advanced treatment plant increased, allowing the city to gradually expand its supply of recycled water. In 2002, it replaced the original recycling plant with a modern system that was about four times larger than the original.[13] In addition to the old treatment methods, the new water recycling plant employed ultrafiltration—a process in which a thin membrane made of a synthetic polymer filters out suspended particles that contain most of the waterborne pathogens as well as organic substances that produce toxic byproducts when water is disinfected with chlorine. As a result of the upgrades, water produced by the system is even cleaner than that produced by its predecessor.

With each upgrade and expansion of the recycling plant, the overall flow of the system increased and the time that the water spent in the holding pond decreased.[14] By 2020, the treated sewage, which typically accounted for about a quarter of the city's supply, spent only two or three days in the dedicated reservoir before heading to the advanced drinking water treatment plant. For all intents and purposes, Windhoek's wastewater and drinking water treatment plants act as a single system, with the storage pond serving as a means of breaking the psychological connection between raw sewage and treated drinking water.

Back in the early twentieth century, when wastewater treatment was still relatively new, the prominent American engineer Allen Hazen questioned the wisdom of using precious public resources to turn sewage into clean water that would likely be recontaminated when it was discharged into polluted rivers and lakes.[15] Although Hazen's hesitation made economic sense when sewage was just one of many pollution sources, it was largely forgotten during the second half of the twentieth century as wealthy countries invested billions of dollars in treatment plants in an effort to stop the algal blooms and fish kills that were decimating waterways. Today, in low- and middle-income countries, where sewage treatment is often rudimentary or completely absent, water managers are facing the same kinds of issues that much of the wealthy world grappled with decades ago. Learning from the experiences of Berlin, Northern Virginia, Atlanta, and Windhoek, cities might feel compelled to heed Hazen's warnings and recycle their wastewater without risking the possibility of recontamination.

In cities that lack the financial resources needed to build and operate modern water recycling plants, more immediate concerns about the public health effects of open defecation in informal settlements might lead to a different set of spending priorities. If sanitation concerns outweigh those related to water scarcity, it makes sense to invest in latrines and other, more sophisticated approaches for keeping disease-carrying human wastes off the streets.[16] Although such measures would be beneficial, surface waters downstream of cities will continue to suffer because even in the poorest of cities, inadequate sanitation is only one of many sources of pollution. It is unlikely that the more affluent people living in modern homes within rapidly growing cities will care to trade flush toilets for communal latrines or sanitation systems that require them to interact with their feces. Even if people in low- and middle-income cities were to convince everyone to adopt new approaches that kept human waste out of the sewers, polluted water from homes, factories, businesses, and city streets would continue to flow into waterways through sewers and ditches.

Ultimately, a singular focus on either water recycling or sanitation misses a larger issue: most of the water brought into cities eventually moves downstream. To protect public health, ensure economic vitality, and restore ecosystems downstream of the world's growing cities, water managers have an obligation to take care of both the quantity and the quality of water emanating from their sewers and drainage canals.

Mexico City provides a good illustration of the effort required to manage the water flowing out of middle-income cities. In the decades after the country's Spanish conquerors began dismantling the Aztec water management system that had been essential to life in Tenochtit-lan, floods periodically inundated the city that the colonizers had recently renamed.[17] During the seventeenth century, the situation improved somewhat when the government installed a tunnel to drain excess water from the volcanic basin. Eventually, population growth and shrinkage of the city's lakes led to an increase in the volume of nuisance water that had to be managed. In 1866, after another set of devastating floods, a network of drainage canals and sewers was built to move water through the tunnel more efficiently.

A century later, after overpumping of groundwater had caused severe land subsidence, parts of the sewer system sank below the height of the exit tunnel. To avoid the backup of water into low-lying parts of Mexico City, engineers built a sewage collection system two hundred meters belowground to route excess water out of the valley. By the mid-1970s this proved to be inadequate. In response, the city's engineers dug another tunnel to provide a second exit for wastewater. By 2020, a network of over twelve thousand kilometers of underground pipes was draining about 1.5 cubic kilometers of sewage and 0.5 cubic kilometer of urban runoff through the tunnels every year.[18]

After it leaves the city, the excess water flows through open channels that eventually meet up with the Tula River. From there, water heads to the Mezquital Valley—an agricultural community located about eighty kilometers north of the capital city. Before the twentieth century, the dry valley had been a quiet place where farmers had survived on rainfall and the modest natural flow of the Tula River. The fortunes of the community began to change in 1896, when the arrival of Mexico City's sewage made it possible for farmers to flood-irrigate greater quantities of corn and alfalfa.[19] As Mexico's capital city rapidly grew with the Great Acceleration, the flow of the Tula River greatly increased, ultimately leading to a fivefold increase in the area of irrigated farmland in the valley.

Although the expanded irrigation system had economic benefits, the water windfall came at a price. Relative to their rural neighbors, people in the Mezquital Valley exhibited substantially higher rates of

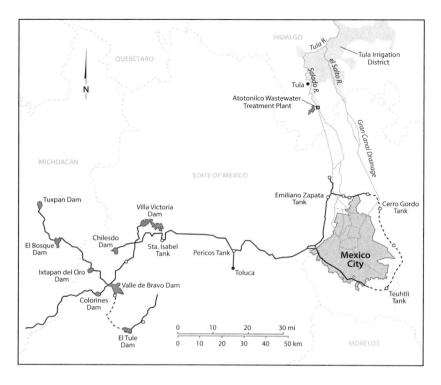

Mexico City imports water into the city from a valley west of the city. Stormwater and sewage generated within the city are sent to the Tula Irrigation District, located north of the city.

infection with waterborne pathogens transmitted by the raw sewage passing through their community.[20] Infiltration of Mexico City's excess water also raised groundwater levels to a point at which springs seeped up to the surface in low-lying areas, where they served as convenient places to obtain drinking water. Because the raw sewage had overwhelmed the treatment capacity of the subsurface, the drinking water obtained from the new springs and shallow wells was contaminated with unsafe levels of waterborne pathogens and nitrate.

After decades of discussion and unrealized plans, the government formed a partnership with a private consortium that spent around nine hundred million dollars to build the largest wastewater treatment plant in Latin America.[21] The Atotonilco Wastewater Treatment Plant, which opened in 2017, is located at the end of one of the two main canals that drain Mexico City. The treatment plant subjects about 60 percent of the megacity's wastewater to conventional sewage treatment before sending it to the Mezquital Valley. It also has a second, less exhaustive treatment system that removes suspended particles from the mixture of sewage and runoff that flows into the drainage canals after rainstorms in Mexico City cause flows in the river to exceed the first plant's treatment capacity.

Installation of a modern treatment plant will go a long way toward alleviating the sewage-related health problems that have beset the people of the Mezquital Valley. It also will enable the valley's farmers to generate higher profits from the production of fruits, vegetables, and herbs that could not be grown legally when raw sewage served as the source of irrigation water. Yet, despite these improvements, it is an imperfect solution. By reinforcing the Mezquital Valley's reliance on wastewater produced upstream, water resource planners may have complicated future efforts to use water more efficiently in Mexico City. To address land subsidence and water shortages, it is likely that the upstream city eventually will rein in its high per capita water use, which, if not balanced by commensurate population increases, will decrease the downstream wastewater flows. If, in the future, the city also manages to recycle more of its wastewater, farmers who rely upon the Tula River may face the same sort of water shortages that Orange County experienced when their upstream neighbors implemented conservation and water recycling programs in the 1990s. Furthermore, the current solution ignores the ecology of the Tula River, which, before the late nineteenth century, carried a much smaller volume of more pristine runoff through the Mezquital Valley. Although future investments might someday make it possible to move treated wastewater to farms in pipes, efforts to restore downstream ecosystems will probably require treatment of the sewage flowing in the second of Mexico City's two major drainage canals as well as measures to return river flows closer to their predevelopment levels.

Although its elevation, arid climate, and massive size complicate matters, Mexico City is not alone when it comes to its struggle to manage the water that it sends downstream. Most of the growing cities of South and Southeast Asia as well as those of sub-Saharan Africa and South America take in clean water from upstream waterways and emit a polluted mixture of sewage and urban runoff, turning once pristine rivers into open sewers. To reduce the impacts of cities on the downstream environment, the United Nation's Sixth Sustainable Development Goal includes a target of treating half of the world's wastewater by 2030.[22]

It is a laudable goal, but one that is proving to be difficult to attain due to a tendency of utilities to focus on water supply and sanitation within the cities where their customers live rather than employing their limited financial resources to protect downstream communities and ecosystems.[23] Without the help of committed national governments that provide funding for wastewater treatment plants, as well as the creation and enforcement of laws that prevent the release of untreated sewage, Allen Hazen's voice will continue to echo over a century after he first argued against wastewater treatment.

If progress cannot be made on this problem, downstream communities may simply resign themselves to the task of converting the mix of sewage, urban runoff, and industrial wastewater emanating from their upstream neighbors into drinking water or water that is suitable for irrigation. This solution might ultimately prove to be technically feasible for downstream water users, but it has serious shortcomings: in addition to polluting the drinking and irrigation water of rural communities that cannot afford modern treatment plants, the excessive quantity of polluted water flowing out of cities plays a major role in the ecological crises facing the world's rivers, lakes, estuaries, and coastal waters.

18

Irrigating Crops with Treated Sewage

THE APPROACH THAT Mexico City has begun to employ to manage its excess water—treating it before using it for irrigation—may be one of the most viable solutions to crises caused by water flowing out of cities. After all, if treatment plants are being built to make sewage safe enough to use for irrigating food crops, it should be easier to justify the additional expense of treating the remainder of the wastewater to make it safe to release back into the environment. In waterways where flows have increased well beyond those that existed before development, the diversion of treated wastewater to agriculture also could provide a way of returning hydrology to more natural conditions.

The use of wastewater to grow food is hardly new. To take advantage of nutrients and water flowing out of cities, humans have been diverting sewers and stormwater drainage to agricultural land for more than three thousand years.[1] The early civilizations of the Indus Valley, Greece, and Rome routed sewage and urban runoff onto farms, while cities in ancient China developed complex systems for collecting, transporting, and fertilizing land with human waste (which when collected and used for this purpose is often termed night soil).

As cities grew during the Industrial Revolution, water distribution pipes made it possible for people to equip their homes with bathtubs and flush toilets. These modern conveniences eliminated the drudgery of fetching water and emptying chamber pots. They also may have made the populace more presentable, but the increased volume of polluted water flowing from sewers fouled rivers that served as drinking water sources. It also was responsible for fish kills and noxious smells that permeated rapidly growing cities.[2] As these problems got worse, enterprising farmers were drawn in to manage the wastewater by the promise of free fertilizer and a reliable source of irrigation water. On the outskirts of the growing cities of Europe and North America, the ancient practice of using wastewater to grow food was reestablished.

The sewer farmers of the second half of the nineteenth century returned the nutrients that urbanites were anxious to get rid of back to them in the form of fruits, vegetables, and nuts. Wastewater recycling even provided fish that had been raised in sewage-fed aquaculture ponds. Although it was profitable, the boom time was short lived; most wealthy countries phased out the use of sewage for food production during the early twentieth century due to concerns about public health. By that time sewer farming already had lost much of its appeal because global trade and advances in mining technology had lowered the cost of mineral fertilizers. But in arid regions, the end of the practice was a hardship for those farmers for whom the water flowing out of cities was just as much of an attraction as the nutrients that it contained. Although some sewage farming continued in defiance of the wishes of public health officials, the sanctioned use of wastewater for agriculture in arid parts of the wealthy world did not resume until well into the second half of the twentieth century, when water from modern treatment plants reduced the likelihood that people would become sick from consuming the crops.

As cities installed pollution control infrastructure, crop irrigation with treated wastewater was adopted with varying degrees of enthusiasm.[3] It was embraced by farmers in Australia and the western United States, who valued the underexploited water resource. Across much of the Mediterranean, agricultural water reuse had fewer takers. Southern European countries gradually increased their use of this new water resource while simultaneously navigating the regulatory hurdles and ambivalent attitudes that had slowed the spread of potable water reuse in

Europe. North African cities reused only a tiny fraction of their treated wastewater due to a lack of social acceptance of the practice and pricing policies that gave farmers little incentive to seek alternative water sources. In contrast to the modest progress being made by their neighbors, one Mediterranean country took up agricultural water reuse with great gusto.

Recycling water made a lot of sense in Israel—a water-stressed country that prioritized economic development and food security. Although agricultural water recycling was eventually adopted, it took a while for it to gain momentum. In the years following the founding of the modern state of Israel, a few sewer farms were established in the countryside. But it was not until about a decade later, when a rapid increase in urban population overwhelmed septic systems in densely populated areas, that the country's water managers got serious about water recycling.[4] By the 1960s, much of the wastewater produced in Israeli cities was being collected in sewers. This solved the immediate problem of overflowing septic systems, but most of the sewage simply drained into rivers, where it killed the fish that had been keeping mosquito populations under control. In response to the stench and the public health risk, the government started investing in wastewater treatment plants, which produced water suitable for irrigation. By the early 1970s, about 20 percent of Israel's wastewater was being treated before being reused on fields of cotton, hay, beans, and other crops that were cooked before being eaten.

Convinced that recycled wastewater could help solve the sewage problem while simultaneously expanding food production, the government used a loan from the World Bank to launch a major agricultural water reuse initiative. The central element of the plan involved conversion of the Dan Sewage Treatment Plant—a rudimentary operation in the sand dunes south of Tel Aviv that had been discharging treated sewage into the Mediterranean Sea since 1973—into the largest modern wastewater treatment plant in the Middle East.[5] After sewage passed through the upgraded treatment plant, it spent an additional six to twelve months undergoing aquifer treatment before being used for irrigation. By 1990, about eighty million cubic meters per year of recycled water was being pumped around one hundred kilometers south to a network of storage reservoirs capable of holding the extra water that was produced during wintertime, when irrigation demand was low. From there, it played a key role in turning barren tracts of the Negev Desert into productive farmland. Elsewhere in the country, where aquifer treatment was less feasible, treated wastewater was subjected to processes used for drinking water purification—sand filtration and disinfection—before being used to grow food.

By 2015, about 85 percent of the sewage being received by Israel's network of more than sixty large treatment plants was being reused. Aside from a modest amount of recycled water that was employed to restore flows to rivers from which upstream water sources had been diverted, this unconventional water source was almost exclusively dedicated to agriculture.[6]

At a national level, recycled water currently accounts for about half of Israel's irrigation water. Although the treated wastewater is essential to the nation's farmers, the food that they grow with it is nowhere near enough to feed a country of more than nine million people. Accounting for water that is not recovered, each person in Israel produces about twenty-five liters of treated wastewater per day, which is a small fraction of the volume of irrigation water needed to sustain a modern diet.[7] Instead of providing food security, Israel's recycled water enables its farmers to grow the fresh produce that fills the shelves of the country's markets.

Farmers in Israel, the western United States, Australia, and Southern Europe have demonstrated that the combination of modern wastewater treatment followed by either aquifer treatment or sand filtration and disinfection can produce irrigation water that does not cause waterborne disease outbreaks. Recycled water can even be used to grow lettuce, strawberries, and other produce that is not cooked before consumption. But water safety does not end with freedom from the risk of digestive discomfort: concerns have been raised about contaminants that are not removed during the treatment process.

In 2021, researchers at the Hebrew University of Jerusalem reported the presence of a suite of pharmaceuticals in fruits and vegetables grown with recycled water, with especially high concentrations being detected in citrus and leafy greens.[8] This may sound dire, but it should be put into context; the dose of a pharmaceutical that people receive by eating fruits and vegetables irrigated with treated wastewater is not much different from what they would take in if they were to obtain their drinking water from a potable water recycling system like the one that serves Berlin.

Although there is not a definitive answer to the question of whether long-term exposure to a cocktail of pharmaceuticals at concentrations that are typically many orders of magnitude lower than a therapeutic dose is a problem, most experts have concluded that it is not a major cause for concern.[9] However, the uptake of pharmaceuticals by crops raises the possibility that other, more toxic chemicals that are sometimes present in treated wastewater, such as PFAS, might find their way into the food supply by way of agricultural water reuse.

The focus on substances that are not removed during treatment has also led to a hypothesis that the reuse of treated wastewater could be playing a role in a growing public health threat—the spread of pathogenic microbes that are resistant to antibiotics.[10] The underlying concern is that minute quantities of genes that provide bacteria with the means of evading antibiotics can survive the treatment processes employed in agricultural water recycling, either within live bacteria or as free-floating bits of genetic material released from inactivated bacteria. After the antibiotic resistance genes reach agricultural soils, it is possible that they can be picked up by other species of bacteria through a process referred to as horizontal gene transfer. If the bacteria that have obtained resistance genes are also capable of causing disease in humans, the antibiotics prescribed to counteract infections that people receive from contaminated food might not be effective.

Concern about the spread of antibiotic-resistant bacteria goes well beyond the practice of agricultural water reuse. In fact, the most concerning pathways that spread antibiotic resistance involve the misuse of antibiotics in human therapy and via animal agriculture, where the drugs are fed to livestock prophylactically.[11] Nonetheless, the possibility that agricultural water reuse might add to the problem is being taken seriously due to the risk of losing the few antibiotics that are effective against disease-causing bacteria.

After about a decade of research, it seems likely that the use of multiple treatment steps, as is the practice in Israel and other wealthy countries, before agricultural reuse greatly reduces the risk that antibiotic resistance will be spread through this pathway.[12] When sewage is applied to agricultural land without prior treatment, as is still the practice in many low- and middle-income countries, the risks of direct exposure to pathogens and the spread of antibiotic resistance are much higher.

While researchers continue to evaluate the risks posed by trace amounts of organic chemicals and antibiotic resistance bacteria in irrigation water, Israeli agronomists are addressing the more immediate concern of soil salinization. To maximize the amount of food produced with limited water resources, most of the country's farmers have adopted home-grown water efficiency measures such as drip irrigation, microsprinklers, and fertigation.[13] When these technologies are used in places where an occasional rainstorm does not wash accumulated salts out of the soil, farmers need to take additional measures to minimize the risk that crops will be damaged.

The effort needed to avoid soil salinization in a dry climate is proportional to the concentration of dissolved ions in the irrigation water. Until the early 2000s, much of the water in Israel's drinking water supply contained relatively high concentrations of salts due to the high rate of evaporation that occurs aboveground as well as the saline intrusions that allow seawater to move into aquifers belowground. When this relatively salty freshwater was recycled, it became even more challenging to avoid soil salinization because use of water for domestic and industrial purposes added dissolved ions that were not removed during wastewater treatment. Under such conditions, even the most prudent of farmers can run into trouble: Israeli researchers warned that the buildup of salts in the country's wastewater-irrigated soils was approaching a point at which crop yields would start decreasing.[14] They also showed that the use of saline irrigation water was leading to potentially unhealthy levels of sodium in fruits and vegetables.

Fortunately, the quality of the treated wastewater started to improve as the country's $15 billion project to transition the drinking water supply to desalinated seawater got underway. The concentration of salts in the recycled water dropped because the desalinated water started out with much lower salt levels than the surface and groundwater that it replaced.

Although salt levels in irrigation water have declined, the widespread adoption of seawater desalination has brought along a new set of agronomic challenges.[15] Much of the problem is related to the fact that the recycled water still contains elevated concentrations of sodium and chloride and unusually low levels of calcium and magnesium. Under these conditions, soil fertility and crop production could still decline in the future if measures are not taken to correct the ion imbalances. The low levels of magnesium in food grown with this recycled water coupled with the nationwide shift to desalinated seawater also contribute to magnesium deficiencies among Israelis that are responsible for increased death rates from heart disease. These new challenges are not insurmountable, but it is becoming clear that intensive agriculture with recycled desalinated water is a lot more complicated than the ancient practice of flood irrigating fields with a city's unwanted water.

Adoption of the water recycling practices that have enabled Israel to expand food production is appealing to many Europeans and North Americans who are committed to the principle of creating a circular economy in which wastes are reused for beneficial purposes.[16] Relative to the alternative of returning highly treated wastewater to the drinking water supply, agricultural water reuse feels like the right thing to do to many circular economy proponents because it gives new life to unwanted nutrients and is more readily accepted by members of the public. But feeling right is not enough to bring about systemic change; overcoming the unfavorable economics of agricultural water reuse and the kinds of water quality issues encountered in Israel will require creativity, sound investment strategies, and stronger societal commitment to the principle of circularity.

One of the biggest challenges facing any effort to employ agricultural water recycling at a meaningful scale is the fact that, like all other fluids, sewage flows downhill. As a result, most wastewater treatment plants are located at the lowest elevations within cities. In urbanized coastal regions, where farms have often been replaced by expensive oceanfront housing, the costs of building a pipeline and pumping wastewater from a seaside treatment plant through a congested city to inland farms can quickly add up. For example, building water recycling plants and installing a pipeline to move treated wastewater from the massive coastal treatment plant that serves most of Los Angeles County over a distance of about fifty kilometers would cost around $3.4 billion.[17] After accounting for materials, construction, and energy required to pump the water uphill, the price of the recycled water produced by such a project would approach that of desalinated seawater. Despite the steep price, the region's water providers are considering a massive recycled water transport project to recharge drinking water aquifers on the inland side of the city. The idea of piping the treated wastewater to farms has received little attention because the nearest location where crops are grown is still a mountain pass and many tens of kilometers farther from the groundwater recharge basins. In other big cities facing water scarcity, such as Phoenix, Perth, and Singapore, there has been little talk about building pipelines for agricultural water reuse because managers can find more economically attractive uses for the water within the city.

With the proper geography and sufficient financial incentives, growing food with treated wastewater can make sense, especially on the outskirts of small- and medium-sized cities in water-stressed regions. But at a national level it is unlikely that any other region or country will reach the extent of agricultural water reuse achieved in Israel because, in most countries, population tends to be concentrated in metropolitan areas. Although there may be some opportunities to send recycled water to farms located on the edges of population centers, the logistical challenges of moving recycled water over long distances combined with the greater attraction for utilities to reuse wastewater locally for landscape irrigation, industrial cooling systems, and drinking are likely to work against the expansion of agricultural water reuse.

In the absence of government subsidies, a water-stressed farmer may prefer options like drip irrigation or a shift to crops that use less water when faced with the prospect of paying the full price of recycled water. Although some financial support may be justified in the name of resource circularity, the more compelling reasons to subsidize agricultural water reuse are related to its public health and environmental benefits. Sending treated wastewater to farms allows water managers to justify investments in sewage treatment in places where it might not otherwise be an investment priority. It also provides a means of reducing the volume of unwanted water that cities release to rivers, lakes, and estuaries. If the original source of water has been diverted for other uses, the judicious implementation of agricultural water reuse may enable the restoration of effluent-dominated water bodies to their original flow conditions while simultaneously reducing sewage pollution.

19

Coastal Cities Turn toward the Sea

WHEN MOST PEOPLE think about desalination, the first things that come to mind are the massive systems that have enabled rich people to live comfortably in coastal cities where water demand exceeds the local supply. Although ocean waters are part of the drinking water supply of more than three hundred million people in the Middle East, Australia, and a host of wealthy places in arid parts of the world, civilization is still in the early stage of a desalination revolution.[1] The decreasing costs of the process along with the growing popularity of its use in the treatment of other unconventional water resources mean that desalination could become the key to solving multiple water crises.

The potential benefits of finding an inexpensive way of removing salt from water motivated the US government to pour more than thirty million dollars per year into desalination research back in the 1960s (an amount equivalent to about two hundred and seventy million dollars annually in today's currency).[2] After government funds made it possible for a generation of scientists to take on the challenge of developing a cost-effective means of desalting water, two technologies emerged that would become the basis for most modern desalination systems. The first was the reverse osmosis membrane—a thin polymeric material that is at the heart of the cartridges used in most modern desalination plants. The second involved the use of electric fields to slow the movement of ions in flowing water—an approach that would eventually lead to electrodialysis, capacitive deionization, and other technologies that are starting to provide even less expensive ways of purifying certain types of unconventional water sources.

In the first three decades after its invention, reverse osmosis could not compete with thermal technologies (various permutations of the energy-intensive practice of taking salt out of water by boiling salty water and condensing the resulting steam) that had been the mainstays of desalination since the start of the Industrial Revolution.[3] Eventually, advances in materials science led to more-permeable membranes that increased the efficiency of the new technology. Reverse osmosis matured with the installation of the first full-scale membrane-based seawater de-salination plants, which provided engineers with further opportunities to figure out ways to lower construction costs, create more-durable components, and reduce energy consumption.

Demand for reverse osmosis membrane cartridges and related equipment grew as the second-generation plants were built, leading to economies of scale in the manufacturing process that further drove down costs.[4] During a ten-year period starting in the early 1990s, the cost of using reverse osmosis to convert seawater into drinking water dropped by about 70 percent. As the technology became less expensive, new facilities were built at a faster rate. By 2018, more than eighteen thousand desalination plants were operating in more than 150 countries, producing around thirty-two cubic kilometers of water per year.

Although the recent expansion of this unconventional water resource has been impressive, seawater desalination remains out of reach for all but the wealthiest of urban and industrial water users. If, as expected, the cost of producing freshwater from the sea continues to drop, an approach that had once been considered the last resort of the rich could become the option of first choice for scores of middle-income coastal communities facing water scarcity.

Predictions of how much further the price of desalinated seawater could drop in the coming decades can be made with learning curves—an approach that has proven useful in projecting the future costs of maturing technologies such as airplanes, computer chips, and solar- and wind-powered electricity plants.[5] By plotting the cost of a new device or facility versus the number of units that have already been built, it is possible to predict the ways that factors such as technological innovation, competition, and economies of scale will further reduce costs.

In most cases, the economics of delivering recently developed technologies tend to follow a predictable pattern where the unit cost of producing an item drops as more of the items are built. Costs drop quickly in the early years following a new product's introduction when there are still many opportunities for design improvements. As more units are built, prices drop further, albeit at a slower rate relative to the number of units built, due to competition and realization of economies of scale in the manufacturing process. After the technology is standardized, costs continue their downward trend, but the rate of technological improvement and business innovation slows even further, meaning that many more units must be built before the significant cost decreases that took place in earlier phases of development reoccur.

Available data indicate that, since the 1970s, the cost of building seawater desalination plants dropped by about 15 percent every time the world's installed treatment capacity doubled.[6] The actual price that consumers pay for desalinated water has dropped at a slower rate than that of plant construction because in addition to construction costs, water prices also reflect operating costs, of which electricity is the main part, along with other more-or-less fixed costs, including the interest charged on loans and labor of skilled professionals who secure permits and manage the projects. Taking all these costs into account, along with expectations about future rates of new plant construction, experts predict that the price of desalinated seawater will drop by about another 50 percent between 2020 and 2040.

Future decisions about whether to build a desalination plant will depend upon how the expected lower prices will stack up against the alternatives. Cities facing growing water demand in the coming decades will have choices to make between further investments in water conservation and efficiency, expansion of traditional sources such as reservoirs and imported water projects, and unconventional sources such as water reuse and seawater desalination. Meeting water needs through restrictions on water use, conservation subsidies, or repairs to leaky pipes will continue to be powerful approaches, but as we have seen, on its own, efficiency is unlikely to prevent water shortfalls. Although the construction of dams, canals, and groundwater wells historically has been the preferred approach for generations of water managers, uncertainties associated with a changing climate along with the paucity of untapped water resources will continue to drive up the costs of traditional water resources. Treated wastewater might fill some needs, but as we have seen, there are limits to how much of it can be reused. Thus, it seems reasonable to assume that desalination will become more attractive to coastal cities in the coming decades.

Considering a middle-of-the-road climate change scenario, current prices for water charged by utilities in different cities, and conservative assumptions about the rate of decrease in the price of seawater desalination, researchers predict that the number of people living in water-stressed cities where desalination will be the least expensive new water source will triple, to more than 1.5 billion people, by 2050.[7] This means that in addition to the wealthy places where seawater desalination has already made serious inroads, the technology is likely to become more economically viable in middle-income cities in northern China, southeastern India, and Southern Africa.

Based on these observations, equipment manufacturers, consulting engineers, and development banks are already planning for a future in which seawater desalination is the main response to the first two water crises (water for the wealthy and water for the many) throughout much of the world.[8] However, there is no guarantee that this will happen. If public concerns about the environmental impacts of seawater desalination overshadow its perceived water security benefits, the diffusion of this seemingly unstoppable technology could be considerably slower than industry predictions.

The main environmental risks associated with desalination are related to the damage that it causes to marine ecosystems and its high energy demand. In terms of the coastal environment, attention is split between two processes: the intake of water and the disposal of brine.

Just like coastal power plants that use massive quantities of seawater for cooling, desalination plants have the potential to kill marine organisms as they take in water. In California, where worries about ecological impacts of water intake systems led to the phase-out of power plants that used once-through seawater cooling systems, new desalination plants are required to use subsurface intakes that filter water through the seafloor.[9] If plant designers can convince state regulators that local conditions make such an approach impractical, they may receive permission to install sophisticated aboveground intake structures that minimize the number of organisms sucked into the plant. Both modifications have proven to be reasonably effective, but environmentalists still express concerns about the long-term impact on marine ecosystems of the unnatural process of pulling large quantities of water into desalination plants.

Improvements in intake systems may assuage some concerns, but they do not address the potential ecological impacts of disposing of the large volume of salty water created by desalination. Modern seawater desalination plants produce about one liter of brine that is twice as salty as seawater for every liter of freshwater that they create. The discharge systems used by the plants are designed to mix this waste into the sea in a manner that prevents the formation of pockets of hypersaline water. Because salty water is denser than normal seawater, hypersaline water that is not properly diluted with normal seawater would sink to the ocean floor, where it could kill off salt-sensitive organisms. A properly designed discharge system can smoothly mix brine back into the sea, but it cannot eliminate the possibility that desalinating too much water in too small of an area will increase the overall salinity across an entire region of the sea.

The most likely places where this will occur are shallow waters where currents minimize brine mixing, such as the southwestern coast of the Persian Gulf.[10] If present trends continue, salt levels in parts of the Gulf will eventually reach a point at which desalination plant discharges will damage coral reefs and sensitive species of fish that are already being stressed by climate change. When discharged into deeper waters, desalination brines are much less likely to lead to measurable increases in salinity. Nonetheless, site-specific assessments of the impacts of desalination plant outfalls will be required if more large treatment plants are to be built.

The second set of concerns about seawater desalination is related to its energy use and the associated release of greenhouse gases. A state-of-the-art reverse osmosis seawater desalination plant consumes about three to four kilowatt hours of electricity for every cubic meter of water that it delivers—an amount that is roughly comparable to that of the energy-intensive imported water systems that serve parts of Southern California, central Arizona, and Mexico City. Moving away from exceptional systems that require water to be pumped over mountain ranges, producing drinking water with a state-of-the-art seawater desalination plant requires about ten times as much energy as what is consumed by a typical urban water supply.[11]

Thus, widespread adoption of seawater desalination has the potential to drive up energy use. However, the overall impact at a local or regional scale is less than one might expect. For example, if California were to build all the projects that have been discussed during the 2010s, its electricity demand would increase by about 1 percent as desalinated seawater grew to approximately 15 percent of the state's urban water supply.[12] The concomitant increase in greenhouse gas production associated with this theoretical expansion of seawater desalination would be only about 0.2 percent. The proportional growth in greenhouse gas emissions would be smaller than the increase in electricity consumption because California generates only about half of its electricity from fossil fuels and a large fraction of the state's greenhouse gas footprint is tied to the burning of gasoline and diesel fuel in cars and trucks. Widespread adoption of seawater desalination might make the price of producing drinking water more vulnerable to swings in electricity-generating costs, but with respect to greenhouse gas emissions, it is unlikely that increases will be large enough to dissuade individual cities from using the technology in response to an imminent water shortage.

To gain support in places where environmental concerns could work against them, the designers of seawater desalination projects are starting to include measures to protect coastal ecosystems and minimize greenhouse gas emissions in their plant designs. For example, in 2015, construction of a seawater desalination facility north of San Diego— the largest such plant in the Western Hemisphere—was accompanied by the restoration of twenty-five hectares of coastal wetlands to compensate for damage that the project might cause to the nearby marine ecosystem.[13] Several of the large seawater desalination plants recently built in Australia were coupled with financing for wind- and solar-powered electricity projects that are designed to produce enough electricity to offset the greenhouse gas emissions from operation of the water projects.

Attempts to make the process greener have not dampened the opposition to seawater desalination voiced by prominent environmental groups.[14] In addition to pointing out ecological risks and energy consumption associated with the process, these nongovernmental organizations have advocated for consideration of water conservation and less energy-intensive approaches, such as water recycling, before turning to this high-tech solution. Local organizations opposed to specific seawater desalination plants have adopted a similar approach in their fights against proposed projects in England, Australia, and Texas.

Capital-intensive seawater desalination plants are often built by private companies that set up partnerships with municipal governments that allow them to operate and profit from the newly built facilities. By placing the burden of financing construction on the companies, these public-private partnerships shift the risk of project failure away from utility customers, but they also cede decision-making powers to organizations that are trying to maximize their revenues. Although the fees that companies can charge for water are negotiated in advance, past experiences with privatization are reason for caution, especially in less affluent cities, where many opportunities remain to enhance water security through improvements in efficiency.

Although the industry ultimately may be able to make a convincing case that properly designed solar- and wind-powered seawater desalination plants can be operated in a manner that does not damage the environment, a community might still decide not to pursue this method of meeting its water needs due to the tendency of the projects to hand partial control of municipal water systems over to the private sector.[15]

20

~~~~~

The Coming Wave of Inland Desalination

DESPITE ITS COSTS AND potential environmental impacts, seawater desalination is likely to become a bigger part of the supply portfolio of many water-stressed coastal cities in the coming decades. But the desalination revolution will not stop there. The technological innovations that are spreading seawater desalination can also be applied to other salty waters. Although these alternative modes of desalination are still unfamiliar to most people, the opportunities that they provide are almost as plentiful as, and, under certain circumstances, may be cheaper and less controversial than, seawater desalination.

A big advantage of non-seawater applications of desalination is related to the fact that the ocean is just about the saltiest water source that anyone would ever care to desalinate. Reverse osmosis produces freshwater by pressurizing the saltwater side of a polymeric membrane enough to overcome the osmotic pressure that would otherwise cause water from the freshwater side to diffuse into the salty side. Because the pressure required to overcome osmotic pressure increases as the salt concentration increases, the energy consumed during desalination is proportional to the salinity of the water being desalinated. After accounting for all of the ingenious ways that engineers have devised to recover the energy used to pressurize reverse osmosis membranes, the desalination of brackish water (by definition, water that contains about 70–97 percent less salt than seawater) typically consumes less than half the energy of seawater desalination.[1] That is good news in terms of cost, but as is typical of situations when a technological answer to a water problem appears to be too good to be true, reality is a bit more complicated.

Numerous factors beyond energy consumption determine the cost and feasibility of brackish water desalination, most of them related to the location of the water source. For brackish surface water formed when tidal action mixes freshwater with seawater at the mouths of rivers, damage to the ecosystem is a major concern because the amount of water taken in by the treatment plant may be significant relative to the overall flow of the river. As a result, the design of the plant must assure that the intake of brackish water and the discharge of brine does not perturb local salinity patterns. To minimize the disturbance of salinity, desalination brine is often sent to an existing wastewater treatment plant—a solution that eliminates the expense of installing dedicated discharge pipes while simultaneously bringing the salinity of the treated wastewater up to levels that more closely match those of the estuarine waters.[2]

Desalination plants treating brackish surface water are still much less common than those that use seawater, but they are becoming more popular due to their lower costs.[3] For example, in 2012, London built one of Europe's largest desalination plants on a part of the Thames River where the water is brackish. By design, the plant remains in idle mode until a drought hits. After the city's other water sources fall below a predetermined threshold, the desalination of brackish river water will provide enough water to meet the needs of almost a million Londoners. Although a few other plants like London's have been built already, the fact that brackish surface water is not always available in large quantities near where it is needed means that this approach will be practical in only a modest number of places. Thus, most cities seeking the benefits of desalination will need to direct their attention underground.

Opportunities for exploiting brackish groundwater are plentiful along the coast. Because water flows downhill, shallow groundwater tends to move toward the ocean, where it often discharges through subsurface springs. As groundwater makes this trip, it often becomes more saline as it mixes with seawater that has worked its way inland. As a result, aquifers along the coast often contain brackish groundwater.

Groundwater wells located farther inland also can become brackish due to overpumping. When too much freshwater is extracted from a coastal aquifer, the water level drops, and saline groundwater migrates inland to fill the void. This process—known as saline groundwater intrusion—is one of the most serious threats to water resources in coastal regions.[4] For example, in the United States, hydrogeologists estimate that saltwater contamination, from saline intrusions caused by overpumping and by natural processes, affects about 15 percent of the shallow aquifers on the coast. Although less information has been collected elsewhere, saline intrusions threaten the water supplies of hundreds of millions of people in coastal communities in the Mediterranean, Asia, and South America. The problem will only worsen in coming decades due to continued overextraction of coastal groundwater and rising sea levels—another force that drives salty groundwater inland.

A second major source of brackish groundwater occurs farther inland in deep aquifers. Groundwater always picks up some dissolved ions from the dissolution of minerals, which explains why well water often contains enough calcium and magnesium to prevent soaps from foaming properly and forms chalky, white precipitates when it is heated. This water, often referred to as hard water, has typically spent tens to hundreds of years belowground. When groundwater spends thousands of years interacting with minerals before it is pumped to the surface, the dissolved ion concentration can increase to levels that approach or exceed those of seawater. Because the composition of this type of brackish water can be quite different from that of brackish water produced when seawater mixes with freshwater, geologists often refer to it as brackish groundwater of mineral origin.[5]

Brackish or saline groundwater of mineral origin is widespread, but in many places, it is found at depths that are too great to be useful as a water supply. Irrespective of its salt content, deep groundwater is not very attractive as a water source because at some point the energy required to bring it to the surface is too much to justify the effort. Accounting for the efficiency of pumps and electric motors, it takes about 4.5 kilowatt hours per cubic meter to pump water to the surface from a depth of one thousand meters, which is almost twice as much as the theoretical minimum energy required to desalinate seawater.[6] As a result, water suppliers rarely construct wells to depths of more than a few hundred meters. Thus, desalination will only make sense when brackish groundwater is located near the surface or where few other options are available.

Considering only groundwater that is present within one thousand meters of the surface, the US Geological Survey estimates that the volume of brackish groundwater under the United States is about thirty-five times greater than the amount of fresh groundwater pumped to the surface each year.[7] Because the recharge of deep aquifers often requires thousands of years, exploitation of brackish groundwater might face the same limitation encountered by Libya's Great Manmade River project, where water that found its way into an aquifer during the most recent ice age will eventually run out. Thus, in many places, brackish groundwater from deep aquifers is a nonrenewable resource that, with proper management, could last anywhere from a few decades to a few centuries.

Although both types of brackish groundwater are plentiful, with respect to their role in meeting urban water needs, the desalination of aquifers affected by saline intrusions is likely to become more common in the near term, whereas brackish groundwater of mineral origin could have a greater impact on water supplies in the future.

The use of desalination in aquifers affected by saline intrusions is attractive because, in most cases, it allows salt-contaminated wells to be reintegrated into existing water supplies. Disposal of the brine produced by desalination at coastal wells also tends to be straightforward provided that a wastewater treatment plant can accommodate the additional flow. If this is not possible, it may be feasible to pipe the water directly to a nearby brackish river, bay, or estuary. Although plentiful, the water that can be obtained from brackish aquifers is finite. If brackish groundwater is extracted too quickly from a coastal well, salinity levels increase as more saltwater flows into the depleted aquifer. When the rate of water extraction exceeds the rate of inflow of freshwater, the plant acts as a seawater desalination plant with a subsurface intake. Thus, desalination can be used to bring a well that has been contaminated by saline intrusion back into service or it can be used to access water from a coastal aquifer that is naturally saline, but the amount of water provided by this form of desalination might not be enough to greatly expand a community's water supply.

In contrast, desalination of brackish groundwater of mineral origin holds considerable promise for meeting water needs because it provides a means of accessing a large, untapped, unconventional water source. However, finding cost-effective ways of exploiting this resource can be quite challenging for several reasons.

First, the composition of brackish groundwater of mineral origin is often quite different from that of seawater or brackish water produced by saline intrusions. Brackish groundwater of mineral origin often contains high concentrations of silicate, calcium, and sulfate—ions that slowly leach out of rocks and minerals. As freshwater is separated from brackish water during the desalination process, concentrations of these ions increase to levels at which minerals such as silica, gypsum, and calcite can precipitate. If these newly formed minerals stick onto the surfaces of the desalination membranes, freshwater production will decrease. Engineers have devised clever ways to minimize such mineral fouling through the addition of tiny amounts of chemicals known as antiscalants that, at very low concentrations, prevent mineral precipitation. They also have learned how to manufacture membranes composed of polymers that are less prone to mineral fouling.[8] In most cases, limitations to water recovery imposed by mineral fouling will determine just how much freshwater can be obtained from this process.

A second complication associated with the desalination of brackish groundwater of mineral origin is related to the fact that the aquifers where it is found are often far from the coast. This means that a large volume of salty water—up to a third of the volume of freshwater being produced—must either be reinjected back into the ground, disposed of in a surface-water body, or dried to a point at which it can be managed as a solid.[9]

Among the places that have turned to brackish water desalination, the state of Florida provides an instructive example of the potential of this unconventional water resource and the challenge of managing brine waste. Despite the region's ample precipitation, Florida faces numerous water supply challenges related to its flat topography (the high point in the state is only about one hundred meters above sea level), which, along with the near absence of freshwater rivers and lakes, makes it difficult to build and operate reservoirs and conventional surface water filtration plants. With few opportunities for accessing surface water, South Florida's water managers relied upon shallow groundwater when the region's population expanded from about a half million to more than three million between 1950 and 1980.[10] Initially, the Biscayne Aquifer, which is located less than a hundred meters below the ground, provided enough freshwater to accommodate the new arrivals. By the late 1990s, saline intrusions threatened many of South Florida's coastal wells.

To provide water for its still-increasing population, water managers took advantage of the Floridan formation—an extensive aquifer that extends below Florida and its three neighboring states to the north. Under the southern half of the state, the formation consists of two separate aquifers: the Upper Floridan, which contains brackish groundwater, and the Lower Floridan, which, due to the local geology, consists mainly of seawater.[11] Pumping water from the Upper Floridan formation at depths of around three hundred meters consumed more than twice as much energy as drawing water from the shallower Biscayne Aquifer. After factoring in the costs of pumping and desalination, brackish groundwater from the Upper Floridan was still cheaper than seawater desalination because there was a place to put the brine. Located below the Lower Floridan aquifer, at a depth of around a thousand meters, another geologic formation known as the Boulder Zone was able to accommodate the brine produced by South Florida's desalination plants. The deep aquifer was ideal for brine disposal because it consisted of extremely porous limestone into which fluids could easily be injected.

By 2013, South Florida's brackish groundwater desalination plants were producing about 0.75 cubic kilometer per year of freshwater (about a hundred liters per person per day when averaged across the entire state), which made it the second most important water source after shallow aquifers like the Biscayne.[12] To put this into perspective, the amount of drinking water produced by desalination of brackish groundwater in Florida is about four times the combined volume of water produced by all US seawater desalination plants.

Due to its massive size and relatively high recharge rates, the Upper Floridan should meet the water needs of South Florida in the coming decades. The northern half of the state faces a greater challenge. Its cities have already been relying upon the Upper Floridan for drinking water because as it moves north, its salinity decreases to a point at which it can be used without desalination. Due to pumping of existing wells, the Upper Floridan is approaching the time when it will no longer provide enough water to support North Florida's continuing growth.[13] As a result, local water managers have been eyeing brackish water in the Lower Floridan aquifer, which also is shallower and less salty in the northern part of the state. However, exploiting this untapped source of brackish groundwater will be a greater challenge because the Boulder Zone does not extend into North Florida. Without a deep, porous aquifer for waste disposal, another brine disposal solution will be needed before North Florida can turn to brackish water desalination.

Notwithstanding the places where brine can be sent to naturally saline rivers and lakes, underground disposal is almost always the least expensive way to get rid of brine produced by inland desalination projects.[14] Deep well injection of brine produced by desalination did not require a lot of research and development because geologists had already been using aquifers to dispose of the salty water produced during the extraction of crude oil. Injecting brine into a deep aquifer requires a specialized well capable of withstanding high pressure, which, along with the energy needed to pressurize the brine enough to get it to flow into the subsurface, is responsible for much of the cost of this method of brine disposal. Deep well injection typically increases the overall price of brackish groundwater desalination by around 30 percent relative to discharge to a sewer or a saline water body. Although the added cost is rarely a dealbreaker, not every deep aquifer can be used for brine disposal: if the aquifer into which the brine is being injected is not overlain by impermeable rock, pressurized salty water can migrate upward, contaminating overlying aquifers. In some situations, deep well injection can even induce seismic activity (as was the case in Oklahoma when this approach was used to dispose of brines from oil and gas production in the 2010s). As a result, many jurisdictions have outlawed brine disposal via deep well injection.

When deep well disposal is impractical or prohibited by law, brine must be dealt with at the surface. One approach to doing this is analogous to the way that nature handles water that cannot find a path to the sea—through evaporation in terminal lakes. Under conditions that are conducive to evaporation, about eighteen thousand cubic meters of water will be lost from each hectare of standing water annually.[15] This means that an evaporation pond used to dispose of the brine from a brackish groundwater desalination system serving a desert town of ten thousand people takes up about as much land as a hundred Olympic-size swimming pools. Although enough cheap land might be available for this purpose on the outskirts of a rural community, the high cost of land acquisition in more densely populated areas usually makes evaporation ponds infeasible. In addition to real estate costs, the piping systems and liners needed to prevent salt from contaminating underlying groundwater add to the expense, with few economies of scale for larger systems.

Due to these constraints, evaporation ponds tend to serve small projects in warm, dry places.[16] In the United States, evaporation ponds have been built as part of a modest number of brackish water desalination projects in the arid Southwest. Evaporation ponds have also been used to dispose of brines in the Middle East and Australia, but the appetite for using this approach has not extended much beyond deserts where water users are affluent. In part, this is because bigger ponds are needed under cooler, wetter conditions to make up for the slower rates of evaporation.

As an alternative to relying upon the sun and wind to evaporate water, brine can be dewatered with machines known as concentrators.[17] Currently, most commercially available concentrators rely upon mechanical vapor compression—a technology that employs a combination of heat and pressure to separate water from salt. When used on desalination brine, the interior surfaces of concentrators must be made from corrosion-resistant steel, titanium, and other expensive materials that are not damaged by continuous exposure to hot, salty water. In addition, getting water out of supersalty brine consumes a lot of energy: under conditions typical of a state-of-the-art concentrator, about 15–25 kilowatt hours of electricity is needed to reduce the volume of each cubic meter of brine by 95 percent. After accounting for the cost of the equipment and the energy needed to operate it, the dewatering of desalination brine in a concentrator adds about a dollar to the price of every cubic meter of freshwater produced, which is over half the cost of producing freshwater by seawater desalination. The process also consumes as much or more energy than seawater desalination.

After passing through the concentrator, the slurry of precipitates and supersalty brine is usually sent to a small evaporation pond. Alternatively, it can be dried in a crystallizer—another mechanical device that uses heat to drive away the residual water.

Irrespective of the method used to process the brine, something needs to be done with the salt produced by the dewatering process. Presently, most dried salts from these so-called zero liquid discharge projects are sent to municipal solid waste landfills (the places where household trash ends up).[18] This approach may be feasible when only a small quantity of salt is being produced by desalination, but it probably will not be a viable approach if inland desalination becomes more popular. If a community were to obtain its entire water supply from brackish groundwater desalination plants equipped with zero liquid discharge processes, the amount of salt needing disposal would be approximately equal to the amount of household trash coming into the landfill.[19]

Beyond the fact that municipal landfill space is limited, adding large quantities of salt to landfills could impede their operation by stressing the microbes that make their living breaking down organics in the trash.[20] It would also complicate efforts to manage the excess water that leaches out of the landfill, especially if the crystallized brine contains toxic elements, such as arsenic, uranium, or selenium.

As a result of its high costs, zero liquid discharge is not very common. A variety of cheaper, less energy intensive alternatives to mechanical vapor compression are in various stages of development.[21] As these technologies mature or as existing concentrator technologies progress along the learning curve, the cost and energy intensity of zero liquid discharge will likely decrease. But without a better way of getting rid of the salt, the spread of brackish water desalination might be limited. As an alternative to landfills, engineers have toyed with the idea of feeding desalination brines into chemical refineries that produce commodity chemicals, including gypsum (calcium sulfate), halite (sodium chloride), and sulfuric acid. Although this approach could generate profits to defray treatment costs while simultaneously reducing the amount of salt needing disposal, technical and logistical challenges have not been overcome. Ultimately, the solution to the salt disposal problem may look a lot like the way that nature disposes of salt—through underground burial (this time in abandoned salt mines) or dilution into the ocean.

Overall, the worldwide volume of water produced by brackish water desalination is still modest compared to that of seawater desalination.[22] Nonetheless, brackish groundwater desalination has great potential in water-stressed cities that are not located on the coast. Coupled with the possibility that future innovations will eventually lower the cost of brine dewatering and solve the salt disposal problem, brackish water desalination is likely to become more important to efforts to address the first two water crises.

Turning our attention to the third and fourth water crises (water for the poor and safe drinking water), desalination would, at first glance, seem to have little to offer. After all, if a community cannot afford groundwater wells or conventional drinking water treatment plants, it seems unlikely that it could afford plants that employ reverse osmosis. Similarly, people struggling with arsenic or PFAS in their tap water will probably find it easier to remove the contaminants than to replace their existing water supply with seawater desalination plants or brackish groundwater treatment systems. But small-scale desalination systems have the potential to expand water access and protect public health by allowing individuals and small communities to remove contaminants from existing water sources.

In the informal settlements and rural villages of low-income countries, water kiosks—operations that refill the twenty-liter plastic containers that are ubiquitous in parts of the world that lack indoor water connections—started to become popular in the early 2000s.[23] In many cases, these operations were enabled by decreases in the cost of small-scale reverse osmosis units that were a side-effect of the increasing popularity of the big desalination systems used to treat seawater and industrial wastewater. The typical infrastructure supporting a reverse osmosis–based water kiosk has at its heart a set of pumps and membrane cartridges capable of producing around twenty thousand liters of clean water per day. At a purchase price of about twenty thousand dollars and monthly electricity costs of several hundred dollars, these systems can turn water that would otherwise be unfit for consumption into safe drinking water that can be sold for less than a penny per liter. With a reverse osmosis system, a locally sourced water kiosk can easily undercut the prices charged by water trucks and bottled water vendors.

Nongovernmental organizations have been working with governments and entrepreneurs in low-income countries to foster the spread of independent water kiosks that are sometimes referred to as Safe Water Enterprises. The idea behind this movement is that with a little initial help, a kiosk can provide an inexpensive source of safe drinking water while simultaneously contributing to the local economy. Despite over two decades of experience and millions of dollars of support from char-

Water kiosks provide a means for nongovernmental organizations and entrepreneurs to sell treated water to people who lack access to improved water sources.

ities and government agencies, the spread of Safe Water Enterprises has been slower than aid agencies had hoped, with only a few million people obtaining water by this approach, mainly in Asia and sub-Saharan Africa. In part, this is because every new operation must overcome a different set of organizational and operational challenges to achieve financial viability.[24]

The nongovernmental organizations helping to spread Safe Water Enterprises have good reasons to be persistent. If they succeed, these locally run businesses could provide affordable water to hundreds of millions of people who still lack access as well as billions more who struggle with water affordability or are served by sources that are unsafe to drink. To become financially viable, kiosk operators will need to overcome challenges associated with financing, operations, and marketing. Over time, Safe Water Enterprises or, if they cannot overcome the aforementioned challenges, commercial kiosk operations could displace water trucks and bottled water purveyors because the cost of purifying water by reverse osmosis systems will continue to drop.

The decreased cost of reverse osmosis has also enabled the spread of the technology to individual homes where the piped water supply originates in poorly run centralized water systems or contaminated wells. Although such point-of-use water purification systems are out of reach of the world's poorest people, they offer an attractive alternative to bottled water for middle- and upper-income families. An under-the-sink reverse osmosis system capable of meeting the drinking and cooking needs of an entire household can be purchased for several hundred dollars in most countries. Because the water that these devices treat is not very salty (tap water typically contains less than 2 percent of the salt content of seawater) and only the water used for drinking and cooking undergoes purification, point-of-use desalination systems are relatively cheap to operate. As a result of their simplicity and ability to remove just about any chemical or waterborne pathogen, the global market for point-of-use water treatment systems is growing by almost 10 percent per year, with annual sales of several billion dollars.[25]

Hundreds of millions of people already employ household reverse osmosis systems to protect themselves from contaminants in their tap water. In China alone more than fourteen million point-of-use water treatment devices employing reverse osmosis were sold in 2019.[26] The growing popularity of household reverse osmosis systems is not limited to middle-income countries: as concerns mount about the presence of PFAS, lead, and other contaminants in tap water, household-scale reverse osmosis units are becoming popular in the United States and other wealthy countries.

Despite their many benefits, household reverse osmosis systems are imperfect long-term solutions to the fourth water crisis for several reasons. First, they may lead to situations in which only those who can afford their own treatment systems will have access to safe drinking water. Although this inequitable outcome could be prevented with subsidies, achieving universal access to clean water will be more difficult with point-of-use reverse osmosis systems than it would be if everyone were receiving their drinking water from the same centralized water distribution system.

Another concern is related to the fact that reverse osmosis produces extremely pure water. This means that in addition to being free from waterborne pathogens and toxic chemicals, reverse osmosis–treated water lacks beneficial ions such as fluoride, which protects children from tooth decay, and nutrients such as magnesium that may not be obtained in sufficient quantities from the food supply.[27] Some epidemiologists have even theorized that communities that obtain their drinking water from sources that are deficient in lithium (as is the case for desalinated water) have higher rates of suicide and violent deaths.

Finally, to minimize the risk of mineral fouling, small-scale reverse osmosis units usually operate at low water recoveries. As a result, per capita water demand increases as the brine rejected by reverse osmosis systems flows down the drain. In India, in recognition of the possibility that this wasteful practice is adding to water stress, Delhi's environmental ministry proposed a ban on household reverse osmosis units in 2020.[28]

The fifth water crisis (water for food) has so far seen little benefit from desalination because its high cost has put the technology out of reach of most farmers. Projects in southern Spain and Israel are the rare exceptions where desalinated seawater has proven to be economically viable for cultivation of high-value agricultural products, such as flowers and tomatoes grown in capital-intensive greenhouses.[29] For outdoor crops selling for lower prices, seawater desalination projects that provide irrigation water have required generous government subsidies. Furthermore, desalinated seawater is not an ideal agricultural water source because it requires additional treatment to remove phytotoxic elements, such as boron and sodium, as well as supplementation with nutrients that plants normally obtain from their water supply, such as magnesium.

If the impact of desalination is going to move beyond niche applications and government-subsidized operations, its proponents will have to get more creative.

Beyond the provision of new supplies, desalination might have a role to play in the future in managing the buildup of salts that often accompanies intensified agricultural practices. As we have seen, more efficient irrigation technologies, including microirrigation and drip irrigation, have provided water-limited farmers with a means of growing more food, but the decreased quantity of water moving through the root zone of precision-irrigated farmland increases the risk of soil salinization. To avoid the accumulation of toxic salts in agricultural soils or the excessive leaching of salts into groundwater, perforated subsurface pipes are often used to drain away the brackish water that remains after crops have taken up their share of the irrigation water. To make this approach viable, the salty water from irrigated fields flows into canals. Finding a place to send the drainage can be difficult due to the risk of contaminating the supply of a downstream neighbor.

The challenge of managing salty drainage water is acute in arid inland regions such as California's San Joaquin Valley. When the imported water system that provided irrigation water to the valley was first built, the federal government's plan included a 450-kilometer canal to drain the unwanted salty drainage water to the ocean by way of San Francisco Bay. As an interim step in the construction process, the first third of the canal, which was completed in 1971, routed drainage water to a set of twelve evaporation ponds.[30] The new surface-water body created in the otherwise lake-free valley quickly became a popular stopover point for migrating waterfowl. Unfortunately, as the salty drainage water evaporated, the naturally occurring element selenium built up to levels that caused birth defects in birds. By the mid-1980s, images of tiny baby ducks with twisted bills in newspapers and on television led to closure of the evaporation ponds, cessation of further construction of the drainage canal, and decades of lawsuits about broken promises made to farmers who had installed tile drains with the expectation that they would have a place to send their salty water.

After years of litigation, the courts sided with the aggrieved farmers. Starting in the early 2000s, government scientists were tasked with finding a solution.

Ultimately, the favored remedy involved the use of microbes capable of converting dissolved selenium ions into insoluble selenium-containing minerals.[31] Because the amount of selenium that the microbes could remove from the salty water was concentration dependent, the best way to minimize costs was to pass the drainage water through reverse osmosis membranes before treatment. After the microbes took care of the selenium, the brine could be sent safely to evaporation ponds while the freshwater passing through the membranes could be sent back to farms. Reverse osmosis treatment also reduced the volume of brine that would need to be sent to the evaporation ponds. Although the federal government's proposal for a selective selenium removal system would have solved the problem of poisoned waterfowl, local groups criticized the high cost of the system and the lack of a sustainable method of disposing of the precipitated salts produced in the ponds.

As an alternative, a consortium of farmers and the state regulators proposed the construction of a pipeline to send the drainage water to San Francisco Bay.[32] The big difference between the newly conceived nine-hundred-million-dollar pipeline project and the original canal plan was the volume of water that would make the trip. Reverse osmosis would reduce the volume of drainage water by about 90 percent, which in turn would lower pumping costs and allow for the use of a pipe instead of a canal. Despite local enthusiasm for the project, it still faces numerous hurdles, including opposition from regulators and environmental groups in the San Francisco Bay region, where over two decades of effort has been underway to get local oil refineries to lower the amount of selenium they are discharging to the bay. Although a consensus solution may be decades away, the approaches being considered for solving the San Joaquin Valley's salt management crisis demonstrate the steady march of desalination technologies into the imagination of agricultural water managers.

While farmers, regulators, and environmentalists were busy debating the merits of using desalination plants to manage drainage water in California's San Joaquin Valley, a giant reverse osmosis plant had already been built for this purpose about six hundred kilometers to the southeast. Completed in 1992 at a cost of approximately $250 million, the Yuma Desalting Plant has a treatment capacity of about three million cubic meters of water per day—about 50 percent more than the country's largest seawater desalination plant. The facility was built in response to a complaint from the Mexican government that Colorado River water originating in the United States was becoming too salty for crops.[33] To comply with the international treaty that dictates the way that the river is shared between the two countries, the United States built a desalination plant in the border town of Yuma, Arizona, to treat water that flowed into the Colorado River from farms located on land that produced a lot of particularly salty drainage.

To dispose of the reverse osmosis concentrate produced at the desalination plant, the government built a ninety-kilometer canal that terminated at a flat spot in Mexico's Sonoran Desert. To keep the salty drainage water out of the river while the desalination plant was being built, the water was routed into the canal, where it created a set of wetlands that became critical habitat for endangered species such as the desert pup fish and the Yuma clapper rail.[34] (Fortunately for the wetland creatures, agricultural drainage from this region did not contain elevated concentrations of selenium or other toxins.) Due to local support for the wetland and the fact that the long-idled desalination plant would need to undergo an extensive modernization process before it could be used, it is unlikely that the Yuma Desalting Plant will ever send clean water into the Colorado River. If rising salt levels once again threaten the livelihood of farmers on the Mexican side of the border, the United States is more likely to release additional freshwater from upstream reservoirs to dilute salts from agricultural drains or pay farmers in other parts of the watershed to stop farming on irrigated land. Although the Yuma desalter proved to be an impractical solution, future drops in the cost of desalination coupled with a desire to grow food on irrigated land in a hotter, drier climate might someday lead to the construction of desalters on drainage canals. Perhaps water draining from farms might someday be subjected to desalination to protect or restore aquatic ecosystems from the effects of salts, nutrients, and toxic elements (the sixth water crisis).

PLANNING FOR A CHANGE

*You can already see the water future
provided you know where to look.*

EXPERTS WHO STUDY the complex systems that provide society with energy, transportation, and water often refer to the brief periods when major changes take place as transitions. Over the past two centuries, water systems have undergone transitions after crises arose that could not be solved by incremental change. Dams, electric pumps, and technologies that increased efficiency addressed crises of water scarcity, while treatment plants alleviated crises involving waterborne diseases and pollution of rivers and lakes. After these transitions took place, the decision to manage water differently seemed obvious, but in the years leading up to transitions, the path forward was unclear.

Facing a series of crises driven by climate change, population growth, and economic development, decision makers are finding that their toolbox of solutions cannot meet many of today's water challenges. The decision to abandon technologies and management practices that worked in the past and take a risk on something new is never easy. When transitions finally take place, they are often justified by the success of communities that have demonstrated the effectiveness of a new approach. In most cases, these influential early adopters are neither visionaries nor heroes. Rather, water trailblazers tend to be rational but somewhat desperate people who experimented with ideas that made sense for their particular circumstances.

To gain insight into some of the most promising new ideas for water provision and treatment and to better understand their potential to spread during future water crises, it is helpful to examine a few concepts that combine technological and policy innovations in ways that could enable the next water transitions. With strategic investments in these approaches coupled with improvements that take place as technologies mature, these approaches may become important to humanity in a water-stressed future.

21

~~~~~~~~~~

Stillsuit for a City

IN 2021, THE MOVIE *Dune* introduced a new generation to Frank Herbert's science fiction classic of 1965. As fans of *Dune* are aware, the story takes place on the desert planet of Arrakis. Due to its limited water supply, Arrakis is sparsely populated, food is scarce, and people go through great lengths to control water. One way that they do this is to wear outfits known as stillsuits when they venture outside. A stillsuit allows its wearer to capture, purify, and reuse water from their breath and bodily wastes. Although no one on earth has built a practical stillsuit, advanced technologies such as the life-support system on the International Space Station make it possible to recycle the urine and moisture produced by exhalation of a small group of astronauts.[1] With a cost of about twenty thousand dollars per liter, it seems unlikely that anyone is going to be employing NASA's high-tech approach to water recycling anytime soon.

The impracticality of building a stillsuit or a version of the system used in space has not stopped communities from attempting to create closed-loop water systems in response to scarcity. As reverse osmosis and other newer technologies mature, the cost of recycling the water from washing machines, showers, and toilets is decreasing to a point at which sewage is often a community's most attractive untapped water resource. By coupling water reuse with unconventional water sources such as rainwater and stormwater runoff plus more radical ways of increasing water use efficiency, it may be possible to wean cities from their historic reliance on imported water.

Due to the technical challenges associated with operating advanced water recycling systems as well as the need for a steady stream of revenue to get through the costly early stages of development, well-funded utilities in water-stressed regions that have already implemented all the conventional approaches for stretching their water resources are ready to take on the challenge of closing the water cycle. In other words, the first stillsuits for cities are likely to be built in affluent, water-stressed cities.

Among the handful of cities that are already on their way to creating closed-loop water systems, Singapore is probably the easiest to understand. Located on a small island without significant groundwater resources, the city-state has long considered water to be essential to its national security.[2] Singapore currently purchases much of its water from Malaysia through a long-term contract that was signed when the two former British colonies were separated into independent states in the early 1960s. Due to the low population density of the watershed that serves as the source of Singapore's water, imports could probably meet the needs of its growing population, but statements from the Malaysian government that it might someday use the water supply to gain leverage over its neighbor motivated the nation's founders to develop other sources. In addition to the imported water source that currently accounts for about half of Singapore's water supply, a few recently constructed seawater desalination plants provide about another 10 percent of the city's water. The remainder comes from an elaborate drainage system that routes rainwater from roofs and streets into reservoirs located on the periphery of the city along with a network of advanced treatment plants that treat nearly all of the city's sewage to a point at which it is clean enough to drink.[3] Singapore's long-term plan is to eliminate its reliance on Malaysian imports by 2060 through the construction of more desalination plants and further expansion of its stormwater capture and water recycling systems.

In parallel with its investments in alternatives to imported water,

Singapore has implemented programs to lower per capita water demand, repair leaks from its water distribution system, and incentivize greater water use efficiency by industries, which account for about half of the country's overall water use.[4] Despite the many gains that have been made in conservation and the capture of local water sources, desalinated seawater or imported water will continue to be part of Singapore's water supply well into the future. This is because stillsuits for cities leak: about 15 percent of the water flowing into the nation-state's recycling plants is lost when reverse osmosis concentrate is discharged to the sea. In addition, much of the water used by Singapore's industries becomes too contaminated to be recycled cost-effectively or is lost to the atmosphere by evaporation from industrial boilers and cooling towers.

At a somewhat larger scale, Southern California is creating a stillsuit for its twenty-four million residents. Orange County—the region's historic leader in efforts to declare independence from imported water—sits at the geographic center of this project.[5] Underlain by an aquifer that is large enough to store and distribute recycled wastewater, stormwater runoff, and water from the effluent-dominated river that bisects the region, the central and northern parts of Orange County have almost achieved water self-sufficiency. In 2023, the potable water recycling system that was built to push back a saline groundwater intrusion grew to a point at which nearly all the wastewater produced by the area's 2.5 million residents is being returned to the drinking water supply. This recycled wastewater provides approximately a third of the drinking water supply. Another third of the supply is derived from water infiltrated from the Santa Ana River—the waterway that for much of the year mostly consists of treated wastewater and runoff from the communities to the east. The remaining third is made up by approximately equal proportions of infiltrated rainwater and water imported from the Colorado River and canals flowing into the region from Northern California.

Water efficiency measures, including the replacement of older plumbing fixtures and appliances with more efficient models, the construction of more multifamily homes with common green spaces, and financial incentives to convert lawns to drought-tolerant landscaping, will help lower the county's per capita water use. But population growth will eventually soak up the gains made through conservation. In anticipation of drier conditions and continued population growth, Orange County's water managers have turned their attention to seawater desalination plants, despite objections from local environmental groups.[6]

Orange County's role as an early adopter of local water sources was driven by its precarious water rights. As one of the last parts of Southern California to undergo development, it found itself at the end of the line for receiving imported water during periods of shortage. Now that climate change and competition for water have increased the likelihood that the more senior water rights holders will also experience cutbacks, the rest of the region has started to follow the path blazed by Orange County.[7] In 2019, during a severe drought, the mayor of Los Angeles pledged that the city would fully recycle its sewage within fifteen years. Driven by the same forces, San Diego also committed to recycling most of its wastewater by 2035. In addition to recycling, Los Angeles is investing in projects to send runoff from city streets to groundwater recharge facilities that historically had received mainly imported water. It is also building hundreds of dry wells and a set of parks where captured stormwater will be treated before being infiltrated into the ground. By 2035, stormwater capture and recharge are expected to make up 10 percent and 20 percent of the city's water supply, respectively. As in Orange County, per capita water use throughout the rest of Southern California is likely to continue to decline through efficiency gains and the disappearance of lawns as more multifamily dwellings are built in response to a shortage of affordable housing.

Although Southern California has far fewer water-intensive industries than Singapore, its stillsuit also leaks. Unlike the Southeast Asian city-state, where tropical downpours greatly reduce the need for landscape irrigation, about half of the water being sent to Southern California's homes and commercial properties currently is used on lawns and gardens. Because irrigation water returns to the atmosphere mostly through evapotranspiration (evaporation from the soil and passage through the leaves of plants) and about 15 percent of the recycled water is sent to sea as reverse osmosis concentrate, at best, Southern California's water recycling projects would ultimately provide for only about a third of regional water needs. Under the most optimistic scenario, another 20 percent of the water supply might eventually be obtained by stormwater recharge. If closing the region's water cycle were the only objective, further conversion of single-family dwellings to apartment buildings coupled with a transition to a desert landscape in the remaining open spaces might provide a path forward. However, a draconian reduction in outdoor water use in such a dry climate would come at a price. Urban greenery keeps neighborhoods cool and makes them more attractive.[8] Financial incentives to remove turfgrass, punitive billing structures to discourage water use, and social pressure to use water responsibly will likely decrease the amount of water used outdoors, but it seems unlikely that Southern Californians will trade their trees and native vegetation for cactuses and rock gardens while they still have access to imported water. If that source dries up, they can build desalination plants at a price they can afford.

The early adopters in Singapore and Southern California may never completely seal up their stillsuits, but the combination of local water resources and conservation will greatly reduce their reliance on imported water. Excluding water used by industry, Singaporeans consume only about seventy-five liters per day of water from external sources (imported water and desalinated seawater). In Southern California, per capita daily use of external water sources could drop to as little as one hundred liters if the region's ambitious plans for water recycling, stormwater capture, and conservation are fully realized in the coming decades. Considering that population growth has slowed in many of the world's wealthy, water-stressed cities, an increased reliance on local water resources coupled with continued water conservation should make it possible to bring consumption into balance with the quantities of imported water that will be available in a drier future. If the stillsuit-for-a-city approach fails to bring water use into balance, desalination of seawater or brackish groundwater might make up the deficit.

Singapore and Southern California are not alone. Atlanta, Barcelona, Perth, and a handful of other water-stressed cities in wealthy countries are poised to build stillsuits. As knowledge increases and costs drop, cities that are not already facing water shortages might also choose to pursue this approach for other reasons. Chief among them is the fact that reducing imported water consumption is good for the environment. With sufficient investments in local water sources, utility managers facing calls to remove aging dams or to release more water to rivers that have been damaged by water supply projects will find it easier to take the environmentally friendly path without subjecting their citizens to greater risks of water shortages. Bringing stormwater into the supply portfolio also reduces ecological damage from wastewater treatment plant and stormwater discharges. Although the current approach for disposing of reverse osmosis concentrate does not improve water quality downstream (the same mass of contaminants is released in a smaller volume of concentrate), the concentrate from water recycling projects is easier to treat than wastewater in its diluted form.

Knowledge gained from the creation of stillsuits for cities in affluent countries will make it easier for cities in low- and middle-income countries to adapt this strategy in response to their own water crises. For example, São Paulo—the Brazilian city that nearly ran out of water in 2015—has not used its largest reservoir as a drinking water source in decades due to pollution from the surrounding favelas.[9] To protect public health while simultaneously bringing the reservoir back into service, the city would need to take on a multiyear project of installing sewers or building decentralized sanitation facilities (that is, latrines) for hundreds of thousands of people. If the city continues to face water shortages like the one it experienced in 2015, the unused water could be accessed sooner by treating the reservoir as what it has become—a giant sewage collection system that is a potential source of recycled water. By installing a sewage treatment plant at the front end of a water recycling system, dirty water from the reservoir could be turned into drinking water while the city initiates the slow process of providing sanitation to the favelas. Over time, water quality in the reservoir would improve as wastewater from the unsewered part of the city is routed directly to the treatment plant.

In Mexico City, where about 60 percent of the sewage is already being recycled for agricultural uses downstream of the city, treatment of the remainder of the wastewater within the city followed by advanced treatment and groundwater injection—a replica of the system used in Orange County—could alleviate downstream sewage pollution problems while simultaneously replenishing the city's rapidly disappearing groundwater. Mexico City's extensive aquifer and ancient tradition of using canals to route stormwater to lakes scattered throughout the city, coupled with more modern approaches of capturing and infiltrating groundwater—as currently practiced in Phoenix, Adelaide, and Los Angeles—could further augment the local water supply. With technological know-how and decreasing costs, these types of local water supply projects may become more attractive than the alternatives of appropriating water from indigenous communities in distant watersheds or taking on the challenge of cutting the Gordian knot of subsidies and political promises that has led to Mexico City's high per capita water use.

Stillsuits might also make sense in sub-Saharan Africa, where urban population growth is expected to accelerate in the coming decades. As sprawling cities that are on their way to becoming megacities, such as Lagos and Kinshasa, face the prospect of spending billions of dollars to expand their water supplies, engineers and city planners likely will recommend that the cities follow the tried-and-true centralized supply approaches used by cities in North America and Europe during the twentieth century. Taking a cue from the cities that are now building stillsuits, the emerging megacities could build integrated water systems that provide water supply, wastewater treatment, and urban drainage. By making water recycling and stormwater capture central to efforts to expand the water supply, these cities may be able to reduce their vulnerability to climate change–induced droughts while simultaneously protecting public health, reducing risks of flooding, and protecting the environment.

Although integrated water planning could be beneficial to emerging megacities, existing infrastructure and established water management institutions will probably make them just as susceptible to the lock-in phenomenon as cities in high-income countries. As a result, the greatest opportunities for rapidly creating urban stillsuits might be found in the small towns where rapid urbanization is just starting to take place. Lacking the established institutions and centralized infrastructure that exist in big cities, growing towns have an opportunity to leapfrog to a new water paradigm.[10] Urua, a rapidly growing town in Uganda, provides an example of the potential for creating a stillsuit for a city in low- and middle-income countries. An analysis of alternative approaches for creating a water supply indicates that Urua could meet the expected increase in water demand through the creation of eight separate water treatment and wastewater recycling facilities distributed around the city. By tapping into local sources of groundwater, surface water, or recycled water, the city could reduce its vulnerability to climate change while simultaneously addressing the public health and environmental damage caused by inadequate sanitation. Ultimately, the overall cost of the distributed water system is projected to be about 30 percent less than that of supplying the entire city with imported water.

Using distributed treatment systems to provide water and sanitation in cities that are not already locked into centralized infrastructure may also make it easier to adapt the water system as the city grows. After all, the exact ways that cities will grow is difficult to predict decades in advance. Rather than oversizing the system and paying for bigger water pipes and treatment plants to accommodate a population that might not arrive or undersizing the system to a point at which expensive modifications will be required to avoid sewage overflows and water shortages, decentralized water systems can be gradually phased in as a city develops. The neighborhood-scale water facilities also can be adapted to meet the needs of different parts of the city, with recycling plants in industrialized areas focusing on nonpotable water reuse while operations in residential neighborhoods employ potable water reuse to restore local groundwater. By distributing the water resource facilities around the city, substantial energy savings can be realized by decreasing the need to pump water over long distances.[11]

22

<span>~~~~~~~</span>

Net Zero Water Buildings

WHEN IT COMES TO providing water to city dwellers, wastewater recycling and stormwater capture are gradually becoming more attractive than imported water. Although this shift may help reduce the frequency of water crises, the cheapest and least environmentally damaging way of meeting growing urban water needs almost always involves some form of conservation. By employing water use efficiency, many cities are providing water to expanding populations without building any new infrastructure at all. Conservation also saves energy by reducing the volume of water that needs to be treated and pumped through pipe networks. The drive toward increased water use efficiency has another less obvious benefit: raising awareness of the value of water can create the public support needed to implement policies that prepare communities for future water crises.

When it comes to realizing water savings, the easiest conservation programs to implement tend to be those that reduce water consumption without making consumers feel as if they are compromising their quality of life. If a smooth path to adoption is the measure of success, the best conservation efforts take place indoors. Few rational people complained when their old twenty-liter-per-flush toilets were replaced by modern versions that accomplished the same task with 75 percent less water. Likewise, more efficient dishwashers and, after fixing some initial design flaws, high-efficiency washing machines, have largely replaced the water hogs that preceded them without a major consumer backlash. In contrast, outdoor conservation, while having the potential to save large quantities of water, has been a bit more challenging to implement in the United States and other wealthy countries where residential irrigation is common because it involves compromises in how people use water. As a result, public education campaigns, political fights, and financial incentives are often required to bring about the replacement of turfgrass and other water-consuming plantings with drought-tolerant landscaping. That is not to say that outdoor water conservation is ineffective. Rather, it demonstrates that water efficiency is easiest when it is nearly invisible to the public.

Cities that have been at the vanguard of the conservation movement are approaching a point of diminishing returns when it comes to personal sacrifice-free conservation measures. Today, a person living in a water-efficient home uses about a hundred liters per day indoors. Opportunities for further water savings still exist at the scale of the entire city because there are almost always a few homes with dripping faucets or inefficient plumbing fixtures and water-wasting appliances. Beyond the stragglers, a water-stressed city can normally find additional savings by repairing leaks in water distribution pipes. By using a combination of financial incentives, public education, and incremental improvements in efficiency, it should be possible to squeeze further reductions in per capita water use from even the most water-efficient cities for a few more decades. With enough commitment, the average per capita daily indoor water use for an entire city might drop to eighty or ninety liters. Although an additional 10–20 percent reduction in water use would be welcome, some people believe that such targets are still too high. For them, a per capita indoor water use goal of zero imported water is the proper goal to strive for, at least in some parts of a city.

The idea of creating buildings that, over the course of a year, do not consume any municipal water has recently captured the imaginations of architects, builders, and engineers around the world. The concept, which is sometimes termed net zero water, is that water-efficient plumbing and appliances, combined with unconventional water sources, such as shallow wells or rainwater harvesting systems, could be coupled with onsite water recycling to radically reduce the need for municipal water.

In most situations, a net zero water building would retain its connection to the municipal water system to provide backup supplies during dry periods. The connection would also provide immediate access to large quantities of pressurized water if the building were to catch on fire. To achieve a "net zero" status while retaining a connection to the municipal supply, a building could provide water to its neighbors or recharge groundwater during periods when it had excess water. Most net zero buildings would also retain a connection to the centralized sewer system to dispose of small quantities of excess water and waste solids produced during the treatment process. On the edges of cities, or in rural locations lacking municipal water and sewer systems, net zero buildings would be equipped with storage tanks that were large enough to prevent service outages during droughts. Additional treatment equipment would also be needed for such buildings to assure that the wastes they discharged to nearby streams or aquifers would not cause any environmental damage.

Recent efforts to employ local water sources and onsite water recycling to reduce the water demand of apartment buildings provide a glimpse into what it might ultimately take to make net zero water a reality. New York City's Battery Park City urban redevelopment project exemplifies just how far a builder can go with off-the-shelf technologies and current regulations.[1] The project, which was built starting in the early 2000s, consists of a set of high-rise buildings that house about ten thousand people, along with schools, retail space, and offices that provide toilets, sinks, and water fountains for around thirty-five thousand people who use the buildings on a typical day. Six buildings at Battery Park City are equipped with rooftop rainwater harvesting systems and miniature sewage treatment plants, known as membrane bioreactors, in their basements. Treated wastewater and rainwater are combined, disinfected, and sent through a dedicated nonpotable pipe network that provides water for toilet flushing, laundry, landscape irrigation, and cooling towers. In total, the onsite water system reduces the amount of water that the building users purchase from the municipal water system by approximately 50 percent.

After accounting for the additional costs needed to obtain permits, monitor water quality, and operate and maintain equipment, the builders reckon that reduced spending on water bills covered the cost of the onsite water system within the first decade of construction. The relatively short payback period was partially attributable to financial incentives provided by state and city governments. Beyond the desire of politicians to encourage the construction of green buildings, grants and discounts on water bills allocated to the project were justified by the benefits that the onsite water systems provide, the main one being that the six buildings comprising Battery Park City discharge significantly less wastewater to the already overburdened sewer system when it rains, which helps New York comply with regulations restricting the number of days that combined sewer overflows release untreated wastes to nearby waterways.

Although Battery Park City was not built to achieve net zero water, it illustrates some of the challenges facing onsite water systems. Due to concerns about possible health risks associated with the use of rainwater or highly treated wastewater for hand washing, bathing, and cooking, the building's potable supply, which accounts for about half of its total water use, is obtained from the municipal water system. The reduced demand for water produced onsite means that only about half of the wastewater is recycled. In addition, the extra efforts required to negotiate permits and document the performance of the system increased the cost of the onsite water systems by about 20 percent.[2] Bringing the project to fruition also took time and required a motivated project developer, along with government regulators who had the staff needed to collaborate on the creation of a system that balanced the need to control project costs with the protection of public health.

Progress also has been made elsewhere in the United States, as exemplified by San Francisco's Salesforce Tower, one of the tallest buildings in the western half of the country, which employs an onsite water system for toilet flushing within the massive office building.[3] The construction of this onsite water system, along with about a dozen systems in new buildings built in the city's downtown business district since 2012, was motivated by San Francisco's ordinance requiring buildings with more than twenty-three thousand square meters of floor space to provide part of their own water supply.

Onsite water reuse is a global phenomenon. Japan has long been a global leader in onsite water systems, with more than 2,500 systems in operation that treat rainwater, gray water (water from kitchens and sinks), or blackwater (sewage) in buildings before using it to flush toilets or irrigate gardens. Municipal governments throughout the country started requiring onsite water systems in newly constructed offices and public buildings in the 1980s both as a means of reducing demands on the municipal water system and as an emergency supply that could be accessed after an earthquake.[4]

In Europe, Barcelona created regulations requiring the installation of gray water treatment systems in newly built multifamily dwellings starting around 2008.[5] Although the Spanish city's effort has not been extended to high-rise buildings, it is building public support for onsite water systems while simultaneously reducing per capita water consumption. A combination of financial incentives, local ordinances, and the promise of savings on water bills along with the public's support for using water in a more sustainable manner is advancing onsite reuse in these and a few other cities. It is likely to drive construction of more of these water-efficient-but-not-quite-net-zero-water buildings in the coming decades. As these efforts become more popular, it is likely that the costs will drop and some of the hesitancy of regulators will dissipate.

Despite growing evidence that onsite water systems can be cost-effective and safe, the spread of policies encouraging or requiring their construction has been slowed by concerns from utility managers that their organizations might lose revenue as buildings disconnect themselves from the municipal water system.[6] In many ways, water utilities are facing a situation similar to what was encountered by electricity providers when rooftop solar systems became popular. To provide incentives for consumers to generate renewable energy, many governments initially required utilities to deduct the value of the excess electricity that homeowners sent into the power grid from their bills. This approach, termed net metering, benefitted early adopters of rooftop solar power because they paid only a small fee for the reliability provided by the electrical grid. The benefit that self-generating customers received from net metering was paid for through higher bills for the remaining utility customers, many of whom were renters or less affluent homeowners who could not afford solar panels.

The advantage that the self-generating utility customers received is an example of a phenomenon that economists call a free rider problem. It can sneak up on the operators of a shared service because the benefit is hardly noticeable when only a few users are getting a free ride. If enough of these systems are built, the people who have not yet taken advantage of the reliability discount shoulder a disproportionate fraction of the cost of maintaining the shared infrastructure. The issue has become particularly contentious in California, where opponents of net metering have attempted to add a monthly reliability charge to newly installed solar panels to account for electricity grid maintenance costs.[7] Proponents of rooftop solar argue that this fee will slow the state's progress toward its goal of reducing fossil fuel use by discouraging the installation of rooftop solar systems.

If onsite water systems become more popular, water utilities may eventually have to address the way that they bill their customers for access to a reliable supply. Yet that presently seems like a distant concern in wealthy countries, where new building construction has slowed and existing structures rarely undergo the kind of remodeling that enables installation of a dedicated nonpotable water system. At current rates of adoption, many decades will be required before onsite water systems have a noticeable effect on utility revenues, provided that the cost-effectiveness of the systems does not drop so low that a building owner can justify the cost of retrofitting a structure that is not being extensively remodeled. In the interim, the benefits that onsite water projects provide to the entire community—including reduced spending on new water infrastructure and avoidance of combined sewer overflows—

should justify the discounts received by the modest number of new buildings equipped with onsite systems.

Concerns that onsite water systems might deprive utilities of revenue are more immediate in low- and middle-income countries, where the construction of new buildings is booming and municipal water and sewer services are often inadequately funded. This issue could become particularly relevant in India, where government mandates to install onsite wastewater treatment and water recycling systems in new buildings were put into place in the early 2000s. These efforts were embraced with great enthusiasm in Bangalore—the rapidly growing water-stressed city that is sometimes called the Silicon Valley of India—where all new developments larger than twenty thousand square meters were required to include onsite water systems. Due to recent growth, Bangalore's onsite water treatment systems already have the capacity to treat 10–20 percent of the sewage produced in the city.[8] Unfortunately, the capacity to treat water does not necessarily translate into an expanded water supply; due to weak regulatory oversight and inadequate funding for maintenance, many of the onsite water systems are not fully operational.

In Beijing, regulators used a more gradual approach to gain experience with onsite water systems. Rather than requiring that all new buildings include their own wastewater recycling systems, the city's initial efforts, which got underway in the late 1980s, were focused on large hotels and resorts, most of which were owned and operated by multinational companies.[9] Driven by a desire to gain access to China's lucrative travel market and a need to avoid odors or service interruptions that might be off-putting to business travelers and tourists, the first generation of onsite water systems in Beijing were well funded and managed. Emboldened by the success of their initial foray into building-scale water systems, government regulators extended the mandate to include large residential buildings in the early 2000s. Although developers competing for new projects in Beijing's profitable housing market complied with the government directive, lax oversight of the newly built systems coupled with the relatively low cost of obtaining water and sewer services from the municipal system did not provide a strong-enough incentive for builders to invest in the robust systems that had been installed in the international hotels. As a result, most of the new onsite water systems were abandoned after a few years. Ultimately, government regulators lost interest in onsite water systems because Beijing addressed its water supply needs by importing water through the South-to-North Project and investing in a set of modern, centralized wastewater treatment plants.

The main lessons learned from early efforts to install onsite water systems in India, China, and other low- and middle-income countries is that providing the ongoing funding and regulatory oversight for thousands of individual treatment systems is difficult and public health and environmental regulations are not uniformly enforced. Furthermore, in cities where water and sewer systems are still inadequate, government efforts to oversee onsite water systems often take a back seat to investments in centralized water infrastructure. If onsite water systems are going to be part of the long-term solution to water crises in the rapidly growing cities of low- and middle-income countries, their proponents will need to find a business model that incentivizes their operation without depriving the larger municipal system of needed financial resources and oversight. This means that governments may have to create larger subsidies for onsite water systems. Alternatively, they can develop the political will needed to force wealthy people in new buildings to contribute twice: first to the construction of onsite water systems and then to upgrades of the systems that provide them with reliability while also serving the rest of the community. In other words, onsite water system owners may have to pay for their systems as well as those of their less affluent neighbors.

Irrespective of where they are located, onsite treatment systems that use half as much water as their conventional counterparts are already technically feasible. With proper management, they can be economically attractive, even after their owners pay their fair share of maintaining the centralized water and sewer system. The question of whether it makes sense for such buildings to strive for a net zero water status has yet to be resolved. If builders are going to make this jump, a source of potable water will be needed. For one- or two-story dwellings, rain-water tanks—a means of supplying potable water that is routinely used in Australia, South America, and parts of Asia—might be a practical solution, but only if they include robust filtration and disinfection systems. Yet rainwater alone will not meet the potable water needs of multistory apartment buildings, because too many people share the same water-collecting roof.[10] Relying upon rainwater harvesting would be especially challenging in places with lengthy dry seasons, such as the American West, much of India, and northeastern Brazil.

As an alternative, it might be possible to exploit shallow ground-water—a resource that has been underused in recent decades due to concerns about contamination. Small-scale reverse osmosis systems, such as those employed by some water kiosks in low- and middle-income countries, could be employed to obtain groundwater that is currently being pumped into sewers. This untapped water resource, which is sometimes termed nuisance groundwater, is extracted as a means of keeping water away from subsurface structures, such as tunnels and building foundations.[11] For example, a developer recently built a reverse osmosis system to treat about 150 million liters per year of water coming from a drainage system that keeps water out of San Francisco's regional transit system. The water will be sent to a district heating system that is one of the city's largest water users, but it could just as easily have supplied drinking water to thousands of people living in net zero water buildings. This underused resource is not unique to San Francisco. London's underground rail system pumps out more than ten billion liters of nuisance groundwater per year, while New York's subway system disposes of close to twenty billion liters of shallow groundwater every year.

Another possible approach for making the limited supply of rain-water or local groundwater go further is to adopt a narrower definition of potable water. In most wealthy countries, the water flowing from the tap serves as potable water because it is safe enough to drink without boiling or some other form of treatment. However, people in low- and middle-income countries frequently do not consume untreated tap water due to concerns about waterborne pathogens. Despite their hesitancy to drink tap water, people who are supplied with this unsafe water bathe and wash their hands with it every day. Although recycled water from a building-scale water system should be safe enough to drink, the risks of waterborne disease from a malfunctioning system would be reduced by restricting its use to the bathroom, where it would be used for showering and hand washing. By saving rainwater or locally sourced groundwater for the kitchen, a limited supply would go a lot farther. For example, in 2013, four students at the University of South Florida lived for two years in an almost net zero water dorm in which recycled water was used for everything except drinking and cooking without any problems with waterborne pathogens or problems with odors from the recycled water.[12] The dorm probably could have achieved a true net zero water status if the local health authorities had allowed the students to consume water from the rainwater tank.

In addition to benefitting their residents, onsite water systems—including those that aspire to achieve a net zero water status—may also serve as niche markets for the developers of devices that take water conservation to the next level because indoor water savings would directly translate into reductions in the size of storage tanks and treatment systems needed for onsite water systems. Thus, a virtuous cycle could be created where water savings from next-generation conservation reduce costs of onsite water systems. In addition to these economic incentives, people who choose to live in water-efficient buildings are likely to be enthusiastic early adopters of water-saving technologies despite the problems that are nearly certain to be encountered in early versions of the devices.

Vacuum toilets are a good example of the kind of next-generation conservation approach that could be particularly beneficial to onsite water systems. If building occupants are willing to put up with the characteristic whooshing sound of the toilets that today are mainly used on airplanes, they may be able to reduce their per capita indoor water use by 20–30 percent. Vacuum toilets, which employ suction to remove solid waste, consume only about one liter per flush, which is approximately 75 percent less than typical water-efficient toilets. The smaller volume of flush water diluting urine and feces makes it cheaper to turn human wastes into biogas—an energy-rich substance that can replace conventional natural gas.[13]

Even at their current stage of development, early adopters are beginning to realize the benefits of these devices: a green housing development consisting of more than two hundred homes equipped with vacuum toilets has been operating in the Netherlands since 2011.[14] The toilets have reduced water consumption by about 25 percent, while the treatment system that converts human wastes into biogas supplies about 10 percent of the energy needed to heat the development's homes and provide its residents with hot water.

For those who are not yet ready for the soothing sound of a vacuum toilet, recirculating showers might provide another way to reduce water consumption. These devices, which currently cost several thousand dollars, recycle water that would otherwise go down the drain, thereby enabling their users to take lengthy, guilt-free showers. During the initial part of the shower, soapy, dirty water is sent down the drain. After the hygienic part of the shower ends, its user flips a switch, or on fancier models a sensor determines when the used water is clean enough to recirculate. When operated in the recirculation mode, water is reheated and disinfected with ultraviolet light before returning to the shower head. The companies that are trying to generate interest in recirculating showers claim that they can reduce shower water use by 90 percent, which is true for people who take ten-minute showers.[15] Sure, a person could get clean with a three-minute shower, but experience has shown that not everyone can be convinced to forsake long showers for water conservation.

Further indoor water savings might someday be obtained by redesigning clothes washing machines.[16] Starting in the 2010s, several of the major manufacturers funded research and development projects on waterless washing machines. One design employed tiny polymers to pull dirt out of soiled clothes; another, not exactly waterless, approach removed dirt by blasting clothes with steam; and a third used pressurized carbon dioxide to extract dirt from fabrics. Although the development of a commercially viable system is a bit further away than the vacuum toilets and recirculating showers, the mere fact that manufacturers are investing in these R&D projects suggests that the amount of water needed to run household appliances might decline in the future.

Finally, borrowing from *Dune's* stillsuits, buildings are being built that can recover the excess moisture exhaled by occupants, the water vapor that is released into the air when they shower, and even the moisture released by their beloved houseplants.[17] Most multifamily dwellings, hotels, and office buildings are already equipped with dehumidifiers as part of the building's climate control systems. Pulling excess moisture out of the air reduces energy use because less-humid air is more comfortable to people at higher temperatures, thereby reducing costs for air conditioning. In most existing buildings, the water that is condensed in the air-handling system is simply sent down the drain. However, a few pioneering companies are reusing this water. For example, Microsoft's new 46,000-square-meter campus in Herzliya, Israel, uses the 237,000 liters of water per year pulled out of office air by its dehumidification system for outdoor landscaping. Although this is equivalent to less than a half-liter per day for each worker in the building complex, every little bit helps in the quest for net zero.

Beyond the initial phase of experimentation when government mandates, subsidies, or simply the novelty of a green building might incentivize onsite water systems, a positive return on investment will be needed if this approach is going to spread beyond the early adopters. The number of net zero water buildings or their less ambitious water-saving cousins will ultimately depend upon their up-front construction costs and reliability. Considering commercially available rainwater harvesting systems for potable water and membrane bioreactors for wastewater recycling, a team of researchers recently estimated that onsite water systems would increase the construction costs of typical multifamily dwellings by 6–12 percent.[18] Accounting for operations, maintenance, and safety monitoring, the researchers estimated that net zero water systems would pay for themselves after only a few years in most parts of North America and Western Europe. In Eastern Europe, Central Asia, and Latin America, where the costs of municipal water services are lower, subsidies would be required to make such projects financially attractive. Thus, net zero water systems have the potential to follow the path blazed by rooftop solar panels, with costs dropping as manufacturers and builders gain more experience. If society is willing to take the plunge, onsite systems might be a good tool for avoiding water supply crises in the world's cities and large towns.

Smaller versions of the systems being developed for office buildings and apartments also may become practical for single-family dwellings. Given the current costs and complexity of onsite water systems, it is likely that the first net zero water homes might find a supportive market among wealthy people who live in remote locations. Like their predecessors who provided a niche market for the manufacturers of small-scale solar panels and storage batteries to lower the costs of self-supplied electricity in the early 2000s, these early adopters might provide the initial funding needed for companies making net zero water technologies to improve their wares.[19] Eventually, high-end systems serving the wealthy could become cheap enough to become accessible to less affluent people struggling with inadequate water supplies in rural settings.

The key to enabling the widespread deployment of onsite water treatment systems for individual homes is modularization. By created a standardized design, equipment providers can take advantage of economies of scale in the manufacturing process while builders can avoid the hassles associated with custom-designed treatment systems. For example, the Dutch company Hydraloop has developed a modular water recycling system that recycles a household's gray water.[20] At a purchase price of around four thousand dollars, the device is already close to a point at which it makes financial sense for homeowners facing high monthly water bills in wealthy countries. In rural settings with inadequate water supplies, such a system could be indispensable. The current version of Hydraloop's recycling system, which requires minimal maintenance, is undergoing a trial in Sydney, with the water utility supervising the installation and operation of the product to about thirty customers. If the development of such household-scale technology continues, it may take a decade or more of experimentation in niche markets populated by early adopters before the concept spreads. If household gray water systems turn out to be as safe and reliable as their inventors claim, these devices could be combined with existing technologies, such rainwater storage tanks and household-scale reverse osmosis systems, to provide millions of people with a cost-effective means of creating their own net zero water homes.

If society pursues net zero water buildings, our relationship with the water supply will get more personal. Onsite water systems make it easier to realize at last the promise of fit-for-purpose water—the idea that water treatment could be adjusted to provide water that is exactly suited for its desired use.[21] With reverse osmosis membranes, sensors, and membrane bioreactors, it may someday be possible for homeowners to adjust the quality of water to meet their individual preferences. Thus, the owner of an onsite treatment system could dial down levels of calcium and magnesium for the washing machine and shower to allow soaps and detergents to work more effectively. Some of those same ions could be added back into water used for cooking or drinking to improve its taste and enhance its nutritional qualities. Nitrogen- and phosphorus-rich water from the onsite waste treatment system could be sent via drip irrigation tubing to the garden, thereby reducing the need for purchasing fertilizer while simultaneously decreasing surface water pollution. The possibilities are nearly endless. Although these are still the early days for onsite systems, local control of water has the potential to address water crises, disrupt the institutions responsible for water supply and sanitation, and return control of water to individuals.

23

A Better Salt Machine

AMONG THE MANY challenges facing water systems, salt management ultimately may prove to be the one that limits humanity's control of the water cycle. At proper levels, plentiful ions such as calcium, magnesium, and sulfate act as nutrients that contribute to water's pleasant taste. Too much is often worse than too little; as evaporation and mineral weathering increase the concentrations of these and other dissolved ions, salts can reach levels that damage plants, make drinking water unpalatable, and even compromise the health of humans and wildlife.

During the Great Acceleration, infrastructure for moving and storing water was created in nearly every corner of the earth. These projects altered the paths of rivers and created lakes where none had previously existed. They turned deserts and grasslands into farmland. Water was pumped out of and recharged back into aquifers that had sat undisturbed for tens of thousands of years. In a host of different ways, these alterations of the water cycle all mobilized salts.[1] Simultaneously, agriculture, mining, manufacturing, and power production released more salt into the environment. Most salts from anthropogenic activities made their way to the ocean, where they mixed with waters that had received continental drainage for millions of years as part of the natural cycle that deposits minerals to the ocean floor. But a small fraction of the salts did not make it to the sea. Some of the salts that remained behind have decreased crop yields, damaged freshwater ecosystems, and affected human health. As climate change and economic development mobilize more salt, salinization of soil and freshwater could become one of the most formidable environmental challenges facing society.

The dangers of improperly managed salt have long been recognized by farmers. In ancient Mesopotamia, the buildup of salts on irrigated farmland led to a shift from the cultivation of wheat to more salt-tolerant crops, such as barley.[2] Ultimately, soil salinization probably played a major role in the decline of Mesopotamia and several other irrigation-dependent civilizations. Recognizing the existential threat of salinization, agronomists have long warned farmers about the risks of salt accumulation on crops and encouraged them to water their crops in a manner that washes salts out of the soil.

Salts tend to build up on irrigated land because dissolved ions are left behind when water evaporates. The risk of salinization is higher in clay-containing soils because salty water causes the minerals to swell, resulting in slower percolation of water. As this trapped water evaporates, more salt-containing water is wicked into the root zone to replace the lost molecules. If measures are not taken to rinse the accumulated salts out of the topsoil, they can reach levels that impede the growth of sensitive crops. Preventing salinization is particularly challenging in arid or semiarid climate zones where evaporation rates are higher and irrigation water often starts out with relatively high concentrations of dissolved ions.

About a quarter of the world's irrigated farmland currently suffers from salinization and the related phenomenon of waterlogging—the term used to describe the accumulation of excess water within the root zone. These twin risks to agricultural productivity are prevalent in some of the world's most important food-producing regions, including Central Asia's Aral Sea Basin, South Asia's Indus Basin, Australia's Murray-Darling Basin, and California's San Joaquin Valley.[3]

To minimize salinization and waterlogging, farmers often install drains underneath their fields. Unfortunately, the placement of ceramic tiles or, in modern times, perforated plastic pipes below the root zone of irrigated fields produces large quantities of salty water that can cause another set of problems.[4] The ecological catastrophes facing Central Asia's Aral Sea and other terminal lakes provide stark examples of what can happen when freshwater that used to feed terminal lakes is replaced by smaller quantities of salty, nutrient-rich agricultural drainage. By disturbing the water balance under which the local ecosystem had developed and introducing a toxic mixture of salts and nutrients, terminal lakes can be turned into barren wastelands, where dried lake beds covered with a crust of salt feed windstorms that expose people to dust enriched in toxic elements, including arsenic and chromium. The impacts of agricultural drainage on rivers that do not flow into terminal lakes may be less dramatic, but this polluted water still damages ecosystems and pollutes lakes and rivers in many parts of the world.

To minimize the threats to agriculture without simply transferring the salt problem downstream, farmers can install subsurface drip irrigation systems that deliver water to roots without wetting the entire soil profile. Soil that has already been damaged by salts can be rehabilitated by adding gypsum (calcium sulfate) and organic matter or by cultivating salt-tolerant plants that gradually enhance soil quality through the decomposition of roots, stems, and leaves left behind after the harvest.[5] Although these practices can restore fields that are prone to salinization and waterlogging, agronomists often face resistance from farmers who have become accustomed to the high crop yields generated by unsustainable practices.

With proper management, farmers can minimize the accumulation of salt in soils, but if there is no means of getting drainage water out of the basin, irrigated agriculture will eventually succumb to salinization. As we have seen, agricultural intensification is often accompanied by radical changes in the quantities of water flowing in and out of watersheds. Typically, the amount of water entering an irrigated region increases when imported water projects are created while, at the same time, less water flows out of the basin as local water bodies are diverted for irrigation. As farmers implement water efficiency measures, flood irrigation gives way to sprinklers and precision irrigation technologies that generate even less runoff. Eventually, watersheds that used to drain to the sea can turn into closed basins—entire regions where little if any salt that entered the system or was mobilized by mineral dissolution escapes through rivers or regional groundwater flow.

The southern part of California's San Joaquin Valley—one of the world's most intensively farmed regions—provides an example of a closed basin that is starting to suffer the effects of salinization.[6] Due to efficient water use and rules designed to minimize the ecological effects of selenium-rich agricultural drainage, nearly all the water coming into the southern half of the valley evaporates from irrigated fields, percolates into local aquifers, or exits in fruits, vegetables, and nuts produced on the region's farms. As a result, much of the salts entering the basin in the imported water as well as those that are added as fertilizers or are released by mineral weathering accumulate in the valley's soil and groundwater. By 2017, about 5 percent of the region's farmland had already been taken out of production due to salinization, while some 30 percent showed signs of salt damage. At current rates, shallow groundwater is predicted to become too salty to use on fruit and nut trees by the middle of the twenty-first century. Although profits from cultivation of valuable crops might pay for the wells and pumps needed to access less-saline deep groundwater, that freshwater source will eventually reach a point when it, too, cannot be used for salt-sensitive crops. Without a way of removing salt, one of the world's most productive agricultural regions will succumb to the same fate as that of ancient Mesopotamia, as farmers will transition to less valuable, salt-tolerant crops or give up on farming altogether.

Salt management is not just an issue for agriculture. A lack of safe, cost-effective tools for managing brine produced by reverse osmosis and other desalination technologies also prevents many communities from accessing brackish groundwater and recycling wastewater produced by inland cities, power plants, and industries. Due to their high costs, concentrators, crystallizers, and evaporation ponds are affordable only to the world's wealthiest inland water users. Without access to a river flowing out of the basin or a deep aquifer that can readily accommodate large quantities of briny waste produced by desalination, an inability to manage brines produced by desalination will continue to limit the potential for using increasingly affordable forms of desalination to solve inland water crises.

If someone could come up with a solution to the salt problem, it might be possible to avoid soil salinization on irrigated farmland while simultaneously expanding the water supply of many water-stressed regions.

If rivers cannot be used to safely move the salt associated with agricultural drainage or the wastes from desalination away from places where they are produced, pipelines might provide a viable alternative. This brute-force solution to salt management works, but at a construction cost somewhere around a million dollars per kilometer combined with additional costs for pumping and maintenance, pipelines quickly become cost prohibitive. Furthermore, to minimize the ecological impacts of nutrients, pesticides, and naturally occurring toxic elements in brine, further treatment may be required before disposal.

When this simple form of brine management is feasible, it can be a game changer. For example, a 114-kilometer pipeline moves more than eighty million kilograms per year of salt produced by brackish groundwater desalination plants, municipal wastewater recycling projects, power plants, and food-processing facilities from a dry, inland valley to the ocean off the coast of Southern California. The Inland Empire Brine Line, a project that was completed in the 1990s, accepts salty waste at a price that is about a fifth of what its users used to pay to truck it out of the basin—the approach that they had been forced to employ before the project was built.[7] Without their brine line, the four million people living in the inland valley would be facing salt disposal challenges that would be stressing the local economy, limiting the ability of water suppliers to tap into brackish groundwater and damaging the ecosystem.

Although brine pipelines can be effective, high costs and the potential environmental impacts often preclude their use. For example, inspired by the success of the Inland Empire Brine Line, a coalition of farmers and cities in the southern part of the San Joaquin Valley proposed the construction of an even more ambitious brine line in the mid-2010s. The group's solution to the closed basin's salt management problem involved the construction of about three dozen desalination plants that would reduce the volume of drainage water needing disposal by around 90 percent. The clean water produced by desalination would be used to recharge local aquifers while the brine would travel 450 kilometers to a discharge point in the San Francisco Bay. At a construction cost of about eight billion dollars and annual operating costs of around two billion dollars, the brine line project seems unlikely to be built anytime soon, even though its advocates have estimated that the project costs would be offset by sales of the desalinated water.[8] If the project's proponents can somehow find the money needed to build the pipeline, they will face another steep challenge: communities at the terminus of the pipeline are unlikely to accept the idea that the San Francisco Bay should serve as a dumping ground for the nutrients, pesticides, and toxic elements in the brine.

Although high construction costs and hesitation about ocean disposal makes it unlikely that many more brine lines like the one serving the Inland Empire will be built anytime soon, salt accumulation is a problem that is not going away. Due to a lack of inexpensive alternatives, this rather simple approach to salt management remains attractive to inland farms and cities if its limitations could be addressed. Perhaps a renewed enthusiasm for brine pipelines will develop when the thousands of kilometers of petroleum pipelines that crisscross the continents become obsolete. If governments and automakers follow through on their pledges to end the production of internal combustion engines over the next two decades, demand for gasoline will drop precipitously.[9] By the second half of the twenty-first century, it might make sense to deliver fuel to the remaining fueling stations for cars, trucks, and airplanes by rail or tanker trucks. Although additional investments would be necessary to repurpose abandoned petroleum pipelines as brine lines, the existence of steel or thick plastic pipes, graded land, rights-of-ways, power supplies, and other related pipeline infrastructure leading from inland areas to the coast could someday make brine lines an attractive option. With a little ingenuity, a pipe dream might turn into a brine management solution.

When sending salty water to the ocean or injecting it underground is impractical, the next best brine disposal option is zero liquid discharge. As already discussed, the existing approaches for turning brine into solid salt rely on distillation in specialized, corrosion-resistant reactors that produce a hypersaline brine that is then either crystallized in another specialized machine or sent to a small evaporation pond. Although this approach is expensive and consumes a lot of energy, it might become more popular as the technologies that support it advance along the learning curve. In recognition of the fact that brine dewatering technologies requiring the heating of large volumes of water will remain relatively expensive, researchers are seeking out more energy-efficient ways of dewatering brine.

About a half dozen companies are currently developing brine concentrating systems that will overcome the barriers that have prevented reverse osmosis from playing a bigger role in brine concentration. Conventional reverse osmosis systems stop functioning when the ion content of the salty side of the membrane reaches levels that are about twice the salinity of seawater for two reasons.[10] First, the pressure that needs to be applied to get water to flow against the osmotic gradient greatly increases as the brine becomes saltier. Many of the components used in conventional membranes simply cannot function at the high pressures needed to dewater brine. The second reason is that as more freshwater is extracted from brines, mineral precipitation (scaling) occurs on membrane surfaces. Equipment manufacturers are attempting to circumvent these limitations by using pressure-resistant membrane materials and by modifying the surfaces of the reverse osmosis membranes to reduce the likelihood of scale formation. They are also lowering energy costs by routing the flow of water through the reactors in clever ways that decrease the salinity difference between the two sides of the membranes. These refinements are likely to yield brine concentration systems that extend the useful range of reverse osmosis to a point at which the volume of brine needing further dewatering will be cut in half.

Another potentially viable approach that does not run the risk of membrane scaling employs organic solvents as a means of pulling water out of brines.[11] When nonpolar organic solvents are mixed with brine, two separate phases are formed, in much the same way that oil droplets separate from vinegar in salad dressing. After a fraction of the water dissolves into the organic solvent, a smaller volume of slightly saltier brine is left behind. If a solvent with a low boiling point, such as dimethyl ether, is used as the organic phase, a modest amount of heat can be applied to distill off pure (water-free) solvent, which is then brought back into contact with the residual brine. This process is repeated until nearly all the water is separated from the brine.

Not all approaches for dropping the cost of brine dewatering involve mechanical devices. Inland communities facing brine management challenges often have an advantage over their coastal counterparts when it comes to managing brine: low humidity, clear skies, and ample amounts of flat, unoccupied land. As we have already seen, evaporation ponds—artificial versions of terminal lakes—typically require so much space that they are rarely a cost-effective means of dewatering brine. If a technology could more efficiently use the energy provided by the sun and wind, costs would decrease as the footprint of these nature-inspired brine dewatering systems shrunk.

The operators of pond systems have experimented with various approaches for enhancing evaporation rates. The inefficiency of evaporation ponds is related to the fact that much of the solar and wind energy reaching the brine heats the entire pond instead of causing the molecules at the surface to evaporate. Due to mixing, much of the energy adsorbed by molecules at the surface is transferred into the entire water column, causing the whole mass of water to become a little warmer. If the energy-absorbing molecules at the surface could be isolated from the rest of the water, evaporation rates would be much higher. Engineers have been able to increase evaporation rates by 10–30 percent by spraying a fine mist of brine into the air or by adding colored dyes to the water to assure that more of the sun's energy is adsorbed closer to the surface.[12] So far these approaches have failed to catch on because they require additional investments and do not always achieve their intended goals.

One promising alternative for maximizing evaporation rates takes its inspiration from trees. By relying upon capillary action—the force that causes water to move from a plant's roots to its leaves—water molecules that receive the sun's energy can be heated to a point at which they evaporate without transferring energy to the rest of the water body.[13] To apply this approach in brine dewatering, an inexpensive, light-absorbing powder is applied to the surface of a short, rigid stalk made of cellulose (think cotton fibers). As the cellulose stalk absorbs energy from the sun or the ambient environment, heated water is transferred into the air. As a molecule of water evaporates, its neighbors are wicked up to replace it. As water evaporates, dissolved salts that cannot enter the gas phase accumulate on the stalk. Eventually they crystallize and fall onto a platform, where they can be collected as part of the zero liquid discharge process. Although this concept is in an early stage of development, it has the potential to cut the area needed for brine dewatering by a factor of a hundred while simultaneously eliminating the crystallization step at the end of the process.

Although this technology has not yet been applied to brine dewatering at a meaningful scale, water managers have employed the natural version of this process by growing real plants on brine. By cultivating salt-tolerant crops, such as wheat grass, on fields equipped with tile drains, the volume of agricultural drainage needing further dewatering in concentrators or evaporation ponds can be reduced by around 80 percent.[14] In terms of economics, the feasibility of using tile-drained farmland to concentrate brines depends upon the value of the land that is being repurposed and the price at which the salty hay produced by the process can be sold. If there is no interest in turning brine into an agricultural commodity, even more salt-tolerant plants might be used to concentrate brines beyond the point that salty hay can no longer grow. Brines can be used as a source of water by thirsty plants such as the salt cedar—a fast-growing tree capable of surviving on water containing salt levels that are about twice as high as seawater.

Reducing the cost of dewatering brines is an exciting prospect, but it is only half of the battle. After the water is removed, something must be done with the resulting piles of salt. As we have already seen, attempts to convert these salts into commodity chemicals such as gypsum, sulfuric acid, and caustic are in their infancy. At this point, the prospect of turning salts produced by zero liquid discharge into products that can compete with chemicals produced by conventional means is daunting; it will be hard to undercut chemicals produced by mining or established manufacturing methods. Lacking a market for salts produced by zero liquid discharge of agricultural drainage water and brines from brackish groundwater desalination, the operators of these projects might be forced to bury the salts underground or move them to the sea on trucks and barges. Perhaps governments might subsidize chemicals produced from brine to account for the environmental damage associated with obtaining these salts by mining and the benefits of employing desalination to solve water problems.

One way or another, the slow progress that is being made in brine dewatering methods will likely cut the cost of safely managing brine in half over the next two to three decades. Even at a lower price, the cost of brine management will likely seem impossibly high to water managers who are accustomed to paying nearly nothing to pipe their wastes into waterways or send it to municipal landfills. In many ways, the approaching era of responsible brine management may be analogous to what happened in the second half of the twentieth century, when newly promulgated environmental regulations forced cities to install sewage treatment plants. The idea of paying for salt disposal might seem to be an extravagance to managers who rely upon dilution to solve their disposal problems. But after society recognizes the benefit of properly managing salts, the additional costs will no longer seem unreasonable.

24

Running the Rivers

PROVIDING THE BILLIONS of people who lived through the Great Acceleration with water, disposing of wastewater from their cities, farms, and industries, protecting them from floods, and providing them with hydropower have all taken a toll on the environment.[1] As a result, with the exception of remote rivers and waterways in places where people have not yet become wealthy enough to afford modern water infrastructure, the needs of humanity largely determine where water flows, when it flows, and what it contains. Unsurprisingly, this widespread reconfiguration of the water cycle has affected aquatic ecosystems. Obvious signs of damage, such as declining populations of salmon and other migratory fish and the growth of hypoxic zones in coastal waters, occasionally capture the public's attention, but the effects of water infrastructure extend to a host of other, more subtle changes that often go unnoticed. As a result of civilization's success in satisfying its water needs, most waterways exhibit reduced biodiversity, contain fewer wetlands, and are less able to meet the needs of communities that historically relied upon them for their economic, physical, and spiritual well-being.

Back when population density was lower and water infrastructure was less extensive, the taming of a river was viewed as a sign of progress. However, as populations and economies grew, healthy streams, rivers, and lakes became more of a rarity. The declining state of waterways finally led to a shift in public sentiment in wealthy parts of the world in the 1970s, when plans for new water infrastructure began to face organized opposition. The increased support for the environment meant that a few lucky rivers were preserved in their natural state. Public concerns about water pollution also brought about other changes, as rich countries built more sewage treatment plants and established more regulations on industrial wastewater, while low- and middle-income countries attempted, often with less success, to reduce pollution emanating from industries, mines, and power plants.

Despite a growing recognition that taking control of the water cycle without making provisions for the environment was a mistake, most of the water infrastructure that had already been built continued to operate because the projects delivered too many benefits to give up on them. Instead, policies were put in place to minimize the damage that they caused. To protect ecosystems, rules were instituted to assure that river flows would not fall below predetermined levels that were deemed deleterious to sensitive fish species. New programs were established to cut back on the pollution emanating from cities and industries. Simultaneously, in places where water infrastructure was yet to be built, engineers designed dams and flood-control structures in a manner that would reduce their impact on the surrounding environment.

The compromises that were reached as part of the effort to balance the environmental damage inflicted by water infrastructure with the human benefits that it provided have created a system that often pits economic development against environmental protection. With the help of concerned citizens and dedicated nongovernmental organizations, ecosystems sometimes prevail in this struggle; occasionally a dam is removed, a wetland is restored, or a watershed is granted protected status. At other times, the needs of water users are prioritized; a dam is built, a growing town takes more water, or farmers divert a river onto their fields as another waterway is sacrificed in the name of progress. More often the needs of both sides are considered and a compromise is reached over the needs of people and the environment.

As the impacts of climate change, population growth, and global development put additional stress on the world's water systems, it will become more difficult to balance the needs of humanity with those of ecosystems. If recent history is any guide, the contentious struggle over scarce water resources will inflict damage on both sides. Communities facing water-supply crises will likely encounter delays in their efforts to secure more water, while environmentalists can anticipate struggles to prevent further damage to already stressed ecosystems. But when it comes to the question of wildlife or humans, people usually prevail. As more water is diverted to meet the needs of humanity, ecosystems will suffer death by a thousand cuts as diminished flows and increased pollution, coupled with warmer temperatures and changing precipitation patterns, diminish habitat quality and provide opportunities for nonnative species to gain a foothold in damaged ecosystems.

Although this scenario is already playing out in some parts of the world, it does not have to be this way. It should be possible to maintain healthy ecosystems while simultaneously providing enough water to satisfy societal needs, provided that we accept the premise that in the Anthropocene, humans run the rivers. Rather than simply putting a few more restrictions on the ways that this great power is exercised, it should be possible to couple the operation of water infrastructure with restoration and protection of landscapes and waterways in a purposeful manner that takes advantage of nature's ability to store and purify water. The discipline of ecological engineering—to the uninitiated, a puzzling oxymoron—employs natural systems to create low-cost solutions to water crises to benefit humanity and the environment.[2]

The idea that humans can or should modify the environment to increase water availability and improve its quality requires a certain amount of hubris. It would be foolish to imagine that anyone could anticipate the many possible impacts of interfering with relationships that have developed over the millennia; yet we need to embrace our role in running the world's rivers if we are to continue using them to deliver water and dispose of our wastes. Because there is little chance that humanity is going to abandon its investments in water infrastructure, there would seem to be little to lose in attempting to make this arrangement work in a more mutually beneficial manner.

To gain insight into the potential for using ecological engineering to alleviate water crises, it is worth considering some of the ways that natural systems are being managed in conjunction with existing infrastructure in places facing crises of water availability and water quality.

Starting at the headwaters, a greater focus on controlling the kind of plants growing in a watershed can sometimes increase the volume of water flowing into reservoirs. Engineering the landscape to increase water yields requires a questioning of the underlying premise behind the way that many watersheds are managed. Throughout the modern era, much of the land surrounding reservoirs had been placed off-limits to protect water quality. This approach preserved undeveloped land and restored areas that had previously been logged, grazed, or turned into farms.[3] This leave-it-alone approach protects drinking water, creates recreational opportunities, and supports threatened and endangered species. Although this approach to land stewardship garners broad public support, it discourages water managers from actively intervening to increase the fraction of the precipitation that ultimately makes its way into their reservoirs.

The response to the drought that took place between 2015 and 2018 in Cape Town, South Africa, illustrates the promise of more actively managing watersheds to increase a water supply while simultaneously protecting the environment.

At the time of the drought, most of Cape Town's drinking water was obtained from five reservoirs located just west of the city. About half of the land surrounding the reservoirs consisted of nature preserves, while the remainder was either dedicated to farming or was held by private landowners who put little effort into managing it. On much of the protected land, eucalyptus, pine, and acacia—nonnative trees—had moved in from timber plantations that had been set up by European colonists.

Before the drought, land managers had expressed a desire to clear the invasive trees to reduce the threat that they posed to the region's unique ecosystem, but their efforts had faltered due to a lack of support from community members who considered the trees to be an aesthetic improvement over the native shrubs and grasses that made up the undisturbed landscape.[4] The drought helped change public attitudes as managers emphasized the tendency of invasive trees to consume large quantities of water.

As part of the city's urgent effort to keep its reservoirs from going dry, Cape Town funded a set of all-female work crews to eradicate invasive trees growing in the preserves.[5] Several hundred young women, who would otherwise have struggled to find good-paying jobs in the city, are now one of the pillars of the city's effort to enhance water security. By bringing chain saws and axes onto protected land, Cape Town's water utility believes that it has found an inexpensive way to prevent its next water crisis. The program's operators estimate that over the next three decades, removal of the invasive trees will increase the amount of water reaching the city's reservoirs by about a million cubic meters per year—enough to meet about 40 percent of the city's current needs. Expressed in terms of spending per unit volume, tree removal costs about a tenth as much as the construction of water recycling systems or desalination plants. It also has the added benefit of supporting a unique ecosystem in one of the world's biodiversity hotspots.

Although Cape Town's project appears to be effective, research conducted in other parts of the world indicates that tree removal does not always provide more water for people.[6] In most watersheds, a higher density of trees means that more water is lost through evapotranspiration. Yet in some places, more trees result in higher water yields because they enhance groundwater recharge or reduce the amount of precipitation that evaporates before it can make its way to the reservoir. In addition, the effect of trees on water flows can vary from year to year. For example, in some mountainous regions, the thinning of dense tree stands—an important strategy for reducing wildfire risk—increases water yields in wet years by allowing more snow to reach the forest floor, where it is protected from evaporation and sublimation (the direct release of water vapor from snow). In years with less snow, when the fraction of water reaching reservoirs really matters, the effect of tree thinning on water yields is minimal.

Even the seemingly straightforward act of removing thirsty, invasive tree species does not guarantee that more water will flow into reservoirs.[7] For example, in the American Southwest, tens of millions of dollars were spent during the second half of the twentieth century on efforts to remove salt cedar trees—an introduced species that proliferates along streambeds in arid landscapes. Much of the justification for government-funded salt cedar removal was based on an erroneous assumption that the trees consumed more water than the native willows and cottonwoods that they displaced. Although decades of research demonstrated that proliferation of the salt cedars was caused by diversion of water to farms and cities, government agencies found it easier to bring in the bulldozers, chain saws, and salt-cedar-eating beetles than to address the root cause of the problem (the drying out of the landscape by overpumping of groundwater and surface water diversion projects). Restoration of native cottonwoods and willows on salt-cedar-invaded land benefits ecosystems, but the promise that getting rid of the thirsty trees will free up large volumes of water is no longer used to justify tree removal.

In addition to increasing the amount of water flowing into reservoirs, more active management of land adjacent to rivers *downstream* of dams can also help resolve water crises. Diverting water onto agricultural land, through practices such as spate irrigation and flood-managed aquifer recharge, enhances groundwater resources by reconnecting rivers with the floodplain. In a similar manner, the flooding of wetlands and low-lying forests next to rivers can recharge aquifers while simultaneously reducing downstream flood risks and providing habitat for wildlife.[8] As with other modes of managed aquifer recharge, the extent to which the flooding of wetlands and forests can augment groundwater depends upon the permeability of the sediments overlying the aquifer. Perhaps of greater significance than enhanced water storage, these natural systems, which are sometimes called nature's kidneys, can remove nutrients and chemicals that threaten downstream water quality.

In recognition of their role in increasing the water supplies and improving water quality, influential organizations such as the United Nations and the World Bank have begun to advocate for investments to protect wetlands, forests, and grasslands as part of their efforts to support water security in rapidly developing countries.[9] The new enthusiasm of development agencies and governments for land preservation has been motivated by research showing that natural systems are responsible for about half of the world's water storage and treatment capacity. Thus, protecting these natural features and assuring that they remain healthy is usually more cost-effective than allowing them to disappear and replacing the services that they provided with artificial reservoirs and treatment plants.

A formal recognition that healthy ecosystems are essential to sustainable water infrastructure is an important first step in employing nature-based solutions in response to water crises. The next big challenge will be to develop the capacity to protect and restore natural systems within water utilities, dam operating agencies, and other institutions that have been configured to operate engineered water storage and delivery systems.

In addition to requiring a shift in attitude among water managers, transforming nature-based solutions from a slogan to an investment strategy will require better tools for quantifying the benefits delivered by new projects. In other words, managers will need help in deciding which projects deliver the greatest water supply and water quality benefits. Given our still incomplete knowledge about the relationship between land preservation, restoration, water quantity, and water quality, those who allocate the funding will need to recognize that projects built during the learning phase may not deliver all the benefits promised by their proponents. Similar to technologies such as desalination and water reuse, which became cheaper and more reliable as they moved along the learning curve, efforts to deploy nature-based solutions may be riskier investments in the early years. The long-term promise is that after experience is gained, nature-based projects will deliver greater benefits at lower costs than conventional concrete and steel alternatives.

The case for investing in forests, grasslands, and wetlands is probably easiest to make in places where ecosystems are still intact and large infrastructure projects have not yet been built. Although the ways that water infrastructure projects are financed, designed, and managed will have to be adjusted to allow funds that might have otherwise gone to the construction of taller dams or more extensive well fields to be spent in pursuit of such less tangible goals as ecosystem protection, development agencies, lenders, and governments have the power to demand the inclusion of nature-based systems in new water infrastructure projects in rapidly growing parts of the world. The idea of including land preservation in water infrastructure projects is also consistent with trends that took hold after the World Commission on Dams released its critique of the status quo in 2000.[10] In contrast, in places where rivers were straightened and wetlands were turned into farm fields decades ago, recovering the benefits of nature-based systems will likely require an even greater effort due to institutional momentum and the economic and social challenges of repurposing working land.

The difficulty inherent in applying nature-based solutions to solve a water crisis in a place where natural systems have already been lost is evident in efforts to control hypoxia in the Gulf of Mexico. In the early 2000s, researchers proposed the restoration of about 1 percent of the historic wetlands in the upper part of the Mississippi River watershed as part of a comprehensive strategy to shrink the Dead Zone.[11] To achieve their goal of reducing the amount of nitrogen discharged by the Mississippi River by about 40 percent, advocates called for the adoption of agricultural practices that would cut nitrogen released by farms, the restoration of riparian zones (the vegetated areas adjacent to rivers), and the reconnection of rivers with low-lying hardwood forests and coastal wetlands in the southern part of the watershed, where levees and dams had turned the river into a transportation artery.

The driver behind the idea of restoring wetlands, forests, and riparian zones was that they remove nitrate—the main form of dissolved nitrogen leached from agricultural fields. Wetlands are particularly well suited for this task because they trap dead leaves, branches, and other plant materials in stagnant water. As this organic material decomposes, microbes convert carbohydrates and sugars into carbon dioxide. To support their metabolism, the bacteria living near the water's surface deplete the dissolved oxygen, forcing the microbes living closer to the sediments to use nitrate—the next best terminal electron acceptor—to break down organic material. The nitrate-metabolizing microbes efficiently convert a form of the element that stimulates algae growth into dinitrogen (the inert gas that makes up about 80 percent of the atmosphere). A similar phenomenon takes place as water passes through the subsurface during its migration across riparian zones or as it recharges aquifers under flooded forests.

Before the nineteenth century, a large part of the Corn Belt was covered with wetlands. Intuition supports the premise that restoring a small fraction of this land to its original state is an effective way to treat the diffuse pollution emanating from the modern agricultural operations that replaced the native wetlands. Unfortunately, turning this hunch into reality has turned out to be a lot harder than simply flooding a few fields and hoping for the best because farmers and the institutions that support them have found that it is usually cheaper and more effective to control nitrogen pollution at its source. In part, this is because more efficient use of fertilizers on farms employs well-established, reliable technologies that increase a farmer's profits by using less fertilizer. The cost-effectiveness of using wetlands and restored riparian zones on the edges of fields to control nitrogen pollution is not as clear because converting working land into nature-based treatment systems decreases the amount of land available for growing crops.[12] Although the societal benefits of wetland restoration likely outweigh the value of the food that is produced on the same land, the individuals and institutions who make the decisions about allocating funds toward controlling agricultural nitrogen pollution prefer to direct their efforts to proven, on-farm practices.

Although source control efforts have been the main focus of nitrogen control since the early 2000s, government funding for wetlands and riparian buffers have restored or given protected status to around half a million hectares of wetlands in the Mississippi River watershed during this period.[13] This experience has provided government officials with valuable insight into how they can effectively work with communities to build support for nature-based solutions, but the land dedicated to wetlands remains less than about 10 percent of the area that scientists projected in their original assessment of the potential for nature-based treatment to control nitrogen. These initial efforts have shown that effective restoration requires cooperation among government entities and farmers and a continued commitment to maintaining the restored wetlands and monitoring their performance.

Despite the billions of dollars that have already been spent on source control and nature-based treatment, there is little evidence that the Dead Zone is shrinking to the degree needed to solve the problem. Because deintensification of agriculture in the upper Mississippi River watershed is unlikely, spending on the problem will need to increase if the hypoxia crisis is going to be resolved. Now that the easiest-to-adopt fertilizer-saving practices have been implemented on most of the region's farms, targeted placement of wetlands in areas where nitrate concentrations are highest appears to be the most cost-effective means of making progress.[14] After two decades of learning how to restore wetlands, the time may finally have arrived when investments in nature-based solutions will play a dominant role in efforts to solve the Gulf's hypoxia crisis.

If skeptics question the wisdom of investing in nature-based solutions to address a diffuse pollution problem at the scale of the largest drainage basin in North America, proponents might take them to Southern California, where wetlands were used to control nitrate pollution in the Santa Ana River watershed. In the early 1990s, diffuse sources of nitrate from dairies and wastewater treatment plants serving the rapidly growing cities of the Inland Empire were causing nitrate concentrations to creep up to levels that made the water unsafe for human consumption. Rather than spending more than a hundred million dollars to build a treatment plant that would remove nitrate before infiltrating the river water into the drinking water aquifer, the downstream water utility invested around five million dollars to convert a network of ponds that had formed behind a flood-control dam into the Prado wetlands.[15] By routing the flow of the river through 140 hectares of constructed wetlands in a manner that maximized the time that the water spent in close contact with decaying vegetation, nitrate concentrations were reduced by over 80 percent during the summer and fall, when the river's flow consisted mainly of wastewater effluent and runoff from dairies. In addition to solving the nitrate pollution problem at a fraction of the cost of building a water treatment plant, the constructed wetlands created wildlife habitat in an area where much of the land had been converted to farms and suburban housing during the twentieth century.

If Southern California is too far for Mississippi River nature-based solutions skeptics to travel, they could visit an even larger system of constructed wetlands that were built south of Dallas. These two nature-based treatment systems that, when considered together, are about ten times larger than the Prado wetlands were built starting in the 1990s to remove nutrients and suspended sediments from the wastewater effluent–dominated Trinity River. After passing through the wetlands, about 250 million cubic meters per year of water (enough to meet the needs of more than a million people) is sent by way of pipelines to the north, where it replenishes the Dallas–Fort Worth region's drinking water reservoirs.[16] Although it might have been technically feasible to achieve many of the water quality benefits of the wetlands by upgrading sewage treatment plants or by installing a smaller water treatment plant at the spot where the river water is put into the pipelines, water managers chose a nature-based solution. In addition to the low cost and the wildlife habitat benefits that this provides, passage of dirty river water through a natural system offered the additional benefit of breaking the psychological connection between the sewage treatment plants, where much of the water originates, and the drinking water treatment plants that draw water out of the reservoirs.

Constructed wetlands have the potential to deliver many of the water quality benefits provided by riverbank filtration and other better-established techniques that take advantage of the natural treatment capacity of the subsurface. Constructed wetlands are more versatile because they can be built in places where the local geology is not conducive to infiltration. Furthermore, wetlands offer habitat and recreational benefits that attract public support that cannot be obtained for infiltration basins and discreetly placed groundwater injection wells.

As a result of their flexibility and popularity with the public, constructed wetlands, restored riparian corridors, and other types of nature-based treatment systems likely have a bigger role to play in future efforts to improve water quality. These systems may not always be as straightforward to create as programs involving modification of agricultural practices or addition of nutrient removal processes to sewage treatment plants. Although they cannot be used for all water crises, nature-based treatment systems provide practical, cost-effective ways of removing the residual contaminants that are too expensive to treat with conventional pollution control methods. Thus, constructed wetlands are best suited for removing the nutrients and organic chemicals remaining in agricultural drainage, wastewater effluent, and street run-off after the reasonable source control measures have been taken. When paired with strategic investments in source control and conventional treatment, nature-based systems really do have the potential to act as nature's kidneys, making the water flowing out of cities and agricultural areas cleaner than the water that flowed into them.

25

The Right Things to Do

THE PREVIOUS CHAPTERS described the importance of global development and climate change to water crises. Considering current trends related to development and climate change along with the ways that nations have responded to recent societal challenges, a pessimist might conclude that efforts to provide safe, affordable water without damaging the environment will fail to keep up with water needs in the coming decades, while an optimist might hold out hope that creative solutions being pioneered by people who are already grappling with crises, coupled with a greater emphasis on the need to adapt to climate change and alleviate poverty, will bring about effective solutions to the world's water woes.

The answer to the question of which of these two possible futures will come to pass cannot be found in a government report, a scientific paper, or a pitch deck from a water technology startup. Turning water from its present status as a commodity that is there for people who can afford it to its rightful place near the center of efforts to create a better world is essential to the future envisioned by the water optimists. The goal of water for all requires a more expansive view of who has the right to water and how those rights are realized. It also requires that society place a greater urgency on the need to address all types of water crises.

Starting with water access, it is important to recognize that much of humanity faces water stress. At the heart of the water access problem are more than eight hundred million people living in poverty who obtain unfiltered water from a river or a hand-dug well or are forced to walk more than a half-hour every day for water. People who lack basic water services face significant health risks and hardships that make it more difficult to escape from poverty. But this is only part of the water access problem. Millions more people who currently have access to piped water face great uncertainty because unsustainable management practices and climate change threaten their continued access to water. Considering just those places where surface and groundwater demand frequently outstrips supply, researchers estimate that around 1.8 billion people are in this situation.[1] If this group is combined with those lacking basic water services, and accounting for a certain amount of overlap, around 2.5 billion people presently lack access to a reliable water source.

With respect to the role that poverty plays in water access, it is worthwhile to consider changes that have taken place over the past two centuries. Before the Industrial Revolution, being poor was the worldwide norm. In 1850, about 80 percent of humanity lived under conditions that fit into what we now consider as extreme poverty.[2] By 1950, that number had shrunk to about 60 percent. During the Great Acceleration, global poverty fell to a point at which fewer than one in ten people now live in extreme poverty. For most of humanity, the exit from poverty was accompanied by access to basic water services and migration to cities equipped with municipal water systems. Thus, from the perspective of global development, many of the people who still lack basic water services will achieve access as economic growth lifts them out of poverty by providing employment in cities. According to the global development narrative, it is the job of governments and development agencies to hasten progress toward achieving the United Nations' sustainable development goals associated with water access through economic development and aid targeted at rural communities. There is plenty of validity in this explanation, but the only hope for more rapidly expanding water access is to increase support for water access while people at the bottom rungs of the income ladder climb out of poverty.

For people with access to improved water sources facing occasional shortages and uncertainty about future supplies, part of the blame for their situation can be traced back to failures of the institutions responsible for water management. For example, rural water shortages are often related to overuse of irrigation water—a problem linked to the inability of governments to control the behavior of individual farmers. Managers who try to prevent excessive water use often lack the power needed to bring about change because farmers tend to have strong political supporters. The less confrontational solution to water shortage of building more dams or drilling deeper wells will offer only temporary relief if there is no mechanism for mangers to prevent the cultivation of ever thirstier crops. Without institutions capable of effectively regulating water use, the Jevons paradox will continue to feed water insecurity.

In addition to the challenges of water access and avoiding shortages, hundreds of millions of people face the prospect that the water available to them will compromise their health. Outside of the world's wealthiest countries, most people accept the need to disinfect their tap water before consuming it. Without major investments to ensure that waterborne pathogens will not contaminate water during its journey from the treatment plant, tap water will remain undrinkable in much of the world. This situation might not constitute a health crisis, but it creates a false sense of security because boiling water, exposing it to ultraviolet light, or adding a tiny amount of bleach rarely protects people from chemical contaminants. Naturally occurring substances, such as arsenic, fluoride, and nitrate, as well as synthetic chemicals, including PFAS, pesticides, and organic solvents, make water unsafe to drink for over half a billion people worldwide. Many of these toxic chemicals can be removed by state-of-the-art drinking water treatment plants, but activated carbon filters, ozonation systems, and other forms of advanced treatment are usually too expensive for residents of cities in low- and middle-income countries. Small towns and domestic well users in all but the richest places also cannot afford advanced treatment because they cannot take advantage of the economies of scale available to their big city counterparts.

The fact that at least 5 percent of the world's population drinks water containing unsafe levels of chemicals and that tap water in much of the world carries the risk of waterborne disease can be traced back to two underlying causes.

The first is an inability to enforce existing water pollution rules. Irrespective of wealth, just about every country has regulations designed to prevent the disposal of toxic chemicals or untreated sewage in waterways. However, the degree to which these rules are enforced varies considerably.[3] When governments do not follow through on water pollution regulations, it falls upon industry to balance the profit motive against the consequences of compromising the health of the communities where they are located. Some companies take this responsibility seriously, but there have been too many cases where the decision-making power was too diffuse or the profit incentive too strong to rely upon corporate goodwill to protect the public.

Even in wealthy countries where pollution laws are strictly enforced, regulators struggle to keep up with the array of chemicals that might contaminate drinking water. Efforts to expand the list of routinely measured chemicals face stiff opposition due to cost of monitoring as well as concerns that manufacturers might be forced to reformulate their products. As a result, many potential threats go undetected. For example, in the United States, Europe, and other wealthy countries, less than 1 percent of the chemicals used in commerce are routinely tested for in drinking water. Only a small subset of those untested chemicals is likely to contaminate drinking water, but the reactionary approach that exists today has too many blind spots. This means that drinking water contamination must often reach a point of crisis before action is taken.

For those struggling with drinking water contamination that cannot be traced back to industrial or agricultural sources, such as arsenic dissolving out of aquifer minerals or lead leaching from old pipes and plumbing fixtures, a lack of will to resolve water quality problems threatens the health of millions of people. Whether the root cause is systemic racism, inadequate funding, or simply a tacit acceptance of the way that things have happened in the past, a lot of people continue to drink unsafe water after contamination has been detected.[4] People whose health is being compromised are often forced to wait until the issue receives sufficient media attention to elevate their struggles to an acknowledged crisis.

Providing water access and making sure that it is safe to drink would be laudable achievements, but stopping there would be a step short of water for all. Universal access means that people can afford the water that is available to them. The exact definition of water affordability differs among experts because it involves value judgments about the fraction of a family's income that should be spent on water, food, shelter, and other essential needs as well as opinions about what exactly constitutes an adequate daily water allotment. Despite room for debate on the best way to measure affordability, it is generally agreed that water is too expensive when meeting the needs for drinking, cooking, and hygiene consumes more than about 4–5 percent of a family's resources.[5] By providing discounts to people at the lower end of the income distribution, utilities can bring the price of tap water down to affordable levels for most of their customers. But that is helpful only to people who are already served by a water utility. A large portion of the billion or so people residing in informal settlements rely upon relatively expensive sources, such as tanker trucks and kiosks. To cope with the high cost of their water, many of these families are forced to reduce the amount of water that they use for hygiene, which lowers their quality of life and contributes to public health problems. It may be challenging to make a precise estimate, but hundreds of millions of people in low- and middle-income countries cannot afford safe water.

Water affordability is also an important issue in some of the world's wealthiest countries. The inability of water utilities to adequately subsidize the water bills of low-income residents adds to the financial burdens of people living in poverty within high-income countries. For example, in the United States, tens of millions of people cannot afford their tap water. In economically struggling cities, such as Cleveland, Ohio, water bills account for over 5 percent of the income of about a third of the population. Utilities in many other less affluent cities find it difficult to subsidize services for their low-income customers because their revenues have been shrinking due to falling populations. It does not help that their perpetually underfunded water infrastructure becomes more expensive to maintain as it ages.[6] Although utilities in these cities are delivering less water, most of the costs of operating the water system, such as payments on loans for water projects and maintenance of the underground pipe network, remain almost as high as they were when the cities had larger populations. Facing their own financial stress, struggling utilities often put the squeeze on their customers, threatening them with water shutoffs if they cannot pay their bills.

The problem is not restricted to cities undergoing economic decline; in America's most prosperous cities, about one in ten residents cannot afford their water. Absent more generous government subsidies, water will likely remain unaffordable for the least affluent families of one of the world's richest countries. Water affordability affects fewer people in most other high-income countries due to the tendency of governments to offer more generous support for low-income water users, but some people at the bottom of the income distribution in just about every wealthy country struggle to pay their bills.[7]

Resolving the problem of unaffordable water will require more than simply waiting for poverty to be alleviated. In low- and middle-income countries, the extension of piped water into informal settlements would go a long way to resolving the affordability problem. However, the pressure on water utilities to improve their balance sheets creates a disincentive to install pipes in neighborhoods where users cannot pay the full price of water. Similarly, the only thing standing between people living in poverty in high-income countries and affordable water is the willingness of middle- and upper-income customers to share some of their good fortune with their less affluent neighbors. Rather than trying to address the existence of the great wealth disparities in the modern world—a topic that merits its own book—it is probably best to consider strategies for elevating the urgency that is placed on achieving universal water access, safety, and affordability.

The most effective approach for adding a sense of urgency to efforts to provide access to safe and affordable water might be found in the idea that water is a right and not a privilege. After a fundamental human right to water is recognized by governments, arguments about the need to treat water provision as a business lose much of their power. Despite competing funding needs and pressure exerted by interest groups opposed to government largesse, few politicians care to be seen as violators of human rights. In addition, recognizing the human right to water provides those who lack access to safe, affordable water with a legal means of challenging the status quo.

The claim that there is a human right to water may be relatively new, but the principle that governments are obliged to provide their poorest citizens with a minimal level of necessities has long been considered by some legal scholars as a fundamental part of the social contract. The International Covenant on Economic, Social and Cultural Rights that was adopted by the United Nations in 1966 included language on a right to an adequate supply of food, clothing, and housing. Proponents of universal water access argued that the right to safe and affordable water was implicit in this statement.[8] Unfortunately, without a specific mention of water they could not make much progress in elevating their efforts to protect, preserve, and provide the liquid necessity to those in need. In the early 2000s, concerns that water transfer projects were depriving communities of water that they had long relied upon invigorated the push for universal water rights at about the same time that more attention was being given to the connection between water access, poverty, and the subjugation of women. In response, the international community became more serious about an explicit statement on a human right to water. Finally, in 2010, the United Nations endorsed the concept and created the position of special rapporteur on the human rights to safe drinking water and sanitation as an advocate for its realization.

Several key UN members, including the United States, Canada, the United Kingdom, and Australia, abstained from voting on the human right to water resolution due to concerns that it could oblige them to alter their internal laws and policies. Recognizing that changing their nations' water management system was the intent of the resolution, governments of 122 of the 159 remaining UN members agreed to respect, protect, and fulfill the right to water and sanitation access for their citizens.[9] In principle, the signatures of the supporters of the resolution means that historic water sources cannot be appropriated from communities without providing affordable alternatives. It also implies that governments are obliged to provide safe water to citizens who cannot afford it.

This was a step in the right direction, but passing a UN resolution is no guarantee of change. In practice, the human right to water is, as former leader of the Soviet Union and founding member of Green Cross International Mikhail Gorbachev said, "not an instant 'silver bullet' solution" because it requires effective laws and policies.[10] Thus, the impact of the UN resolution is limited to those signatories that are committed to realizing the human right to water because there is no mechanism to force compliance on uncooperative countries. Yet that is not the point. The resolution signals a recognition among nations that water and sanitation are not merely commodities; it creates a moral obligation for governments to protect existing resources and expand access to safe and affordable water. The clearest manifestation of the power of the human right to water is the seriousness with which many countries treat the UN's Sixth Sustainable Development Goal (SDG 6)— the targets associated with access to water and sanitation for all. Perhaps SDG 6 would have been created without a formal recognition of a human rights, but that framing helped elevate water to one of the central endeavors of the international development community.

The human right to water has implications that go beyond people living in low- and middle-income countries. Despite a lack of support of the rights declaration from their federal government, California, Massachusetts, and Pennsylvania each adopted legislation recognizing a human right to water.[11]

This act has been particularly impactful in California, where at least a million people—over 2 percent of the population—lack access to safe and affordable water. Although it took seven years to gather the political will to fund the state's commitment, in 2019, California's budget allocated over $1.4 billion (about $1,000 for each person lacking access) to a ten-year effort to realize the human right to water.[12] It can be argued that the state was already subsidizing water systems in low-income communities, but the formal commitment to a human right to water and the additional financial resources that followed have provided a new tool to community leaders seeking a long-term solution to a set of problems that had never before received sustained attention from an easily distracted legislature. Much like the approach that the United Nations employs to chart its progress toward achieving SDG 6, California now has a timeline for achieving safe and affordable water, along with a system for measuring its progress.

The human right to water is not going to solve all problems faced by communities that lack access to safe and affordable water, but it is worth considering how adoption of a human right to water might have altered a few contemporary water crises.[13] A human right to water in Michigan could have made it more difficult for state officials presiding over Flint's struggling utility to put the health of residents in jeopardy in the name of restoring financial self-sufficiency. Maybe a federal government that was fully committed to realizing water as a human right would now be putting a higher priority on cutting through the bureaucratic morass that is making it difficult to fund water access for the two million parched Americans in Texas's colonias, Arizona's Navajo reservations, and rural communities of Puerto Rico and Appalachia. Beyond the United States, recognition of a human right to water would be a useful tool for people fighting dams and water transfer projects that threaten Indigenous communities. It also could serve as a counterbalance against the push to make water utilities behave more like for-profit businesses. On its own, the human right to water cannot eliminate racism, malfeasance, incompetence, or greed, but it can empower communities that, for a variety of reasons, have been shut out in their quest for access to safe and affordable water.

The right to an ample quantity of clean water is such a compelling idea that some people have attempted to extend it to the environment.

It has long been recognized that taking too much water out of a river or an aquifer or failing to adequately treat wastewater can push an ecosystem into a state of crisis. From a legal standpoint, the power to stop this from happening normally stems from the idea that damage to the environment affects property held by a person or group who has downstream water rights. Thus, rules and regulations governing water extraction and wastewater disposal allow the government to balance the property rights of upstream water users against those of downstream rights holders whose abilities to obtain drinking water, go fishing, and navigate could be damaged by overextraction of water or the release of pollutants.

Inherent in the government's ability to limit what upstream property owners can do with their water is a controversial legal interpretation asserting that all citizens, and not just those who own downstream property, have a collective right to enjoy a healthy environment. According to the public trust doctrine—an idea that traces its origins back to the Roman Empire—the state cannot assign property owners rights that interfere with certain resources that it holds in trust for the benefit of society. The less contested part of the public trust doctrine supports the idea that a property owner cannot interfere with a citizen's right to access a beach or navigate on waters that cross private property. The more controversial part, which was first articulated by American lawyer Joseph Sax in 1970, asserts that the public's right to a healthy environment is also held in trust by the government.[14] According to Sax's argument, citizens can have legal standing to bring lawsuits against their government when it fails to protect the environment, even if they do not own downstream property that has been damaged.

This interpretation of the public trust doctrine first captured the attention of the legal community in 1983, when the Audubon Society, a nongovernmental organization dedicated to protecting birds and their habitats, won a lawsuit compelling the City of Los Angeles to cut back on the amount of water that it was diverting from tributaries of Mono Lake—a terminal lake that was slowly drying up due to the city's exercise of a water right that had been established in the 1940s.[15] By acting as a representative for the collective right of citizens to enjoy a healthy lake, the Audubon Society protected a part of the environment that the state had been willing to sacrifice in the name of progress.

Although it has been argued that the court's interpretation of the public trust doctrine was a misinterpretation of a legal concept limited to navigation, the idea that a healthy environment provides intangible benefits that can supersede established water rights has proven to be a potent tool in fights over water in the United States.[16] In some parts of the country, the idea that the state has a public trust obligation to protect the environment has even become official policy. For example, Hawaii formally adopted a broad interpretation of the public trust doctrine into its state constitution in 1978, thereby codifying the state's long-held tradition of government management of natural resources for the benefit of the community. Elsewhere, government officials have begun to refer to their responsibility to protect the environment as stemming from the public trust doctrine.

Since the Mono Lake decision, the public trust doctrine has become part of the legal landscape in parts of the United States, but Joe Sax's legacy may be of greater consequence in countries that trace parts of their legal systems back to their European colonizers. For example, in 1997, India's supreme court invoked the public trust doctrine when it ruled in favor of an activist who sued the government to revoke a permit granting a resort the right to divert a flood-prone river around its property.[17] Elsewhere, the idea that environmental protection is a public trust responsibility was endorsed by the Supreme Court of the Philippines in 2008, when it issued a ruling compelling the government to build sewage treatment plants, restock native fish, and engage in public education about pollution in Manila Bay. In their opinion the justices noted that, "Even assuming the absence of a categorical legal provision specifically prodding petitioners to clean up the bay, they [the government] and the men and women representing them cannot escape their obligation to future generations of Filipinos to keep the waters of the Manila Bay clean and clear as humanly as possible. Anything less would be a betrayal of the trust reposed in them." Since these early victories, courts in Uganda, Kenya, Nigeria, and South Africa have invoked the public trust doctrine and the government's role as a protector of rivers, lakes, and forests in successful citizen challenges of rights claimed by private entities.

The public trust doctrine has provided advocates with a powerful tool for compelling their governments to protect the environment, but it has not turned the tide on environmental degradation. Some of these shortcomings can be tied to the fact that under the public trust doctrine, bodies of water are property controlled by the citizens in whose name the government acts. As a result, there may be times when most members of the public are willing to accept some damage to the environment in exchange for the economic benefits that a new project might deliver. Over time, the impacts of small compromises made in the name of progress can add up to a greatly diminished ecosystem. Even under circumstances where communities are supportive of environmental protection, the defenders of waterways may lack the financial resources or training needed to initiate legal challenges. For these reasons, natural systems might be better off if they had their own rights and someone whose sole job it was to look after their interests.

Most people are a bit puzzled when they encounter the idea that nature (and not just the people who derive benefits from its enjoyment) can have rights, especially when they learn that a river or a forest has obtained legal personhood. Yet for those familiar with Western legal systems, this should be unremarkable. Civil courts would not function without allowances for nonhuman entities, including nations, religious organizations, and corporations, to have rights and responsibilities that are distinct from those of the people who temporarily oversee their affairs. Thus, the extension of personhood to rivers and forests can be viewed as the next step in the fight for legal protection for excluded groups. Before their acquisition of such rights, the idea that legal standing could be granted to Jews, women, enslaved people, Indigenous people, children, and persons who are incapable of managing their own affairs seemed inconceivable to members of society who had already secured their own rights. But the arc of history bent a little further in the direction of justice each time rights were extended to a group that previously had been deemed as unworthy of legal status.

The idea that the environment should have its own set of legal rights can be traced back to Christopher Stone, another American legal scholar, who wrote a paper in 1972 arguing that trees are entitled to legal standing.[18] According to Stone's logic, treating natural systems as property fails to capture an emerging societal consensus that a healthy environment can supersede the short-term interests of individuals and their governments. Providing nature with its own set of rights extends environmental protection beyond the constraints of the public trust doctrine because it acknowledges that the short-term interest of the community in economic benefits can shortchange the environment. The granting of personhood to natural systems also flows from spiritual beliefs about the place of humans in the universe and the essential role that a healthy environment plays in sustaining civilization. For proponents of this way of thinking, the act of giving forests, grasslands, and waterways personhood and designating human guardians whose sole function is to represent nature is simply the right thing to do.

In the early days, the idea that the environment could have legal standing was dismissed by the establishment as a fringe notion that had little relevance to such serious matters as water allocation and pollution control. But the declaration of personhood for the environment resonated with communities that had never fully bought into the Western way of seeing the world. In 2008 and 2010, Ecuador and then Bolivia amended their constitutions to recognize the rights of nature.[19] The extension of these protections was driven by Indigenous Andean communities seeking recognition of their perspective that nature and society are not distinct entities. Although the granting of rights to nature empowered local Indigenous communities and clarified the state's obligation to protect the environment, the ultimate effect of the constitutional amendments was not much different than what might have been accomplished by strengthening environmental rules according to the public trust doctrine. The more profound effect on water of this new way of looking at society's legal relationship with nature became evident only in 2017, when New Zealand granted personhood to a river.

In retrospect, it makes sense that the granting of personhood to nature had its greatest impact in a country where the government's authority is derived from an agreement that established shared governance according to the laws and traditions of the Māori people and the British colonists who signed the Treaty of Waitangi in 1840. The Māori approach to governance became more prominent after the country started to grapple with its failure to live up to the treaty in the 1970s. By the mid-2010s, the Māori perspective had become embedded in the workings of New Zealand's government, especially with respect to laws and policies affecting natural resources.

For decades, the iwi (Māori tribe) living adjacent to the North Island's Whanganui River had invoked a clause in the Treaty of Waitangi that gave them property rights to river beds in their struggle to protect the Whanganui from hydroelectric dam construction and the mining of gravel.[20] Aside from the fact that they were not particularly successful at stopping development, the idea that the river was property was inconsistent with the way that the Whanganui iwi saw the world. According to Māori thinking, rivers and streams are living ancestors with their own personalities, wants, and needs.

The Whanganui iwi understood the river to be "an indivisible and living whole extending from the mountains to the sea" that could not be broken up into parts that are owned by different groups of people.[21] Thus, legal personhood for the river was an appropriate way to ensure that the entire system would be treated properly. In 2017, the Te Awa Tupua (Whanganui River Claims Settlement) Act recognized the Whanganui River as a legal entity and appointed two representatives to speak on its behalf. As specified by the act, one of the two river guardians is appointed by the Whanganui iwi and the other by the federal government. Supported by an advisory board and ample financial resources, the representatives are now working on behalf of the river.

The establishment of personhood for natural systems is just one of the ways that Māori perspectives are altering water governance in New Zealand.[22] The other ways that the Māori approach of treating nature as something other than property has affected efforts to protect New Zealand's natural heritage while simultaneously meeting the economic and social needs of its citizens. For example, engineers on the North Island recently redesigned a wastewater treatment plant to bring it into harmony with a Māori belief that prohibits the direct discharge of human waste into a body of water. Working with the local iwi, the engineers created a treatment system that removes all signs of waste from the water before discharging it into a specially designed channel containing blessed rocks that allow the purified water to reconnect with the earth and regain its life force before returning to the river. Elsewhere in the country, the holistic Māori view of water offers a stark contrast to the reductionist approach of diagnosing problems and protecting a river's health by focusing on chemical and biological parameters that are measured in laboratories. Māori representation in the decision-making process adds a new layer of complexity to efforts to manage the country's water resources. But as local and national government agencies adjust their water management plans and regulations to account for the needs of the environment, there is optimism that the Māori way of thinking will lead to more robust and sustainable solutions.

In the years since the Whanganui River received personhood, legal standing has been extended to waterways in India, Bangladesh, Colombia, and the United States.[23] However, the impact has not been as profound as the changes in New Zealand because the new rights have been claimed within systems where the environment is still considered as property. Furthermore, the guardians assigned to protect the water bodies outside of New Zealand often lack the independence and financial resources needed to follow through on their assigned mission. Thus, the true power of personhood for waterways may be limited to lands that are controlled by Indigenous people who embrace a more holistic way of seeing the world, such as North America's native people. In the United States, the Yurok Tribe granted personhood to the Klamath River in 2019. Two years later, Canada's Ekuanitshi granted personhood to a river in Quebec. The future success of these efforts will depend on the seriousness with which the governments surrounding tribal nations take their obligation to share power with the people who have been stewards of the land for thousands of years.

Epilogue

RECASTING THE STRUGGLE to provide an ample quantity of clean water to people and ecosystems in terms of universal rights might help draw attention to water crises that often fail to receive the attention they deserve. But this alone would be insufficient. Major investments in new ways of using existing resources more efficiently and accessing previously underused water sources (the approaches described throughout this book) will be essential in the coming decades if the world is to avoid water crises caused by population growth, global development, and a changing climate. Considering the powerful tools at society's disposal and the potential for innovation to further decrease the costs of building and operating water systems, none of the six water crises is insurmountable provided that the inadequacies of the existing system are recognized. Avoiding severe crises will require society to replace some of the water management approaches that came about during the Great Acceleration with approaches that are better suited for a new reality.

Breaking free of a mindset that no longer makes sense is never easy. This is especially true when the necessary change might be expensive and socially disruptive. To illustrate the challenges that the world's water systems will face in coming decades, consider the situation along the Colorado River, a place where water infrastructure and the institutions that manage it were built on the premise that there would always be an adequate supply of water for farms, cities, and ecosystems provided that enough money could be directed toward water infrastructure.

Throughout most of the twentieth century, proponents of this way of thinking touted the economic development that water infrastructure investments had brought to the region. Warnings about overallocation of water resources and environmental damage caused by water diversions largely went unheeded by powerful politicians who represented rapidly growing Sunbelt cities and prosperous farmers. Despite a few successes for environmentalists fighting to protect ecosystems, the pro-development forces usually prevailed. By the 2010s, it had become evident that water demand was exceeding the capacity of the region's dams and aquifers. As dry conditions persisted, meteorologists began to refer to the prevailing conditions as aridification rather than just an extended drought.

The initial reaction of many Colorado River–dependent communities to their new climatic reality was to double down on the system they had inherited. For some, this meant calling in lawyers to defend rights to the remaining water. Others invested in water efficiency measures and aquifer storage and recovery systems as a means of continuing to meet demand in the face of shrinking supplies. These responses—reinforcing a legacy system that no longer provided enough water—might have made sense if the problem was simply a matter of competition among water users for resources that had been overallocated through overly optimistic projections of water availability. Without climate change, water managers might have been able to figure out how to conserve their way out of the shortfall while simultaneously renovating the river's aging dams and reducing their impacts on the ecosystem. But the increasingly hotter and drier climate means that the twentieth-century approach may have run its course in the Colorado River Basin as managers contemplate cutbacks in agriculture and stricter water budgets for cities.

The situation on the Colorado River may be dire, but it is hardly unique. The infrastructures created during the first phase of the Great Acceleration in Mediterranean Europe and Australia are facing, or likely will soon face, similar challenges from aridification. Brazil, India, and China—nations that entered the Great Acceleration a few decades after the OECD countries—have also created systems for water supply, hydroelectric power production, and flood control that are in just as precarious a situation as those that were built in Western countries earlier in the twentieth century. Like most people facing a water crisis, the initial response of managers running these increasingly stressed water systems will be to build more of what they already have while attempting to operate existing infrastructure more efficiently. But as the impacts of climate change intensify, they, too, will realize that these are only temporary solutions. Intensifying water crises will eventually force society to face a new reality: start doing things differently or face a future with smaller cities, less industry, and fewer farms.

Considering the reluctance of society to accept defeat and the creative solutions that people have started to use in response to water supply crises, change is the likely path forward. Wealthy regions on the front lines of water supply crises are likely to be the first places where this new approach to water management will emerge.

Motivated by scarcity and supported by robust economies, wealthy communities will have a myriad of choices for creating next-generation water systems. With approaches including stillsuits for cities, net zero water buildings, and desalination plants, cities can greatly reduce their reliance on imported water. If they invest wisely in new infrastructure and embrace the next stage of conservation, urbanites in wealthy arid regions can be surrounded by greenery with confidence that everyone in their community has access to safe and affordable water.

Efforts to address agricultural water shortfalls in rich parts of the world can be supported by precision irrigation, advanced plant breeding, managed aquifer recharge, and desalination, but the resolution of water shortfalls will require a recognition that water consumption must be brought into line with its availability. Solving the coming water supply crises will be possible only through the resolution of long-standing issues related to water rights, political power, and food security. If people living in affluent countries are willing to pay a little more for locally grown produce, the surrounding rural communities can continue to thrive in a hotter, drier climate. Prosperity may mean that a little less land is cultivated as farmers adopt the more-crop-per-drop mentality while they shift their attention to high-value products. Although these regions may have once grown their own staples, living within their means will likely require importation of grains and cereals from places where irrigation is not a necessity.

The new solutions will also require a different approach to environmental stewardship in water-stressed parts of wealthy countries. As the effects of rising temperatures and changing precipitation patterns intensify, simply protecting nature from further damage will no longer suffice. Ecosystem decline caused by water projects and inadequate land stewardship can be reversed. Active intervention—through forest management, removal of obsolete dams, and restoration of connections between rivers and floodplains—will be necessary for wealthy regions seeking coexistence with a healthy environment. Although these measures will not come cheap, a recognition of the precarious state of natural systems coupled with changing perspectives on the right to a healthy environment is needed to turn the tide.

Water-stressed regions in low- and middle-income countries that have already committed to the same sort of infrastructure that exists in high-income countries will face an even greater challenge due to continued population growth, increasing demand for water driven by higher incomes, and a desire to achieve food security. In these countries, the creation of institutions that can effectively foster water use efficiency, reduce pollution, and promote more equitable water access will be a lot more effective than investments in advanced technologies. But new technologies will still play a role as attitudes about water shift in low- and middle-income countries. Although these countries will likely continue to invest in additional infrastructure to serve their growing economies, water managers will do so with the knowledge that building their own version of the Colorado River system is a recipe for disaster. Learning from the successes and failures of other regions facing water crises and empowered with technologies that become cheaper as they move along the learning curve, water managers can create infrastructure that sidesteps many of the failures that have come to light in wealthier parts of the world. Although the needs for food security and drinking water provision may drive behavior in the near term, robust solutions will require a recognition that the hard work of creating sustainable cities and food systems while simultaneously avoiding environmental destruction is essential to the long-term project of fostering prosperity and avoiding water crises.

The adoption of new approaches to water management will not be restricted to regions facing shortages. Although it may not be as obvious in wetter regions, the infrastructure that generates power, delivers water, and prevents flooding has put humanity in control of most of the world's waterways. Infrastructure built during the Great Acceleration is essential to modern life, but it has come at a high price. It may not be feasible to stop running the rivers, but it is possible to run them in a manner that does not cause water crises. In places where waterways flow with the wastes of upstream cities and farms, new treatment technologies—many developed as part of efforts to access unconventional water sources—can remove contaminants that threaten human health and ecosystems. The old beliefs that it is too expensive to remove arsenic, lead, or PFAS at the tap or that pesticide- and nutrient-laden runoff is the cost of growing food can be rejected by a society that understands that water pollution is not inevitable. In places where dams, canals, and flood control structures cannot be removed, they can be operated in a manner that helps restore the environment by allocating a fraction of the water and land to ecosystem restoration. Seeing the damage caused by failures in water management as resulting from a lack of imagination rather than from technological and institutional impossibilities is a first step in resolving crises related to our inability to properly manage the rivers that we now operate.

During the early stages of the Great Acceleration, our predecessors embarked on ambitious projects that remade the world's water systems with confidence that they were creating a better life for the generations that would follow them. Although the outcomes of their efforts led to a host of new problems, modern water systems have enabled the growth of cities, fostered public health, and supported food systems that help feed more than eight billion people. As inheritors of this legacy, we have clung to the water infrastructure and institutions that developed during that period of rapid growth. But inadequacies in the approaches developed by our ancestors along with a climate that they had not anticipated are forcing us to rethink nearly every facet of water management. Decades of experience gained by communities that are already facing water crises coupled with technological innovations and scientific knowledge that was not available to previous generations have prepared us to head in a new direction. Although we might resist it for a few more years, change is inevitable.

If we can meet the challenge, decades from now, people will turn on their taps confident in the knowledge that the water that flows through the pipes is safe to drink. They will have learned that if they use only what they need, the water will not stop flowing during a dry year. They also will know that the act of obtaining this water has not created a crisis somewhere else. After the water has been used, they will watch it drain away with an awareness that it will be put to a productive use. I hope that as they watch the water, they will remember us—the generation that built their remarkable water system.

NOTES

1 WATER FOR HOUSEHOLD USE

1. L. Cannon, "Santa Barbara Greets Big Desalination Plant with Praise, Criticism," *Washington Post,* February 28, 1992.

2. L. Rodriguez and R. Lamb, *Water Resources of Santa Barbara County* (Santa Barbara, CA: SBCWA, 2000).

3. R. B. McKinstry, H. D. Prior, J. E. Drust, A. C. Montalbán, and K. D. Magrini, "Unpave a Parking Lot and Put Up a Paradise: Using Green Infrastructure and Ecosystem Services to Achieve Cost-Effective Compliance," *Environmental Law Reporter* 42 (2012): 10824–39.

4. *The Role of Desalination in an Increasingly Water-Scarce World,* World Bank Group, Washington, DC, 2019.

5. C. R. Azzoni, *São Paulo Metropolitan Area: Size, Competitiveness and the Future,* São Paulo, 2005; A. Cashman and R. Ashley, "Costing the Long-Term Demand for Water Sector Infrastructure," *Foresight* 10 (2008): 9–26; J. Kelman, "Water Supply to the Two Largest Brazilian Metropolitan Regions," in *At the Confluence,* vol. 5, *Selections from the 2014 World Water Week in Stockholm,* ed. J. Lundqvist, 13–21 (Amsterdam: Elsevier, 2015).

6. B. Braga and J. Kelman, "Facing the Challenge of Extreme Climate: The Case of Metropolitan São Paulo," *Water Policy* 18 (2016): 52–69.

7. S. Böhm and R. K. Flores, "São Paulo Water Crisis Shows the Failure of Public-Private Partnerships," The Conversation, May 6, 2015, https://theconversation.com/sao-paulo-water-crisis-shows-the-failure-of-public-private-partnerships-39483.

8. G. N. de Lima, M. A. Lombardo, and V. Magana, "Urban Water Supply and the Changes in the Precipitation Patterns in the Metropolitan Area of São Paulo—Brazil," *Applied Geography* 94 (2018): 223–29.

9. De Lima, Lombardo, and Magana, "Urban Water Supply."

10. J. Welty and X. Zeng, "Does Soil Moisture Affect Warm Season Precipitation over the Southern Great Plains?," *Geophysical Research Letters* 45 (2018):

7866–73; J. Diamond, *Collapse: How Societies Choose to Fail or Succeed* (New York: Viking, 2005).

11. J. M. Shepherd, H. Pierce, and A. J. Negri, "Rainfall Modification by Major Urban Areas: Observations from Spaceborne Rain Radar on the TRMM Satellite," *Journal of Applied Meteorology and Climatology* 41 (2002): 689–701.

12. D. Phillips, "Brazil's Terrible, Horrible, No Good, Very Bad Year," *Washington Post*, July 29, 2016; T. Waldron, "Everything Is Going Wrong in Brazil ahead of the Olympics," Huffington Post, May 23, 2016, https://www.huffpost.com /entry/rio-olympics-2016-brazil-crises_n_573b53e7e4b0646cbeeb02c8.

13. Braga and Kelman, "Facing the Challenge of Extreme Climate."

14. Kelman, "Water Supply to the Two Largest Brazilian Metropolitan Regions."

15. J. Watts, "Brazil's Worst Drought in History Prompts Protests and Blackouts," *Guardian*, January 23, 2015.

16. A. Dhillon, "Chennai in Crisis as Authorities Blamed for Dire Water Shortage," *Guardian*, June 19, 2019; K. Ritter, "Drought, Pollution, and Expansion Imperil Istanbul's Best-Laid Water Plans," Circle of Blue, April 19, 2018, https:// www.circleofblue.org/2018/water-management/cities/drought-pollution -and-expansion-imperil-istanbuls-best-laid-water-plans/; M. Kimmelman, "Mexico City, Parched and Sinking, Faces a Water Crisis," *New York Times*, February 17, 2017; "Millions Hit in Manila's 'Worst' Water Shortage," Phys.org, March 15, 2019, https://phys.org/news/2019-03-millions-manila-worst-shortage .html; M. Florke, C. Schneider, and R. I. McDonald, "Water Competition between Cities and Agriculture Driven by Climate Change and Urban Growth," *Nature Sustainability* 1 (2018): 51–58.

17. *Progress on Household Drinking Water, Sanitation and Hygiene, 2000–2017: Special Focus on Inequalities,* UNICEF, New York, 2019.

18. *Human Development Report 2006: Beyond Scarcity: Power, Poverty and the Global Water Crisis,* United Nations Development Programme, New York, 2006.

19. *Progress on Household Drinking Water;* O. Cumming, M. Elliott, A. Overbo, and J. Bartram, "Does Global Progress on Sanitation Really Lag behind Water? An Analysis of Global Progress on Community- and Household- Level Access to Safe Water and Sanitation," *PLoS One* 9 (2014): 16.

20. E. Royte, "Nearly a Billion People Still Defecate Outdoors: Here's Why," *National Geographic,* August 2017; E. G. Wagner and J. N. Lanoix, *Excreta Disposal for Rural Areas and Small Communities,* World Health Organization, Geneva, 1958, 95.

21. D. Hulme, *The Millennium Development Goals (MDGs): A Short History of*

the *World's Biggest Promise,* Brooks World Poverty Institute, BWPI Working Paper 100, Manchester, UK, September 2009.

22. *Progress on Household Drinking Water;* M. Ait-Kadi, in *Water for Development and Development for Water: Realizing the Sustainable Development Goals (SDGs) Vision,* 106–10, World Water Week: Water for Development, Stockholm, August 23–28, 2015.

23. J. Abbink, "The Ethiopian Second Republic and the Fragile 'Social Contract,'" *Africa Spectrum* 44 (2009): 3–28.

24. *One WaSH—Consolidated WaSH Account Project (One WaSHCWA) (P167794),* World Bank, Washington, DC, April 30, 2019; *Ethiopia Poverty Assessment,* World Bank Group, Washington, DC, 2015.

25. *Final Project Report: Water Harvesting for Multiple Use in Ethiopia (MUStRAIN),* IRC, The Hague, 2014; T. Oyedotun, "Ensuring Water Availability in Mekelle City, Northern Ethiopia: Evaluation of the Water Supply Sub-Project," *Applied Water Science* 7 (2017): 4165–68.

26. S. Ali, "Ethiopia's Imperfect Growth Miracle," Carnegie Endowment for International Peace, October 20, 2011, https://carnegieendowment.org/2011/10/20/ethiopia-s-imperfect-growth-miracle-pub-45776.

27. *Ethiopia Poverty Assessment.*

28. *Progress on Household Drinking Water.*

29. J. Kurtzer, H. F. Abdullah, and S. Ballard, *Concurrent Crises in the Horn of Africa,* Center for Strategic and International Studies, Washington, DC, June 2022.

30. *Progress on Household Drinking Water.*

2 SAFE DRINKING WATER

1. M. McGuire, "Boiled in China: A Personal Source of Safe Drinking Water," Safedrinkingwater.com, January 13, 2014, https://safedrinkingwaterdotcom.wordpress.com/2014/01/13/boiled-in-china-a-personal-source-of-safe-drinking-water/comment-page-1/.

2. D. L. Sedlak, *Water 4.0: The Past, Present and Future of the World's Most Vital Resource* (New Haven: Yale University Press, 2014).

3. E. Kumpel and K. L. Nelson, "Intermittent Water Supply: Prevalence, Practice, and Microbial Water Quality," *Environmental Science and Technology* 50 (2016): 542–53.

4. *Nutrients in Drinking Water,* Water, Sanitation and Health Protection and the Human Environment, World Health Organization, Geneva, 2005.

5. A. H. Smith, E. O. Lingas, and M. Rahman, "Contamination of Drinking-Water by Arsenic in Bangladesh: A Public Health Emergency," *Bulletin of the World Health Organization* 78 (2000): 1093–103.

6. A. M. R. Chowdhury, "Arsenic Crisis in Bangladesh," *Scientific American* 291 (2004): 86–91.

7. M. F. Hossain, "Arsenic Contamination in Bangladesh: An Overview," *Agriculture Ecosystems and Environment* 113 (2006): 1–16.

8. Chowdhury, "Arsenic Crisis in Bangladesh."

9. Smith, Lingas, and Rahman, "Contamination of Drinking-Water"; A. H. Smith, G. Marshall, Y. Yuan, C. Ferreccio, J. Liaw, O. von Ehrenstein, C. Steinmaus, et al., "Increased Mortality from Lung Cancer and Bronchiectasis in Young Adults after Exposure to Arsenic in Utero and in Early Childhood," *Environmental Health Perspectives* 114 (2006): 1293–96; E. M. Hall, J. Acevedo, F. G. Lopez, S. Cortes, C. Ferreccio, A. H. Smith, and C. M. Steinmaus, "Hypertension among Adults Exposed to Drinking Water Arsenic in Northern Chile," *Environmental Research* 153 (2017): 99–105.

10. Smith, Lingas, and Rahman, "Contamination of Drinking-Water"; S. V. Flanagan, R. B. Johnston, and Y. Zheng, "Arsenic in Tube Well Water in Bangladesh: Health and Economic Impacts and Implications for Arsenic Mitigation," *Bulletin of the World Health Organization* 90 (2012): 839–46.

11. Flanagan, Johnston, and Zheng, "Arsenic in Tube Well Water."

12. M. F. Ahmed, S. Ahuja, M. Alauddin, S. J. Hug, J. R. Lloyd, A. Pfaff, T. Pichler, et al., "Epidemiology—Ensuring Safe Drinking Water in Bangladesh," *Science* 314 (2006): 1687–88.

13. F. Ahmed, "Arsenic Mitigation Technologies in South and East Asia," World Bank Water and Sanitation Program, World Bank, Washington, DC, 2005.

14. N. B. Jamil, H. Feng, K. M. Ahmed, I. Choudhury, P. Barnwal, and A. van Geen, "Effectiveness of Different Approaches to Arsenic Mitigation over 18 Years in Araihazar, Bangladesh: Implications for National Policy," *Environmental Science and Technology* 53 (2019): 5596–604.

15. Ahmed et al., "Epidemiology."

16. Jamil et al., "Effectiveness of Different Approaches."

17. H. Brammer and P. Ravenscroft, "Arsenic in Groundwater: A Threat to Sustainable Agriculture in South and South-East Asia," *Environment International* 35 (2009): 647–54.

18. J. D. Ayotte, L. Medalie, S. L. Qi, L. C. Backer, and B. T. Nolan, "Estimating the High-Arsenic Domestic-Well Population in the Conterminous United States," *Environmental Science and Technology* 51 (2017): 12443–54.

19. M. Amini, K. Mueller, K. C. Abbaspour, T. Rosenberg, M. Afyuni, K. N.

Moller, M. Sarr, et al., "Statistical Modeling of Global Geogenic Fluoride Contamination in Groundwaters," *Environmental Science and Technology* 42 (2008): 3662–68; R. M. Coyte, R. C. Jain, S. K. Srivastava, K. C. Sharma, A. Khalil, L. Ma, and A. Vengosh, "Large-Scale Uranium Contamination of Groundwater Resources in India," *Environmental Science and Technology Letters* 5 (2018): 341–47; D. M. Hausladen, A. Alexander-Ozinskas, C. McClain, and S. Fendorf, "Hexavalent Chromium Sources and Distribution in California Groundwater," *Environmental Science and Technology* 52 (2018): 8242–51; P. K. Hopke, T. B. Borak, J. Doull, J. E. Cleaver, K. F. Eckerman, L. C. S. Gundersen, N. H. Harley, et al., "Health Risks Due to Radon in Drinking Water," *Environmental Science and Technology* 34 (2000): 921–26.

20. S. Preunkert, J. R. McConnell, H. Hoffmann, M. Legrand, A. I. Wilson, S. Eckhardt, A. Stohl, et al., "Lead and Antimony in Basal Ice from Col du Dome (French Alps) Dated with Radiocarbon: A Record of Pollution during Antiquity," *Geophysical Research Letters* 46 (2019): 4953–61; C. S. L. Lee, S. H. Qi, G. Zhang, C. L. Luo, L. Y. L. Zhao, and X. D. Li, "Seven Thousand Years of Records on the Mining and Utilization of Metals from Lake Sediments in Central China," *Environmental Science and Technology* 42 (2008): 4732–38.

21. Sedina Banks, "The 'Erin Brockovich Effect': How Media Shapes Toxics Policy," *Environs* 26 (2003): 219–51.

22. Lois Gibbs, *Love Canal: My Story* (Albany: State University of New York Press, 1982).

23. *Report to Congress: Disposal of Hazardous Wastes*, US Environmental Protection Agency, Washington, DC, 1973; "114 Toxic Waste Sites Listed as the Nation's Most Dangerous," *New York Times*, October 23, 1981.

24. Perry L. McCarty, "Groundwater Contamination by Chlorinated Solvents: History, Remediation Technologies and Strategies," in *In Situ Remediation of Chlorinated Solvent Plumes*, ed. Hans F. Stroo and C. Herb Ward, 1–28 (New York: Springer, 2010).

25. *Alternatives for Managing the Nation's Complex Contaminated Groundwater Sites*, National Research Council, National Academies of Science, Engineering and Medicine, Washington, DC, 2013.

26. Tara Lohan, "A Climate-Resilient Los Angeles Must First Address Its Polluted Past," The Revelator, Center for Biological Diversity, July 25, 2019, https://therevelator.org/los-angeles-groundwater/.

27. W. Giger, "The Rhine Red, the Fish Dead—The 1986 Schweizerhalle Disaster, a Retrospect and Long-Term Impact Assessment," *Environmental Science and Pollution Research* 16 (2009): 98–111.

28. *The Songhua River Spill China, December 2005*, United Nations Environment

Programme, Nairobi, 2005; A. J. Whelton, L. McMillan, M. Connell, K. M. Kelley, J. P. Gill, K. D. White, R. Gupta, et al., "Residential Tap Water Contamination following the Freedom Industries Chemical Spill: Perceptions, Water Quality, and Health Impacts," *Environmental Science and Technology* 49 (2015): 813–23.

29. M. M. Schultz, D. F. Barofsky, and J. A. Field, "Fluorinated Alkyl Surfactants," *Environmental Engineering Science* 20 (2003): 487–501.

30. *Report: Up to 100 Million Americans Could Have PFAS-Contaminated Drinking Water,* Environmental Working Group, Washington, DC, 2018.

3 WATER TO GROW FOOD

1. "Water Footprint of Food," Water Footprint Network, https://waterfootprint .org/en/resources/interactive-tools/.

2. P. B. deMenocal, "Cultural Responses to Climate Change during the Late Holocene," *Science* 292 (2001): 667–73.

3. A. van Dijk, H. E. Beck, R. S. Crosbie, R. A. M. de Jeu, Y. Y. Liu, G. M. Podger, B. Timbal, et al., "The Millennium Drought in Southeast Australia (2001–2009): Natural and Human Causes and Implications for Water Resources, Ecosystems, Economy, and Society," *Water Resources Research* 49 (2013): 1040–57; J. Quiggin, *Drought, Climate Change and Food Prices in Australia* (Brisbane: University of Queensland, 2007).

4. C. M. Marquette, "Current Poverty, Structural Adjustment, and Drought in Zimbabwe," *World Development* 25 (1997): 1141–49; C. Benson and E. Clay, *The Impact of Drought on Sub-Saharan African Economies: A Preliminary Examination,* Overseas Development Institute, Regent's College, London, 1994.

5. M. Roser and H. Ritchie, "Food Prices," Our World in Data, October 10, 2019, https://ourworldindata.org/food-prices; *The State of Food Insecurity in the World,* United Nations Food and Agriculture Organization, Rome, 2011.

6. R. Arezki and B. C. Markus, *Food Prices and Political Instability,* International Monetary Fund, Washington, DC, 2011.

7. J. Selby, O. S. Dahi, C. Frohlich, and M. Hulme, "Climate Change and the Syrian Civil War Revisited," *Political Geography* 60 (2017): 232–44.

8. K. J. Mach, C. M. Kraan, W. N. Adger, H. Buhaug, M. Burke, J. D. Fearon, C. B. Field, et al., "Climate as a Risk Factor for Armed Conflict," *Nature* 571 (2019): 193–97.

9. B. La Shier and J. Stanish, *The National Security Impacts of Climate Change,* Environmental and Energy Policy Institute, Washington, DC, 2017; "Climate

Change Recognized as 'Threat Multiplier': UN Security Council Debates Its Impact on Peace," *UN News*, December 22, 2019, https://news.un.org /en/story/2019/01/1031322; *High and Dry: Climate Change, Water, and the Economy*, World Bank, Washington, DC, 2016.

10. L. W. Mays, "A Brief History of Water Technology during Antiquity: Before the Romans," in *Ancient Water Technologies*, ed. L. W. Mays, 1–28 (Dordrecht: Springer, 2010); *Encyclopaedia Brittanica*, s.v. "Canals and Inland Waterways."

11. K. Barton, "Challenge, Promise for Nation's 'Winter Salad Bowl,'" *California Agriculture* 51 (1997): 4–6.

12. A. S. Qureshi, "Water Management in the Indus Basin in Pakistan: Challenges and Opportunities," *Mountain Research and Development* 31 (2011): 252–60.

13. M. Cohen, J. Christian-Smith, and J. Berggren, *Water to Supply the Land: Irrigated Agriculture in the Colorado River Basin*, Pacific Institute, Oakland, CA, 2013.

14. D. R. Cayan, T. Das, D. W. Pierce, T. P. Barnett, M. Tyree, and A. Gershunov, "Future Dryness in the Southwest US and the Hydrology of the Early 21st Century Drought," *Proceedings of the National Academy of Sciences* 107 (2010): 21271–76; T. P. Barnett and D. W. Pierce, "When Will Lake Mead Go Dry?," *Water Resources Research* 44 (2008): W03201.

15. S. I. Yannopoulos, G. Lyberatos, N. Theodossiou, W. Li, M. Valipour, A. Tamburrino, and A. N. Angelakis, "Evolution of Water Lifting Devices (Pumps) over the Centuries Worldwide," *Water* 7 (2015): 5031–60.

16. M. J. Jones, *Thematic Paper 8: Social Adoption of Groundwater Pumping Technology and the Development of Groundwater Cultures: Governance at the Point of Abstraction*, Groundwater Governance, Rome, 2012.

17. Yannopoulos et al., "Evolution of Water Lifting Devices."

18. Jones, *Thematic Paper 8*.

19. Jones, *Thematic Paper 8*.

20. S. S. Kepfield, "The Liquid-Gold Rush: Groundwater Irrigation and Law in Nebraska, 1900–93," *Great Plains Quarterly* 13 (1993): 237–50.

21. *India-Water Resources Management Sector Review*, World Bank, Washington, DC, 1998.

22. Jones, *Thematic Paper 8*.

23. Jones, *Thematic Paper 8*; T. Shah, "Climate Change and Groundwater: India's Opportunities for Mitigation and Adaptation," *Environmental Research Letters* 4 (2009): 035005.

24. A. S. Richey, B. F. Thomas, M. H. Lo, J. T. Reager, J. S. Famiglietti, K. Voss, S. Swenson, et al., "Quantifying Renewable Groundwater Stress with GRACE," *Water Resources Research* 51 (2015): 5217–38; B. R. Scanlon, C. C. Faunt,

L. Longuevergne, R. C. Reedy, W. M. Alley, V. L. McGuire, and P. B. Mc-Mahon, "Groundwater Depletion and Sustainability of Irrigation in the US High Plains and Central Valley," *Proceedings of the National Academy of Sciences* 109 (2012): 9320–25.

25. *Feeding the World in 2050,* Food and Agriculture Organization of the United Nations, Rome, 2009.

26. J. Jagermeyr, D. Gerten, S. Schaphoff, J. Heinke, W. Lucht, and J. Rockstrom, "Integrated Crop Water Management Might Sustainably Halve the Global Food Gap," *Environmental Research Letters* 11 (2016): 025002.

4 WATER FOR NATURE

1. T. Oki and S. Kanae, "Global Hydrological Cycles and World Water Resources," *Science* 313 (2006): 1068–72; P. Greve, T. Kahil, J. Mochizuki, T. Schinko, Y. Satoh, P. Burek, G. Fischer, et al., "Global Assessment of Water Challenges under Uncertainty in Water Scarcity Projections," *Nature Sustainability* 1 (2018): 486–94.

2. L. Hill, *The Chicago River: A Natural and Unnatural History* (Chicago: Lake Claremont, 2000); Daniel Egan, *The Death and Life of the Great Lakes* (New York: W. W. Norton, 2017).

3. P. Micklin and N. V. Aladin, "Reclaiming the Aral Sea," *Scientific American* 298 (2008): 64–71; P. Micklin, "The Future Aral Sea: Hope and Despair," *Environmental Earth Sciences* 75 (2016): 844.

4. B. D. Richter, S. Postel, C. Revenga, T. Scudder, B. Lehner, A. Churchill, and M. Chow, "Lost in Development's Shadow: The Downstream Human Consequences of Dams," *Water Alternatives* 3 (2010): 14–42.

5. R. Sabalow and D. Kasler, "Can an Uneasy Truce Hold Off Another Water Rebellion on California's Northern Border?," *Sacramento (CA) Bee,* May 18, 2018.

6. B. Kaye, "A Look at the Klamath River and Those Who Depend on It," *Siskiyou (CA) Daily News,* September 25, 2019.

7. N. Kirkpatrick, L. Karklis, J. Cornsilk, M. Trinca, and A. Li, "Climate Change Fuels a Water Rights Conflict Built on over a Century of Broken Promises," *Washington Post,* November 22, 2021; G. Flaccus, "Major Hurdle Cleared in Plan to Demolish 4 Klamath River Dams," Oregon Public Broadcasting, February 26, 2022, https://www.opb.org/article/2022/02/26/major-hurdle-cleared-in-plan-to-demolish-4-klamath-river-dams/.

8. S. Jackson and L. Head, "Australia's Mass Fish Kills as a Crisis of Modern Water: Understanding Hydrosocial Change in the Murray-Darling Basin,"

Geoforum 109 (2020): 44–56; S. Lovgren and D. Guttenfelder, "Southeast Asia May Be Building Too Many Dams Too Fast," National Geographic, August 23, 2018, https://www.nationalgeographic.com/environment/article/news -southeast-asia-building-dams-floods-climate-change; L. Castello and M. N. Macedo, "Large-Scale Degradation of Amazonian Freshwater Ecosystems," *Global Change Biology* 22 (2016): 990–1007.

9. *Dams and Development: A New Framework for Decision-Making*, World Commission on Dams, London, 2000.

10. Richter et al., "Lost in Development's Shadow."

11. J. A. Foley, N. Ramankutty, K. A. Brauman, E. S. Cassidy, J. S. Gerber, M. Johnston, N. D. Mueller, et al., "Solutions for a Cultivated Planet," *Nature* 478 (2011): 337–42.

12. *70 Years of F.A.O.*, Food and Agriculture Organization of the United Nations, Rome, 2015; *Feeding the World in 2050*, Food and Agriculture Organization of the United Nations, Rome, 2009; P. L. Pingali, "Green Revolution: Impacts, Limits, and the Path Ahead," *Proceedings of the National Academy of Sciences* 109 (2012): 12302–8.

13. M. Roser and H. Ritchie, "Food Prices," Our World in Data, 2021, https://our worldindata.org/food-prices; H. Steinfeld, P. Gerber, T. Wassenaar, V. Castel, M. Rosales, and C. de Haan, *Livestock's Long Shadow: Environmental Issues and Options*, Food and Agriculture Organization of the United Nations, Rome, 2006; J. Mateo-Sagasta, S. Marjani Zadeh, and H. Tyurral, *More People, More Food, Worse Water? A Global Review of Water Pollution from Agriculture*, Food and Agriculture Organization of the United Nations, Rome, 2018.

14. Steinfeld et al., "Livestock's Long Shadow."

15. *North Carolina's Statewide Water and Wastewater Infrastructure Master Plan: The Road to Viability*, State Water Infrastructure Authority, North Carolina Department of Environmental Quality, Raleigh, 2017; D. W. Hamilton, B. Fathepure, C. D. Fulhage, W. Clarkson, and W. Lalman, "Treatment Lagoons for Animal Agriculture," in *Animal Agriculture and the Environment*, ed. J. M. Rice, D. F. Caldwell, and F. J. Humenik, 547–74 (St. Joseph, MI: ASABE, 2006).

16. T. Buford, "A Hog Waste Agreement Lacked Teeth, and Some North Carolinians Say They're Left to Suffer," ProPublica, November 23, 2018, https:// www.propublica.org/article/a-hog-waste-agreement-lacked-teeth-and-some -north-carolinians-say-left-to-suffer.

17. S. R. Carpenter, N. F. Caraco, D. L. Correll, R. W. Howarth, A. N. Sharpley, and V. H. Smith, "Nonpoint Pollution of Surface Waters with Phosphorus

and Nitrogen," *Ecological Applications* 8 (1998): 559–68; L. Lassaletta, G. Billen, B. Grizzetti, J. Anglade, and J. Garnier, "50 Year Trends in Nitrogen Use Efficiency of World Cropping Systems: The Relationship between Yield and Nitrogen Input to Cropland," *Environmental Research Letters* 9 (2014): 105011.

18. Steinfeld et al., "Livestock's Long Shadow"; T. P. Van Boeckel, C. Brower, M. Gilbert, B. T. Grenfell, S. A. Levin, T. P. Robinson, A. Teillant, et al., "Global Trends in Antimicrobial Use in Food Animals," *Proceedings of the National Academy of Sciences* 112 (2015): 5649–54.

19. *Feeding the World in 2050*; P. M. Vitousek, J. D. Aber, R. W. Howarth, G. E. Likens, P. A. Matson, D. W. Schindler, W. H. Schlesinger, et al., "Human Alteration of the Global Nitrogen Cycle: Sources and Consequences," *Ecological Applications* 7 (1997): 737–50.

20. J. Hatfield, "Agriculture in the Midwest," in *U.S. National Climate Assessment Midwest Technical Input Report*, Great Lakes Integrated Sciences and Assessments (GLISA) Center, 2012.

21. *Mississippi River Water Quality and the Clean Water Act: Progress, Challenges, and Opportunities*, Committee on the Mississippi River and the Clean Water Act, Water Science and Technology Board, Division of Earth and Life Sciences, National Research Council, Washington, DC, 2008.

22. *Mississippi River Water Quality.*

23. *Large 'Dead Zone' Measured in Gulf of Mexico*, National Oceanographic and Atmospheric Administration, Washington, DC, 2019; N. N. Rabalais, R. E. Turner, and W. J. Wiseman, "Gulf of Mexico Hypoxia, aka 'the Dead Zone,'" *Annual Review of Ecology and Systematics* 33 (2002): 235–63.

24. *Mississippi River Water Quality.*

25. *Mississippi River/Gulf of Mexico Watershed Nutrient Task Force: 2017 Report to Congress*, United States Environmental Protection Agency, Washington, DC, 2017.

26. R. J. Diaz and R. Rosenberg, "Spreading Dead Zones and Consequences for Marine Ecosystems," *Science* 321 (2008): 926–29.

27. D. J. Sobota, J. E. Compton, M. L. McCrackin, and S. Singh, "Cost of Reactive Nitrogen Release from Human Activities to the Environment in the United States," *Environmental Research Letters* 10 (2015): 025006; M. A. Sutton, O. Oenema, J. W. Erisman, A. Leip, H. van Grinsven, and W. Winiwarter, "Too Much of a Good Thing," *Nature* 472 (2011): 159–61.

28. *Feeding the World in 2050.*

29. Charles Duhigg, "Debating How Much Weed Killer Is Safe in Your Water Glass," *New York Times*, August 22, 2009; T. Hayes, K. Haston, M. Tsui, A. Hoang, C. Haeffele, and A. Vonk, "Atrazine-Induced Hermaphroditism

at 0.1 ppb in American Leopard Frogs (*Rana pipiens*): Laboratory and Field Evidence," *Environmental Health Perspectives* 111 (2003): 568–75.

30. L. Allen, M. J. Cohen, D. Abelson, and B. Miller, "Fossil Fuels and Water Quality," in *The World's Water*, vol. 7, *The Biennial Report on Freshwater Resources*, ed. P. H. Gleick, with L. Allen, M. J. Cohen, H. Cooley, J. Christian-Smith, M. Heberger, J. Morrison, et al., 73–96 (Washington, DC: Island Press, 2012); T. A. Larsen, S. Hoffmann, C. Luthi, B. Truffer, and M. Maurer, "Emerging Solutions to the Water Challenges of an Urbanizing World," *Science* 352 (2016): 928–33.

5 THE GREAT ACCELERATION

1. J. R. McNeill, "Social, Economic, and Political Forces in Environmental Change Decadal Scale (1900 to 2000)," in *Sustainability of Collapse? An Integrated History and Future of People on Earth*, ed. R. Costanza, L. J. Graumlich, and W. Steffen, 301–29 (Cambridge, MA: MIT Press, 2005).

2. W. Steffen, W. Broadgate, L. Deutsch, O. Gaffney, and C. Ludwig, "The Trajectory of the Anthropocene: The Great Acceleration," *Anthropocene Review* 2 (2015): 81–98; W. Steffen, A. Sanderson, P. Tyson, J. Jäger, P. Matson, B. Moore III, F. Oldfield, et al., *Global Change and the Earth System: A Planet under Pressure* (Berlin: Springer, 2004).

3. "World Population Prospects 2019," United Nations, Population Division, https://population.un.org/wpp/Graphs/DemographicProfiles/Line/947 (April 3, 2020).

4. D. M. Cutler and E. Meara, "Changes in the Age Distribution of Mortality over the Twentieth Century," in *Perspectives on the Economics of Aging*, ed. D. A. Wise, 333–65 (Chicago: University of Chicago Press, 2004).

5. J. Bongaarts, "Human Population Growth and the Demographic Transition," *Philosophical Transactions of the Royal Society, B* 364 (2009): 2985–90.

6. O. Varis, A. K. Biswas, C. Tortajada, and J. Lundqvist, "Megacities and Water Management," *International Journal of Water Resources Development* 22 (2006): 377–94; S. Heblich, S. J. Redding, and D. M. Sturm, *The Making of a Modern Metropolis: Evidence from London*, NBER Working Paper 25047, National Bureau of Economic Research, Cambridge, MA, September 2018; M. Hoff, "The 15 Fastest-Growing Cities in the World," *Business Insider*, February 16, 2020.

7. Varis, Biswas, Tortajada, and Lundqvist, "Megacities and Water Management."

8. *The World's Cities in 2018: Data Booklet*, United Nations, Department of Economic and Social Affairs, Population Division, New York, 2018.

9. L. N. Chete, J. O. Adeoti, F. M. Adeyinka, and O. O. Ogundele, *Industrial Development and Growth in Nigeria: Lessons and Challenges,* WIDER Working Paper 2014/019, Helsinki, 2014; A. Leke, R. Fiorini, R. Diobbs, F. Thompson, A. Suleiman, and D. Wright, *Nigeria's Renewal: Delivering Inclusive Growth in Africa's Largest Economy,* McKinsey Global Institute, New York, 2014.

10. *More, and More Productive, Jobs for Nigeria: A Profile of Work and Workers,* World Bank, Washington, DC, 2015.

11. F. van der Ploeg, "Natural Resources: Curse or Blessing?," *Journal of Economic Literature* 49 (2011): 366–420; J. D. Sachs and A. M. Warner, *Natural Resource Abundance and Economic Growth,* NBER Working Paper 5398, National Bureau of Economic Research, Cambridge, MA, December 1995.

12. X. Sala-i-Martin and A. Subramanian, "Addressing the Natural Resource Curse: An Illustration from Nigeria," *Journal of African Economies* 22 (2013): 570–615; "Annual Percentage Growth Rate of GDP at Market Prices Based on Constant Local Currency," World Bank, https://data.worldbank.org/indicator/NY.GDP.MKTP.KD.ZG?locations=NG (April 16, 2020).

13. *Regional Economic Outlook: Sub-Saharan Africa: Recovery amid Elevated Uncertainty,* International Monetary Fund, Washington, DC, 2019; N. Jensen and L. Wantchekon, "Resource Wealth and Political Regimes in Africa," *Comparative Political Studies* 37 (2004): 816–41.

14. M. Sarraf and M. Jiwanji, *Beating the Resource Curse: The Case of Botswana,* World Bank, Washington, DC, 2001; *Ethiopia Poverty Assessment,* World Bank Group, Washington, DC, 2015.

15. *The State of African Cities, 2014: Re-Imagining Sustainable Urban Transitions,* UN-Habitat, Nairobi, 2014.

16. *State of African Cities, 2014;* J. Vidal, "The 100 Million City: Is 21st Century Urbanisation Out of Control?," *Guardian,* March 19, 2018.

17. *State of African Cities, 2014.*

18. B. Batinge, J. K. Musango, and A. C. Brent, "Leapfrogging to Renewable Energy: The Opportunity for Unmet Electricity Markets," *South African Journal of Industrial Engineering* 28 (2017): 32–49; K. Vairavamoorthy, "How Africa Can Leapfrog the World's Stagnant Water Paradigm," *Source,* August 12, 2019.

19. *MENA Generation 2030: Investing in Children and Youth Today to Secure a Prosperous Region Tomorrow,* UNICEF, Division of Data, Research and Policy, New York, 2019.

20. *OECD-FAO Agricultural Outlook, 2018–2027,* OECD and Food and Agricultural Organization of the United Nations, Rome, 2018.

21. P. Rogers, "The Triangle: Energy, Water and Food Nexus for Sustainable Security in the Arab Middle East," in *Water, Energy and Food Sustainability in the Middle East*, ed. A. Badran, S. Murad, and N. Daghir, 21–43 (Cham, Switzerland: Springer, 2017); J. Waterbury, "Water and Water Supply in the MENA: Less of the Same," in Adnan, Murad, and Daghir, *Water, Energy and Food Sustainability in the Middle East*, 57–84.

22. A. Y. Hoekstra and M. M. Mekonnen, "The Water Footprint of Humanity," *Proceedings of the National Academy of Sciences* 109 (2012): 3232–37; N. Madi, *Cultivating a Crisis: The Political Decline of Agriculture in Syria*, European University Institute, Robert Schuman Centre for Advanced Studies, San Domenico di Fiesole, Italy, 2019.

23. S. A. Topol, "Libya's Qaddafi Taps 'Fossil Water' to Irrigate Desert Farms," *Christian Science Monitor*, August 23, 2010; "GMR (Great Man-Made River) Water Supply Project," Water Technology, https://www.water-technology.net/projects/gmr/; *Libya's Great Manmade River Project: Plans and Realities*, Directorate of Intelligence, Washington, DC, 1987.

24. Topol, "Libya's Qaddafi Taps 'Fossil Water'"; *Libya's Great Manmade River Project*.

25. *Inventory of Shared Water Resources in Western Asia*, UN-ESCWA and BGR (United Nations Economic and Social Commission for Western Asia and Bundesanstalt für Geowissenschaften und Rohstoffe), Beirut, 2013; *Ambitious Plans in Egypt to Improve Food Security Involve Reclaiming Desert Land*, Oxford Business Group, London, 2017.

6 POWERING THE ACCELERATION

1. H. Ritchie and M. Roser, "Energy," Our World in Data, https://ourworldindata.org/energy.

2. C. A. Dieter, M. A. Maupin, R. R. Caldwell, M. A. Harris, T. I. Ivahnenko, J. K. Lovelace, N. L. Barber, et al., *Estimated Use of Water in the United States in 2015*, US Department of the Interior, US Geological Survey, Washington, DC, 2017; D. Magagna, G. I. Hidalgo, G. Bidoglio, S. Peteves, M. Adamovic, B. Bisselink, M. De Felice, et al., eds., *Water–Energy Nexus in Europe*, Publications Office of the European Union, Luxembourg, 2019; D. Tan, F. Hu, H. Theriot, and D. McGregor, *Towards a Water and Energy Secure China: Tough Choices Ahead In Power Expansion with Limited Water Resources*, China Water Risk, Hong Kong, 2015.

3. J. Andrew, "Thomas Newcomen (1664–1729) and the First Recorded Steam Engine," *Proceedings of the Institution of Civil Engineers—Transport* 168

(2015): 570–78; H. F. Massey and R. I. Barnhisel, "Copper, Nickel, and Zinc Released from Acid Coal Mine Spoil Materials of Eastern Kentucky," *Soil Science* 113 (1972): 207–12; K. C. Rice and J. S. Herman, "Acidification of Earth: An Assessment across Mechanisms and Scales," *Applied Geochemistry* 27 (2012): 1–14.

4. *Principles and Guide to Practices in the Control of Acid Mine-Drainage Supplemented by Case Histories,* Ohio River Valley Water Sanitation Commission, Cincinnati, 1964; *Stream Pollution by Coal Mine Drainage in Appalachia,* US Department of the Interior, Federal Water Pollution Control Administration, Cincinnati, 1969; W. H. J. Strosnider, J. Hugo, N. L. Shepherd, B. K. Holzbauer-Schweitzer, P. Herve-Fernandez, C. Wolkersdorfer, and R. W. Nairn, "A Snapshot of Coal Mine Drainage Discharge Limits for Conductivity, Sulfate, and Manganese across the Developed World," *Mine Water and the Environment* 39 (2020): 165–72.

5. J. Kemp, "Water Is the Biggest Output of U.S. Oil and Gas Wells: Kemp," Reuters, November 18, 2014.

6. Brandt, A. R. Oil Depletion and the Energy Efficiency of Oil Production: The Case of California. *Sustainability* 3 (2011): 1833–1854.

7. T. Cook and J. Perrin, "Hydraulic Fracturing Accounts for about Half of Current U.S. Crude Oil Production," Energy Information Agency, March 15, 2016, https://www.eia.gov/todayinenergy/detail.php?id=25372; "Natural Gas Explained: Where Our Natural Gas Comes From," Energy Information Agency, https://www.eia.gov/energyexplained/natural-gas/where-our-natural-gas-comes-from.php; J. M. Estrada and R. Bhamidimarri, "A Review of the Issues and Treatment Options for Wastewater from Shale Gas Extraction by Hydraulic Fracturing," *Fuel* 182 (2016): 292–303.

8. J. Eaton, "Oklahoma Grapples with Earthquake Spike—and Evidence of Industry's Role," National Geographic, August 2, 2014, https://www.national geographic.com/science/article/140731-oklahoma-earthquake-spike-waste water-injection; N. Chokshi and H. Fountain, "Oklahoma Orders Shutdown of Wells after Record-Tying Earthquake," *New York Times,* September 3, 2016.

9. Estrada and Bhamidimarri, "Review of the Issues and Treatment Options."

10. A. Vaughan, "Fracking—The Reality, the Risks and What the Future Holds," *Guardian,* February 26, 2018; A. Maddocks and P. Reig, "A Tale of 3 Countries: Water Risks to Global Shale Development," Insights: WRI's Blog, September 5, 2014, https://www.wri.org/insights/tale-3-countries-water-risks -global-shale-development.

11. Dieter et al., *Estimated Use of Water;* A. Kondash and A. Vengosh, "Water

Footprint of Hydraulic Fracturing," *Environmental Science and Technology Letters* 2 (2015): 276–80.

12. *International Energy Outlook, 2016,* US Department of Energy, Washington, DC, 2016.

13. N. Madden, A. Lewis, and M. Davis, "Thermal Effluent from the Power Sector: An Analysis of Once-Through Cooling System Impacts on Surface Water Temperature," *Environmental Research Letters* 8 (2013): 035006.

14. J. Macknick, R. Newmark, G. Heath, and K. C. Hallett, "Operational Water Consumption and Withdrawal Factors for Electricity Generating Technologies: A Review of Existing Literature," *Environmental Research Letters* 7 (2012): 045802.

15. S. Ray, "Some U.S. Electricity Generating Plants Use Dry Cooling," Energy Information Agency, August 29, 2018, https://www.eia.gov/todayinenergy /detail.php?id=36773; N. T. Carter, *Energy's Water Demand: Trends, Vulnerabilities, and Management,* Congressional Research Service, Washington, DC, 2010.

16. L. Poon, "Ask CityLab: What's the Deal with Steam Rising from the NYC Streets?," Bloomberg CityLab, October 23, 2015, https://www.bloomberg .com/news/articles/2015-10-23/why-steam-rises-from-the-new-york-city -pavement; "Combined Heat and Power (CHP)," European Environment Agency, updated May 11, 2021, https://www.eea.europa.eu/data-and-maps /indicators/combined-heat-and-power-chp-1/combined-heat-and-power -chp-2; M. Walton, *Desalinated Water Affects the Energy Equation in the Middle East,* International Energy Agency, Paris, 2019.

17. M. E. Weber, *Thirst for Power: Energy, Water, and Human Survival* (New Haven: Yale University Press, 2016).

18. J. McCall, J. Macknick, and D. Hillman, *Water-Related Power Plant Curtailments: An Overview of Incidents and Contributing Factors,* National Renewable Energy Laboratory, Golden, CO, 2016; G. Garfin, A. Jardine, R. Merideth, M. Black, and S. LeRoy, *Assessment of Climate Change in the Southwest United States* (Washington, DC: Island Press, 2013); J. Kanter, "Climate Change Puts Nuclear Energy into Hot Water," *New York Times,* May 20, 2007.

19. Magagna et al., *Water–Energy Nexus in Europe;* J. Macknick, S. Sattler, K. Averyt, S. Clemmer, and J. Rogers, "The Water Implications of Generating Electricity: Water Use across the United States Based on Different Electricity Pathways through 2050," *Environmental Research Letters* 7 (2012): 045803.

20. N. Zhou, D. Fridley, M. McNeil, N. Zheng, J. Ke, and M. Levine, *China's*

Energy and Carbon Emissions Outlook to 2050, Lawrence Berkeley National Laboratory, Berkeley, CA, 2011.

21. Tan et al., *Towards a Water and Energy Secure China;* M. Hibbs, *The Future of Nuclear Power in China,* Carnegie Endowment for International Peace, Washington, DC, 2018.

22. K. Dubin, "EIA Projects Less Than a Quarter of the World's Electricity Generated from Coal by 2050," Energy Information Agency, https://www.eia.gov /todayinenergy/detail.php?id=42555; S. Srinivasan, N. Kholod, V. Chaturvedi, P. P. Ghosh, R. Mathur, L. Clarke, M. Evans, et al., "Water for Electricity in India: A Multi-Model Study of Future Challenges and Linkages to Climate Change Mitigation," *Applied Energy* 210 (2018): 673–84.

23. Y. P. Wang, E. Byers, S. Parkinson, N. Wanders, Y. Wada, J. F. Mao, and J. M. Bielicki, "Vulnerability of Existing and Planned Coal-Fired Power Plants in Developing Asia to Changes in Climate and Water Resources," *Energy and Environmental Science* 12 (2019): 3164–81; V. Chaturvedi, R. Sugam, P. Nagar Koti, and K. Neog, *Energy-Water Nexus and Efficient Water-Cooling Technologies for Thermal Power Plants in India,* Council on Energy, Environment and Water, New Delhi, 2019.

24. E. Roston, M. Rojanasakul, P. Murray, B. Harris, D. Pogkas, and A. Tartar, "Real-Time Power Mix," Bloomberg, https://www.bloomberg.com/graphics /climate-change-data-green/power-mix.html.

7 IMPACTS OF CLIMATE CHANGE ON WATER RESOURCES

1. N. Popovich and B. Plumer, "Who Has the Most Historical Responsibility for Climate Change?," *New York Times,* November 12, 2021.

2. C. Funk and B. Kennedy, "The Politics of Climate," in *Numbers, Facts and Trends Shaping the World,* Pew Research Center, Washington, DC, 2016; B. Stokes, R. Wilke, and J. Carle, *Global Concern about Climate Change, Broad Support for Limiting Emissions,* Pew Research Center, Washington, DC, 2015.

3. *Resilience to Climate Change?,* Economist Intelligence Unit, London, 2019.

4. W. Nordhaus, "Climate Change: The Ultimate Challenge for Economics," *American Economic Review* 109 (2019): 1991–2014.

5. T. Schneider, T. Bischoff, and G. H. Haug, "Migrations and Dynamics of the Intertropical Convergence Zone," *Nature* 513 (2014): 45–53.

6. B. Bloeschl, J. Hall, A. Viglione, R. A. P. Perdigao, J. Parajka, B. Merz, D. Lun, et al., "Changing Climate Both Increases and Decreases European River Floods," *Nature* 573 (2019): 108–11; W. Kron and G. Berz, "Flood Disasters

and Climate Change: Trends and Options: A (Re-)Insurer's View," in *Global Change: Enough Water for All?*, ed. J. L. Lozán, H. Grassl, P. Hupfer, L. Menzel, and C.-D. Schönwiese, 268–73 (Hamburg: Wissenschaftliche Auswertungen, 2007).

7. N. Ehsani, C. J. Vorosmarty, B. M. Fekete, and E. Z. Stakhiv, "Reservoir Operations under Climate Change: Storage Capacity Options to Mitigate Risk," *Journal of Hydrology* 555 (2017): 435–46.

8. B. E. Jiménez Cisneros, T. Oki, N. W. Arnell, G. Benito, J. G. Cogley, P. Döll, T. Jiang, et al., "Freshwater Resources," in *Climate Change 2014: Impacts, Adaptation, and Vulnerability; Part A: Global and Sectoral Aspects; Contribution of Working Group II to the Fifth Assessment Report of the Intergovernmental Panel on Climate Change,* ed. C. B. Field, V. R. Barros, D. J. Dokken, K. J. Mach, M. D. Mastrandrea, T. E. Bilir, M. Chatterjee, et al., 229–69 (Cambridge: Cambridge University Press, 2014).

9. P. W. Staten, J. Lu, K. M. Grise, S. M. Davis, and T. Birner, "Re-Examining Tropical Expansion," *Nature Climate Change* 8 (2018): 768–75; D. A. Post, B. Timbal, F. H. S. Chiew, H. H. Hendon, H. Nguyen, and R. Moran, "Decrease in Southeastern Australian Water Availability Linked to Ongoing Hadley Cell Expansion," *Earth's Future* 2 (2014): 231–38.

10. I. Smith and S. Power, "Past and Future Changes to Inflows into Perth (Western Australia) Dams," *Journal of Hydrology-Regional Studies* 2 (2014): 84–96; Lauren Nicole Core, "Perth's Fresh Water Thinking for Urban Water Security," World Bank Blogs, February 5, 2020, https://blogs.worldbank.org /water/perths-fresh-water-thinking-urban-water-security.

11. Brigitte Meueller and Sonia I. Seneviratne, "How Soils Send Messages on Heat Waves," *Global Change* 81 (2013): 14–17; L. Samaniego, S. Thober, R. Kumar, N. Wanders, O. Rakovec, M. Pan, M. Zink, et al., "Anthropogenic Warming Exacerbates European Soil Moisture Droughts," *Nature Climate Change* 8 (2018): 421–26.

12. A. De Bono, G. Giuliani, S. Kluser, and P. Peduzzi, *Impacts of Summer 2003 Heat Wave in Europe,* United Nations Environment Programme DEWA/ GRID-Europe, Nairobi, 2004.

13. F. Lloret, A. Escudero, J. M. Iriondo, J. Martinez-Vilalta, and F. Valladares, "Extreme Climatic Events and Vegetation: The Role of Stabilizing Processes," *Global Change Biology* 18 (2012): 797–805.

14. T. P. Barnett, J. C. Adam, and D. P. Lettenmaier, "Potential Impacts of a Warming Climate on Water Availability in Snow-Dominated Regions," *Nature* 438 (2005): 303–9; D. Y. Li, M. L. Wrzesien, M. Durand, J. Adam, and D. P. Letten-

maier, "How Much Runoff Originates as Snow in the Western United States, and How Will That Change in the Future?," *Geophysical Research Letters* 44 (2017): 6163–72.

15. Nicholas Casey, "In Peru's Deserts, Melting Glaciers Are a Godsend (until They're Gone)," *New York Times,* November 26, 2017; "Chavimochic Irrigation Project—Peru," World Bank, https://ppp.worldbank.org/public-private-partnership/library/chavimochic-irrigation-project-peru, last updated October 25, 2021; "Water Works: Irrigation Schemes Are Increasing the Amount of Land Available for Cultivation," Oxford Business Group, https://oxfordbusinessgroup.com/analysis/water-works-irrigation-schemes-are-increasing-amount-land-available-cultivation.

16. M. Huss and R. Hock, "Global-Scale Hydrological Response to Future Glacier Mass Loss," *Nature Climate Change* 8 (2018): 135–40.

17. H.-O. Pörtner, D. C. Roberts, V. Masson-Delmotte, P. Zhai, E. Poloczanska, K. Mintenbeck, M. Tignor, et al., "Technical Summary," in *IPCC Special Report on the Ocean and Cryosphere in a Changing Climate,* ed. H.-O. Pörtner, D. C. Roberts, V. Masson-Delmotte, P. Zhai, M. Tignor, E. Poloczanska, K. Mintenbeck, et al., 39–69 (Cambridge: Cambridge University Press, 2019); J. A. Church, P. U. Clark, A. Cazenave, J. M. Gregory, S. Jevrejeva, A. Levermann, M. A. Merrifield, et al., "Sea Level Change," in *Climate Change 2013: The Physical Science Basis; Working Group I Contribution to the Fifth Assessment Report of the Intergovernmental Panel on Climate Change,* ed. T. F. Stocker, D. Qin, G.-K. Plattner, M. Tignor, S. K. Allen, J. Boschung, A. Nauels, et al., 1137–216 (Cambridge: Cambridge University Press, 2013).

18. M. Kimmelman, "The Dutch Have Solutions to Rising Seas: The World Is Watching," *New York Times,* June 15, 2017.

19. Pörtner et al., "Technical Summary."

20. Carol Davenport and Campbell Robertson, "Resettling the First American 'Climate Refugees,'" *New York Times,* May 2, 2016.

21. Kevin Sack and John Schwartz, "Left to Louisiana's Tides, a Village Fights for Time," *New York Times,* February 24, 2018.

22. Z. D. Tessler, C. J. Vorosmarty, M. Grossberg, I. Gladkova, H. Aizenman, J. P. M. Syvitski, and E. Foufoula-Georgiou, "Profiling Risk and Sustainability in Coastal Deltas of the World," *Science* 349 (2015): 638–43.

23. Mark Scialla, "Meet the Mekong Delta Rice Farmers Who Are on the Frontline of Sea Level Rise," Vice, May 13, 2015, https://www.vice.com/en/article/8x39xk/meet-the-mekong-delta-rice-farmers-who-are-on-the-frontline-of-sea-level-rise; P. S. J. Minderhoud, L. Coumou, G. Erkens, H. Middelkoop, and E. Stouthamer, "Mekong Delta Much Lower Than Previously Assumed

in Sea-Level Rise Impact Assessments," *Nature Communications* 10 (2019): 3847.

8 REDUCING WATER USE IN WEALTHY COMMUNITIES

1. *2019–2028 Water Conservation Program Planning Document,* Saving Water Partnership, 2018.
2. *Water Conservation Report, 2018–2019,* Sydney Water, Sydney, 2020; K. G. Low, S. B. Grant, A. J. Hamilton, K. Gan, J. D. Saphores, M. Arora, and D. L. Feldman, "Fighting Drought with Innovation: Melbourne's Response to the Millennium Drought in Southeast Australia," *Wiley Interdisciplinary Reviews—Water* 2 (2015): 315–28.
3. R. Hoo, "Managing Water Demand in Singapore through a Systems Perspective," *International Journal of Water Resources Development* 36 (2020): 879–87.
4. "Total Water Delivered for House Holds," International Water Association, http://waterstatistics.iwa-network.org/graph/5.
5. *Adapting to Change: Utility Systems and Declining Flows,* California Urban Water Agencies, Walnut Creek, 2017.
6. F. Santos, "An Arid Arizona City Manages Its Thirst," *New York Times,* June 16, 2013.
7. E. H. and M. Davis, "Lawns and Water Demand in California," *California Economic Policy* (2006): 1–22.
8. K. Drysdale, M. D'ukowitz, and D. Frost, *Phoenix Metropolitan Area Multi-City Water Use Study: Single-Family Residential Sector Executive Report,* City of Phoenix, City of Glendale, and Town of Gilbert, AZ, 2019.
9. "MAG Fast Facts—Population and Growth," Maricopa Association of Governments, https://webadmin.azmag.gov/About-Us/Divisions/Regional-Analytics-Division/MAG-Fast-Facts-Population-and-Growth.
10. S. M. Hermitte and R. E. Mace, *The Grass Is Always Greener . . . Outdoor Residential Water Use in Texas,* Texas Water Development Board, Austin, 2012; *New Jersey Water Supply Plan, 2017–2202,* New Jersey Department of Environmental Protection, 2017.
11. *Potable Reuse Compendium,* US Environmental Protection Agency, Washington, DC, 2017; *Wetlands Transform a Murky Mess into Viable Water Supply,* Tarrant Regional Water District, Fort Worth, TX, 2018; Craig Pittman, "Desalination Plant, Reservoir Helping Tampa Bay Endure Florida's Fiery Drought," *Tampa Bay (FL) Times,* April 18, 2017.
12. *Dallas Comprehensive Environmental and Climate Action Plan,* City of Dallas,

2020; Carlos Placencia, "How Dallas Is Approaching Water Conservation as the Climate Changes," in *Save Water: Nothing Can Replace It,* Dallas Water Utilities, 2020.

13. V. Parsons, "Water—When It Comes to Tampa Bay's Water Supplies, Is the Glass Half Full or Half Empty?," *Bay Soundings* (Tampa Bay, FL), 2007.

14. *Water Resource Management Plan for Metropolitan North Georgia Water Planning District,* CH2M and Black & Veatch, 2017; K. Benfield, "The Country's Most Ambitious Smart Growth Project," *Atlantic,* July 26, 2011.

15. E. Osann, "25 Years of Water Efficiency across the US," NRDC Expert Blog, October 25, 2017, https://www.nrdc.org/experts/ed-osann/celebrating-25 -years-water-efficiency.

16. W. B. DeOreo, "The Truth about Water Efficiency in the United States," *Journal of the American Water Works Association* 112 (2020): 60–65.

17. M. A. Dickinson, *Water Conservation in the United States: A Decade of Progress,* California Urban Water Conservation Council, 2001; D. L. Sedlak, *Water 4.0: The Past, Present and Future of the World's Most Vital Resource* (New Haven: Yale University Press, 2014).

18. D. Wroclawski, "The Great Washer Debate: Are Front-Loaders Really Better?," *USA Today,* 2014; Osann, "25 Years of Water Efficiency"; DeOreo, "Truth about Water Efficiency."

19. S. Malpezzi, "Population Density: Some Facts and Some Predictions," *Cityscape* 15, no. 3 (2013): 183–201; BIO Intelligence Service, *Study on Water Efficiency Standards,* European Commission, Paris, 2009.

20. "The World Factbook," United States Central Intelligence Agency, https:// www.cia.gov/the-world-factbook/; C. R. Wilkes, A. D. Mason, and S. C. Hern, "Probability Distributions for Showering and Bathing Water-Use Behavior for Various US Subpopulations," *Risk Analysis* 25 (2005): 317–37; *Managing Water for All—An O.E.C.D. Perspective on Pricing and Financing: Key Messages for Policy Makers,* Organisation for Economic Co-Operation and Development, Paris, 2009; A. A. Makki, R. A. Stewart, K. Panuwatwanich, and C. Beal, "Revealing the Determinants of Shower Water End Use Consumption: Enabling Better Targeted Urban Water Conservation Strategies," *Journal of Cleaner Production* 60 (2013): 129–46.

21. A. F. Colombo and B. W. Karney, "Energy and Costs of Leaky Pipes: Toward Comprehensive Picture," *Journal of Water Resources Planning and Managemen* 128 (2002): 441–50; *Control and Mitigation of Drinking Water Losses in Distribution Systems,* US Environmental Protection Agency Office of Water, Washington, DC, 2010.

22. W. Tenney, "Arizona Pilot Project Could Help Find More 'Lost' Water,"

AMWUA Blog, October 16, 2017, https://www.amwua.org/blog/arizona
-pilot-project-could-help-find-more-lost-water; *2019–2028 Water Conserva-*
tion Program Planning Document; J. F. Ferguson, *2017 Estimated Water Use*
Report, Southwest Florida Water Management District, Tampa, 2018; *Perfor-*
mance Audit: Department of Watershed Management Efforts to Reduce Water
Loss, City Auditor's Office, Atlanta, 2017.

23. P. Rao, D. Sholes, and J. Cresko, "Evaluation of US Manufacturing Subsectors
at Risk of Physical Water Shortages," *Environmental Science and Technology*
53 (2019): 2295–303.

24. *Decoding the Evolution of the U.S. Industry from 1950 to 2020,* SDR Ventures,
Greenwood, CO, 2020; "Trends in Water Use in the United States, 1950 to
2015," Water Science School, USGS, June 18, 2018, https://www.usgs.gov
/special-topic/water-science-school/science/trends-water-use-united-states
-1950-2015; L. Marston, Y. F. Ao, M. Konar, M. M. Mekonnen, and A. Y.
Hoekstra, "High-Resolution Water Footprints of Production of the United
States," *Water Resources Research* 54 (2018): 2288–316.

25. A. Shehabi, S. Smith, D. Sartor, R. Brown, M. Herrlin, J. Koomey, E. Masanet,
et al., *United States Data Center Energy Usage Report,* Lawrence Berkeley
National Laboratory, Berkeley, CA, 2016.

26. Shehabi et al., *United States Data Center Energy Usage Report.*

27. N. Sattiraju, "Google Data Centers' Secret Cost: Billions of Gallons of
Water," Bloomberg, April 1, 2020, https://www.bloomberg.com/news
/features/2020-04-01/how-much-water-do-google-data-centers-use-billions
-of-gallons.

28. K. Lu and K. Liu, "Taiwan: The Water-Starved Island," *CommonWealth,*
March 9, 2018; N. Porzucki and C. Woolf, "Water, Water Everywhere, but
in Taiwan Today There's Just a Drop to Drink," The World, April 8, 2015,
https://theworld.org/stories/2015-04-08/water-water-everywhere-taiwan
-today-theres-just-drop-drink.

9 REDUCING WATER USE IN LOW-
AND MIDDLE-INCOME COMMUNITIES

1. T. Johnson, "Mexico City Copes with That Sinking Feeling," *Seattle Times,*
September 24, 2011; "Water Security and Resilience for the Valley of Mexico
(Proseghir)," in *Combined Project Information Documents / Integrated Safe-*
guards Datasheet (PID/ISDS), World Bank, Washington, DC, 2018; C. Torta-
jada and E. Castelan, "Water Management for a Megacity: Mexico City
Metropolitan Area," *Ambio* 32 (2003): 124–29.

2. *Mexico City's Water Supply: Improving the Outlook for Sustainability*, National Academies of Sciences, Engineering and Medicine, Washington, DC, 1995.

3. C. D. Torres, *The Future of Water in African Cities: Why Waste Water? Urban Access to Water Supply and Sanitation in Sub-Saharan Africa, Background Report*, World Bank, Washington, DC, 2012; G. Hutton and M. Varughese, *The Costs of Meeting the 2030 Sustainable Development Goal Targets on Drinking Water, Sanitation, and Hygiene*, World Bank Water and Sanitation Program, Washington, DC, 2016; *U.N.-Water Global Analysis and Assessment of Sanitation and Drinking-Water (GLAAS) 2017 Report: Financing Universal Water, Sanitation and Hygiene under the Sustainable Development Goals*, World Health Organization, Geneva, 2017.

4. B. Vucijak, *Tariff Setting Methodology for Water Supply and Sewerage Services in Bosnia and Herzegovina*, Stockholm International Water Institute, 2015.

5. D. Torres, *Future of Water in African Cities; Key Issues and Recommendations for Consumer Protection: Affordability, Social Protection, and Public Participation in Urban Water Sector Reform in Eastern Europe, Caucasus and Central Asia*, Organisation for Economic Co-Operation and Development, Paris, 2003.

6. D. Mitlin and A. Walnycki, "Informality as Experimentation: Water Utilities' Strategies for Cost Recovery and Their Consequences for Universal Access," *Journal of Development Studies* 56 (2020): 259–77.

7. B. Kingdom, R. Liemberger, and P. Marin, *The Challenge of Reducing Non-Revenue Water (N.R.W.) in Developing Countries: How the Private Sector Can Help: A Look at Performance-Based Service Contracting*, World Bank, Washington, DC, 2006.

8. A. W. Bivins, T. Sumner, E. Kumpel, G. Howard, O. Cumming, I. Ross, K. Nelson, et al., "Estimating Infection Risks and the Global Burden of Diarrheal Disease Attributable to Intermittent Water Supply Using QMRA," *Environmental Science and Technology* 51 (2017): 7542–51.

9. Kingdom, Liemberger, and Marin, *Challenge of Reducing Non-Revenue Water*.

10. S. Tully, "Water, Water Everywhere Today Companies Like France's Suez Are Rushing to Privatize Water, Already a $400 Billion Global Business; They Are Betting That H_2O Will Be to the 21st Century What Oil Was to the 20th," *Fortune*, May 15, 2000.

11. J. Vidal, "Water Privatisation: A Worldwide Failure?," *Guardian*, January 30, 2015.

12. W. Finnegan, "Leasing the Rain," *New Yorker*, April 1, 2002.

13. X. Wu and N. A. Malaluan, "A Tale of Two Concessionaires: A Natural Ex-

periment of Water Privatisation in Metro Manila," *Urban Studies* 45 (2008): 207–29.

14. S. Haughn, "Making Connections in the Philippines: Water Privatization across Manila's East Zone," Circle of Blue, June 6, 2012, https://www.circle ofblue.org/2012/world/making-connections-in-the-philippines-water -privatization-across-manilas-east-zone/.

15. L. Heller, *A/75/208: Human Rights and the Privatization of Water and Sanitation Services,* report presented at the 75th Session of the UN General Assembly, New York, July 21, 2020; D. Hall and E. Lobina, *Pipe Dreams: The Failure of the Private Sector to Invest in Water Services in Developing Countries,* Public Services International Research Unit, London, 2006.

16. D. A. McDonald, "To Corporatize or Not to Corporatize (and If So, How?)," *Utilities Policy* 40 (Jun 2016): 107–14.

17. "International Decade for Action 'Water for Life' 2005–2015," United Nations Department of Economic and Social Affairs, https://www.un.org/waterfor lifedecade/human_right_to_water.shtml.

18. Hutton and Varughese, *Costs of Meeting the 2030 Sustainable Development Goal Targets.*

19. *U.N.-Water Global Analysis and Assessment of Sanitation and Drinking-Water (GLAAS) 2017 Report.*

20. *Seizing the Water Opportunity,* World Wildlife Fund, ING, and Boston Consulting Group, 2018; "Blended Finance Is Struggling to Take Off," *Economist,* August 13, 2020.

21. *U.N.-Water Global Analysis and Assessment of Sanitation and Drinking-Water (GLAAS) 2017 Report.*

22. *U.N.-Water Global Analysis and Assessment of Sanitation and Drinking-Water (GLAAS) 2017 Report.*

23. *J.I.C.A.'s Cooperation Strategy for Water Resources Sector,* Japan International Cooperation Agency, 2017; *Global Water and Development Report of Water and Sanitation Activities F.Y. 2018/2019,* US AID, 2020; *Water—The Source of Development,* Federal Ministry for Economic Cooperation and Development, Bonn, Germany, 2019.

24. *J.I.C.A.'s Cooperation Strategy for Water Resources Sector.*

25. *Water: Where Most Needed Fund Annual Report,* World Vision, 2020.

26. *Annual Report 2019,* Water.org, 2020.

27. *U.N.-Water Global Analysis and Assessment of Sanitation and Drinking-Water (GLAAS) 2017 Report.*

28. T. Nagpal, M. Eldridge, and A. A. Malik, "Global Water Access Fund: A New Idea to Bridge Operations and Maintenance Shortfalls for the Poorest Water

Utilities," *Journal of Water Sanitation and Hygiene for Development* 9 (2019): 774–79; *Global Investment Fund for Water: A Partnership with the Bottled Water Sector to End Water Poverty*, Rockefeller Foundation, Surrey, UK, 2018.

29. *Water Unite Impact Report 2019/2020*, Water Unite, Surrey, UK, 2020.
30. H. Ritchie, M. Roser, J. Mispy, and E. Ortiz-Ospina, "Sustainable Development Goal 6: Ensure Access to Water and Sanitation for All," SDG Tracker, Our World in Data, https://sdg-tracker.org/water-and-sanitation.

10 REDUCING AGRICULTURAL WATER DEMAND

1. A. K. Chapagain, A. Y. Hoekstra, H. H. G. Savenije, and R. Gautam, "The Water Footprint of Cotton Consumption: An Assessment of the Impact of Worldwide Consumption of Cotton Products on the Water Resources in the Cotton Producing Countries," *Ecological Economics* 60 (2006): 186–203; Y. Wada, L. P. H. van Beek, and M. F. P. Bierkens, "Nonsustainable Groundwater Sustaining Irrigation: A Global Assessment," *Water Resources Research* 48 (2012): W00L06; R. J. Diaz and R. Rosenberg, "Spreading Dead Zones and Consequences for Marine Ecosystems," *Science* 321 (2008): 926–29.
2. M. S. Bowman and D. Zilberman, "Economic Factors Affecting Diversified Farming Systems," *Ecology and Society* 18 (2013): 33.
3. Editorial, "How to Feed a Hungry World," *Nature* 466 (2010): 531–32.
4. J. A. Foley, R. DeFries, G. P. Asner, C. Barford, G. Bonan, S. R. Carpenter, F. S. Chapin, et al., "Global Consequences of Land Use," *Science* 309 (2005): 570–74; P. S. Thenkabail, M. A. Hanjra, V. Dheeravath, and M. Gumma, "A Holistic View of Global Croplands and Their Water Use for Ensuring Global Food Security in the 21st Century through Advanced Remote Sensing and Non-Remote Sensing Approaches," *Remote Sensing* 2 (2010): 211–61.
5. T. Sauer, P. Havlik, U. A. Schneider, E. Schmid, G. Kindermann, and M. Obersteiner, "Agriculture and Resource Availability in a Changing World: The Role of Irrigation," *Water Resources Research* 46 (2010): W06503.
6. M. Stubbs, *Irrigation in U.S. Agriculture: On Farm Technologies and Best Management Practices*, Congressional Research Service, Washington, DC, 2016.
7. G. N. Tindula, M. N. Orang, and R. L. Snyder, "Survey of Irrigation Methods in California in 2010," *Journal of Irrigation and Drainage Engineering* 139 (2013): 233–38.
8. R. Taylor and D. Zilberman, "Diffusion of Drip Irrigation: The Case of California," *Applied Economic Perspectives and Policy* 39 (2017): 16–40.
9. E. Stokstad, "Deep Deficit," *Science* 368 (2020): 230–33.

10. M. Kiparsky, A. Milman, D. Owen, and A. T. Fisher, "The Importance of Institutional Design for Distributed Local-Level Governance of Groundwater: The Case of California's Sustainable Groundwater Management Act," *Water* 9 (2017): 755.

11. E. Hanak, A. Escriva-Bou, B. Gray, S. Green, T. Harter, J. Jezdimirovic, J. Lund, et al., *Water and the Future of the San Joaquin Valley,* Public Policy Institute of California, San Francisco, 2019.

12. D. Wichelns and M. Qadir, "Achieving Sustainable Irrigation Requires Effective Management of Salts, Soil Salinity, and Shallow Groundwater," *Agricultural Water Management* 157 (2015): 31–38.

13. Hanak et al., *Water and the Future of the San Joaquin Valley.*

14. J. Mount, B. Gray, C. Chappelle, T. Grantham, P. Moyle, N. Seavy, L. Szeptycki, et al., *Managing California's Freshwater Ecosystems: Lessons from the 2012–16 Drought,* Public Policy Institute of California, San Francisco, 2017.

15. Dale Kasler and Ryan Sabalow, "Sites Reservoir Is Sacramento Valley's Water Project. But L.A. Is Taking a Huge Role," *Sacramento Bee,* February 15, 2019.

16. S. Sese-Minguez, H. Boesveld, S. Asins-Velis, S. van der Kooij, and J. Maroulis, "Transformations Accompanying a Shift from Surface to Drip Irrigation in the Canyoles Watershed, Valencia, Spain," *Water Alternatives: An Interdisciplinary Journal on Water Politics and Development* 10 (2017): 81–99; E. Lopez-Gunn, P. Zorrilla, F. Prieto, and M. R. Llamas, "Lost in Translation? Water Efficiency in Spanish Agriculture," *Agricultural Water Management* 108 (2012): 83–95.

17. M. R. Llamas and A. Garrido, "Lessons from Intensive Groundwater Use in Spain: Economic and Social Benefits and Conflicts," in *The Agricultural Groundwater Revolution: Opportunities and Threats to Development,* ed. M. Giordano and K. G. Villhoth, 266–95 (Wallingford, UK: CAB International, 2007).

18. T. E. Grantham, R. Figueroa, and N. Prat, "Water Management in Mediterranean River Basins: A Comparison of Management Frameworks, Physical Impacts, and Ecological Responses," *Hydrobiologia* 719 (2013): 451–82.

19. "Aquastat Database," Food and Agriculture Organization of the United Nations, http://www.fao.org/aquastat/statistics/query/index.html?lang=en.

20. "Farm and Ranch Irrigation Survey (2013)," in *2012 Census of Agriculture,* US Department of Agriculture, Washington, DC, 2014.

21. "Irrigation and Water Use," USDA Economic Research Service, updated May 6, 2022, https://www.ers.usda.gov/topics/farm-practices-management /irrigation-water-use/; L. Pfeiffer and C.-Y. C. Lin, "Perverse Consequences of Incentive-Based Groundwater Conservation Programs," *Agricultural and*

Resource Economics Update 12, no. 6 (2009): 1–8; L. Pfeiffer and C.-Y. C. Lin, "Does Efficient Irrigation Technology Lead to Reduced Groundwater Extraction? Empirical Evidence," *Journal of Environmental Economics and Management* 67 (2014): 189–208.

22. I. E. Houk, *Irrigation Engineering*, vol. 1, *Agricultural and Hydrological Phase* (New York: Wiley, 1951); R. Koech and P. Langat, "Improving Irrigation Water Use Efficiency: A Review of Advances, Challenges and Opportunities in the Australian Context," *Water* 10 (2018): 1771.

23. C. J. Kucharik and N. Ramankutty, "Trends and Variability in U.S. Corn Yields over the Twentieth Century," *Earth Interactions* 9 (2005): 29; A. F. Troyer, "Background of US Hybrid Corn," *Crop Science* 39 (1999): 601–26; P. Ranum, J. P. Peña-Rosas, and M. N. Garcia-Casal, "Global Maize Production, Utilization, and Consumption," in *Technical Considerations for Maize Flour and Corn Meal Fortification in Public Health*, ed. J. P. Peña-Rosas, M. N. GarciaCasal, and H. Pachon, Annals of the New York Academy of Sciences, 105–12 (Oxford: Blackwell Science, 2014); B. Bouman, R. Barker, E. Humphreys, and T. P. Tuoong, "Rice: Feeding the Billions," in *Water for Food, Water for Life: A Comprehensive Assessment of Water Management in Agriculture*, ed. D. Molden, 515–50 (London: Earthscan and International Water Management Institute, 2007).

24. P. L. Pingali, "Green Revolution: Impacts, Limits, and the Path Ahead," *Proceedings of the National Academy of Sciences* 109 (2012): 12302–8.

25. G. Carr, "Technology Quarterly: The Future of Agriculture," *Economist*, June 11, 2016.

26. D. Schimmelpfennig, *Farm Profits and Adoption of Precision Agriculture*, US Department of Agriculture, Washington, DC, 2016.

27. Pingali, "Green Revolution."

11 NAVIGATING THE JEVONS PARADOX

1. L. Sears, J. Caparelli, C. Lee, D. Pan, G. Strandberg, L. Vuu, and C.-Y. C. Lin Lawell, "Jevons' Paradox and Efficient Irrigation Technology," *Sustainability* 10 (2018): 1590; R. Q. Grafton, J. Williams, C. J. Perry, F. Molle, C. Ringler, P. Steduto, B. Udall, et al., "The Paradox of Irrigation Efficiency," *Science* 361 (2018): 748–50; J. F. Song, Y. N. Guo, P. T. Wu, and S. K. Sun, "The Agricultural Water Rebound Effect in China," *Ecological Economics* 146 (2018): 497–506; R. Koech and P. Langat, "Improving Irrigation Water Use Efficiency: A Review of Advances, Challenges and Opportunities in the Australian Context," *Water* 10 (2018): 1771.

2. *The 2020 Basin Plan Evaluation,* Murray-Darling Basin Authority, Canberra, 2020.

3. A. Ross and D. Connell, "The Evolution and Performance of River Basin Management in the Murray-Darling Basin," *Ecology and Society* 21 (2016): 29; J. Bolorinos, "Lessons Australia's Water Reform Offers in Science, Politics and Sustainable Watersheds," Stanford, Water in the West, August 21, 2019, https://waterinthewest.stanford.edu/news-events/news -insights/lessons-australias-water-reform-offers-science-politics-and -sustainable.

4. Q. J. Wang and Avril Horne, "Murray-Darling Water Plan Walks a Fine Line between Efficiency and the Environment," ABC News (Australia), July 9, 2019, https://www.abc.net.au/news/2019-07-09/murray-darling-basin-water -plan-whats-next/11290060; B. Gawne, J. Hale, M. J. Stewardson, J. A. Webb, D. S. Ryder, S. S. Brooks, C. J. Campbell, et al., "Monitoring of Environmental Flow Outcomes in a Large River Basin: The Commonwealth Environmental Water Holder's Long-Term Intervention in the Murray-Darling Basin, Australia," *River Research and Applications* 36 (2020): 630–44.

5. Q. Grafton, D. H. MacDonald, D. Paton, G. Harris, H. Bjornlund, J. D. Connor, J. Quiggin, et al., "The Murray Darling Basin Plan Is Not Delivering— There's No More Time to Waste," The Conversation, February 4, 2018, https:// theconversation.com/the-murray-darling-basin-plan-is-not-delivering -theres-no-more-time-to-waste-91076.

6. A. Davies, "Water Wars: Will Politics Destroy the Murray-Darling Basin Plan 9 and the River System Itself?," *Guardian,* December 13, 2019.

7. Q. Q. Huang, S. Rozelle, B. Lohmar, J. K. Huang, and J. X. Wang, "Irrigation, Agricultural Performance and Poverty Reduction in China," *Food Policy* 31 (2006): 30–52; X. F. Zhu, Y. Z. Li, M. Y. Li, Y. Z. Pan, and P. J. Shi, "Agricultural Irrigation in China," *Journal of Soil and Water Conservation* 68 (2013): 147A–54A.

8. L. Zhang, F. Chen, and Y. D. Lei, "Climate Change and Shifts in Cropping Systems Together Exacerbate China's Water Scarcity," *Environmental Research Letters* 15 (2020): 104060; K. Nowakowski, "Why Corn—Not Rice—Is King in China," National Geographic, May 18, 2018, https://www.nationalgeo graphic.com/culture/article/why-corn-not-rice-is-king-in-china.

9. W. Feng, M. Zhong, J. M. Lemoine, R. Biancale, H. T. Hsu, and J. Xia, "Evaluation of Groundwater Depletion in North China Using the Gravity Recovery and Climate Experiment (GRACE) Data and Ground-Based Measurements," *Water Resources Research* 49 (2013): 2110–18; J. Barnett, S. Rogers, M. Webber, B. Finlayson, and M. Wang, "Sustainability: Transfer Project Cannot Meet

China's Water Needs," *Nature* 527 (2015): 295–97; D. Long, W. T. Yang, B. R. Scanlon, J. S. Zhao, D. G. Liu, P. Burek, Y. Pan, et al., "South-to-North Water Diversion Stabilizing Beijing's Groundwater Levels," *Nature Communications* 11 (2020): 3665.

10. T. Shah, "Climate Change and Groundwater: India's Opportunities for Mitigation and Adaptation," *Environmental Research Letters* 4 (2009): 035005; K. D. Morrison, "Dharmic Projects, Imperial Reservoirs, and New Temples of India: An Historical Perspective on Dams in India," *Conservation and Society* 8 (2010): 182–95; "Irrigation and Railways," in *The Cambridge Economic History of India,* ed. D. Kumar and M. Desai (Cambridge: Cambridge University Press, 1983).

11. H. Farooqi and K. Wegerich, "Institutionalizing Inequities in Land Ownership and Water Allocations During Colonial Times in Punjab, Pakistan," *Water History* 7 (2015): 131–46.

12. *Transboundary River Basin Overview—Indus,* Food and Agriculture Organization of the United Nations, Rome, 2011; G. S. Hira, "Water Management in Northern States and the Food Security of India," *Journal of Crop Improvement* 23 (2009): 136–57.

13. R. Jain, P. Kishore, and D. K. Singh, "Irrigation in India: Status, Challenges and Options," *Journal of Soil and Water Conservation* 18 (2020): 354–63; "Rs 80,000 Crore, World's Biggest! All About the Kaleshwaram Irrigation Project That Will Make You Proud of Telangana," *Financial Express,* June 27, 2018; M. Bhardwaj, "Modi's $87 Billion River-Linking Gamble Set to Take Off as Floods Hit India," Reuters, September 1, 2017, https://www.reuters.com/article/india-rivers/modis-87-billion-river-linking-gamble-set-to-take-off-as-floods-hit-india-idUSL4N1L940G.

14. T. Shah, M. Giordano, and A. Mukherji, "Political Economy of the Energy-Groundwater Nexus in India: Exploring Issues and Assessing Policy Options," *Hydrogeology Journal* 20 (2012): 995–1006.

15. M. J. Jones, "Thematic Paper 8: Social Adoption of Groundwater Pumping Technology and the Development of Groundwater Cultures: Governance at the Point of Abstraction," in *Groundwater Governance: A Global Framework for Country Action,* Groundwater Governance, Rome, 2012; Jain, Kishore, and Kumar Singh, "Irrigation in India."

16. Shah, Giordano, and Mukherji, "Political Economy of the Energy-Groundwater Nexus."

17. Jones, "Thematic Paper 8"; Shah, Giordano, and Mukherji, "Political Economy of the Energy-Groundwater Nexus."

18. K. Narula, R. Fishman, V. Modi, and L. Polycarpou, *Addressing the Water Crisis in Gujarat, India,* Columbia Water Center, New York, 2011.

19. Shah, Giordano, and Mukherji, "Political Economy of the Energy-Groundwater Nexus."

20. T. Shah and S. Verma, "Co-Management of Electricity and Groundwater: An Assessment of Gujarat's Jyotirgram Scheme," *Economic and Political Weekly* 43, no. 7 (2008): 59–68.

21. M. Jena, *Intelligent Power Rationing Eases Indian State's Irrigation Woes,* Ministry of External Affairs, Government of India, 2014.

22. P. M. Patel, D. Saha, and T. Shah, "Sustainability of Groundwater through Community-Driven Distributed Recharge: An Analysis of Arguments for Water Scarce Regions of Semi-Arid India," *Journal of Hydrology: Regional Studies* 29 (2020): 100680; M. D. Kumar and C. J. Perry, "What Can Explain Groundwater Rejuvenation in Gujarat in Recent Years?," *International Journal of Water Resources Development* 35 (2019): 891–906.

23. Kumar and Perry, "What Can Explain Groundwater Rejuvenation?"

24. M. Sally, "Budget Gives Push to Micro-Irrigation Sector," *Economic Times,* February 1, 2021; R. Fishman, N. Devineni, and S. Raman, "Can Improved Agricultural Water Use Efficiency Save India's Groundwater?," *Environmental Research Letters* 10 (2015): 084022.

25. J. M. Kerr, *Sustainable Development of Rainfed Agriculture in India,* International Food Policy Research Institute, Washington, DC, 1996.

26. D. Molden, K. Frenken, R. Bariker, C. de Fraiture, B. Mati, M. Svendsen, C. Sadoff, et al., "Trends in Water and Agricultural Development," in *Water for Food, Water for Life: A Comprehensive Assessment of Water Management in Agriculture,* ed. D. Molden, 57–89 (London: Earthscan and International Water Management Institute, 2007).

27. T. P. Higginbottom, R. Adhikari, R. Dimova, S. Redicker, and T. Foster, "Performance of Large-Scale Irrigation Projects in Sub-Saharan Africa," *Nature Sustainability* 4 (2021): 501–8.

28. E. Harrison, "Engineering Change? The Idea of 'the Scheme' in African Irrigation," *World Development* 111 (2018): 246–55.

29. J. Rockstrom, L. Karlberg, S. P. Wani, J. Barron, N. Hatibu, T. Oweis, A. Bruggeman, et al., "Managing Water in Rainfed Agriculture—The Need for a Paradigm Shift," *Agricultural Water Management* 97 (2010): 543–50.

30. C. de Fraiture, L. Karlberg, and J. Rockström, "Can Rainfed Agriculture Feed the World? An Assessment of Potentials and Risk," in *Rainfed Agriculture:*

Unlocking the Potential, ed. S. P. Wani, J. Rockström, and T. Oweis, 124–32 (Wallingford, UK: CAB International, 2009).

12 A DAM LEGACY

1. D. Perera, V. Smakhtin, S. Williams, T. Nort, and A. Curry, *Ageing Water Storage Infrastructure: An Emerging Global Risk,* United Nations University Institute for Water, Environment and Health, Hamilton, ON, 2021.
2. B. Lehner, C. R. Liermann, C. Revenga, C. Vorosmarty, B. Fekete, P. Crouzet, P. Doll, et al., "High-Resolution Mapping of the World's Reservoirs and Dams for Sustainable River-Flow Management," *Frontiers in Ecology and the Environment* 9 (2011): 494–502; N. L. Poff and D. D. Hart, "How Dams Vary and Why It Matters for the Emerging Science of Dam Removal," *Bioscience* 52 (2002): 659–68.
3. R. W. Righter, *The Battle over Hetch Hetchy: America's Most Controversial Dam and the Birth of Modern Environmentalism* (New York: Oxford University Press, 2005); M. W. T. Harvey, "Echo Park, Glen Canyon, and the Postwar Wilderness Movement," *Pacific Historical Review* 60 (1991): 43–67.
4. E. Shah, J. Vos, G. J. Veldwisch, R. Boelens, and B. Duarte-Abadía, "Environmental Justice Movements in Globalising Networks: A Critical Discussion on Social Resistance against Large Dams," *Journal of Peasant Studies* (2019): 1–25; N. J. Torrecilla and J. Martínez-Gil, "The New Water Culture in Spain: A Philosophy towards a Sustainable Development," *E-Water: Official Publication of the European Water Association (EWA),* May 13, 2005.
5. J. D. Tabara and A. Ilhan, "Culture as Trigger for Sustainability Transition in the Water Domain: The Case of the Spanish Water Policy and the Ebro River Basin," *Regional Environmental Change* 8 (2008): 59–71.
6. E. Shah, J. Vos, G. J. Veldwisch, R. Boelens, and B. Duarte-Abadia, "Environmental Justice Movements in Globalising Networks: A Critical Discussion on Social Resistance against Large Dams," *Journal of Peasant Studies* 48 (2019): 1008–32.
7. P. S. Bose, "Critics and Experts, Activists and Academics: Intellectuals in the Fight for Social and Ecological Justice in the Narmada Valley, India," *International Review of Social History* 49 (2004): 133–57; H. Sims, "Moved, Left No Address: Dam Construction, Displacement and Issue Salience," *Public Administration and Development* 21 (2001): 187–200.
8. "Modi Inaugurates World's Second Biggest Dam on His Birthday," Huffing-

ton Post, September 17, 2017, https://www.huffpost.com/archive/in/entry
/modi-to-inaugurate-worlds-second-largest-dam-on-his-birthday_in
_5c10c720e4b09dcd67fc2bb3.

9. C. Schulz and W. M. Adams, "Debating Dams: The World Commission on Dams 20 Years On," *Wiley Interdisciplinary Reviews—Water* 6 (2019): e1396.

10. "Dams and Development: A New Framework for Decision-Making" (London: World Commission on Dams, 2000).

11. O. Shumilova, K. Tockner, M. Thieme, A. Koska, and C. Zarfl, "Global Water Transfer Megaprojects: A Potential Solution for the Water-Food-Energy Nexus?," *Frontiers in Environmental Science* 6 (2018): 150; C. Zarfl, A. E. Lumsdon, J. Berlekamp, L. Tydecks, and K. Tockner, "A Global Boom in Hydropower Dam Construction," *Aquatic Sciences* 77 (2015): 161–70; A. Kuriqi, A. N. Pinheiro, A. Sordo-Ward, M. D. Bejarano, and L. Garrote, "Ecological Impacts of Run-of-River Hydropower Plants? Current Status and Future Prospects on the Brink of Energy Transition," *Renewable and Sustainable Energy Reviews* 142 (2021): 110833; H. Hudek, K. Zganec, and M. T. Pusch, "A Review of Hydropower Dams in Southeast Europe—Distribution, Trends and Availability of Monitoring Data Using the Example of a Multinational Danube Catchment Subarea," *Renewable and Sustainable Energy Reviews* 117 (2020): 109434.

12. Perera et al., *Ageing Water Storage Infrastructure.*

13. B. Henn, K. N. Musselman, L. Lestak, F. M. Ralph, and N. P. Molotch, "Extreme Runoff Generation from Atmospheric River Driven Snowmelt during the 2017 Oroville Dam Spillways Incident," *Geophysical Research Letters* 47 (2020): e2020GL088189; *Independent Forensic Team Report. Oroville Dam Spillway Incident,* California Department of Water Resources, Sacramento, 2018.

14. *Report Card for America's Infrastructure,* American Society of Civil Engineers, Reston, VA, 2021; J. Cai, "China Says It Will Spend US$15 Billion over Five Years to Fix 'Sick and Dangerous' Dams," *South China Morning Post,* December 1, 2020; "Cabinet Nod for Dam Rehabilitation and Improvement Project Worth Rs 10,211 Cr," Construction Week, October 21, 2020, https://www.constructionweekonline.in/projects-tenders/15607-cabinet-nod-for-dam-rehabilitation-and-improvement-project-worth-rs-10211-cr.

15. *Dam Removal: A Viable Solution for the Future of Our European Rivers,* Dam Removal Europe, 2018; F. J. Magilligan, C. S. Sneddon, and C. A. Fox, "The Social, Historical, and Institutional Contingencies of Dam Removal," *Environmental Management* 59 (2017): 982–94; P. Glamann and K. Kan, "China

Has Thousands of Hydropower Projects It Doesn't Want," Bloomberg, August 14, 2021, https://www.bloomberg.com/news/features/2021-08-14/china-wants -to-shut-down-thousands-of-dams.

16. J. R. Shuman, "Environmental Considerations for Assessing Dam Removal Alternatives for River Restoration," *Regulated Rivers—Research and Management* 11 (1995): 249–61; T. Mann, "GE Nears End of Hudson River Cleanup," *Wall Street Journal,* November 11, 2015.

17. Shuman, "Environmental Considerations."

18. M. M. Foley, J. R. Bellmore, J. E. O'Connor, J. J. Duda, A. E. East, G. E. Grant, C. W. Anderson, et al., "Dam Removal: Listening In," *Water Resources Research* 53 (2017): 5229–46; "American Rivers Dam Removal Database" (American Rivers, Berkeley, CA), figshare, dataset, https://doi.org/10.6084 /m9.figshare.5234068.v9; Q. Schiermeier, "Dam Removal Restores Rivers," *Nature* 557 (2018): 290–91.

19. Foley et al., "Dam Removal."

20. M. Nijhuis, "World's Largest Dam Removal Unleashes U.S. River after Century of Electric Production," National Geographic, August 26, 2014, https://www.nationalgeographic.com/science/article/140826-elwha-river -dam-removal-salmon-science-olympic; D. Westneat, "Gorton Threatens to Block Removal of Elwha River Dam," *Seattle Times,* April 3, 1998; A. E. East, J. B. Logan, M. C. Mastin, A. C. Ritchie, J. A. Bountry, C. S. Magirl, and J. B. Sankey, "Geomorphic Evolution of a Gravel-Bed River under Sediment-Starved versus Sediment-Rich Conditions: River Response to the World's Largest Dam Removal," *Journal of Geophysical Research—Earth Surface* 123 (2018): 3338–69.

21. "San Vincente Dam Raise, San Diego, California," Water Technology, https://www.water-technology.net/projects/san-vicente-dam-raise-san-diego -california-us/; J. Adams, "Reviewing FERC's Final Federal Nod of Approval for Gross Reservoir Expansion," Denver Water, July 17, 2020, https://www .denverwater.org/tap/reviewing-fercs-final-federal-nod-approval-gross -reservoir-expansion; "Shasta Dam and Reservoir Enlargement Project," US Bureau of Reclamation, https://www.usbr.gov/mp/ncao/shasta-enlargement. html; "Los Vaqueros Reservoir Expansion Project," California Water Commission, https://cwc.ca.gov/Water-Storage/WSIP-Project-Review-Portal /All-Projects/Los-Vaqueros-Reservoir-Expansion-Project; "Valley Water Evaluating Five Dam Alternatives for Proposed Expansion of the Pacheco Reservoir," Santa Clara Valley Water News, March 26, 2021, https://valley waternews.org/2021/03/26/valley-water-evaluating-five-dam-alternatives -for-proposed-expansion-of-pacheco-reservoir/.

22. P. Hannam, "'Expensive Brain Fart': Cost of Dam Project May Triple, Documents Show," *Sydney Morning Herald,* January 21, 2021.

13 A SECOND CHANCE FOR DAMS

1. C. J. Vorosmarty, M. Meybeck, B. Fekete, K. Sharma, P. Green, and J. P. M. Syvitski, "Anthropogenic Sediment Retention: Major Global Impact from Registered River Impoundments," *Global and Planetary Change* 39 (2003): 169–90; D. Wisser, S. Frolking, S. Hagen, and M. F. P. Bierkens, "Beyond Peak Reservoir Storage? A Global Estimate of Declining Water Storage Capacity in Large Reservoirs," *Water Resources Research* 49 (2013): 5732–39.
2. A. Palmieri, F. Shah, G. W. Annandale, and A. Dinar, *Reservoir Construction: The Rescon Approach,* vol. 1 (Washington, DC: International Bank for Reconstruction and Development/World Bank, 2003).
3. G. M. Kondolf, Y. X. Gao, G. W. Annandale, G. L. Morris, E. H. Jiang, J. H. Zhang, Y. T. Cao, et al., "Sustainable Sediment Management in Reservoirs and Regulated Rivers: Experiences from Five Continents," *Earth's Future* 2 (2014): 256–80.
4. Z. Y. Wang and C. H. Hu, "Strategies for Managing Reservoir Sedimentation," *International Journal of Sediment Research* 24 (2009): 369–84; B. Q. Hu, Z. S. Yang, H. J. Wang, X. X. Sun, N. S. Bi, and G. G. Li, "Sedimentation in the Three Gorges Dam and the Future Trend of Changjiang (Yangtze River) Sediment Flux to the Sea," *Hydrology and Earth System Sciences* 13 (2009): 2253–64.
5. Kondolf et al., "Sustainable Sediment Management."
6. J. Waldman, "Blocked Migration: Fish Ladders on U.S. Dams Are Not Effective," *Yale Environment 360,* April 4, 2013, https://e360.yale.edu/features /blocked_migration_fish_ladders_on_us_dams_are_not_effective; D. A. Algera, T. Rytwinski, J. J. Taylor, J. R. Bennett, K. E. Smokorowski, P. M. Harrison, K. D. Clarke, et al., "What Are the Relative Risks of Mortality and Injury for Fish during Downstream Passage at Hydroelectric Dams in Temperate Regions? A Systematic Review," *Environmental Evidence* 9 (2020): 3.
7. A. T. Silva, M. C. Lucas, T. Castro-Santos, C. Katopodis, L. J. Baumgartner, J. D. Thiem, K. Aarestrup, et al., "The Future of Fish Passage Science, Engineering, and Practice," *Fish and Fisheries* 19 (2018): 340–62.
8. A. Matei, "What Is the 'Salmon Cannon' and How Do the Fish Feel about It?," *Guardian,* August 15, 2019.
9. A. Matthews, "The Largest Dam-Removal in US History," BBC Future Planet, November 10, 2020, https://www.bbc.com/future/article/20201110-the-largest -dam-removal-project-in-american-history.

10. Silva et al., "Future of Fish Passage."

11. S. Postel and B. Richter, *Rivers for Life: Managing Water for People and Nature* (Washington, DC: Island Press, 2003); A. H. Arthington, S. E. Bunn, N. L. Poff, and R. J. Naiman, "The Challenge of Providing Environmental Flow Rules to Sustain River Ecosystems," *Ecological Applications* 16 (2006): 1311–18.

12. B. D. Richter and G. A. Thomas, "Restoring Environmental Flows by Modifying Dam Operations," *Ecology and Society* 12 (2007): 26.

14 STORING WATER UNDERGROUND

1. B. A. Faber and J. R. Stedinger, "Reservoir Optimization Using Sampling Sdp with Ensemble Streamflow Prediction (Esp) Forecasts," *Journal of Hydrology* 249 (2001): 113–33.

2. C. J. Delaney, R. K. Hartman, J. Mendoza, M. Dettinger, L. Delle Monache, J. Jasperse, F. M. Ralph, et al., "Forecast Informed Reservoir Operations Using Ensemble Streamflow Predictions for a Multipurpose Reservoir in Northern California," *Water Resources Research* 56 (2020): e2019WR026604.

3. F. van Steenbergen, P. Lawrence, A. M. Haile, M. Salman, and J.-M. Faurés, *Guidelines on Spate Irrigation,* Food and Agriculture Organization of the United Nations, Rome, 2010.

4. F. van Steenbergen, O. Verheijen, S. van Aarst, and A. M. Haile, *Spate Irrigation, Livelihood Improvement and Adaptation to Climate Variability and Change,* International Fund for Agricultural Development, Rome, 2008.

5. F. van Steenbergen and A. al-Weshali, "A New World, More Equity: Changing Water Allocation in Wadi Zabid, Yemen," The Water Channel, March 10, 2021, https://thewaterchannel.tv/thewaterblog/a-new-world-more-equity -changing-water-allocation-in-wadi-zabid-yemen/.

6. D. Charles, "As Rains Soak California, Farmers Test How to Store Water Underground," *All Things Considered,* National Public Radio, January 13, 2017.

7. P. A. M. Bachand, S. B. Roy, N. Stern, J. Choperena, D. Cameron, and W. R. Horwath, "On-Farm Flood Capture Could Reduce Groundwater Overdraft in Kings River Basin," *California Agriculture* 70 (2016): 200–207.

8. S. Alam, M. Gebremichael, R. P. Li, J. Dozier, and D. P. Lettenmaier, "Can Managed Aquifer Recharge Mitigate the Groundwater Overdraft in California's Central Valley?," *Water Resources Research* 56 (2020): e2020WR027244.

9. R. Sakthivadivel, "The Groundwater Recharge Movement in India," in *The Agricultural Groundwater Revolution: Opportunities and Threats to Development,* ed. M. Giordano and K. G. Villholth, 195–210 (Wallingford, UK: CAB International, 2007).

10. P. Dillon, P. Stuyfzand, T. Grischek, M. Lluria, R. D. G. Pyne, R. C. Jain, J. Bear, et al., "Sixty Years of Global Progress in Managed Aquifer Recharge," *Hydrogeology Journal* 27 (2019): 1–30.

11. Sakthivadivel, "Groundwater Recharge Movement."

12. T. Shah, "India's Master Plan for Groundwater Recharge: An Assessment and Some Suggestions for Revision," *Economic and Political Weekly* 43, no. 51 (2008): 41–49; *Master Plan for Artificial Recharge to Groundwater in India*, Central Ground Water Board, Ministry of Water Resources, New Delhi; *Master Plan for Artificial Recharge to Groundwater in India—2020*, Central Ground Water Board Department of Water Resources, New Delhi, 2020.

13. Shah, "India's Master Plan"; A. Richard-Ferroudji, T. P. Raghunath, and G. Venkatasubramanian, "Managed Aquifer Recharge in India: Consensual Policy but Controversial Implementation," *Water Alternatives—An Interdisciplinary Journal on Water Politics and Development* 11 (2018): 749–69.

14. L. Muthuwatta, U. A. Amarasinghe, A. Sood, and L. Surinaidu, "Reviving the 'Gangeswater Machine': Where and How Much?," *Hydrology and Earth System Sciences* 21 (2017): 2545–57.

15. M. Dinesh Kumar, A. Patel, R. Ravindranath, and O. P. Singh, "Chasing a Mirage: Water Harvesting and Artificial Recharge in Naturally Water-Scarce Regions," *Economic and Political Weekly* 43, no. 35 (2008): 61–71.

16. J. E. Zuniga, *The Central Arizona Project*, US Bureau of Reclamation, Lakewood, CO, 2000; J. Keane, "Managing Water Supply Variability: The Salt River Project," in *Managing Water Resources in the West under Conditions of Climate Uncertainty: A Proceedings*, National Research Council, Water Science and Technology Board, Washington, DC, 1991.

17. B. R. Scanlon, R. C. Reedy, C. C. Faunt, D. Pool, and K. Uhlman, "Enhancing Drought Resilience with Conjunctive Use and Managed Aquifer Recharge in California and Arizona," *Environmental Research Letters* 11 (2016): 035013.

18. A. Lustgarten and N. Sadasivam, "Holy Crop: How Federal Dollars Are Financing the Water Crisis in the West," ProPublica, May 27, 2015, https://projects.propublica.org/killing-the-colorado/story/arizona-cotton-drought-crisis/.

19. *Why in God's Name Are We Growing Cotton in the Desert?*, Arizona Farm Bureau, Gilbert, 2016.

20. Lustgarten and Sadasivam, "Holy Crop."

21. Zuniga, *Central Arizona Project*.

22. Dillon et al., "Sixty Years of Global Progress."

23. H. Bouwer, "Artificial Recharge of Groundwater: Hydrogeology and Engineering," *Hydrogeology Journal* 10 (2002): 121–42.

24. A. Milman, C. Bonnell, R. Maguire, K. Sorensen, and W. Blomquist, "Groundwater Recharge for Water Security: The Arizona Water Bank, Arizona," *Case Studies in the Environment* 5 (2021): 1113999.

25. Scanlon et al., "Enhancing Drought Resilience."

26. K. Friedrich, R. L. Grossman, J. Huntington, P. D. Blanken, J. Lenters, K. D. Holman, D. Gochis, et al., "Reservoir Evaporation in the Western United States: Current Science, Challenges, and Future Needs," *Bulletin of the American Meteorological Society* 99 (2018): 167–88.

27. H. Fountain, "In a First, U.S. Declares Shortage on Colorado River, Forcing Water Cuts," *New York Times*, August 16, 2021; *2021 Update: Recovery of Water Stored by the Arizona Water Banking Authority,* AWBA, ADWR and CAP, 2021.

28. J. Simes, L. Alexanderson, and D. Bradbury, *Summary Report: Los Angeles Basin Study,* US Department of the Interior, Bureau of Reclamation, and County of Los Angeles Department of Public Works, Los Angeles County Flood Control District, 2016.

29. K. Miller, P. Goulden, M. Kiparsky, and A. Milman, *Case Study: Kern County Water Bank,* Berkeley Law Center for Law, Energy and the Environment, 2019; J. Parker, *Kern Water Bank Storage Project within the Kern County Groundwater Authority Groundwater Sustainability Plan,* 2020.

15 A NEW SOURCE OF WATER FALLING FROM THE SKY

1. According to Stephen Malpezzi, the population density of metropolitan Houston is approximately eleven people per hectare; S. Malpezzi, "Population Density: Some Facts and Some Predictions," *Cityscape* 15 (2013): 183–201. The US National Weather Service reports that Houston receives an average of 131 cm of precipitation per year; National Weather Service, https://www.weather.gov/wrh/climate?wfo=hgx. Thus, capturing 20 percent of the annual precipitation would yield about 652 L/person day. For comparison, the North Texas Council of Governments reported average residential water use for Houston of 260 L/person day and total municipal water use of 540 L/person day; Conserve North Texas, http://conservenorthtexas.org/regional-indicators/municipal-capita-water-use-selected-texas-cities.

2. According to Malpezzi, "Population Density," the population density of metropolitan Los Angeles is approximately twenty-two people per hectare. The US National Weather Service reports that Los Angeles receives an average of 32.6 cm of precipitation per year; National Weather Service, https://www.weather.gov/wrh/Climate?wfo=lox. Thus, capturing 20 percent of the annual precip-

itation would yield about 82 L/person day. According to the International Water Association, the average daily per capita household water use in Los Angeles in 2016 was 428 L; https://waterstatistics.iwa-network.org.

3. Malpezzi, "Population Density."

4. *Using Graywater and Stormwater to Enhance Local Water Supplies: An Assessment of Risks, Costs, and Benefits,* National Academies of Sciences, Engineering, and Medicine, Washington, DC, 2016; S. Ozdemir, M. Elliott, J. Brown, P. K. Nam, V. T. Hien, and M. D. Sobsey, "Rainwater Harvesting Practices and Attitudes in the Mekong Delta of Vietnam," *Journal of Water Sanitation and Hygiene for Development* 1 (2011): 171–77; L. M. Fry, J. R. Cowden, D. W. Watkins, T. Clasen, and J. R. Mihelcic, "Quantifying Health Improvements from Water Quantity Enhancement: An Engineering Perspective Applied to Rainwater Harvesting in West Africa," *Environmental Science and Technology* 44 (2010): 9535–41.

5. L. Mays, G. P. Antoniou, and A. N. Angelakis, "History of Water Cisterns: Legacies and Lessons," *Water* 5 (2013): 1916–40; *Using Graywater and Stormwater.*

6. A. K. Sharma, S. Cook, T. Gardner, and G. Tjandraatmadja, "Rainwater Tanks in Modern Cities: A Review of Current Practices and Research," *Journal of Water and Climate Change* 7 (2016): 445–66; *Guidance on the Use of Rainwater Tanks,* Australian Government Department of Health and Aged Care, 2010.

7. Sharma et al., "Rainwater Tanks in Modern Cities."

8. A. Campisano, D. Butler, S. Ward, M. J. Burns, E. Friedler, K. DeBusk, L. N. Fisher-Jeffes, et al., "Urban Rainwater Harvesting Systems: Research, Implementation and Future Perspectives," *Water Research* 115 (2017): 195–209; T. Schuetze, "Rainwater Harvesting and Management—Policy and Regulations in Germany," *Water Science and Technology—Water Supply* 13 (2013): 376–85; M. Denchak, "Green Infrastructure: How to Manage Water in a Sustainable Way," NRDC Our Stories, July 25, 2022, https://www.nrdc.org/stories/green-infrastructure-how-manage-water-sustainable-way.

9. U. A. F. Gomes, L. Heller, S. Cairncross, L. Domenech, and J. L. Pena, "Subsidizing the Sustainability of Rural Water Supply: The Experience of the Brazilian Rural Rainwater-Harvesting Programme," *Water International* 39 (2014): 606–19.

10. *Master Plan for Artificial Recharge to Groundwater in India—2020,* Central Ground Water Board Department of Water Resources, New Delhi; P. Dillon, P. Stuyfzand, T. Grischek, M. Lluria, R. D. G. Pyne, R. C. Jain, J. Bear, et al., "Sixty Years of Global Progress in Managed Aquifer Recharge," *Hydrogeology Journal* 27 (2019): 1–30.

11. S. Spahr, M. Teixido, D. L. Sedlak, and R. G. Luthy, "Hydrophilic Trace Organic Contaminants in Urban Stormwater: Occurrence, Toxicological Relevance, and the Need to Enhance Green Stormwater Infrastructure," *Environmental Science—Water Research and Technology* 6 (2020): 15–44; J. R. Masoner, D. W. Kolpin, I. M. Cozzarelli, L. B. Barber, D. S. Burden, W. T. Foreman, K. J. Forshay, et al., "Urban Stormwater: An Overlooked Pathway of Extensive Mixed Contaminants to Surface and Groundwaters in the United States," *Environmental Science and Technology* 53 (2019): 10070–81.

12. D. A. Aronson and R. C. Prill, "Analysis of Recharge Potential of Storm-Water Basins on Long-Island, New-York," *Journal of Research of the US Geological Survey* 5 (1977): 307–18.

13. M. S. Fischler, "What Lurks Beneath: Cesspools That Time Forgot," *New York Times,* May 27, 2007.

14. L. Leuzzi, "A Discussion about Suffolk's Wastewater Treatment Systems," *Suffolk County (NY) News,* May 27, 2021.

15. D. Winzelberg, "Suffolk Officials Mark Start of $400m Sewer Expansion," *Long Island Business News,* November 1, 2021; "Septic Improvement Program," Reclaim Our Water, https://reclaimourwater.info/Septic-Improvement -Program.

16. "Long Island Inflow to the Groundwater System," New York Water Science Center, USGS, May 9, 2017, https://www.usgs.gov/centers/ny-water/science /long-island-inflow-groundwater-system.

17. H. T. Buxton and D. A. Smolensky, *Simulation of the Effects of Development of the Ground-Water Flow System of Long Island, New York,* Water-Resources Investigations Report 98-4069, USGS, Coram, NY, 1999.

18. E. K. Larson and N. B. Grimm, "Small-Scale and Extensive Hydrogeomorphic Modification and Water Redistribution in a Desert City and Implications for Regional Nitrogen Removal," *Urban Ecosystems* 15 (2012): 71–85.

19. *Preliminary Assessment of Increased Natural Recharge Resulting from Urbanization and Stormwater Retention within the City of Chandler,* GeoSystems Analysis, Tucson, AZ, 2004.

20. "RDA Adelaide Metropolitan," Regional Development Australia, https:// profile.id.com.au/rda-adelaide/about; P. Kretschmer, *Managed Aquifer Recharge Schemes in the Adelaide Metropolitan Area,* Government of South Australia, Department of Environment, Water and Natural Resources, Adelaide, 2017; "Stormwater," Government of South Australia, Department of Environment and Water, https://www.environment.sa.gov.au/topics/water /resources/stormwater.

21. A. Alam, A. Borthakur, S. Ravi, M. Gebremichael, and S. K. Mohanty, "Man-

aged Aquifer Recharge Implementation Criteria to Achieve Water Sustainability," *Science of the Total Environment* 768 (May 2021): 144992.

22. J. E. Grebel, S. K. Mohanty, A. A. Torkelson, A. B. Boehm, C. P. Higgins, R. M. Maxwell, K. L. Nelson, et al., "Engineered Infiltration Systems for Urban Stormwater Reclamation," *Environmental Engineering Science* 30 (2013): 437–54; *Using Graywater and Stormwater;* Kretschmer, *Managed Aquifer Recharge Schemes.*

23. E. F. Houtz and D. L. Sedlak, "Oxidative Conversion as a Means of Detecting Precursors to Perfluoroalkyl Acids in Urban Runoff," *Environmental Science and Technology* 46 (2012): 9342–49; D. Page, J. Vanderzalm, A. Kumar, K. Y. Cheng, A. H. Kaksonen, and S. Simpson, "Risks of Perfluoroalkyl and Polyfluoroalkyl Substances (PFAS) for Sustainable Water Recycling via Aquifers," *Water* 11 (2019): 1737; X. D. C. Hu, D. Q. Andrews, A. B. Lindstrom, T. A. Bruton, L. A. Schaider, P. Grandjean, R. Lohmann, et al., "Detection of Poly- and Perfluoroalkyl Substances (PFASs) in US Drinking Water Linked to Industrial Sites, Military Fire Training Areas, and Wastewater Treatment Plants," *Environmental Science and Technology Letters* 3 (2016): 344–50.

24. *Perfluorochemical Contamination in Lake Elmo and Oakdale, Washington County, Minnesota,* Minnesota Department of Health and US Department of Health and Human Services Agency for Toxic Substances and Disease Registry, 2008.

25. *California Drywell Guidance: Research and Recommendations,* Geosyntec Consultants, Sacramento, CA, 2020; P. J. Squillace, J. S. Zogorski, W. G. Wilber, and C. V. Price, "Preliminary Assessment of the Occurrence and Possible Sources of MTBE in Groundwater in the United States, 1993–1994," *Environmental Science and Technology* 30 (1996): 1721–30; C. Nelson and B. Lock, *Separating Fact from Fiction: Assessing the Use of Dry Wells as an Integrated Low Impact Development (LID) Tool for Reducing Stormwater Runoff while Protecting Groundwater Quality in Urban Watersheds City of Elk Grove, California,* City of Elk Grove, CA, 2017.

26. *Pesticide Industry Sales and Usage: 2008–2012 Market Estimates,* US Environmental Protection Agency, Washington, DC, 2017; M. Burkhardt, S. Zuleeg, R. Vonbank, K. Bester, J. Carmeliet, M. Boller, and T. Wangler, "Leaching of Biocides from Facades under Natural Weather Conditions," *Environmental Science and Technology* 46 (2012): 5497–503; Masoner et al., "Urban Stormwater."

27. R. G. Luthy, S. Sharvelle, and P. Dillon, "Urban Stormwater to Enhance Water Supply," *Environmental Science and Technology* 53 (2019): 5534–42; Y. Duan and D. L. Sedlak, "An Electrochemical Advanced Oxidation Process for the Treatment of Urban Stormwater," *Water Research* 13 (2021): 100127.

28. J. E. Grebel, S. K. Mohanty, A. A. Torkelson, A. B. Boehm, C. P. Higgins, R. M. Maxwell, K. L. Nelson, et al., "Engineered Infiltration Systems for Urban Stormwater Reclamation," *Environmental Engineering Science* 30 (2013): 437–54; B. A. Ulrich, E. A. Im, D. Werner, and C. P. Higgins, "Biochar and Activated Carbon for Enhanced Trace Organic Contaminant Retention in Stormwater Infiltration Systems," *Environmental Science and Technology* 49 (2015): 6222–30; J. A. Charbonnet, Y. H. Duan, C. M. van Genuchten, and D. L. Sedlak, "Regenerated Manganese-Oxide Coated Sands: The Role of Mineral Phase in Organic Contaminant Reactivity," *Environmental Science and Technology* 55 (2021): 5282–90; J. A. Charbonnet, Y. H. Duan, and D. L. Sedlak, "The Use of Manganese Oxide-Coated Sand for the Removal of Trace Metal Ions from Stormwater," *Environmental Science: Water Research and Technology* 6 (2020): 593–603.

29. B. Kerkez, C. Gruden, M. Lewis, L. Montestruque, M. Quigley, B. Wong, A. Bedig, et al., "Smarter Stormwater Systems," *Environmental Science and Technology* 50 (2016): 7267–73.

16 REPLENISHING GROUNDWATER WITH TREATED SEWAGE

1. P. Salian and B. Anton, *Making Urban Water Management More Sustainable: Achievements in Berlin,* SWITCH, ICLEI European Secretariat, Freiburg, 2011; S. Kulaksiz and M. Bau, "Anthropogenic Gadolinium as a Microcontaminant in Tap Water Used as Drinking Water in Urban Areas and Megacities," *Applied Geochemistry* 26 (2011): 1877–85.

2. "Water Quality," Berliner Wasserbetriebe, https://www.bwb.de/en/2471.php.

3. C. Sprenger, N. Hartog, M. Hernandez, E. Vilanova, G. Grutzmacher, F. Scheibler, and S. Hannappel, "Inventory of Managed Aquifer Recharge Sites in Europe: Historical Development, Current Situation and Perspectives," *Hydrogeology Journal* 25 (2017): 1909–22.

4. C. K. Schmidt, F. T. Lange, H.-J. Brauch, and W. Kühn, *Experiences with Riverbank Filtration and Infiltration in Germany,* DVGW-Water Technology Center [TZW], Karlsruhe, 2003; T. Grischek, D. Schoenheinz, C. Sandhu, and P. Eckert, "Sustainability of Riverbank Filtration in Germany," *Proceedings of the International Conference on Water, Environment, Energy and Society,* 2009.

5. Sprenger et al., "Inventory of Managed Aquifer Recharge Sites."

6. J. E. Drewes, S. Karakurt, L. Schmid, M. Bachmaier, U. Hübner, V. Clausnitzer, R. Timmermann, et al., *Dynamik der Klarwasseranteile in Oberflächengewässern und Mögliche Herausforderung für die Trinkwassergewinnung in Deutschland* (Dessau-Roßlau, Germany: Umwelt Bundeamt, 2018).

7. P. Dillon, P. Stuyfzand, T. Grischek, M. Lluria, R. D. G. Pyne, R. C. Jain, J. Bear, et al., "Sixty Years of Global Progress in Managed Aquifer Recharge," *Hydrogeology Journal* 27 (2019): 1–30.

8. Grischek et al., "Sustainability of Riverbank Filtration in Germany."

9. H. Bouwer, "About Herman Bouwer," *Ground Water* 41 (2003): 709–13.

10. T. A. Johnson, "Ground Water Recharge Using Recycled Municipal Waste Water in Los Angeles County and the California Department of Public Health's Draft Regulations on Aquifer Retention Time," *Ground Water* 47 (2009): 496–99.

11. M. Gasca and E. Hartling, "Montebello Forebay Groundwater Recharge Project Using Recycled Water, Los Angeles County, California," in *2012 Guidelines for Water Reuse,* US Environmental Protection Agency, Washington, DC, 2012.

12. B. A. Milkovich, *A History of the Orange County Water District,* 2nd ed., Fountain Valley, CA, 2014.

13. C. A. Burton, J. A. Izbicki, and K. S. Paybins, *Water Quality Trends in the Santa Ana River at MWD Crossing and below Prado Dam, Riverside County, California,* US Geological Survey, Sacramento, CA, 1998.

14. A. Hutchinson, "Transforming Wastewater to Drinking Water: How Two Agencies Collaborated to Build the World's Largest Indirect Potable Reuse Project," presentation at the College of Agriculture and Life Sciences Cooperative Extension Water Resources Research Center, Tucson, AZ, April 13, 2017.

15. "Recharge Operations," Orange County Water District, https://www.ocwd .com/media/6975/recharge-operations-fact-sheet_082018.pdf.

16. E. Wilson, "Pharmaceutical Drugs in European Drinking Water," *Science News Magazine,* March 21, 1998.

17. W. H. Alley and R. Alley, *The Water Recycling Revolution* (Latham, MD: Rowman and Littlefield, 2022).

18. Alley and Alley, *Water Recycling Revolution;* "The Sustainable Water Initiative for Tomorrow (SWIFT): A Forward-Looking Solution to Tackle Today's Problems," Hampton Roads Sanitary District, https://www.hrsd.com/swift /about.

19. N. V. Paranychianakis, M. Salgot, S. A. Snyder, and A. N. Angelakis, "Water Reuse in EU States: Necessity for Uniform Criteria to Mitigate Human and Environmental Risks," *Critical Reviews in Environmental Science and Technology* 45 (2015): 1409–68; A. Jiricka and U. Probstl, "One Common Way— the Strategic and Methodological Influence on Environmental Planning across Europe," *Environmental Impact Assessment Review* 29 (2009): 379–89.

20. R. Marcé, J. Honey-Rosés, A. Manzano, L. Moragas, B. Catllar, and S. Sabater, "The Llobregat River Basin: A Paradigm of Impaired Rivers under Climate Change Threats," in *The Llobregat: The Story of a Polluted Mediterranean River,* ed. S. Sabater, A. Ginebreda, and D. Barceló, 1–26 (Heidelberg: Springer, 2012); R. Mujeriego, M. Gullon, and S. Lobato, "Incidental Potable Water Reuse in a Catalonian Basin: Living Downstream," *Journal of Water Reuse and Desalination* 7 (2017): 253–63.

21. T. Cazurra, "Water Reuse of South Barcelona's Wastewater Reclamation Plant," *Desalination* 218 (2008): 43–51.

22. D. Skutlarek, M. Exner, and H. Farber, "Perfluorinated Surfactants in Surface and Drinking Water," *Environmental Science and Pollution Research* 13 (2006): 299–307; M. Behrooz, "Status of PFAS Investigations in the Santa Ana Region," in *2020 California PFAS Virtual Conference,* Groundwater Resources Association of California, 2020.

23. S. Harris-Lovett and D. Sedlak, "Protecting the Sewershed as Cities Use Sewage as a Water Source, Proactive Policies Must Safeguard Public Health," *Science* 369 (2020): 1429–30.

17 REFILLING RESERVOIRS WITH TREATED SEWAGE

1. R. I. McDonald, K. Weber, J. Padowski, M. Florke, C. Schneider, P. A. Green, T. Gleeson, et al., "Water on an Urban Planet: Urbanization and the Reach of Urban Water Infrastructure," *Global Environmental Change—Human and Policy Dimensions* 27 (2014): 96–105.

2. *Fulfilling the Promise: The Occoquan Watershed in the New Millennium,* Report of the New Millennium Occoquan Watershed Task Force, Fairfax County Board of Supervisors, Fairfax, VA, 2003.

3. R. W. Angelotti and T. J. Grizzard, "34 Years of Experience with Potable Water Reuse in the Occoquan Reservoir," in *Milestones in Water Reuse: The Best Success Stories,* ed. V. Lazarova, T. Asano, A. Bahri, and J. Anderson, 323–38 (London: IWA, 2013).

4. Metcalf & Eddy, Inc., T. Asano, F. Burton, and H. Leverenz, "Indirect Potable Reuse through Surface Water Augmentation," in *Water Reuse: Issues, Technologies, and Applications,* chap. 23 (New York: McGraw-Hill, 2007).

5. C. W. Randall and T. J. Grizzard, "Management of the Occoquan River Basin: A 20-Year Case History," *Water Science and Technology* 32 (1995): 235–43; "No Simple Answer," *Northern Virginia Sun* (Arlington, VA), July 7, 1971.

6. *Fulfilling the Promise;* Angelotti and Grizzard, "34 Years of Experience."

7. P. P. Maldonado and G. E. Moglen, "Low-Flow Variations in Source Water

Supply for the Occoquan Reservoir System Based on a 100-Year Climate Forecast," *Journal of Hydrologic Engineering* 18 (2013): 787–96.

8. Angelotti and Grizzard, "34 Years of Experience."

9. W. H. Alley and R. Alley, *The Water Recycling Revolution* (Latham, MD: Rowman and Littlefield, 2022).

10. T. Wilkins, "Lake Lanier Pollution Could Cause Odd Odor and Taste in Drinking Water," *Atlanta Journal-Constitution,* March 16, 2021; *Final Total Maximum Daily Load Evaluation for Lake Lanier in the Chattahoochee River Basin for Chlorophyll a,* Georgia Department of Natural Resources, Environmental Protection Division, Atlanta, 2017.

11. *State of Technology of Water Reuse,* Report to the Texas Water Development Board, Alan Plummer Associates, Dallas, 2010.

12. P. L. du Pisani, "Direct Reclamation of Potable Water at Windhoek's Goreangab Reclamation Plant," *Desalination* 188 (2006): 79–88; *50 Years of Direct Potable Reuse: The Windhoek Experience,* City of Windhoek, [Namibia, 2016].

13. J. Lahnsteiner, P. du Pisani, J. Menge, and J. Esterhuizen, "More Than 40 Years of Direct Potable Reuse Experience in Windhoek," in *Milestones in Water Reuse: The Best Success Stories,* ed. V. Lazarova, T. Asano, A. Bahri, and J. Anderson, 351–64 (London: IWA, 2013).

14. Lahnsteiner et al., "More Than 40 Years"; "50 Years of Direct Potable Reuse."

15. A. Hazen, *Clean Water and How to Get It* (New York: John Wiley and Sons, 1909).

16. T. A. Larsen, S. Hoffmann, C. Luthi, B. Truffer, and M. Maurer, "Emerging Solutions to the Water Challenges of an Urbanizing World," *Science* 352 (2016): 928–33.

17. J. E. Becerril and B. Jimenez, "Potable Water and Sanitation in Tenochtitlan: Aztec Culture," paper presented at the 1st IWA International Symposium on Water and Wastewater Technologies in Ancient Civilization, Iraklio, Greece, October 28–30, 2006; B. Jiménez-Cisneros, "Improving the Air Quality in Mexico City through Reusing Wastewater for Environmental Restoration," in *Milestones in Water Reuse: The Best Success Stories,* ed. V. Lazarova, T. Asano, and J. Anderson, 283–91 (London: IWA, 2020).

18. B. Jimenez and A. Chavez, "Quality Assessment of an Aquifer Recharged with Wastewater for Its Potential Use as Drinking Source: 'El Mezquital Valley' Case," *Water Science and Technology* 50 (2004): 269–76.

19. A. N. Angelakis, T. Asano, A. Bahri, B. E. Jimenez, and G. Tchobanoglous, "Water Reuse: From Ancient to Modern Times and the Future," *Frontiers in Environmental Science* 6 (2018), https://doi.org/10.3389/fenvs.2018.00026.

20. J. D. Contreras, R. Meza, C. Siebe, S. Rodriguez-Dozal, Y. A. Lopez-Vidal,

G. Castillo-Rojas, R. I. Amieva, et al., "Health Risks from Exposure to Untreated Wastewater Used for Irrigation in the Mezquital Valley, Mexico: A 25-Year Update," *Water Research* 123 (2017): 834–50.

21. *Wastewater: From Waste to Resource—the Case of Atontonilco de Tula, Mexico,* World Bank, Washington, DC, 2018.

22. *Summary Progress Update 2021: SDG 6—Water and Sanitation for All,* UN-Water, Geneva, 2021.

23. C. Tortajada, "Contributions of Recycled Wastewater to Clean Water and Sanitation Sustainable Development Goals," *npj Clean Water* 3 (2020): 22.

18 IRRIGATING CROPS WITH TREATED SEWAGE

1. A. N. Angelakis, T. Asano, A. Bahri, B. E. Jimenez, and G. Tchobanoglous, "Water Reuse: From Ancient to Modern Times and the Future," *Frontiers in Environmental Science* 6 (2018), https://doi.org/10.3389/fenvs.2018.00026.

2. D. L. Sedlak, *Water 4.0: The Past, Present and Future of the World's Most Vital Resource* (New Haven: Yale University Press, 2014).

3. D. Stevens and J. Anderson, "Irrigation of Crops in Australia," in *Milestones in Water Reuse: The Best Success Stories,* ed. V. Lazarova, T. Asano, A. Bahri, and J. Anderson, 201–8 (London: IWA, 2013); R. Crites, R. Beggs, and H. Leverenz, "Perspective on Land Treatment and Wastewater Reuse for Agriculture in the Western United States," *Water* 13 (2021): 1822; N. V. Paranychianakis, M. Salgot, S. A. Snyder, and A. N. Angelakis, "Water Reuse in EU States: Necessity for Uniform Criteria to Mitigate Human and Environmental Risks," *Critical Reviews in Environmental Science and Technology* 45 (2015): 1409–68; D. Frascari, G. Zanaroli, M. A. Motaleb, G. Annen, K. Belguith, S. Borin, R. Choukr-Allah, et al., "Integrated Technological and Management Solutions for Wastewater Treatment and Efficient Agricultural Reuse in Egypt, Morocco, and Tunisia," *Integrated Environmental Assessment and Management* 14 (2018): 447–62.

4. A. Tal, *Pollution in a Promised Land: An Environmental History of Israel* (Berkeley: University of California Press, 2002).

5. S. M. Siegel, *Let There Be Water* (New York: St. Martin's, 2015); P. Marin, S. Tal, J. Yeres, and K. Ringskog, *Water Management in Israel: Key Innovations and Lessons Learned for Water-Scarce Countries,* World Bank, Washington, DC, 2017; N. Ickeson-Tal, O. Avraham, J. Sack, and H. Cikurel, "Water Reuse in Israel—The Dan Region Project: Evaluation of Water Quality and Reliability of Plant's Operation," paper presented at the IWA Regional Symposium on

Water Recycling in the Mediterranean Region, Iraklion, Greece, September 26–29, 2002.

6. Marin et al., *Water Management in Israel.*

7. A. Y. Hoekstra and M. M. Mekonnen, "The Water Footprint of Humanity," *Proceedings of the National Academy of Sciences* 109 (2012): 3232–37.

8. E. Ben Mordechay, V. Mordehay, J. Tarchitzky, and B. Chefetz, "Pharmaceuticals in Edible Crops Irrigated with Reclaimed Wastewater: Evidence from a Large Survey in Israel," *Journal of Hazardous Materials* 416 (2021): 126184.

9. A. Christou, P. Karaolia, E. Hapeshi, C. Michael, and D. Fatta-Kassinos, "Long-Term Wastewater Irrigation of Vegetables in Real Agricultural Systems: Concentration of Pharmaceuticals in Soil, Uptake and Bioaccumulation in Tomato Fruits and Human Health Risk Assessment," *Water Research* 109 (2017): 24–34; J. B. Brown, J. M. Conder, J. A. Arblaster, and C. P. Higgins, "Assessing Human Health Risks from Per- and Polyfluoroalkyl Substance (PFAS)-Impacted Vegetable Consumption: A Tiered Modeling Approach," *Environmental Science and Technology* 54 (2020): 15202–14; M. C. S. Costello and L. S. Lee, "Sources, Fate, and Plant Uptake in Agricultural Systems of Per- and Polyfluoroalkyl Substances," *Current Pollution Reports* (2020), https://doi.org/10.1007/s40726-020-00168-y.

10. P. J. Vikesland, A. Pruden, P. J. J. Alvarez, D. Aga, H. Burgmann, X. D. Li, C. M. Manaia, et al., "Toward a Comprehensive Strategy to Mitigate Dissemination of Environmental Sources of Antibiotic Resistance," *Environmental Science and Technology* 51 (2017): 13061–69; Y. Negreanu, Z. Pasternak, E. Jurkevitch, and E. Cytryn, "Impact of Treated Wastewater Irrigation on Antibiotic Resistance in Agricultural Soils," *Environmental Science and Technology* 46 (2012): 4800–4808.

11. A. T. B. Abadi, A. A. Rizvanov, T. Haertle, and N. L. Blatt, "World Health Organization Report: Current Crisis of Antibiotic Resistance," *Bionanoscience* 9 (2019): 778–88.

12. S. Slobodiuk, C. Niven, G. Arthur, S. Thakur, and A. Ercumen, "Does Irrigation with Treated and Untreated Wastewater Increase Antimicrobial Resistance in Soil and Water: A Systematic Review," *International Journal of Environmental Research and Public Health* 18 (2021): 11046.

13. A. Tal, "Rethinking the Sustainability of Israel's Irrigation Practices in the Drylands," *Water Research* 90 (2016): 387–94.

14. Tal, "Rethinking the Sustainability of Israel's Irrigation Practices."

15. E. Raveh and A. Ben-Gal, "Leveraging Sustainable Irrigated Agriculture via Desalination: Evidence from a Macro-Data Case Study in Israel," *Sustainability*

10 (2018): 974; M. Shlezinger, Y. Amitai, A. Akriv, H. Gabay, M. Shechter, and M. Leventer-Roberts, "Association between Exposure to Desalinated Sea Water and Ischemic Heart Disease, Diabetes Mellitus and Colorectal Cancer: A Population-Based Study in Israel," *Environmental Research* 166 (2018): 620–27.

16. N. Voulvoulis, "Water Reuse from a Circular Economy Perspective and Potential Risks from an Unregulated Approach," *Current Opinion in Environmental Science and Health* 2 (2018): 32–45.

17. R. B. Chalmers, M. Tremblay, and R. Soni, "A New Water Source for Southern California: The Regional Recycled Water Program," *Journal of the American Water Works Association* 112 (2020): 6–19.

19 COASTAL CITIES TURN TOWARD THE SEA

1. *The Role of Desalination in an Increasingly Water-Scarce World,* World Bank Group, Washington, DC, 2019.

2. *Using Desalination Technologies for Water Treatment,* US Congress, Office of Technology Assessment, Washington, DC, 1988.

3. D. L. Sedlak, *Water 4.0: The Past, Present and Future of the World's Most Vital Resource* (New Haven: Yale University Press, 2014).

4. S. Lattemann, M. D. Kenney, J. C. Schippers, and G. Amy, "Global Desalination Situation," in *Sustainable Water for the Future: Water Recycling versus Desalination,* ed. I. C. Escobar and A. I. Schäfer, 7–39, Elsevier, 2010; *Role of Desalination.*

5. U. Caldera and C. Breyer, "Learning Curve for Seawater Reverse Osmosis Desalination Plants: Capital Cost Trend of the Past, Present, and Future," *Water Resources Research* 53 (2017): 10523–38.

6. Caldera and Breyer, "Learning Curve"; N. Voutchkov, "Energy Use for Membrane Seawater Desalination—Current Status and Trends," *Desalination* 431 (2018): 2–14.

7. L. Gao, S. Yoshikawa, Y. Iseri, S. Fujimori, and S. Kanae, "An Economic Assessment of the Global Potential for Seawater Desalination to 2050," *Water* 9 (2017): 763.

8. *Role of Desalination.*

9. L. Wong and A. Le, *Tracking Progress: Once-Through Cooling Phaseout,* California Energy Commission, Sacramento, 2019; T. M. Missimer and R. G. Maliva, "Environmental Issues in Seawater Reverse Osmosis Desalination: Intakes and Outfalls," *Desalination* 434 (2018): 198–215.

10. F. D. Ibrahim and E. A. B. Eltahir, "Impact of Brine Discharge from Seawater Desalination Plants on Persian/Arabian Gulf Salinity," *Journal of Environ-*

mental *Engineering* 145 (2019), https://doi.org/10.1061/(ASCE)EE.1943
-7870.0001604; W. J. F. Le Quesne, L. Fernand, T. S. Ali, O. Andres,
M. Antonpoulou, J. A. Burt, W. W. Dougherty, et al., "Is the Development of
Desalination Compatible with Sustainable Development of the Arabian
Gulf?," *Marine Pollution Bulletin* 173 (2021): 112940.

11. D. Giammar, S. Jiang, P. Xu, R. Breckenridge, T. Edirisooriya, W. Jiang, L. Lin,
et al., *National Alliance for Water Innovation (NAWI) Technology Roadmap:
Municipal Sector,* National Renewable Energy Laboratory, 2021.

12. H. Cooley and M. Heberger, *Key Issues for Seawater Desalination in California
Energy and Greenhouse Gas Emissions,* Pacific Institute, Oakland, CA, 2013.

13. *Role of Desalination.*

14. S. Martinez and K. Viswanathan, "Proceed with Caution: California's
Droughts and Desalination in Context," NRDC, March 28, 2016, https://
www.nrdc.org/resources/proceed-caution-californias-droughts-and-desali
nation-context; P. Dickie, *Desalination: Option or Distraction for a Thirsty
World?,* World Wildlife Fund, 2007; E. Leckie and B. Neindorf, "'It Can't Happen': Out to Sea Protest Warns SA Water Its Desal Plans Aren't Welcome,"
ABC News (Australia), October 13, 2021, https://www.abc.net.au/news/2021
-10-13/desal-protest-aquaculture/100536348; N. Sadasivam, "Why Environmental Groups Are Salty on Corpus Christi's Pricey Desalination Plan," *Texas
Observer,* October 9, 2018.

15. J. Williams and E. Swyngedouw, *Tapping the Oceans: Seawater Desalination
and the Political Ecology of Water* (Cheltenham, UK: Edward Elgar, 2018);
R. A. Greer, K. Lee, A. Fencl, and G. Sneegas, "Public-Private Partnerships in
the Water Sector: The Case of Desalination," *Water Resources Management* 35
(2021): 3497–511.

20 THE COMING WAVE OF INLAND DESALINATION

1. D. Curto, V. Franzitta, and A. Guercio, "A Review of the Water Desalination
Technologies," *Applied Sciences* 11 (2021): 670; P. Rao, A. Aghajanzadeh,
P. Sheaffer, W. R. Morrow, S. Brueske, C. Dollinger, K. Price, et al., *Volume 1:
Survey of Available Information in Support of the Energy-Water Bandwidth
Study of Desalination Systems,* Lawrence Berkeley National Laboratory,
Berkeley, CA, 2016.

2. N. Cahill, "Pressed by Drought and Climate Change, a California City Turns
to Desalination," Courthouse News Service, September 1, 2021, https://www
.courthousenews.com/pressed-by-drought-and-climate-change-a-california
-city-turns-to-desalination/.

3. S. J. Bell, "The Place That Will Save Us When There's a Drought: London's Desalination Plant," Londonist, last updated December 7, 2017, https://londonist.com/2015/10/london-s-desalination-plant; A. Crawford, "How Brockton's Desalination Plant Cost Them Millions," *Boston Magazine,* May 28, 2013.

4. S. Jasechko, D. Perrone, H. Seybold, Y. Fan, and J. W. Kirchner, "Groundwater Level Observations in 250,000 Coastal US Wells Reveal Scope of Potential Seawater Intrusion," *Nature Communications* 11 (2020): 3229; C. C. Li, X. B. Gao, S. Q. Li, and J. Bundschuh, "A Review of the Distribution, Sources, Genesis, and Environmental Concerns of Salinity in Groundwater," *Environmental Science and Pollution Research* 27 (2020): 41157–74.

5. Li et al., "Review of the Distribution, Sources, Genesis."

6. J. Foley, *Fundamentals of Energy Use in Water Pumping,* National Centre for Engineering in Agriculture, Brisbane, 2015.

7. J. S. Stanton, D. W. Anning, C. J. Brown, R. B. Moore, V. L. McGuire, S. L. Qi, A. C. Harris, et al., *Brackish Groundwater in the United States,* US Geological Survey, 2017.

8. A. Matin, F. Rahman, H. Z. Shafi, and S. M. Zubair, "Scaling of Reverse Osmosis Membranes Used in Water Desalination: Phenomena, Impact, and Control; Future Directions," *Desalination* 455 (2019): 135–57.

9. E. Jones, M. Qadir, M. T. H. van Vliet, V. Smakhtin, and S. M. Kang, "The State of Desalination and Brine Production: A Global Outlook," *Science of the Total Environment* 657 (2019): 1343–56.

10. "South Florida Region Resident Population Estimates and Projections, 1920–2040," South Florida Regional Planning Council, https://sfregionalcouncil.org/our-region/; A. Bradner, B. F. McPherson, R. L. Miller, G. Kish, and B. Bernard, *Quality of Ground Water in the Biscayne Aquifer in Miami-Dade, Broward, and Palm Beach Counties, Florida, 1996–1998, with Emphasis on Contaminants,* US Geological Survey, Reston, VA, 2005.

11. F. W. Meyer, *Hydrogeology, Ground-Water Movement, and Subsurface Storage in the Floridan Aquifer System in Southern Florida,* US Geological Survey, Denver, 1988.

12. C. P. Hill, "Florida Brackish Water and Seawater Desalination: Challenges and Opportunities," *Florida Water Resources Journal,* September 2012, 22–28.

13. J. C. Bellino, E. L. Kuniansky, A. M. O'Reilly, and J. F. Dixon, *Hydrogeologic Setting, Conceptual Groundwater Flow System, and Hydrologic Conditions, 1995–2010, in Florida and Parts of Georgia, Alabama, and South Carolina,* US Geological Survey, Washington, DC, 2018.

14. A. Panagopoulos, K. J. Haralambous, and M. Loizidou, "Desalination Brine

Disposal Methods and Treatment Technologies—A Review," *Science of the Total Environment* 693 (2019): 133545; N. Voutchkov and G. N. Kaiser, *Management of Concentrate from Desalination Plants* (Amsterdam: Elsevier, 2020).

15. Voutchkov and Kaiser, *Management of Concentrate.*

16. M. C. Mickley, *Membrane Concentrate Disposal: Practices and Regulation,* 2nd ed., US Department of the Interior, Bureau of Reclamation, Denver, 2006; M. Ahmed, W. H. Shayya, D. Hoey, and J. Al-Handaly, "Brine Disposal from Reverse Osmosis Desalination Plants in Oman and the United Arab Emirates," *Desalination* 133 (2001): 135–47.

17. Voutchkov and Kaiser, *Management of Concentrate;* Panagopoulos, Haralambous, and Loizidou, "Desalination Brine Disposal Methods."

18. M. C. Mickley, *Treatment of Concentrate,* US Department of the Interior, Bureau of Reclamation, Denver, 2009.

19. Assuming brackish groundwater that initially contains 5,000 mg/L of total dissolved solids (that is, salt) is desalinated until the salt concentration decreases to 500 mg/L, about 4.5 grams of salt would be produced by zero liquid discharge for each liter of water that a community member uses. If the per capita water consumption for the community is 400 liters per day (a value typical of communities in the arid part of the United States), each person's water use would result in the production of 1.8 kilograms of waste salt. For reference, the EPA estimates that Americans produce approximately 2.2 kilograms of municipal solid waste each day; "National Overview: Facts and Figures on Materials, Wastes and Recycling," EPA, https://www.epa.gov/facts-and-figures-about-materials-waste-and-recycling/national-overview-facts-and-figures-materials.

20. M. S. Hossain, Y. S. Sivanesan, S. Samir, and L. Mikolajczyk, "Effect of Saline Water on Decomposition and Landfill Gas Generation of Municipal Solid Waste," *Journal of Hazardous Toxic and Radioactive Waste* 18 (2014): 04014002.

21. Panagopoulos, Haralambous, and Loizidou, "Desalination Brine Disposal Methods."

22. Y. D. Ahdab and J. H. Lienhard, "Desalination of Brackish Groundwater to Improve Water Quality and Water Supply," in *Global Groundwater: Source, Scarcity, Sustainability, Security, and Solutions,* ed. A. Mukherjee, B. R. Scanlon, A. Aureli, S. Langan, H. Guo, and A. A. McKenzie, chap. 41 (Amsterdam: Elsevier, 2021).

23. "The Story behind the Jerry Can," Charity: Water (blog), December 9, 2011, https://blog.charitywater.org/post/143491921667/the-story-behind-the-jerry-can; "Community Safe Water Solutions: India Sector Review," Safe Water

Network, August 2014, https://safewaternetwork.org/knowledge-hub/india
-sector-review-2014/.

24. *The Untapped Potential of Decentralized Solutions to Provide Safe, Sustainable Drinking Water at Large Scale,* Dalberg Global Development Advisors, Geneva, 2017.

25. "Point-of-Use Water Treatment Systems Market by Device, Technology, Application and Region—Global Forecast to 2025," GlobeNewswire, November 23, 2020, https://www.globenewswire.com/news-release/2020/11/23/2131620/0/en/Point-of-Use-Water-Treatment-Systems-Market-by-Device-Technology-Application-Region-Global-Forecast-to-2025.html.

26. B. Y. Chen, J. Y. Jiang, X. Yang, X. R. Zhang, and P. Westerhoff, "Roles and Knowledge Gaps of Point-of-Use Technologies for Mitigating Health Risks from Disinfection Byproducts in Tap Water: A Critical Review," *Water Research* 200 (2021): 117265.

27. D. L. Sedlak, "The Unintended Consequences of the Reverse Osmosis Revolution," *Environmental Science and Technology* 53 (2019): 3999–4000; N. D. Kapusta, N. Mossaheb, E. Etzersdorfer, G. Hlavin, K. Thau, M. Willeit, N. Praschak-Rieder, et al., "Lithium in Drinking Water and Suicide Mortality," *British Journal of Psychiatry* 198 (2011): 346–50.

28. J. Koshy, "Why Does the Environment Ministry Want to Regulate RO-Based Water Filtration Systems?" The Hindu, February 9, 2020, https://www.thehindu.com/sci-tech/health/why-does-the-environment-ministry-want-to-regulate-ro-based-water-filtration-systems/article61633342.ece.

29. V. Martinez-Alvarez, B. Martin-Gorriz, and M. Soto-Garcia,"Seawater Desalination for Crop Irrigation—a Review of Current Experiences and Revealed Key Issues," *Desalination* 381 (2016): 58–70; T. Navarro, "Water Reuse and Desalination in Spain—Challenges and Opportunities," *Journal of Water Reuse and Desalination* 8 (2018): 153–68.

30. "San Luis Drain," Water Education Foundation, https://www.watereducation.org/aquapedia/san-luis-drain; "Kesterson Reservoir," Water Education Foundation, https://www.watereducation.org/aquapedia/kesterson-reservoir.

31. R. Stratten, "Selenium Removal Key to Water Reuse and Sustainable Agriculture in the Central Valley," HDR Incorporated, https://www.hdrinc.com/insights/central-valleys-demo-treatment-process; T. S. Presser and S. E. Schwarzbach, *Technical Analysis of In-Valley Drainage Management Strategies for the Western San Joaquin Valley, California,* Open-File Report 2008-1210, US Geological Survey, Reston, VA, 2008; M. Weiser, "Pressure Mounts to Solve California's Toxic Farmland Drainage Problem," The New Humanitarian, May 2, 2018, https://deeply.thenewhumanitarian.org/water/articles

/2018/05/02/pressure-mounts-to-solve-californias-toxic-farmland-drainage
-problem.

32. *Phase 3 Report—Evaluate Potential Salt Disposal Alternatives to Identify
Acceptable Alternatives for Implementation,* Strategic Salt Accumulation
Land and Transportation Study (SSALTS), CDM Smith, 2016; "'White Death'
Threatens Central Valley," *Water Desalination Report,* May 16, 2016; "25th
Anniversary Flash from the Past—Refineries Compelled to Stop Selenium
Pollution," Baykeeper, San Francisco, July 22, 2014, https://baykeeper.org
/blog/25th-anniversary-flash-past%E2%80%94refineries-compelled-stop
-selenium-pollution.

33. M. Lopez, "The Yuma Desalting Plant," *Desalination* 30 (1979): 15–21.

34. J. Howe, "The Great Southwest Salt Saga," *Wired,* November 1, 2004.

21 STILLSUIT FOR A CITY

1. L. Carter, J. Williamson, C. A. Brown, J. Bazley, D. Gazda, R. Schaezler,
F. Thomas, et al., "Status of ISS Water Management and Recovery," paper
presented at the 49th International Conference on Environmental Systems,
Boston, 2019; "Pancopia NASA Success Story," https://www.ars.usda.gov/ARS
UserFiles/ott/New%20Website/Partnerships/SBIR%20-%20TT/Pancopia%20
NASA%20Success%20Story.pdf.

2. K. N. Irvine, L. H. C. Chua, and H. S. Eikass, "The Four National Taps of
Singapore: A Holistic Approach to Water Resources Management from
Drainage to Drinking Water," *Journal of Water Management Modeling* (2014),
https://doi.org/10.14796/JWMM.C375; S. Chin, "Water War of Words," *Asean
Post,* July 18, 2018, https://theaseanpost.com/article/water-war-words-0.

3. M.-H. Lim and H. Seah, "NEWater: A Key Element in Singapore's Water
Sustainability," in *Milestones in Water Reuse: The Best Success Stories,* ed.
V. Lazarova, T. Asano, A. Bahri, and J. Anderson, 53–62 (London: IWA, 2013).

4. T. Y. Soon, *Clean, Green and Blue: Singapore's Journey towards Environmental
and Water Sustainability* (Singapore: ISEAS, 2009).

5. G. Ayala and R. Long, "Orange County Water and Sanitation Districts Break
Ground on Project That Recycles 100% of Available Wastewater Flows into
Drinking Water for 1 Million People," press release, Groundwater Replenish-
ment System, Fountain Valley, CA, November 8, 2019; A. Hutchinson, "Trans-
forming Wastewater to Drinking Water: How Two Agencies Collaborated to
Build the World's Largest Indirect Potable Reuse Project," presentation at the
College of Agriculture and Life Sciences Cooperative Extension Water Re-
sources Research Center, Tucson, AZ, April 13, 2017.

6. D. Trotta, "Desalination Advances in California Despite Opponents Pushing for Alternatives," Reuters, July 30, 2021, https://www.reuters.com/world/us /desalination-advances-california-despite-opponents-pushing-alternatives-2021 -07-28/; B. Staggs, "Coastal Commission Approves Ocean Desalination Plant Off Orange County Coast," *Orange County (CA) Register,* October 13, 2022.

7. W. H. Alley and R. Alley, *The Water Recycling Revolution* (Latham, MD: Rowman and Littlefield, 2022); *Stormwater Capture Master Plan,* Los Angeles Department of Water and Power, 2015.

8. P. Gober, A. Brazel, R. Quay, S. Myint, S. Grossman-Clarke, A. Miller, and S. Rossi, "Using Watered Landscapes to Manipulate Urban Heat Island Effects: How Much Water Will It Take to Cool Phoenix?," *Journal of the American Planning Association* 76 (2010): 109–21.

9. R. Johnson and R. Jelmayer, "To Fix Water Crisis, Brazil Turns to Big Projects," *Wall Street Journal,* April 6, 2015.

10. K. Vairavamoorthy, J. Eckart, S. Tsegaye, K. Ghebremichael, and K. Khatri, "A Paradigm Shift in Urban Water Management: An Imperative to Achieve Sustainability," in *Sustainability of Integrated Water Resources Management,* ed. S. G. Setegn and M. C. Donoso, 51–64 (Cham, Switzerland: Springer, 2015); S. Tsegaye, T. M. Missimer, J. Y. Kim, and J. Hock, "A Clustered, Decentralized Approach to Urban Water Management," *Water* 12 (2020): 185.

11. M. S. Mauter and P. S. Fiske, "Desalination for a Circular Water Economy," *Energy and Environmental Science* 13 (2020): 3180–84.

22 NET ZERO WATER BUILDINGS

1. V. D'Amato, E. Clerico, E. Dietzmann, M. Clark, and E. Striano, "When to Consider Distributed Systems in an Urban and Suburban Context," *Proceedings of the Water Environment Foundation* 10 (2009): 5441–60; *On-Site Water Systems: Financial Case Studies,* International Living Future Institute, Seattle, 2019; Y. Liu, E. Giraldo, and M. W. LeChevallier, "Water Reuse in the America's First Green High-Rise Residential Building—The Solaire," in *Milestones in Water Reuse: The Best Success Stories,* ed. V. Lazarova, T. Asano, A. Bahri, and J. Anderson, 161–68 (London: IWA, 2013).

2. *On-Site Water Systems.*

3. P. Sisson, "Facing Severe Droughts, Developers Seek to Reuse the Water They Have," *New York Times,* August 3, 2021; *San Francisco's Onsite Water Reuse System Projects,* San Francisco Public Utilities Commission, 2021.

4. K. Kimura, N. Funamizu, and Y. Oi, "On-Site Water Reclamation and Reuse in Individual Buildings in Japan," in *Milestones in Water Reuse: The Best*

Success Stories, ed. V. Lazarova, T. Asano, A. Bahri, and J. Anderson, 169–74 (London: IWA, 2013).

5. L. Domenech and M. Valles, "Local Regulations on Alternative Water Sources: Greywater and Rainwater Use in the Metropolitan Region of Barcelona," *Investigaciones Geográficas—Spain,* no. 61 (2014): 87–96; K. Pakizer, M. Fischer, and E. Lieberherr, "Policy Instrument Mixes for Operating Modular Technology within Hybrid Water Systems," *Environmental Science and Policy* 105 (2020): 120–33.

6. *Making the Utility Case for Onsite Non-Potable Water Systems,* National Blue Ribbon Commission for Onsite Non-Potable Water Systems, US Water Alliance and Water Research Foundation, 2018.

7. S. Roth, "Should California Make Solar More Expensive? Inside the Climate Justice Battle," *Los Angeles Times,* November 2, 2021.

8. P. Reymond, P. Chandragiri, and L. Ulrich, "Governance Arrangements for the Scaling up of Small-Scale Wastewater Treatment and Reuse Systems—Lessons from India," *Frontiers in Environmental Science* 8 (2020), https://doi.org/10.3389/fenvs.2020.00072.

9. C. Binz and B. Truffer, "Path Creation as a Process of Resource Alignment and Anchoring: Industry Formation for on-Site Water Recycling in Beijing," *Economic Geography* 92 (2016): 172–200.

10. M. Garrido-Baserba, I. Barnosell, M. Molinos-Senante, D. L. Sedlak, K. Rabaey, O. Schraa, M. Verdaguer, et al., "The Third Route: A Techno-Economic Evaluation of Extreme Water and Wastewater Decentralization," *Water Research* 218 (2022): 118408.

11. G. Judd and D. Chiovoloni, "Challenge: Can a 100 Year Old District Heating System Cut Water Use by 100%?," paper presented at the International District Energy Association 2019 Conference, Pittsburgh, PA; "TFL Joins Danone in Giving Out Bottles of Evian on the Tube," press release, Transport for London, July 23, 2014; S. M. Nir, "Water, Water Everywhere in New York Subway; and with It, Problems," *New York Times,* February 12, 2018.

12. T. T. Wu and J. D. Englehardt, "Mineralizing Urban Net-Zero Water Treatment: Field Experience for Energy-Positive Water Management," *Water Research* 106 (2016): 352–63.

13. G. Zeeman, K. Kujawa, T. de Mes, L. Hernandez, M. de Graaff, L. Abu-Ghunmi, A. Mels, et al., "Anaerobic Treatment as a Core Technology for Energy, Nutrients and Water Recovery from Source-Separated Domestic Waste(Water)," *Water Science and Technology* 57 (2008): 1207–12.

14. M. Blanken, C. Verweij, and K. Mulder, "Why Novel Sanitary Systems Are Hardly Introduced?," *Journal of Sustainable Development of Energy, Water and*

Environment Systems 7 (2019): 13–27; "Noorderhoek, Sneek, the Netherlands," Urban Green-Blue Grids, 2011, https://www.urbangreenbluegrids.com /projects/noorderhoek-sneek-the-netherlands/?s=sneek.

15. T. Woody, "The Next Green Must-Have: Showers That Use Recycled Water," *Time,* January 31, 2022.

16. J. Fuller, "The Present and Future of Waterless Washing Machines," Global-Spec, June 2, 2017, https://insights.globalspec.com/article/5337/the-present -and-future-of-waterless-washing-machines; N. Garun, "LG's New Washing Machine Doesn't Use Water or Detergent," Digital Trends, April 17, 2013, https://www.digitaltrends.com/home/lgs-new-washing-machine-doesnt-use -water-or-detergent/; K. Lee, "LG Electronics Gears Up to Develop Commercial 'Waterless' Washing Machine," Korea Bizwire, December 31, 2021, http:// koreabizwire.com/lg-electronics-gears-up-to-develop-commercial-waterless -washing-machine/207953.

17. M. K. McGowan, "Don't Sweat It: Comfort Conditioning Can Increase Thermal Comfort, Decrease Energy Use," *ASHRAE Journal Newsletter,* July 10, 2018; C. Malloy, "Air Conditioners Might Be One Water Source of Our Urban Future," Bloomberg City Lab, May 11, 2021, https://www.bloomberg .com/news/articles/2021-05-11/dry-cities-look-to-reuse-air-conditioner-water; T. Kohnstamm, "How Microsoft Designed a Campus with the Evolution of Work in Mind," Microsoft, December 10, 2020, https://news.microsoft.com /features/israel-campus/.

18. Garrido-Baserba et al., "Third Route."

19. I. Penn, "Frustrated with Utilities, Some Californians Are Leaving the Grid," *New York Times,* March 13, 2022.

20. C. Velazco, "This In-Home Water Recycler Is Meant to Help the Planet, and Your Wallet," Engadget, January 8, 2020, https://www.engadget.com/2020 -01-08-hydraloop-home-water-recycler-ces-sustainabilty.html; C. Harris, "Hydraloop Trial to Reduce Sydney Water Use," Australian Water Association, October 29, 2021, https://www.awa.asn.au/resources/latest-news /hydraloop-trial-to-reduce-sydney-water-use.

21. K. Rabaey, T. Vandekerckhove, A. Van de Walle, and D. L. Sedlak, "The Third Route: Using Extreme Decentralization to Create Resilient Urban Water Systems," *Water Research* 185 (2020): 116276.

23 A BETTER SALT MACHINE

1. G. Ondrasek and Z. Rengel, "Environmental Salinization Processes: Detection, Implications and Solutions," *Science of the Total Environment* 754 (2021):

142432; M. Canedo-Arguelles, B. Kefford, and R. Schafer, "Salt in Freshwaters: Causes, Effects and Prospects—Introduction to the Theme Issue," *Philosophical Transactions of the Royal Society B* 374 (2019): 20180002.

2. T. Jacobsen and R. M. Adams, "Salt and Silt in Ancient Mesopotamian Agriculture," *Science* 128 (1958): 1251–58.

3. S. A. Shahid, M. Zaman, and L. Heng, "Soil Salinity: Historical Perspectives and a World Overview of the Problem," in *Guideline for Salinity Assessment, Mitigation and Adaptation Using Nuclear and Related Techniques,* ed. M. Zaman, S. A. Shahid, and L. Heng, 43–53 (Cham, Switzerland: Springer, 2018).

4. V. Dukhovny, P. Umarov, H. Yakubov, and C. A. Madramootoo, "Drainage in the Aral Sea Basin," *Irrigation and Drainage* 56 (2007): S91–S100; P. Micklin and N. V. Aladin, "Reclaiming the Aral Sea," *Scientific American,* April 2008, 64–71; K. L. Blann, J. L. Anderson, G. R. Sands, and B. Vondracek, "Effects of Agricultural Drainage on Aquatic Ecosystems: A Review," *Critical Reviews in Environmental Science and Technology* 39 (2009): 909–1001.

5. Ondrasek and Rengel, "Environmental Salinization Processes."

6. E. Hanak, A. Escriva-Bou, B. Gray, S. Green, T. Harter, J. Jezdimirovic, J. Lund, et al., "Water and the Future of the San Joaquin Valley," Public Policy Institute of California, San Francisco, 2019; R. A. Pauloo, G. E. Fogg, Z. L. Guo, and T. Harter, "Anthropogenic Basin Closure and Groundwater Salinization (ABSCAL)," *Journal of Hydrology* 593 (2021): 125787.

7. J. Mosher, "SAWPA's Inland Empire Brine: An Engine for Economic Growth," *IDA Global Connections,* Spring 2021.

8. *Central Valley Salt and Nitrate Management Plan Economic Analysis,* Larry Walker Associates, 2016.

9. B. Plumer and H. Tabuchi, "6 Automakers and 30 Countries Say They'll Phase Out Gasoline Car Sales," *New York Times,* November 9, 2021.

10. D. M. Davenport, A. Deshmukh, J. R. Werber, and M. Elimelech, "High-Pressure Reverse Osmosis for Energy-Efficient Hypersaline Brine Desalination: Current Status, Design Considerations, and Research Needs," *Environmental Science and Technology Letters* 5 (2018): 467–75; "RO Systems Make Their Case for Brine Concentration Applications," *Global Water Intelligence,* June 20, 2019.

11. C. Boo, R. K. Winton, K. M. Conway, and N. Y. Yip, "Membrane-Less and Non-Evaporative Desalination of Hypersaline Brines by Temperature Swing Solvent Extraction," *Environmental Science and Technology Letters* 6 (2019): 359–64; J. S. McNally, Z. H. Foo, A. Deshmukh, C. J. Orme, J. H. Lienhard, and A. D. Wilson, "Solute Displacement in the Aqueous Phase of Water-

NaCl-Organic Ternary Mixtures Relevant to Solvent-Driven Water Treatment," *RSC Advances* 10 (2020): 29516–27.

12. N. Voutchkov and G. N. Kaiser, *Management of Concentrate from Desalination Plants* (Amsterdam: Elsevier, 2020).

13. C. Finnerty, L. Zhang, D. L. Sedlak, K. L. Nelson, and B. X. Mi, "Synthetic Graphene Oxide Leaf for Solar Desalination with Zero Liquid Discharge," *Environmental Science and Technology* 51 (2017): 11701–9; C. T. K. Finnerty, A. K. Menon, K. M. Conway, D. Lee, M. Nelson, J. J. Urban, D. Sedlak, et al., "Interfacial Solar Evaporation by a 3D Graphene Oxide Stalk for Highly Concentrated Brine Treatment," *Environmental Science and Technology* 55 (2021): 15435–45.

14. A. Singh, N. W. T. Quinn, S. E. Benes, and F. Cassel, "Policy-Driven Sustainable Saline Drainage Disposal and Forage Production in the Western San Joaquin Valley of California," *Sustainability* 12 (2020): 6362.

24 RUNNING THE RIVERS

1. G. Grill, B. Lehner, M. Thieme, B. Geenen, D. Tickner, F. Antonelli, S. Babu, et al., "Mapping the World's Free-Flowing Rivers," *Nature* 569 (2019): 215–21; D. Tickner, J. J. Opperman, R. Abell, M. Acreman, A. H. Arthington, S. E. Bunn, S. J. Cooke, et al., "Bending the Curve of Global Freshwater Biodiversity Loss: An Emergency Recovery Plan," *Bioscience* 70 (2020): 330–42.

2. W. J. Mitsch, "What Is Ecological Engineering?," *Ecological Engineering* 45 (2012): 5–12.

3. *New Strategies for America's Watersheds,* National Research Council, Washington, DC, 1999.

4. B. W. van Wilgen, "Evidence, Perceptions, and Trade-Offs Associated with Invasive Alien Plant Control in the Table Mountain National Park, South Africa," *Ecology and Society* 17 (2012): 23.

5. A. Crawford, "Cliff Hanger," *Nature Conservancy Magazine,* Fall 2020; L. Stafford, D. Shemie, T. Kroeger, T. Baker, and C. Apse, *Greater Cape Town Water Fund: Assessing the Return on Investment for Ecological Infrastructure,* Nature Conservancy, Cape Town, 2019.

6. S. Filoso, M. O. Bezerra, K. C. B. Weiss, and M. A. Palmer, "Impacts of Forest Restoration on Water Yield: A Systematic Review," *PLOS One* 12 (2017), https://doi.org/10.1371/journal.pone.0183210; R. R. Bart, R. L. Ray, M. H. Conklin, M. Safeeq, P. C. Saksa, C. L. Tague, and R. C. Bales, "Assessing the Effects of Forest Biomass Reductions on Forest Health and Streamflow," *Hydrological Processes* 35 (2021): e14114.

7. P. B. Shafroth, V. B. Beauchamp, M. K. Briggs, K. Lair, M. L. Scott, and A. A. Sher, "Planning Riparian Restoration in the Context of Tamarix Control in Western North America," *Restoration Ecology* 16 (2008): 97–112; M. L. Sevigny, "The Thirsty Tree," Terrain.org (blog), April 1, 2011, https://www.terrain.org /2011/nonfiction/the-thirsty-tree/.

8. M. G. Chung, K. A. Frank, Y. Pokhrel, T. Dietz, and J. G. Liu, "Natural Infrastructure in Sustaining Global Urban Freshwater Ecosystem Services," *Nature Sustainability* 4 (2021): 1068–75.

9. *Making Every Drop Count: An Agenda for Water Action,* High Level Panel on Water, United Nations and World Bank, Washington, DC, 2018; C. J. Vorosmarty, B. Stewart-Koster, P. A. Green, E. L. Boone, M. Florke, G. Fischer, D. A. Wiberg, et al., "A Green-Gray Path to Global Water Security and Sustainable Infrastructure," *Global Environmental Change—Human and Policy Dimensions* 70 (2021): 102344.

10. C. Schulz and W. M. Adams, "Debating Dams: The World Commission on Dams 20 Years On," *Wiley Interdisciplinary Reviews: Water* 6 (2019): e1396.

11. M. J. Mitsch, J. W. Day, J. W. Gilliam, P. M. Groffman, D. L. Hey, G. W. Randall, and N. M. Wang, "Reducing Nitrogen Loading to the Gulf of Mexico from the Mississippi River Basin: Strategies to Counter a Persistent Ecological Problem," *Bioscience* 51 (2001): 373–88.

12. S. S. Rabotyagov, T. D. Campbell, M. White, J. G. Arnold, J. Atwood, M. L. Norfleet, C. L. Kling, et al., "Cost-Effective Targeting of Conservation Investments to Reduce the Northern Gulf of Mexico Hypoxic Zone," *Proceedings of the National Academy of Sciences* 111 (2014): 18530–35; W. A. Jenkins, B. C. Murray, R. A. Kramer, and S. P. Faulkner, "Valuing Ecosystem Services from Wetlands Restoration in the Mississippi Alluvial Valley," *Ecological Economics* 69 (2010): 1051–61.

13. Mississippi River/Gulf of Mexico Watershed Nutrient Task Force 2017 Report to Congress, US Environmental Protection Agency, Washington, DC, 2017; A. T. Hansen, T. Campbell, S. J. Cho, J. A. Czuba, B. J. Dalzell, C. L. Dolph, P. L. Hawthorne, et al., "Integrated Assessment Modeling Reveals Near-Channel Management as Cost-Effective to Improve Water in Watersheds," *Proceedings of the National Academy of Sciences* 118 (2021): e2024912118.

14. Hansen et al., "Integrated Assessment Modeling."

15. R. G. Luthy, D. L. Sedlak, M. H. Plumlee, D. Austin, and V. H. Resh, "Wastewater-Effluent-Dominated Streams as Ecosystem-Management Tools in a Drier Climate," *Frontiers in Ecology and the Environment* 13 (2015): 477–85.

16. E. Rosenblum, F. Matrcus, R. Raucher, B. Sheikh, and S. Spurlock, *Multi-Agency Water Reuse Program: Lessons for Successful Collaboration,* PG Envi-

ronmental LLC and Eastern Research Group, US Environmental Protection Agency, 2022.

25 THE RIGHT THINGS TO DO

1. H. Dormido, "These Countries Are the Most at Risk from a Water Crisis," Bloomberg, August 6, 2019, https://www.bloomberg.com/graphics/2019 -countries-facing-water-crisis/.
2. M. Moatsos, "Global Extreme Poverty: Present and Past since 1820," in *How Was Life?*, vol. 2, *New Perspectives on Well-Being and Global Inequality since 1820*, chap. 9 (Paris: OECD, 2021).
3. S. Olmstead and J. Zheng, *Policy Instruments for Water Pollution Control in Developing Countries*, World Bank Group, Washington, DC, 2019.
4. J. Keller, "Flint's Horrifying Water Crisis Is Bigger Than Just Flint," Pacific Standard, January 25, 2016, https://psmag.com/news/flints-horrifying-water -crisis-is-way-bigger-than-just-flint.
5. L. A. Patterson and M. W. Doyle, "Measuring Water Affordability and the Financial Capability of Utilities," *AWWA Water Science* 3 (2021): e1260.
6. N. Lakhani, "Revealed: Millions of Americans Can't Afford Water as Bills Rise 80% in a Decade," *Guardian,* June 23, 2020; B. Walton, "Millions of Americans Are in Water Debt," Circle of Blue, August 5, 2020, https://www .circleofblue.org/2020/world/millions-of-americans-are-in-water-debt/.
7. *Water Affordability—Public Operators Views and Approaches on Tackling Water Poverty,* Aqua Publica Europea, 2016.
8. C. de Albuquerque, *Realising the Human Rights to Water and Sanitation: A Handbook by the UN Special Rapporteur,* UN Special Rapporteur on the Human Right to Safe Drinking Water and Sanitation, Portugal, 2014.
9. "UN Declares Clean Water a 'Fundamental Human Right,'" BBC, July 29, 2010, https://www.bbc.com/news/world-us-canada-10797988.
10. M. Gorbachev, "The Right to Water," *New York Times,* July 16, 2010.
11. C. Balazs, J. J. Goddard, C. Chang, L. Zeise, and J. Faust, "Monitoring the Human Right to Water in California: Development and Implementation of a Framework and Data Tool," *Water Policy* 23 (2021): 1189–210.
12. Drinking Water, 2019–2020, SB-200, California Senate, Balazs et al., "Monitoring the Human Right to Water."
13. B. E. Hill, "Human Rights, Environmental Justice, and Climate Change: Flint, Michigan," *Human Rights Magazine,* June 14, 2021; Z. Roller, S. Gasteyer, N. Nelson, W. Lai, and M. Shingne, *Closing the Water Access Gap in the United States: A National Action Plan,* Dig Deep and US Water Alliance, 2019.

14. J. L. Sax, "The Public Trust Doctrine in Natural Resource Law: Effective Judicial Intervention," *Michigan Law Review* 68 (1970): 471–566.
15. B. E. Gray, "Ensuring the Public Trust," *University of California at Davis Law Review* 973 (2012): 973–1019.
16. J. L. Huffman, "Speaking of Inconvenient Truths—A History of the Public Trust Doctrine," *Duke Law and Policy Forum* 18 (2007): 1–103; A. Ching, "Charting the Boundaries of Hawai'i's Extensive Public Trust Doctrine Post-*Waiāhole Ditch*," *Environmental Law* 52 (2022): 115–60.
17. M. C. Blumm and R. D. Guthrie, "Internationalizing the Public Trust Doctrine: Natural Law and Constitutional and Statutory Approaches to Fulfilling the Saxion Vision," *University of California Davis Law Review* 44 (2012): 741–808.
18. C. D. Stone, "Should Trees Have Standing? Towards Legal Rights for Natural Objects," *Southern California Law Review* 45 (1972): 450–510.
19. E. L. O'Donnell and J. Talbot-Jones, "Creating Legal Rights for Rivers: Lessons from Australia, New Zealand, and India," *Ecology and Society* 23 (2018): 7.
20. *Iwi/Hapū Rights and Interests in Fresh Water: Recognition Work-Stream: Research Report,* Iwi Chairs Forum, 2015.
21. O'Donnell and Talbot-Jones, "Creating Legal Rights for Rivers."
22. *Iwi/Hapū Rights and Interests in Fresh Water;* "Working 'Shoulder-to-Shoulder' with Local Māori for a Culturally-Sound Wastewater Solution," Stantec, August 9, 2018, https://www.stantec.com/en/ideas/careers/standing-shoulder-to-shoulder-working-with-the-mauri-community-to-create-a-wastewater-solution-that-returns-mauri-life-force-to-hawke-bay-stantec; "Three Waters Reform Programme: Iwi/Māori Interests," Te Tari Taiwhenua, Department of Internal Affairs of New Zealand, https://www.dia.govt.nz/three-waters-reform-programme-iwi-maori-interests.
23. E. O'Donnell, A. Poelina, A. Pelizzon, and C. Clark, "Stop Burying the Lede: The Essential Role of Indigenous Law(s) in Creating Rights of Nature," *Transnational Environmental Law* 9 (2020): 403–27; A. V. Smith, "The Klamath River Now Has the Legal Rights of a Person," *High Country News,* September 24, 2019; J. Townsend, A. Bunten, C. Iorns, and L. Borrows, "Rights for Nature: How Granting a River 'Personhood' Could Help Protect It," The Conversation, June 3, 2021, https://theconversation.com/rights-for-nature-how-granting-a-river-personhood-could-help-protect-it-157117.

ACKNOWLEDGMENTS

This book would not have been possible without all the people who shared their wisdom, experiences and time with me.

I am especially appreciative of the hospitality of my hosts during the sabbatical in 2019 that shaped this book. These include Professor Xiangdong Li, from Hong Kong Polytechnic University, who opened my eyes to the history and complexities of water management in China; Professors Wei-Quin Zhuang and Shan Yi, from the University of Auckland and Fulbright New Zealand for helping me discover the ways that Māori conceptions of the world are being integrated into water management in New Zealand; Professor Laurent Charlet, University of Grenoble Alpes, for showing me the ways that geochemistry, culture, and history can affect water crises; Professor Jelena Radjenović at Institut Català de Recerca de l'Aigua (ICRA) for teaching me that electrochemical water treatment is not quite magic; and finally, Professor Korneel Rabaey, Ghent University, for continuing to challenge me with ideas about creating a better water future.

In addition, I am extremely grateful to the innovators, collaborators, and inspirational characters who are making *Water for All* into a reality. These include Professors Lisa Alvarez-Cohen, Baoxia Mi, Alex Horne, Kara Nelson, David Zilberman, and Dr. Michael Kiparsky at UC Berkeley; Dr. Peter Fiske, Dr. Jenn Stokes-Draut, and Dr. Newsha Ajami at Lawrence Berkeley National Laboratories; Professors Meagan Mauter, William Mitch, and Richard Luthy at Stanford University; Professors Josh Sharp, Tzahi Cath, Chris Bellona, and Chris Higgins at the Colorado School of Mines; Dr. Christian Binz, Professors Janet Hering and Urs von Gunten at the Swiss Federal Institute for Environmental Science & Technology (Eawag); Dr. Jordan Macknick at NREL; Professors Meny Elimelech and Jaehong Kim at Yale University; Professor Eric Hoek at UCLA; Professor Jeffrey McCutcheon at the University of Connecticut; Professors Sunny Jiang and Diego Rosso at UC Irvine; Professor Dan Giammar at Washington University; Professor Pei Xu at New Mexico State University; Professor Lynn Katz at UT Austin; Professor Dion Dionysiou at the University of Cincinnati; Professor Shankar Chellam at Texas A&M; and Dr. Yarom Polsky at Oak Ridge National Laboratory.

I am also indebted to the water professionals who grapple with the practical aspects of bringing about transformations in water systems. Your wisdom and willingness to share your experiences and occasional frustrations have helped me calibrate my expectations and understand the risks and rewards of being an earlier adopter. These exceptional people include the horizontal levee crew: Jason Warner, Jeremy Lowe, Mark Lindley, Carlos Diaz, Donna Ball, and Jackie Zipkin; Jason Dadakis, Megan Plumlee, and Scott Nygren at the Orange County Water District; Hossein Ashktorab and Medi Sinaki at Valley Water; Paula Kehoe at the San Francisco Public Utilities Commission; Tom Mumley at the San Francisco Bay Regional Water Quality Control Board; and David Smith, Luisa Valiela, and Rabia Chaudhry at the USEPA.

Members of my research team have taught me more about water systems than could be learned from a secondary source. Sasha Harris-Lovett, Joe Charbonnet, Rachel Scholes, Carsten Prasse, Emily Marron, Jean Van Buren, Yanghua Duan, Angela Stiegler, Aidan Cecchetti, Marc Planes, Jess Ray, Emily Kraemer, and Tzipora Wagner inspired me with the discoveries that they were making as I wrote this book.

I also appreciate discussions and comments on this manuscript from Dr. Mike Kavanaugh, Dr. Paul O'Callaghan, Eric Rosenblum, Felicia Marcus, and Dr. Peter David. It is important to have extra sets of eyes from people who have considerable wisdom about the way that the world works. Meg, Jane, and Adam Sedlak also offered invaluable insights into the writing and framing of issues throughout the process as well as welcome distractions on days when writing was not going as well as I had hoped.

Finally, I am grateful to my book agent, Andy Ross, my editor, Jean E. Thomson Black, my illustrator extraordinaire, Bill Nelson, and the staff of Yale University Press. Once again, you showed me that a book is much more than carefully chosen words.

ILLUSTRATION CREDITS

p. 1: The six water crises: (1) RODNAE Productions; (2) Kritsada Seekham; (3) Kate Holt/AusAID (CC BY 2.0); (4) Vicki Francis/DFID—UK Department for International Development (CC BY 2.0); (5) Chris Austin: Maven's Notebook; (6) NASA/Goddard Space Flight Center.

p. 37: NASA.

p. 42: NASA/Goddard Space Flight Center.

p. 48: Bill Nelson.

p. 53: © Cameron Davidson.

p. 57: Bill Nelson. Redrawn from data included in W. Steffen, W. Broadgate, L. Deutsch, O. Gaffney, and C. Ludwig, "The Trajectory of the Anthropocene: The Great Acceleration," *Anthropocene Review* 2 (2015): 81–98.

p. 66: Bill Nelson. Data on locations of desalination plants from M. A. Dawoud and M. M. Al Mulla, "Environmental Impacts of Seawater Desalination: Arabian Gulf Case Study," *International Journal of Environment and Sustainability* 1 (2012): 22–37; and S. Lattemann and T. Höpner, "Environmental Impact and Impact Assessment of Seawater Desalination," *Desalination* 220 (2008): 1–15.

p. 69: Bill Nelson. Data source: Our World in Data based on Vaclav Smil, *Energy Transitions: Global and National Perspectives* (2017); and BP's *Statistical Review of World Energy* (2022).

p. 83: Wikimedia Commons, modified by user Kaidor (CC BY-SA 3.0).

p. 88: Edubucher (CC BY-SA 3.0).

p. 93: Chris Austin, Maven's Notebook, mavensnotebook.com.

p. 103: Bill Nelson. Data source: International Water Association Statistics and Economics Specialist Group.

p. 127: Bill Nelson. Data source: AQUASTAT database, Food and Agriculture Organization of the United Nations.

p. 142: Bill Nelson. Data source: Location of South-to-North Water Transfer Project redrawn from J. Barnett, S. Rogers, M. Webber, B. Finlayson, and M. Wang, "Sustainability: Transfer Project Cannot Meet China's Water Needs," *Nature* 527 (2015): 295–97.

p. 153: PRA (CC BY-SA 3.0).

p. 160: Bill Nelson. Data source: ICOLD (International Committee on Large Dams) database as summarized by W. Steffen, W. Broadgate, L. Deutsch, O. Gaffney, and C. Ludwig, "The Trajectory of the Anthropocene: The Great Acceleration," *Anthropocene Review* 2 (2015): 81–98.

p. 189: USDA.

p. 192: Sustainable Sanitation Alliance (CC BY-SA 4.0).

p. 208: Bill Nelson. Data source: Santa Ana Water Project Authority, One Water One Watershed 2.0 Plan.

p. 222: Bill Nelson. Data source: B. Jiménez, "Unplanned Reuse of Wastewater for Human Consumption: The Tula Valley, Mexico," in *Water Reuse—An International Survey: Contrasts, Issues and Needs around the World* (London: IWA, 2008), 4133; and T. Tortajada and E. Castelán, "Water Management for a Megacity: Mexico City Metropolitan Area," *AMBIO: A Journal of the Human Environment* 32 (2003): 124–29.

p. 253: Sustainable Sanitation Alliance (CC BY-SA 4.0).

p. 261: Gryffindor (CC BY-SA 3.0).

INDEX

Figures are indicated by italicized page numbers.

agriculture (*continued*)
rainfed, 86, 135, 140, 148–50; runoff, 26, 33–34, 44–47, 124, 218; salinization effects of, 131–32, 230–31, 287–90; soil moisture sensors, use of, 135, 136; specialty crops, 128, 133–34, 136; strategies to avoid water crises, 33–39; tax revenue used for, 30; technology to expand food production, 136; wastewater use for, 225–33; waterlogging as threat to, 287; water shortages and, 28–30, 125–26. *See also* fertilizers; irrigation; *specific locations*

aid and assistance. *See* international aid groups; subsidies; technical assistance

air pollution, 51, 76. *See also* greenhouse gas emissions

Akkadian Empire, drought impact on, 29

Alaska, oil spills in, 52

al-Assad, Bashar, 32

algae, 47–50, 163, 171, 215–16, 218, 220, 304

Amazon River, 40, 43, 106

American Midwest, modern agriculture's impact on, 48–49, *48*

American Society of Civil Engineers, 162

American South, landscape irrigation and, 99

American Southwest: climate change effects on, 91, 186; evaporation ponds in, 249; groundwater recharge in, 182–87; overusing water resources and damaging environment, 326; population growth in, 98; rainfall in, 85; soil moisture, loss of, 86

American West: agricultural use of treated wastewater in, 226, 228; center pivot irrigation system in, 36, 134; dam expansion projects in, 165–66; fishways in, 172; infrequent heavy rainstorms in, 175; rainwater harvesting as challenge in, 280; snowmelt-fed rivers in, 87

Anaheim (California), sewage treatment to provide drinking water for, 209

ancient civilizations: agricultural irrigation in Egypt, 34; Aztec water management system, 220–21; droughts and, 29; Mesopotamian dam building, 33; Mesopotamian soil salinization, 287, 289; sewage and urban runoff use by, 225; underground water storage by Yemeni farmers, 176–77

animal waste, pollution from, 45–46

antibiotics, 47, 58, 229–30

antiglobalization movement, 114, 158

antimony, 22

antiscalants, 246

Appalachia, access to affordable safe drinking water in, 316

aquifers. *See* groundwater

Aral Sea and Sea Basin, 41–42, *42*, 287–88

Argentina: fluoride contamination in, 22; fracking in, 72

aridification, 326–27

Arizona: Colorado River and, 182–86, 258; cotton production in, 183–84; drought in, 184; groundwater regulations and priorities in, 185; Navajo reservations, access to affordable safe drinking water in, 316; stormwater use in, 199; underground recharge systems in, 182–87

Arizona Water Banking Authority, 185

Armenia, residential water costs in, 111

arsenic, 17–22, 27, 251, 252, 288, 310–11, 329

Asia: cheaper food and rural wealth in, 136; commodity crop production in, 135; dams in, 155, 161, 162, 167; Green Revolution in, 136; meat consumption in, 45; metal contamination in, 22; precipitation amounts in, 85, 107–8; rainfed agriculture in, 140, 150; rainwater harvesting in, 191; rainwater storage in, 280; residential water use in, 103, 107–8; saltwater contamination in, 244; underfunding of water utilities in, 110; water kiosks in, 253. *See also specific regions and countries*

Asian Development Bank, 11, 116–17

Asian Financial Crisis (1997), 114

Association of People Affected by Large Reservoirs and Water Transfers (COAGRET), 157

Atlanta: closed-loop water system in, 268; growth of, 99, 102; outdoor water use in, 99–100; wastewater recycling in, 217–18, 220; water leaks reduced in, 104

Atotonilco Wastewater Treatment Plant (Mexico), 222, 223

atrazine, 51

Audubon Society, 317–18

Australia: agricultural use of treated wastewater in, 226, 228; climate change effects in, 91, 326; conservation strategies in, 96, 107; dam expansion in, 166; desalination in, 85–86, 234, 240; environmental opposition to seawater desalination in, 240; evaporation ponds in, 249; fish population decline in, 43; microirrigation in, 133; Millennium Drought in, 30, 85–86, 96, 107, 138–40; Murray-Darling Basin Plan, 43, 139–40, 166, 287; rainwater storage in, 193–94, 280; residential water use in, *103,* 107; on UN resolution of human right to water, 314–15; Water Act (2007), 139

Bangalore (India), adoption of onsite water systems in, 278

Bangladesh: arsenic contaminated water in, 17–22; legal standing of waterways in, 322

Barcelona: closed-loop water system in, 268; onsite water systems in, 276; water recycling plant built in, 212

Basel, Switzerland, chemical factory fire, 26–27

bathing. *See* showers and bathing water

Bechtel (American company), 113–15

Beijing: groundwater depletion in, 141; onsite water systems in, 278–79; residential water use in, 107, 108

Belgium, household water cost in, 103

Berlin: consumer water usage in, 96;
population density in, 102; trace
amounts of pollutants in drinking water of, 210, 229; water
recycling system in Cold War,
204–5
biochar, 203
biogas, 282
blended financing, 117
Bolivia: constitutional rights of nature
in, 320; privatization of water
systems in, 113–14; spate irrigation in, 177
Bouwer, Herman, 207
brackish water, 242–49; brackish
groundwater of mineral origin,
244–47; costs of recycling, 190,
289–90; desalination of, 251–52;
future role of, 251–52, 268; as
nonrenewable resource, 245–46;
zero-liquid discharge and waste
salt production, 379n19
Brazil: climate change and water crisis
in, 327; commodity crop production in, 135; dams in, 155, 160;
hydroelectric power in, 78;
irrigation in, *127*; One Million
Cisterns program in, 195; rainwater harvesting as challenge in,
280; São Paulo drought (2014),
7–10, 268–69
BRICS, 56, *57,* 79, 91, *160. See also
individual countries*
brine removal and disposal, 289–95;
inland communities' approach
to, 293–94; market for salts produced by, 295; pipeline removal,
290–92; reverse osmosis treatment, 257–58, 289; seawater

desalination plants, 238–39;
underground disposal, 248–50;
water stress increased by, 255,
289–90; zero liquid discharge,
292–93
British East India Company, 143
Brockovich, Erin, 23
Brower, David, 156
Brown's Ferry nuclear power plant
(Alabama), 74

calcium, 17, 231, 244, 246, 285
California: banking of groundwater
in, 186–87; canal system for drainage water in, 256–57; closed-loop
water systems in, 265–68; dam
removal in, 172; dams in, 42–43,
162; desalination in, 131–32,
290–91; droughts in, 4–5, 128–29,
132, 187, 266; flood irrigation
in, 178–79; fossil fuels and pollution in, 239; fracking in, 70–71;
groundwater overexploitation in,
38; human right to water acknowledged in, 315–16; imported water
systems in, 128, 186, 239, 265–67;
indoor water use reductions,
incentives for, 101; infiltration
systems in, 208–9, *208;* inland
desalination in, 256–58; Inland
Empire Brine Line, 209, 290–91,
305; irrigation methods in, 42,
43, 128–30; Kern Water Bank,
187; net metering in, 277; rainwater storage in, 193; residential
lawns and landscaping in,
266–67; seawater desalination
in, 238, 239; sewage treatment to
produce drinking water, 208–9;

China (*continued*)
140–42; water transfer projects in, 141–42, *142*

chlorine, 16, 205, 210

chromate and chromium, 22, 25, 288

cities: conservation strategies in, 95–104, 273; desalination as water source in, 237, 239–40; megacities' future water needs, 269–70; net zero water buildings, 273–85; population growth in, 62–63; population loss affecting water affordability in, 312–13; precipitation patterns and, 8–9; rainwater harvesting in, 180, 191–96, *192*, 274; small towns presenting opportunity for new water paradigm, 270; stormwater runoff captured in, 196–202; temporary water shortages in, 11. *See also* downstream communities and ecosystems; lawns and landscaping; *specific cities by name*

Cleveland (Ohio), water affordability in, 312

climate change, 79–92; agriculture and, 124, 130; droughts induced by, 32, 165, 269–70; economic factors in decision-making for countering, 80–81; as factor affecting water resources, x, 2, 51, 91–92, 172, 262, 297–98, 309, 326–27, 330; floods and, 83–84, 89–90; glaciers, shrinking of, 87–88; Hadley cells and, 82–83, *83*, 85; lawns and urban landscape, water demands of, 98; public disagreement over, 80–81;

rainfall and, 8, 83–87; sea-level rise, 88–91, 211; snowmelt and, 86–87; water management opportunities presented by, 270–71, 325–26; watersheds and, 86–87; water supplies, impact on, 11, 82, 107. *See also* greenhouse gas emissions

closed-loop water systems, 263–70, 327; in California, 265–68; in low- and middle-income countries, 268–70; in Singapore, 264–68

COAGRET (Association of People Affected by Large Reservoirs and Water Transfers), 157

coal and coal mining, 68–70, 72; in China, 75–76; in India, 77

coastal areas: sea-water rise, 88–91, 211. *See also* seawater desalination

Cochabamba Water War (Bolivia), 113–14

Colombia, legal standing of waterways in, 322

Colorado River: Arizona's underground recharge system and, 182–86; climate change and economic development affecting, 325–26; dam construction on, 156; lessons learned from failure to manage, 33–34; Orange County (California) importing water from, 265; Yuma Desalting Plant (Arizona) built to address saltiness, 258

Colorado River Compact (1944), 182

commodity, water treated as, 116, 118, 308, 314, 315

dams (*continued*)
160, 164–65, 167, 174; negative
impacts of, 154, 171–74; removal
of, 163–65, 170, 174, 268; sedimentation and, 163, 165, 167–71,
174; small, 14, 147, 156, 161–64. *See
also* hydroelectric power; World
Commission on Dams; *specific
locations or names of dams*
Dan Sewage Treatment Plant (Israel),
227
Danube River and riverbank filtration, 206
data centers, water demands of, 105–6
DDT. *See* pesticides
Dead Sea, 66–67
Dead Zone (US), *48,* 49–51, 303
decentralization, 270–71
Defense Department, US, 25
dehumidification systems, 283
deltas, 49, 90, 154, 168. *See also specific
rivers and delta formations*
demographic dividend, 62
demographic transition, 58–60, 64
Denver, riverbank filtration system
in, 210
Denver Water's reservoir capacity,
166
Department of ___. *See name of
specific department*
desalination, inland. *See* inland
desalination
desalination, seawater. *See* seawater
desalination
dinitrogen, 46, 198, 304
disease and illness. *See* human
health; waterborne diseases
and pathogens
Disi Water Project (Jordan), 66

downstream communities and
ecosystems, threats to, 173–74,
177–81, 209, 220, 223–24, 256, 301
drinking water. *See* access to safe and
affordable water; safe drinking
water
droughts, ix, 28–31; agricultural
effects of, 28–29; ancient civilizations and, 29; anticipatory
action to avoid, 3, 274; aridification vs., 326–27; in Arizona,
184; in California, 4–5, 128–29,
132, 187, 266; climate change-
induced, 32, 165, 269–70; development of new water resources
during, 6; economic impact of,
30–31; in India, 144, 148, 180;
rainwater harvesting as poor
choice for, 193–94; rationing
during, 123; in São Paulo, 7–10,
268–69; in South Africa,
299–300; in Spain, 212; in
Zimbabwe, 30–31. *See also*
Millennium Drought
Dune (film), 263, 283

early adopters, 126, 129, 262, 266–67,
277, 281–85, 327
East Asia, access to water in, 11
East China Sea, 51, 169
Eastern Europe: commodity crop
production in, 135; hydroelectric
dam construction in, 161; net
zero water systems' cost in, 284
Ebro River (Spain), 157, 158
ecological engineering, 298–99
economic growth/decline: adaptation
of water system to, 262; environmental protection vs. economic

development, 297; Ethiopia's improved economy, 14–15; GDP growth during Great Acceleration, *57*; in Zimbabwe drought (1991–92), 30–31. *See also* Great Acceleration; poverty; wealthy communities

ecosystems, 40–52; agricultural intensification's effect on, 47–51, 126, 305; copper as algicide and, 216; dams, impact of, 44, 154, 156, 163, 167, 171–74; desalination, impact of, 131–32, 240–41, 243, 268; as driving force for water efficiency, ix, 1, 41; ecological engineering, 298–99; environmental regulations to protect, 297; fish and aquatic life, 41–44; future of, 296–307; Great Acceleration's impact on, 296; invasive trees, removal of, 299–301; nature-based solutions, learning curve of using, 302–7; nitrate removal and, 303–6; nutrient pollution of, 47–48, 215; overextraction of water, effect on, 317; public trust doctrine and, 317–20; rainfed agriculture's effect on, 150; restoration, 132–33, 164–65, 328–29; salt buildup's effect on, 287–95; wastewater pollution of, 317; watershed management, 299–303. *See also* wetlands

Ecuador: constitutional rights of nature in, 320; oil spills in, 52

education programs. *See* public education campaigns

Egypt: agricultural irrigation in ancient Egypt, 34; Nile water distribution in, 67; riverbank filtration in, 206

Ekuanitshi people (Canada), 322–23

electricity. *See* energy; hydroelectric power; thermoelectric power

electrodialysis, 235

El Niño–Southern Oscillation, 92

Elwha Dam (Washington), 164–65

energy: alternative energy sources, 68, 81; biogas, 282; data centers' use of electricity, 105–6; fossil fuels and pollution, 51–52, 68–72, 79, 239, 297; fracking, 70–72; groundwater pumping, use of, 38; Indian expansion of electrical service, 145–48; injection wells from oil production, 71; net metering, 277; Nigeria's economic over-reliance on oil and gas industry, 60–61; oil drilling, 70–71; seawater desalination, 239–40; steam heat, 74; usage (1950–2020), *69*; water management challenges to production of, 68–72. *See also* coal and coal mining; greenhouse gas emissions; hydroelectric power; power plants; solar power; thermoelectric power

Energy Policy Act (1992), 101

Environmental Defense Fund, 158

environmental movement, 156–57, 173, 184, 238, 240, 296–97; public trust doctrine and, 317–20

Environmental Protection Agency (EPA), 23–24; WaterSmart Program, 101–2

Ethiopia: access to water for the poor in, 13–15; economic growth in,

Ethiopia (*continued*)
62; ethnic-federalism system of,
14; poverty reduction in, 14–15
European Investment Bank, 11
Europe/European Union: antidam
movement in, 157; chemical
contamination in, 26–27; climate
change effects in, 80, 84, 326–27;
commodity crop production in,
135; compared to Australia and
Asia, *103,* 107; dams in, 155–57;
demographic transition in,
58–59; ecosystem protection in,
133; energy sector's water use
in, 68; fishways in, 172; flooding
in, 84; heat waves in, 86; irrigation using wastewater effluent in,
211; metal contamination in, 22;
monitoring for water contamination in, 311; net zero water
systems, financial return on, 284;
population growth during Great
Acceleration in, 58; power plants,
decrease in water usage by, 75;
precautionary principle, adoption in, 211; rainwater harvesting
in, 191, 194; residential water use
in, 102–4, *103,* 107; riverbank
filtration in, 206–7, 209; steam
heat in, 74; treated wastewater as
drinking water source in, 211–12;
wastewater agriculture in, 226,
228, 231; Water Framework
Directive, 133. *See also specific
countries*
evaporation, 82, 86, 186, 265, 287,
294–95
evaporation ponds, 249–50, 256–57,
289, 293–94

farms and farming. *See* agriculture;
fertilizers; irrigation
favelas. *See* informal settlements
feedlots, 45–47
fertigation, 129, 230
fertilizers: animal waste as, 46–47;
contamination by, 44–45, 196,
217, 304; cost of, 226; Great
Acceleration usage of, *57;* human
waste as, 225; precision agriculture and, 136
filters, 16, 18, 20, 310. *See also* infiltration structures; reverse osmosis
financial incentives: for early
adopters, 283–85; for removal
of turfgrass, 267, 273; for urban
conservation, 273
fish and aquatic life: Aral Sea disappearance and, 41; dam removal
to restore, 165; desalination,
impact of, 131–32, 238–39; fish
ladders and elevators, 171–72;
Klamath River system and,
42–43; "salmon cannon," 172;
water projects, impact of, 154,
171–74, 296
fit-for-purpose water, 285
Flint (Michigan) water crisis, 316
floods and flood control: cities rerouting roof drains into wells,
180; city use of water from, 190;
climate change and, 83–84,
89–90, 165; dams constructed for,
155–56; flood plains, purpose of,
176, 301; levees, 41, 49, 90, 176,
303; reservoirs and, 170; river
deltas and, 90
Florida: brackish water desalination
in, 247–48; University of South

Great Acceleration (*continued*)
changes, 56, *57*; spate irrigation
in, 177; treated wastewater
effluent in, 212. *See also* population growth
Great Lakes, 49
Great Manmade River project
(Libya), 65–66, *66*, 245
Greece, climate change effects in, 86
greenhouse gas emissions: desalination production of, 239–40;
equatorial region, effect on, 82;
Great Acceleration producing,
79–80; optimistic scenario in
second half of twenty-first
century, 91; power sources,
changes due to, 75; vehicular
production of, 72
Greenpeace, 157
Green Revolution, 37, 47, 135–36, 144,
158, 180; Second Green Revolution, 136–37
groundwater: agricultural use of,
34–39, *37*, 132–33, 144–45; Arizona regulations on, 185; brackish groundwater of mineral
origin, 244–47; contamination,
18–19, 202–3; cost of extracting
deep groundwater, 244–45; hard
water, 244–47; India's access to,
142–48; overexploitation of,
36–39, 109, 138, 154; recharge, 147,
179–87, 198–201, 204, 206, 207,
209–12, 327; salinity of, 243–44;
sewage treatment for, 204–13;
shallow, 280, 289; water shortages and, 11. *See also* brackish
water; droughts; irrigation; safe
drinking water; wells

Gujarat (India): groundwater level
decrease in, 38; Sardar Sarovar
project, 146–47, 157–58; underground water storage in, 180, 182
Gulf of Mexico, 49–50, 303–5
gypsum, 246, 251, 288

Hadley cells, 82–83, *83*, 85
halogenated solvents, 24–25
Hampton Roads Sanitary District
(Virginia), 211
Harbin (China), chemical factory
accident in, 27
hard water, 244–47
Hawaii, public trust doctrine in, 318
Hazen, Allen, 219–20, 224
health issues. *See* human health
heat waves, 86
Herbert, Frank: *Dune*, 263, 283
Hinkley (California), 22
Hong Kong, residential water use in,
107
horizontal gene transfer, 229
household appliances, 93, 95, 101–2,
265, 272–73, 282–83. *See also*
specific types of appliances
household use of water. *See* access to
safe and affordable water; safe
drinking water
Houston: growth of, 102, 366n1;
precipitation per year, 366n1;
rainwater harvesting in, 191
Hudson River, PCB contamination
in, 163–64
human health: access to water and,
309; dams creating ideal environment for disease, 154; desalinated
seawater, health problems from,
231; as driving force for water

efficiency, 1; Great Acceleration, impact on, 58; sanitation and, 12–13; water treatment and, ix. *See also* access to safe and affordable water; pollution *and specific pollutants and toxins in drinking water*

human right to water, 313–16

Hungary, riverbank filtration in, 206

hurricanes, 46, 49, 83

Hydraloop (Dutch company), 284

hydraulic fracturing. *See* fracking

hydroelectric power: in Brazil, 78; in China, 76, 168–69; dams providing, 76, 155, 161, 172; desalination and, 66–67; fish populations, impact on, 43–44; during Great Acceleration, 68; in Jordan, 66–67; Oregon/California, 42–43, 172; in São Paulo, 10; in Zimbabwe, 30

imported water: in California, 128, 186, 239, 265–67; in Mexico City, 109–10, 239; reducing reliance on, 268, 273, 327; reliance on, 123, 264–68; salt introduced in, 289; in Singapore, 264–65, 267

India: agricultural access to water in, 33, 37–38, 142–48; canals in, 143–45, 147; Central Groundwater Board, 181; check dams in, 180–81; climate change and water crisis in, 32, 80, 327; colonial sharecropper system in, 143; commodity crop production in, 135; dams in, 155, 157–58, 160, 163; desalination as viable option in, 237; droughts in, 144, 148, 180;

electricity demand in, 77, 145–48; fluoride contamination in, 22; Green Revolution in, 37–38; groundwater overexploitation in, 37–38, 124; Indus Basin Irrigation System, 33, 143, 287; irrigation in, 127, *127;* Jevons paradox in, 147–48; Jyotirgram Yojana (village lighting) scheme, 146–47; Kaleshwaram Lift Irrigation Project, 144; legal standing of waterways in, 322; *Master Plan for Artificial Recharge into Groundwater in India,* 181, 196; onsite water systems in, 278–79; public trust doctrine in, 318; rainfed agriculture in, 148; rainwater harvesting as challenge in, 280; reservoirs in, 143, 179; reverse osmosis units in households in, 255; riverbank filtration in, 206; Sardar Sarovar project, 147, 157–58; surface irrigation in, 124–25, 140, 143–45; underground water storage in, 179–82

Indigenous peoples, 157, 165, 185; rights of nature recognized by, 320–22. *See also specific peoples*

Indo-Gangetic Plain, 40

Indonesia, electricity demand in, 77

indoor water use. *See* household appliances; safe drinking water; showers and bathing water; toilets; washing machines

Indus Basin Irrigation System, 33, 143, 287

industrial pollution, 17, 19, 25–26, 213, 297

Industrial Revolution, 163, 225, 235

industrial sector: drinking water polluted by, 17, 19, 25–26, 213, 297; regulations on, 213; untreated industrial waste, 52; US decline in, 105; water conservation by, 104–5

infiltration structures, 180–85, 197–99; in California, 208–9, *208;* cities foregoing use of, 214; contamination concerns, 201–3; for urban runoff, 200

informal settlements: open defecation as public health challenge in, 220; piping water into, 313; reservoir pollution from, 268; in São Paulo, 7; waste collection in, 196; water access stations in, 115; water infrastructure challenges in, 59, 63, 119; water kiosks in, 252–54, *253, 312*

infrastructure: blended financing for, 117; conservation in lieu of development of, 94; cost of, 153–54; innovation and benefits of, x, 63, 330; nature-based solutions and, 302–7; privatization of water systems, 113–15, 117–18; raising financing for, 116–18; underfunding of, 110–12, 116. *See also* Great Acceleration; low- and middle-income countries; wealthy communities; *specific projects and types of infrastructure*

inland desalination, 242–59, 327; advantages of, 242–43; antiscalants, use of, 246; brackish groundwater of mineral origin, 244–47; in California, 256–58; compared to seawater desalination, 251;

concentrators, use of, 250–51, 289, 292, 294; cost of, 190, 234, 249–50, 251, 289; crystallizers, use of, 250, 289; environmental impact of, 243; evaporation ponds and, 249–50; in Florida, 247–48; limitations on, 245–46, 251; saline groundwater intrusion, 244–47, 265; zero-liquid discharge projects, 250–51, 292–95. *See also* brine removal and disposal

Inland Empire (California), 209, 305; Brine Line, 290–91

innovation, x, 63, 330. *See also* future needs and planning

Inter-American Development Bank, 116–17

international aid groups: in Ethiopia, 13–15; on household water costs, 111; privatization of water systems and, 113–15, 149; rainfed agriculture viewed as risky by, 150; reconsideration of big water projects, 158–59; subsidies for water utilities in low- and middle-income countries, 112, 118–19; wetlands protection, advocacy for, 302; in Zimbabwe, 31. *See also specific aid organizations*

International Covenant on Economic, Social and Cultural Rights (1966), 314

International Finance Corporation, 113

International Water Management Institute, 146

invasive species: fish, 131; removal of invasive trees, 299–301

Manila: climate change and, 11; Manila Bay pollution ruling, 318; privatization of water systems in, 114–15

manufacturing sector. *See* industrial sector

Māori holistic view of water, 321–22

Massachusetts, human right to water recognized in, 315

Mayans, drought impact on, 29

meat consumption, 45, 141

Mediterranean: agricultural use of treated wastewater in, 226, 228; climate change effects on, 91, 326–27; irrigation improvements in, 132–33; rainfall in, 40, 85; rainwater storage in, 193; saltwater contamination in, 244; soil moisture, loss of, 86

Mekong River, 43, 90–91

meltwater dividend, 87–88, *88,* 92

membrane bioreactors, 274, 283, 285

membrane reverse osmosis. *See* reverse osmosis

MENA. *See* Middle East and North Africa

Mesopotamia: ancient dam building in, 33; soil salinization in, 287, 289

Mexico and Mexico City: Atotonilco Wastewater Treatment Plant, *222, 223;* Aztec water management system in, 220–21; canal system in, 220–21, 223, 269; cost of water in, 110; future challenges for, 223; imported water systems in, 109–10, 239; irrigation, treated sewage used for, 221–25; population growth in, 221; salinization of Colorado River, impact of,

258; water conservation challenges in, 109–10; water management in, 11, 220–24, *222;* water recycling potential in, 269

Mezquital Valley (Mexico), 221–23

microirrigation. *See* irrigation

micro-levy on bottled water, 121–22

Middle East and North Africa (MENA): agricultural use of treated wastewater in, 227; brine waste disposal in, 249–50; climate change, impact on, 32; dams in, 161; desalination in, 74, 234; evaporation ponds in, 249; fluoride contamination in, 22; food security in, 64–67; population growth in, 56, 64; spate irrigation in, 177; trading in virtual water as policy of, 65; underfunding of water utilities in, 110; water infrastructure projects in, 65–67, *66;* water management challenges in, 63–67. *See also specific countries*

middle-income countries. *See* low- and middle-income countries

migration trends, 29, 59–60, 136, 309

Millennium Development Goals, 13

Millennium Drought (Australia), 30, 85–86, 96, 107, 138–40

Mississippi River, 49–50, 303–6

Mississippi River–Gulf of Mexico Watershed Nutrient Task Force (1997), 50

Mochica civilization (Peru), drought impact on, 29

Modi, Narendra, 158

Mono Lake (California) lawsuit (1983), 317–18

monsoons, 83, 92, 142, 148, 179

Montana, fracking in, 71

Morocco, demographic transition in, 64

mortality rates during Great Acceleration, 58

MTBE (gasoline additive), 202

Muir, John, 156

Murray-Darling Basin Plan (Australia), 43, 139–40, 166, 287

Namibia, wastewater plant in, 218–20

NAPL (non-aqueous phase liquid), 24–25

natural gas, 22, 68, 70, 72, 75, 77, 282

Navajo reservations (Arizona), access to affordable safe drinking water in, 316

Nehru, Jawaharlal, 157–58

Netherlands: drinking water contamination from fire at chemical factory, 26; green housing development with vacuum toilets in, 282; groundwater recharge projects in, 207; riverbank filtration in, 206

net zero water buildings, 273–85; backup connection to municipal water system, 274; Bangalore (India) as example, 278; Battery Park City urban redevelopment project as example, 274–75; Beijing as example, 278–79; dehumidification systems, 283; financial incentives for, 283–84; gray water recycling, 276, 284–85; lessons learned, 279; membrane bioreactors for sewage treatment, 274, 283, 285; next-generation conservation measures, 281–83, 327; onsite water systems, 274–79, 281; rainwater harvesting, 274; recirculating showers, 282; San Francisco's Salesforce Tower as example, 275–76; storage tanks of, 274; subsidies for, 275; University of South Florida dorm as example, 281

New England, aging dams in, 163

New Jersey, water demands of lawns and residential landscape in, 98–99

New Orleans: levees and water diversion projects, 90; Mississippi delta, 49

New York: Fort Edward Dam demolition, 163; Long Island storm runoff and drinking water supply, 196–200

New York City: Battery Park City urban redevelopment project, 262, 274–75; steam heat in, 74; subway's removal of nuisance groundwater, 280

New Zealand, personhood granted to river in, 321–22

next-generation water systems, 281–83, 327

Niger Delta, oil spills in, 52

Nigeria: demographic transition in, 60–61; public trust doctrine in, 319

night soil, 225

Nile River, 67

nitrate, 47, 197–99, 203, 209, 222, 303–6, 310

pesticides, 23, 26, 44–45, 47, 135, 136,
140, 196, 202–3, 213, 310, 329
PFAS (poly- and perfluoroalkyl substances), 27, 201–2, 213, 229, 252,
254, 310, 329
Philippines: Manila Bay pollution
ruling in, 318; privatization of
water systems in, 114–15
Phoenix: data centers, construction
in, 106; outdoor water use in,
97–100; precipitation in, 199;
treated wastewater, uses for, 232;
water allocation and, 182, 184;
water leaks reduced in, 104;
water recycling in, 207, 269
phosphorus, 47, 215, 285
pipes and pipe networks: brine line
project and, 290–92; in Ethiopia,
14; lead contamination from, 311;
leaking and water loss from, 104,
110, 112–13, 123, 134–35, 265, 273;
recontamination in, 16–17; salt
management and, 256–58, 288;
urban sprawl and, 59; water
usage levels and, 96–97
planning. See future needs and
planning
point-of-use water treatment, 254–55
Poland, aging dams in, 163
pollution: from agricultural runoff, ix,
45–46, 124; coal mining as source
of, 69–70; industrial, ix, 17, 19,
25–26, 297; from naturally occurring substances, 310–11; not
inevitable, 329; pharmaceutical,
210, 229; from power plants, 73;
regulation, 297, 311; of rivers,
lakes, and estuaries, 44, 51, 297;
saltwater contamination, 243–44;

sensors to detect water contaminants, 203; from stormwater runoff, 196, 199–203; trace amounts,
205, 210, 230. *See also specific
types of pollutants and toxins as
well as methods of purification*
population growth: adaptation of
water system to, 11, 262, 297–98;
demographic dividend, 62; demographic transition, 58–60, 64;
density in Asian cities, 107; density in US vs. European cities,
102; food demand and, 37, 39, 51,
124; during Great Acceleration,
56–59, *57*; loss of population
affecting water affordability, 313;
projecting trends in, x, 63–65;
slowing in water-stressed cities,
267; in southern US urban
areas, 98; urban migration and,
59. *See also specific regions and
countries*
poverty: access to water and, 11–12,
308–9; droughts and, 30–31;
Great Acceleration and, 59–60,
309; within high-income countries, 12, 312–13; inland desalination as way to address water
crisis of, 251–52; investments in
water and sanitation to alleviate,
13, 120–21; rights of the poor
ignored in water project construction, 157; rural poor, ix, 12,
14–15. *See also* access to safe and
affordable water; Sustainable
Development Goals
power plants: decrease in water
usage by, 75; location near water
source, 74; run-of-the-river, 161,

171; in São Paulo, 10; thermoelectric power, 72–77, 105–6. *See also* nuclear energy and power plants

precautionary principle, 211

precipitation: Asian abundance translating into low conservation initiatives, 107–8, 147; climate change effects on, 8–9, 83–87; contaminants in, 196; rainwater harvesting, 180, 191–96, *192*, 274; storage, 14, 192–96, *192*, 274, 280; as water source, 40, 190, 191–203. *See also* agriculture, *at* rainfed

privatization of water systems, 113–15, 117–18, 149; seawater desalination plants, 240–41

public education campaigns, 98, 150, 273, 318

public trust doctrine, 317–20

Puerto Rico, access to affordable safe drinking water in, 316

pumps: brackish water produced by overpumping, 244; submersible, 36–37, 177, 180; water shortage addressed by, 35–37, *37*, 109, 144–48, 183

qanat (Syrian irrigation tunnel), 35

rainfall. *See* precipitation

rainfed agriculture. *See* agriculture

rainwater cisterns and tanks, 14, 192–96, *192*, 274, 280

Rajkot (India), consequences of upstream water capture on, 181

rationing: in California, 5; during droughts, 123; as strategy to avoid crises, 6–7; in Taipei, 107

recreational water uses, 170, 186, 299

recycling system. *See* sewage treatment; water recycling

Red Sea–Dead Sea project (Jordan), 66–67

reservoirs: agrarian investment in, ix; Australian drought and, 85; in California, 4–5, 132, 166; copper sulfate as algicide for, 215–16; "dead storage," access of, 9; displacement of people by, 154; in Ethiopia, 14; expansion needs, 8, 165; forecast-informed reservoir operation, 175–76; Great Acceleration construction of, 153–54; in India, 143, 179; lifetime of, 169–70; recreational, 170, 186, 299; risk of overfilling, 84, 175; sediments in, 168–70; small, 156; treated sewage used to refill, 214–24; in Virginia, 214–17; water supplies increased by, 6, 165

Resource Conservation and Recovery Act (1976), 23

Resource Curse, 61–62

reverse osmosis: cost of, 252, 254, 289; disadvantages of, 242, 255, 265; energy requirements of, 239, 242; fit-for-purpose water and, 285; household use of, 254–55; membrane, 234–35, 242, 257, 285, 292–93; salinity rendering inoperable, 292–93; selenium buildup from salty runoff water and, 257–58; small-scale, 252, 255, 280; treated wastewater and, 212; wastewater from, 267–68

Rhine River, flow from sewage treatment plants, 206, 207

Rio Hondo Coastal Basin Spreading Grounds (California), 207, 210
riverbank filtration, 205–7, 210, 213–14, 306
rivers and lakes: chemical spills and, 26–27; coal mining as source of pollution in, 69–70; dams, impact of, 155, 164, 171–74; effluent-dominated rivers, 204; environmental movement's protection of, 157; European cities clustering on, 206; glacier-fed, 87–88, *88;* metal contamination of, 22; New Zealand granting personhood to river, 321–22; preservation in natural state, 297; terminal (endorheic) lakes, 41–42, 124, 288, 317; water diversion, impact of, 41–44, 296–98; water shortages and, 11. *See also* dams; *specific pollutants*
Roman Empire, 35, 225, 317
Ruhr River (Germany), 213
runoff: agricultural, 26, 33–34, 44–47, 124, 218; stormwater runoff, 196–202. *See also* stormwater runoff
rural poor. *See* poverty
Russia: climate change, attitude on, 80; commodity crop production in, 135; fracking in, 72; Soviet Union's diversion of water from Aral Sea, 41

Sachs, Jeffrey, 61
safe drinking water, 16–27; Berlin's water recycling system, 204–5; boiling water for, 16–17, 310; bottled water for, 17, 121–22, 252,

254; chemical spills and, 26–27; contamination of, ix, 12, 17–25, 112, 213, 222, 280–81, 310–11; definition of, 16, 280–81; energy needed to produce, 5; fluoride contamination of, 22; illness from, ix, 12, 22; inland desalination as way to address water crisis of, 251–52; synthetic organic chemicals as pollutants of, 23–27, 196, 310; tap water, ix, 16–17, 310, 312; treated sewage as, 204–11; water kiosks providing, 252–54, 253, 280, 312. *See also* access to safe and affordable water; *specific sources of drinking water*
Safe Water Enterprises, 252–54, 253
Sahara Desert, 82
salinization: crops endangered by, 131–32, 230–31, 287–90; Great Acceleration's effect, 286; irrigation producing, 131–32, 230–31, 256; management, 251, 286–95; saline groundwater intrusion, 244–47, 265; selenium buildup from salty runoff water, 256–57; zero liquid discharge projects as solution possibility, 292, 295. *See also* brine removal and disposal; evaporation ponds; inland desalination; seawater desalination
salmon. *See* fish and aquatic life
salt. *See* inland desalination; salinization; seawater desalination
salt cedar trees, 294, 301
Salton Sea (California), 42
sand filtration, 218, 228
San Diego: desalination facility in,

shaduf (Egyptian irrigation tool), 34
Shasta Reservoir (California), 166
showers and bathing water, 103–4,
    263, 275, 281–83
Sierra Club, 156
Sierra Nevada mountain range, 87, 162
siltation, 167–71, 177. *See also*
    sedimentation
Singapore: closed-loop water system
    in, 264–68; conservation strategy
    in, 96; imported water in,
    264–65, 267; residential water
    use in, 107–8; treated wastewater,
    uses for, 232
Sites Reservoir (California), 132
small towns presenting opportunity
    for new water paradigm, 270
snowmelt, 33–34, 86–87, 144, 205, 208,
    209, 300
sodium, 231, 251, 255
soil moisture sensors, 135, 136
soil salinization. *See* salinization
solar power, 68, 75–77, 106, 236,
    240–41, 277, 284, 293
solutions to water crises: connections
    among, x; effectiveness of cur-
    rent solutions, xii, 1–2; next-
    generation water systems,
    281–83, 327; one-size-fits-all
    solution, 2; salt management,
    286–95; variety of approaches to,
    x; wealthy city dwellers generat-
    ing, 3–4, 284, 327. *See also* brine
    removal and disposal; closed-
    loop water systems; inland
    desalination; net zero water
    buildings; seawater desalination
South Africa: drought in, 299–300;
    microirrigation in, 133; public

trust doctrine in, 319; water man-
    agement in, 159
South America: arsenic in drinking
    water in, 21; cheaper food and
    rural wealth in, 136; dams in, 155,
    167; forecast for dealing with
    water stress in, 91; funding rural
    water and sanitation projects in,
    120; Green Revolution in, 136;
    rainwater storage in, 280; resi-
    dential water use in, *103;* salt-
    water contamination in, 244. *See
    also* Latin America and Central
    America; *specific countries*
South Asia: arsenic in drinking water
    in, 21; downstream environment,
    impact on, 224; funding rural
    water and sanitation projects in,
    120; groundwater overexploita-
    tion in, 37–38. *See also* Indus
    Basin Irrigation System; *specific
    countries*
Southeast Asia: access to water in, 11;
    arsenic in drinking water in, 21;
    downstream environment, impact
    on, 224; forecast for dealing with
    water stress in, 91; population
    growth in, 56; precipitation in,
    40. *See also specific countries*
Southeastern Europe, hydroelectric
    dam construction in, 161
Southern Africa: climate change
    effects on, 91; dams in, 161; de-
    salination as viable option in,
    237; rainfall in, 85. *See also
    specific countries*
South Korea: Great Acceleration in,
    62; residential water use in Seoul,
    107

South Platte River, riverbank filtration system on, 210

Soviet Union's diversion of water from Aral Sea, 41

Spain: aging dams in, 163; climate change effects in, 86; conservation strategy in, 96, 133; dam opposition movement in, 157, 158; desalination in, 157, 255; irrigation in, 127, 132–33; Jevons paradox in, 138; reverse osmosis in, 212, 255; treated wastewater effluent in, 212; wetlands in, 133

sprinklers. See irrigation

stewardship, 41, 52, 105, 130, 299, 323, 328

stillsuits. See closed-loop water systems

Stone, Christopher, 320

stormwater runoff, 196–202; as alternative source, 268; chemical contamination of, 196, 199–203; in future megacities, 269–70; in Virginia reservoir, 216–17

sub-Saharan Africa: access to water in, 11; climate change, impact on, 32, 80; closed-loop water systems as alternatives for, 269–70; conservation measures in, 149–50; crop yields, possibility to increase, 149; demographic dividend in, 62; downstream environment, impact on, 224; electricity demand in, 77; funding rural water and sanitation projects in, 120; population growth in, 56, 59–60, 62–63, 148, 269; rainfed agriculture in, 148–50; Resource Curse in, 61–62; surface water projects in, 148–49; terracing and drainage construction in, 149; underfunding of water utilities in, 110; urban growth in, 62–63; water kiosks in, 253. See also specific countries

subsidies: for affordable safe drinking water, 312–13, 316; Arizona cotton farmers receiving, 184; Australia's support of rainwater tanks, 193; Brazil's support of rainwater tanks, 195; Indian farmers receiving to drill water wells, 144; international aid groups paying in low- and middle-income countries, 112; Mexico City's payments to water utilities, 110; New York City's net zero water buildings, 275; seawater desalination requiring, 255; Spain's drip irrigation funded by, 132; taxes used for, 116

Suez (French company), 114–15

sulfate, 215, 246, 286

sulfuric acid, 69

Superfund (CERCLA), 25

sustainability challenges. See climate change; Jevons paradox

Sustainable Development Goals (SDGs), 13, 116, 119, 121, 224, 309, 315

Sustainable Groundwater Management Act (California 2015), 130

Sustainable Water Initiative for Tomorrow (SWIFT), 211

Switzerland, riverbank filtration in, 206

Sydney (Australia): conservation strategy to address Millennium

Sydney (Australia) (*continued*)
Drought in, 96; household
modular system trial in, 284–85
synthetic organic chemicals, 23–27,
196, 310
Syrian drought (2006–09), 31–32

Taipei, water rationing in, 107
Tampa: outdoor water use in,
99–100; water leaks reduced
in, 104
tanks. *See* rainwater cisterns and
tanks; water storage
Tanzania, rehabilitation of failed
water projects in, 149
tap water. *See* access to safe and
affordable water; safe drinking
water
TCE (trichloroethylene), 24–25
Te Awa Tupua (Whanganui River
Claims Settlement) Act (New
Zealand 2017), 321
technical assistance, 14, 95, 120
Tel Aviv, 5, 227
terminal lakes. *See* rivers and lakes
Terranova Ranch (California), 178
Texas: access to affordable safe drinking water in, 316; environmental
opposition to seawater desalination in, 240; fracking in, 71;
groundwater overexploitation in,
38; lawns and residential landscape, water demands of, 98
Thailand, riverbank filtration in, 206
thermoelectric power, 72–77; China's
increasing use of, 75–77; closed-
loop cooling, 73; cooling water,
increased use of, 105–6; dry
cooling, 73–74, 77; India's

increasing use of, 77; once-
through cooling, 73, 75, 77, 106
Three Gorges Dam (China), 168
Tiwanaku (Peru), drought impact
on, 29
toilets: Industrial Revolution's introduction of, 225–26; nonpotable
water used for, 192; onsite water
systems for, 276; in poor rural
communities, 12, 120; vacuum
toilets, 281–82; water conservation and, 96, 101, 272, 281–83;
water recycling and, 263, 274,
275. *See also* sanitation
Tokyo, residential water use in, 107
topography. *See* geographic and
topographic factors
toxins and toxicity: in crystallized
brine, 251–52; in drinking water,
17–27, 310; in urban aquifers, 202.
See also specific toxins
trachoma, 13
trading in virtual water, 65
transitions to meet water crises,
261–62
treated sewage. *See* sewage treatment
treated wastewater: for agriculture,
225–33; in Atlanta, 217–18;
groundwater recharge with, 184,
204, 206, 209–12; infiltration
systems and, 208–9, *208*; in
Virginia, 214–17. *See also*
wastewater treatment plants
Treaty of Waitangi (New Zealand
1840), 321
trees: legal standing of, 320; removal
of, 299–301
trichloroethylene (TCE), 24–25
Trinity River (Texas), 306

United States (*continued*)
water recycling in, 207–11, 220.
*See also specific regions (starting
with "American"), states, and
cities*
uranium, 22, 251
urban areas. *See* cities; *specific cities
by name*
urban heat island effect, 8
urban sprawl, 59
US Agency for International Development (USAID), 119
US Geological Survey, 245
US Water Conservation Laboratory,
184

vacuum toilets, 281–82
Vietnam, electricity demand in, 77
Virginia: groundwater recharge
project, treatment processes for,
211; Occoquan Reservoir, wastewater in, 214–17

Wadi Zabid (Yemen), capture of flood
waters, 177–78
Warner, Andrew, 61
washing machines, x, 101–2, 198, 263,
272–73, 282, 285
wastewater effluent. *See* sewage
treatment
wastewater recycling: for agriculture,
225–33; in Atlanta, 99, 217–18,
220; in Australia, 86; cost of,
289–90; in Dallas, 99; implementation of, 6; in Israel, 227–32;
in Mexico City, 221–23; Sixth
Sustainable Development Goal
and, 224; in Tampa, 99. *See also*
brine removal and disposal;

membrane bioreactors; sewage
treatment
wastewater treatment plants: investment in, ix, 213, 215–18; in Long
Island, 197; in Mexico City,
222–24; in Namibia, 218–20.
See also treated wastewater
waterborne diseases and pathogens:
drinking water and, ix, 12, 18–19,
112, 222, 280–81, 310–11; fecal
contamination and, 196, 220–22;
processes removing, 16–17, 215,
262; reverse osmosis as protection against, 254–55; stormwater
runoff and, 200–201
water conservation. *See* conservation
policies
water crises: avoidance of, xi, 3, 6–7,
33–39, 126, 190, 325, 329; categories of, x–xi, 2; ecological
engineering to address, 298–99;
failure of conservation to fully
address, 151; forcing policymak-
ers to confront Jevons paradox,
138–39; history of, ix; lack of
single solution, ix; local nature
of, 2; nature-based solutions to,
302–7; transitions to address,
261–62; uniqueness of, xii, 2. *See
also* droughts; water shortages
water efficiency, 93–94, 109–23,
265–66. *See also* conservation
policies; Sustainable Development Goals
water kiosks, 252–54, 253, 280, 312
waterlogging, 287–88
Water.org, 120
water pollution. *See* pollution; *specific
types of pollutants*

water pressure reduction, 9–10, 104

water quality. *See* pollution; safe drinking water

water recycling: cost of, 263–64; drinking water, 204–11; in future megacities, 269–70; in Germany, 204–6, 213, 220; gray water, 276, 284–85; household modular system, 284–85; irrigation using, 225–33; in Israel, 227–32; onsite in net zero water buildings, 274; in United States, 207–11, 220

water rights: as complicating factor in access to water, 5, 54, 158, 178, 266; food cost and, 28; Klamath River system, 42–43, 172; purchase of, 6; universal, 312–14

watersheds: agreements to share water, 178; best practices for rainfed agriculture in, 150; climate change and, 86–87; dam construction in, 76; management of, 7–8, 299–303; salmon migration and watershed modification, 42–43; water quantity in, 85–88; water retention and, 175–77, 300. *See also* dams; downstream communities and ecosystems, threats to; *specific locations and rivers*

water shortages: agriculture and, 29, 149; climate change and, 84; groundwater and, 109–10; methods to address, 261; underground water storage to address, 175–87. *See also* droughts; water crises

WaterSmart Program (EPA), 101–2

water sources and supplies. *See* dams; groundwater; inland desalination; precipitation; reservoirs; rivers and lakes; seawater desalination; sewage treatment; unconventional water resources; underground water storage

water storage: consumers using tanks for, 10; India's use of farm-sized storage tanks, 143; for net zero water buildings, 274, 280; rainwater storage tanks, 191–92, *192*; strategy to avoid water shortage, 33; sub-Saharan African small-scale systems of, 149. *See also* rainwater cisterns and tanks; underground water storage

water transfer projects. *See* canals; dams; pipes and pipe networks; reservoirs

water treatment plants. *See* inland desalination; safe drinking water; seawater desalination; wastewater treatment plants

Water Unite, 122

water utilities. *See* infrastructure

wealthy communities, x, 3–10; affordability of water for low-income residents in, 312; anticipatory actions by, 3; big water projects, slowing investment in, 154; conservation policies in, 95–108, 266–67, 273, 327; desalination efforts of, 4–6, 237, 289–90; as driving force for water efficiency, 1, 327; failure to enforce water regulation, 311; food shortage and, 29; meat consumption by, 45; monitoring for water contamination in, 311; new solutions

wealthy communities (*continued*)
    generated by, 3–4, 284, 327; population forecast for, 91; precision agriculture in, 136, 256, 289, 327; rainwater tanks in, 193–95; river and water diversions, opposition to, 296–97; safe drinking water in, 280, 310–11; stewardship of water-stressed parts, 328; wastewater agriculture in, 226, 230; wastewater treatment concerns of, 213. *See also specific countries and cities*
weather forecasts, 175–76. *See also specific weather events*
wells: agricultural use of, 35–36; community, 14; depth limitations for, 245; dry well storage, 196–97, 199–200; Great Acceleration construction of, 153–54; hand-dug, 11–14, 17, 179–80, 309; injection, 71, 248–49, 269, 307; shallow, 34, 111, 144, 177, 222, 274; tube, 18–21; water supplies increased by, x, 4, 6, 14
Western Europe. *See* Europe/European Union
wetlands: desalinated water used in, 258; flood plains and, 176, 301; groundwater overexploitation and, 154; nitrate removal and, 303–6; protection and restoration of, 302–7; in Spain, 133; treated wastewater used in, 212
Whanganui River (New Zealand), 321–22

wildfires, 79, 86, 300
wind power, 68, 75, 77, 106, 236, 241
World Bank: India's groundwater recharge projects, funding to coordinate, 182; Israeli sewage treatment plant financing from, 227; privatization of water systems favored by, 113; reconsideration of decision-making process for big water projects, 159; Sardar Sarovar Dam project abandoned by, 158; Wadi Zabid (Yemen) flood capture funded by, 177; water crises, response to, 11; water system improvement funding from, 116–17; wetlands protection, advocacy for, 302
World Commission on Dams, 44, 159–61, 303
World Health Organization (WHO), 19–21
World Vision, 120

Yangtze River, 168–69
Yemen, spate irrigation in, 176–77, 208
Yosemite National Park, 156
Yuma Desalting Plant (Arizona), 258–59
Yurok Tribe, 322

zero liquid discharge projects, 250–51, 292–95, 379n19
Zika virus, 9
Zimbabwe drought (1991–92), 30–31